More praise for *Warlord Democrats*

"A major work. This book tells us exactly how and why wartime leaders play significant roles in post-war politics. Extremely insightful and clear, it is likely to spur a new research programme in the study of post-conflict politics and state-building. It should be widely read."
William Reno, Northwestern University

"An excellent collection of essays. The political economy analysis it offers should be of particular interest to those – quite especially the UN and those charged with running its peace operations – trying to build peace and secure durable political settlements to long-running conflicts."
Mats Berdal, King's College London

Africa Now

Africa Now is published by Zed Books in association with the internationally respected Nordic Africa Institute. Featuring high-quality, cutting-edge research from leading academics, the series addresses the big issues confronting Africa today. Accessible but in-depth, and wide-ranging in its scope, Africa Now engages with the critical political, economic, sociological and development debates affecting the continent, shedding new light on pressing concerns.

Nordic Africa Institute

The Nordic Africa Institute (Nordiska Afrikainstitutet) is a centre for research, documentation and information on modern Africa. Based in Uppsala, Sweden, the Institute is dedicated to providing timely, critical and alternative research and analysis of Africa and to co-operation with African researchers. As a hub and a meeting place for a growing field of research and analysis the Institute strives to put knowledge of African issues within reach for scholars, policy makers, politicians, media, students and the general public.

www.nai.uu.se

Forthcoming titles

Paul Higate and Mats Utas (eds), *Private Security in Africa*

Mimmi Söderberg Kovacs and Jesper Bjarnesen (eds), *Violence in African Elections*

Atakilte Beyene (ed.), *Agricultural Transformation in Ethiopia*

Titles already published

Fantu Cheru and Cyril Obi (eds), *The Rise of China and India in Africa*

Ilda Lindell (ed.), *Africa's Informal Workers*

Iman Hashim and Dorte Thorsen, *Child Migration in Africa*

Prosper B. Matondi, Kjell Havnevik and Atakilte Beyene (eds), *Biofuels, Land Grabbing and Food Security in Africa*

Cyril Obi and Siri Aas Rustad (eds), *Oil and Insurgency in the Niger Delta*

Mats Utas (ed.), *African Conflicts and Informal Power*

Prosper B. Matondi, *Zimbabwe's Fast Track Land Reform*

Maria Eriksson Baaz and Maria Stern, *Sexual Violence as a Weapon of War?*

Fantu Cheru and Renu Modi (eds), *Agricultural Development and Food Security in Africa*

Amanda Hammar (ed.), *Displacement Economies in Africa*

Mary Njeri Kinyanjui, *Women and the Informal Economy in Urban Africa*

Liisa Laakso and Petri Hautaniemi (eds), *Diasporas, Development and Peacemaking in the Horn of Africa*

Margaret Lee, *Africa's World Trade*

Godwin R. Murunga, Duncan Okello and Anders Sjögren (eds), *Kenya: The Struggle for a New Constitutional Order*

Lisa Åkesson and Maria Eriksson Baaz (eds), *Africa's Return Migrants*

Thiven Reddy, *South Africa: Settler Colonialism and the Failures of Liberal Democracy*

Cedric de Coning, Linnéa Gelot and John Karlsrud (eds), *The Future of African Peace Operations*

Tobias Hagmann and Filip Reyntjens (eds), *Aid and Authoritarianism in Africa*

Henning Melber, *The Rise of Africa's Middle Class*

About the editor

Anders Themnér is a senior researcher at the Nordic Africa Institute and an assistant professor at the Department of Peace and Conflict Research, Uppsala University. His research focus is on post-civil war democratization; disarmament, demobilization and reintegration of ex-combatants (DDR); and informal military networks in post-civil war societies.

Warlord democrats in Africa

Ex-military leaders and electoral politics

edited by Anders Themnér

Nordiska Afrikainstitutet
The Nordic Africa Institute

Zed Books
LONDON

Warlord Democrats in Africa: Ex-Military Leaders and Electoral Politics
was first published in association with the Nordic Africa Institute,
PO Box 1703, SE-751 47 Uppsala, Sweden in 2017 by Zed Books Ltd,
The Foundry, 17 Oval Way, London SE11 5RR, UK.

www.zedbooks.net
www.nai.uu.se

Editorial copyright © Anders Themnér 2017
Copyright in this collection © Zed Books 2017

The right of Anders Themnér to be identified as the editor of this
work has been asserted by him in accordance with the Copyright,
Designs and Patents Act, 1988.

Typeset in Minion Pro by seagulls.net
Printed and bound by CPI Group (UK) Ltd, Croydon, CR0 4YY
Index by Ed Emery
Cover design by Alice Marwick
Cover photo © Sven Torfinn/Panos

A catalogue record for this book is available from the British Library.

ISBN 978-1-78360-249-0 hb
ISBN 978-1-78360-248-3 pb
ISBN 978-1-78360-250-6 pdf
ISBN 978-1-78360-251-3 epub
ISBN 978-1-78360-252-0 mobi

Contents

Acknowledgements | ix

Introduction: Warlord democrats: wartime investments, democratic returns?
ANDERS THEMNÉR 1

1 *Pompier-pyromanocracy*: Mbusa Nyamwisi and the DR Congo's inflammable post-settlement political order
JUDITH VERWEIJEN 41

2 Apotheosis of a warlord: Paul Kagame
LARS WALDORF. .68

3 Discourses of peace and fear: the electoral navigations of Sekou Conneh and Prince Johnson in post-war Liberia
CARRIE MANNING AND ANDERS THEMNÉR 95

4 Afonso Dhlakama and RENAMO's return to armed conflict since 2013: the politics of reintegration in Mozambique
ALEX VINES 121

5 From warlord to drug lord: the life of João Bernardo "Nino" Vieira
HENRIK VIGH 156

6 Shape-shifters in the struggle for survival: post-war politics in Sierra Leone
MIMMI SÖDERBERG KOVACS AND IBRAHIM BANGURA 177

7 Riek Machar: warlord-doctor in South Sudan
JOHAN BROSCHÉ AND KRISTINE HÖGLUND 199

Conclusion: Ambiguous peacelords: the diminishing returns of post-war democracy
ANDERS THEMNÉR 222

About the contributors | 246

Index | 247

Acknowledgements

This volume grew out of a rich and stimulating research environment at the Nordic Africa Institute (NAI), and particularly its "Conflict Cluster". It was through constant discussions about Big Men, informalities, post-civil war dynamics and processes of democratization that the idea for analyzing warlord democrats as electoral navigators developed. For this reason, I am eternally grateful to colleagues such as Maria Eriksson Baaz, Linnéa Gelot, Ilmari Käihkö, Maria Malmström, Anders Sjögren and Mimmi Söderberg Kovacs. I am particularly indebted to Mats Utas for introducing the Big Man framework to me and for constantly pushing me to look beyond my positivist inclinations. In a similar vein, I also want extend my appreciation to the current and former directors of NAI, Iina Soiri and Carin Norberg, as well as NAI's head of research, Victor Adetula, who have supported the process throughout. I would also like to express my gratitude to my "other" workplace – the Department of Peace and Conflict Research (DPCR) at Uppsala University. It has been a luxury to have DPCR as an alternative source of inspiration. From some of the brightest scholars on the dynamics of war and peace I have received insights about how, in a systematic manner, to try to capture, compare and analyze something as fluid and ambiguous as individual agency in a largely informal setting.

The book began to take shape in September 2012, with the organization of a two-day workshop entitled Warlord Democrats: Agents of Change or Instigators of Insecurity? During the workshop, a number of scholars and practitioners were present who are not part of this book. These individuals did, however, undoubtedly infuse valuable ideas and perspectives into the project. I therefore owe thanks to Bola Amoke Awotide, Maria Eriksson Baaz, Tumba Tuseku Diuedonné, Nura Jibo, Trice Kabundi, Maria Malmström, Carin Norberg, Daniel Poon, Koko Sadiki, Pierre Schori, Anders Sjögren, Roxanna Sjöstedt, Ari Baghdassar Tatian, James Tar Tsaaior and Mats Utas. This workshop could not have been organized without the generous economic support of the Swedish International Development Cooperation Agency (Sida) and the organizational assistance of NAI. We are truly indebted to both organizations. From the latter, I particularly want to mention Ingrid Andersson, whose administrative expertise made all the difference.

During the writing of this volume, we have received invaluable comments, reflections and assistance from a number of people. Three research assistants have on several occasions literally pushed the project forward with their enthu-siasm, input and administrative help. Without the work done by Alexandra Brandner, Claudia Forster-Towne and Sayra van den Berg it would have taken twice as long to finalize this book. I am also extremely grateful to Hanne Fjelde, Roxanna Sjöstedt, Lotta Themnér and three anonymous reviewers who through their insightful suggestions and reflections have undoubtedly increased the quality of the book. I would furthermore like to extend my warm appreciation to Zed Books for having made this project possible. Throughout the process, I have benefited from the wisdom and guidance of the editor of Zed's Africa Now series, Ken Barlow, as well as NAI's head of communications, Elnaz Alizadeh. The writing of the book would, furthermore, not have been possible without the generous economic support provided by Stiftelsen Marcus och Amalia Wallenbergs Minnesfond and the Swedish Research Council.

In the end, this has been a collaborative effort involving ten researchers, coming from various scholarly traditions. The interdisciplinary dialogue generated by this meeting has undoubtedly enriched the volume by providing alternative perspectives and interpretations. I therefore want to extend my gratitude to all chapter authors.

On a final note, I would like to dedicate my own contribution to a set of people who mean the world to me. Without the unwavering love and patience of my wife Lotta and my lovely daughter Teresa this project would never have been possible. In addition, the tireless encouragement and support of "fyrklövern" – Farmor, Bu, Mojmoj and Offa – made all the difference. Thank you!

Anders Themnér
Uppsala, September 2016

Introduction | Warlord democrats: wartime investments, democratic returns?

Anders Themnér

> The hope of the international community is that the experience of
> electoral politics will somehow result in the changes of former rebels,
> so that they move away from the militaristic and corrupt practices that
> characterized their previous activities and accept a new democratic culture.
> (Chris Melville, Global Insight, quoted in Menezes 2005)

In 2005 former General Adolphus Dolo made Liberian and international
headlines when he declared his intention to contest one of the senate seats
allotted to Nimba County. Running under the slogan "Let him butter your
bread", he cleverly alluded to his nom de guerre "General Peanut Butter" and
by extension his past as a wartime leader. For Dolo it was natural that he as
a Big Man should participate in the country's first post-civil war elections.
In an interview he declared that "people [Liberians] owe their allegiance to
individuals ... and all our institutions are broken down" (Toweh 2005). Seen
by some as a local war hero due to his role in defending Nimba County
against rebel incursions in 2003, and being a successful local businessman,
Dolo could count on the allegiance of many (Inquirer 2005; The Analyst
2005). However, for others Dolo represented all the evils that had afflicted the
country since the start of the civil war in 1989. Not only was he accused of
murder and recruiting child combatants during the war, he was also suspected
to have enlisted ex-combatant mercenaries on behalf of his former employer
ex-President Charles Taylor only five months prior to the elections (CIJ 2005:
15; Toweh 2005; TRC 2009: 352). Despite the labors of local and international
media to depict Dolo as a danger to peace and security, he eventually succeeded
in winning at the polls and entering the senate.

Dolo's efforts to transform himself from wartime general to post-war democrat highlights a central problem facing many war-torn countries: with facade
institutions and weak or authoritarian political parties, electoral politics often
becomes a game contested by Big Men – more seldom women[1] – who have
committed horrendous atrocities. A central question is therefore what happens
when the likes of Dolo come to dominate electoral politics. Do such individuals
continue to employ wartime tactics, such as inciting fear, orchestrating violence,

committing abuses and engaging in criminal activities to gain an edge over their opponents? Or is it more common that they build their electoral careers on embodying discourses and behaviors attuned to democracy, seeking to reconcile war-affected groups and convince their followers of the benefits of peace? In this book we seek to address these questions.

With the advent of post-war democratization as a conflict resolution mechanism during the last twenty-five years, warlord democrats (WDs) – former military or political leaders of armed groups (armed forces, rebel movements, militias or paramilitaries) who take part in electoral politics – have become a common feature in many post-civil war countries in Africa. In fact, it has become popular for ex-military leaders to reinvent themselves as "democrats". Former leaders of armed groups – such as Jean-Pierre Bemba (Democratic Republic of Congo), Julius Maada Bio (Sierra Leone), Afonso Dhlakama (Mozambique), Pierre Nkurunziza (Burundi) and Charles Taylor (Liberia) – have contested national elections to gain office. With the international community increasingly insisting that democracy is "the only game in town", electoral participation has become the safest route through which ex-military men and women can transform military might into post-war political influence. In fact, African ex-militaries habitually seek to "convert their gains made during the war into material security and social status" and "seek political office to consolidate their military exploits" (Anders 2012: 159-160). To this end, they have a myriad of different strategies at their disposal; transforming their armed groups into political parties, joining political parties already in existence, creating new parties or running as independents. In order to maximize their political leverage, they often switch between these strategies, promising to bring their networks of clients – frequently composed of ex-fighters – to the highest bidder.

The usage of the term "warlord democrat" stems from a conscious decision to provoke. It raises immediate questions about whether an individual can simultaneously be a warlord and democrat, and challenges natural inclinations to categorize actors and practices into stylized dichotomies – war/peace, democracy/autocracy and corrupt/accountable. Put differently, hybridity causes confusion and is analytically messy. However, in many developing countries in general, and post-civil war African societies in particular, any effort to assign adjectives to political actors soon becomes a disorderly affair. This is largely due to the dynamics of domestic elite formation. First, few Big Men can afford to put all of their eggs in one basket. For instance, by "only" being a politician a Big Man becomes vulnerable. In societies where power is amassed by increasing the number of social networks – political, economic, military, ethnic, religious, regional or sport – at one's disposal, it is vital to have multiple leadership roles. Having access to several networks allows leaders to mobilize clients from various social groups. This explains why most African elites are not only politicians, but also businessmen, pastors, (ex-)generals, informal security providers, or presidents of football clubs. In this sense, elites cannot afford to be "only" democrats. Second, since independence most African countries have been in more or less perpetual transition, moving between various forms of authoritarian and democratic rule, planned and liberal economies, and different levels of societal violence. As a consequence, elites must possess a canny ability to constantly reinvent themselves to sustain political power; without being able to transform different types of social capital they soon risk becoming marginal figures (Bourdieu 1986). In this sense, it is rational for post-war elites not to shed their military credentials too quickly. Depending on the audience and prevailing circumstances, they may need to give greater emphasis to their role as "warlords" or "democrats". In trying to provide a more nuanced view of leadership in war-to-peace transitions, this volume adheres to a larger and growing body of literature that stresses the hybrid nature of contemporary peace and democratization processes in Africa and beyond (Mac Ginty 2006; Moran 2006; Richards 2005; Richmond and Mitchell 2012).

The agency and power of ex-militaries as individuals in electoral politics has so far largely been neglected in the literature on peacebuilding and post-war democratization. When it comes to electoral politics, these bodies of literature have instead foremost emphasized its formal, organizational aspects, focusing on the importance of constructing state institutions and political parties that can channel popular dissent through ballots rather than bullets (see e.g. Manning 2004, 2007; Paris 2004; Chesterman et al. 2005; Doyle and Sambanis 2006; Söderberg Kovacs 2007, 2008; Zeeuw 2007; Call 2008; Jarstad and Sisk 2008; Paris and Sisk 2009). To the extent that the agency of individual military leaders is acknowledged, scholars commonly frame it in negative terms, where the goal of peacemaking should be to find ways to channel "political power thorough parties rather than individuals, and through civilians rather than the military" (Chesterman et al. 2005: 383). Even if the creation of institutions and political parties are desirable social goods that peacemakers should strive for, post-war politics are seldom – at least in the short run – that neat and manageable. More often than not, institutions and political parties are, in the aftermath of war, weak or non-existent, as they have been systematically undermined or targeted by the armed belligerents. In instances where political parties are strong – for instance when liberation movements or well-organized rebel groups have been transformed into political parties – they tend to be dominated by one leader and be authoritarian by nature. Within these contexts electoral politics becomes a question of Big Man politics, where political, economic and military elites – each controlling their own networks of dependents – compete for influence (Nugent 1995; Daloz 2003; Utas 2012). During such competitions, WDs often possess a competitive advantage over other Big Men. Thanks to the spoils

3

of war, and peace, that they have amassed, the communal loyalties that they command and the informal, and sometimes formal, military networks that they head, WDs are often well placed to navigate the political landscape being built and have a profound impact on political processes. As former commander of the African Party for the Independence of Guinea and Cape Verde (Partido Africano da Independência da Guiné e Cabo Verde, PAIGC) and ex-president, Nino Vieira was, for instance, able to use the military and criminal networks that he had maintained since the liberation struggle against Portugal to buy political and military allies and be re-elected as president in 2005 (see e.g. Chapter 5).

Considering the political influence of WDs, it is questionable whether we can truly understand the dynamics of post-war politics and assess the ability of "democratic" systems[2] to promote peace and security without acknowledging their agency as individuals and including them in the analysis. This is especially true when considering that former military leaders are arguably the category of individuals with the greatest capacity to sponsor insecurity and undermine the ability of democracy to function as a conflict resolution mechanism. The lack of attention given to WDs is part of a larger research lacuna that often obscures the role and responsibility of individual elites in the study of war and peace.[3] According to Brown (2001: 220), this risks creating a:

"No fault" history that leaves out the pernicious effect of influential individuals. ... Leaving elite decisions and actions out of the equation, as many social scientists do, is analytically misguided. It also has important policy implications: underappreciating the importance of elite decisions and actions hinders conflict management efforts and fails to place blame where blame is due.

Post-war democratization may therefore – at least in the short run –have less to do with building institutions and political parties than with making "warlords" into "peacelords".

But what do we see when we start analyzing the actions and choices of WDs as they maneuver within the context of electoral politics? Do we see leaders that embrace democratic norms, refrain from sponsoring violence and function as agents of change? A recurring theme in the literature on conflict resolution is the centrality of good leadership (see e.g. Gormley-Heenan 2006). According to this perspective, peace becomes possible only when military leaders come to the conclusion that war is no longer in their or their movements' interest (Zartman 1989; Stedman 1991). Not only does this realization push wartime leaders to agree to peace, but frequently also to commit themselves to building democratic institutions and holding regular elections. According to this perspective WDs – still caught in the mindset of the futility of war – have incentives to mobilize support for the peace process and convince their followers to settle future conflicts through the ballot box (see e.g. Zartman 1995: 19; Darby and Mac Ginty 2000: 239; Jarstad and Sisk 2008: 23). Scholars have, however, increasingly come to question the wisdom of using wartime actors and structures as the basis for building peace and democracy. According to this perspective democratic consolidation is most likely to occur when "a new leadership emerges, seeking to organize politics in a different way from those adopted by discredited parties and leaders in the past" (Clapham and Wiseman 1995: 226), otherwise there is an imminent risk that democratization processes are prematurely closed (Ottaway 1997). This seems to imply that WDs are best seen as Machiavellian-like politicians who for strategic reasons embrace democratic traits and, when given the chance, show their true colors by engaging in more destructive and aggressive behavior. However, perhaps the answer lies somewhere in between these two ideal types of WDs – being either shepherds of peace or democratic spoilers. Could it be that ex-military turned politicians eventually become socialized into responsible democrats if they partake in recurring elections? This would entail observable shifts over time, where belligerent WDs eventually moderate their behavior and discourses according to the rules and norms of democratic politics (Michels 1962; Manning 2004: 69; Jervis 2013: 155).

In this book, we seek to address these questions by introducing a framework for how to analyze WDs in a post-war electoral setting. More specifically, we do this by conducting an in-depth, systematic study of a number of ex-militaries in the Democratic Republic of Congo (DRC) (Antipas Mbusa Nyamwisi), Guinea-Bissau (João Bernardo Vieira), Liberia (Sekou Conneh and Prince Johnson), Mozambique (Afonso Dhlakama), Rwanda (Paul Kagame), Sierra Leone (Julius Maada Bio, Eldred Collins and Samuel Hinga Norman) and South Sudan (Riek Machar) to assess the two following questions: does the electoral participation of WDs tend to have a positive or negative effect on post-civil war security; and, if there are negative implications, how do they manifest themselves? Here we have a broad take on security, assessing whether WDs have: (1) positively contributed to long-term efforts at building peace and democracy; (2) supported organized violence; (3) securitized wartime identities; (4) criminalized politics; or (5) fostered human rights abuses – where the four latter actions are arguably detrimental to post-war stability. It is important to note that the WDs analyzed in this volume operate in what can best be described as semi-democratic, rather than democratic states. For this reason, we prefer to employ the term electoral politics when describing the context in which they partake. By this we mean political systems that have recurring elections and where at least some opposition parties or leaders are allowed to take part. Such systems are, however, often characterized by a number of democratic deficiencies, ranging from electoral fraud and harassment of political opponents to biased electoral commissions and judiciaries.

The aim of the book is not only to establish whether ex-militaries who run for office promote or undermine security, but also to inductively trace the trajectories through which they do so. We thereby also hope to say something about which factors – for instance, electoral constraints, capacity to misbehave, costs of misbehaving and personality traits – influence ex-militaries' choices to become either peacelords or instigators of insecurity. The ultimate aim of this volume is therefore to make a contribution to the literature on peacebuilding and post-war democratization that has so far overlooked this important topic and to say something about what strategies peacemakers can employ when faced with different kinds of WDs.

Institutions, political parties and the building of post-civil war democracy

Before further developing the role WDs play in post-civil war politics, it is first necessary to say something about why peacemakers invest so many resources in democratizing war-ridden societies and why it is so difficult to build state institutions and political parties that are both strong and democratic.

Since the advent of large-scale peacekeeping and peacebuilding operations – in countries such as Cambodia, El Salvador, Namibia and Mozambique – in the early 1990s, peacemakers have turned to the democratic template to construct new systems of governance that can ensure long-term stability. In fact, this tendency has gone so far that post-war democratization has become "the default approach of the international community in its response to end contemporary wars" (Jarstad and Sisk 2008: 3). The underlying assumption of such policies is that the origins of most civil wars can be traced back to different forms of political marginalization. Peacemaking thereby becomes a quest for inclusive institutional designs that tie different groups to the state being (re)built (Zartman 1995; Jarstad and Sisk 2008).[4] As the centerpiece of electoral democracy, many peacemakers – at least initially – equated democracy building with holding elections. In fact, the latter is often expected to provide multiple and reinforcing social goods. First, it provides belligerents with an alternative avenue for settling disputes: instead of confronting each other on the battlefield, the combatants agree to let the public decide whose political visions should prevail. Second, elections are commonly seen as providing legitimacy for peace processes by clearly signaling a break with the past and opening up space for political actors who were marginalized during the war. Third, the mere participation in elections is sometimes expected to have a moderating effect on extremist parties. In order to have a chance at the polls, former belligerents need to appeal to broader segments of society than their wartime constituencies (Manning 2004: 59, 69). Finally, peacemakers – at least in the early days of peacebuilding – saw the organization of elections as an indicator for success and consequently an excuse to disengage manpower and economic support. In conjuncture these multiple expectations meant that peacemakers often pushed for early elections in war-torn countries (see e.g. Paris 2004; Brancati and Snyder 2013).

However, experiences have shown that holding elections in post-war societies is not only difficult, but commonly results in renewed forms of violence. This is due to multiple reasons. For instance, incumbent elites – who may have benefited from the creation of a war economy (siphoning off of funds intended for the military, land appropriations, illegal exploitation of natural resources and pillaging) – may fear holding free and fair elections. A loss at the polls would in all likelihood mean yielding control of their economic networks and by extension their ability to retain their support base (Jarstad and Sisk 2008: 25; Zürcher et al. 2013: 24). In addition, in many war-ridden societies – just as in most developing countries – it is critical who controls the reins of power. It is often through political connections that people gain access to contracts, employment, education and land. Elections are thus not only an issue of which policy direction a state should choose, but also about everyday economics that can have a decisive impact on citizens' wellbeing and even survival (Chabal and Daloz 1999; Lindberg 2003). Furthermore, post-war political systems habitually lack the institutions and resources needed to provide security guarantees for the losing side. Electoral defeat may therefore have dire consequences, ranging from harassment and arrest, to exile and even execution (Höglund 2008: 84). Finally, elections are always competitive by nature and tend to polarize even peaceful societies. Organizing such events in war-afflicted countries, fraught with fear, suspicion and inter-group hatred, usually results in political mobilization along old conflict lines. Elections can therefore create a sense of heightened insecurity, rather than generate support for the new political system being built (Paris 2004). In conjunction these processes often push or tempt political actors to employ different forms of electoral violence, either to maximize their chances of winning or to ensure their physical survival. Such tendencies are particularly likely to unfold during the first post-war elections, when communal fears and anxieties generally run higher and many wartime actors continue to retain their (informal) command structures and arms (Lyons 2005; Brancati and Snyder 2013; Themnér 2015).

To minimize the risk of elections fueling, rather than preventing, new violence, peacemakers have increasingly sought to address the structural deficiencies that enable such forms of aggression. This has usually meant supporting efforts to build strong state institutions and political parties. Interventions to do the former have traditionally focused on what is commonly referred to as statebuilding or "actions undertaken by international or national actors to establish, reform, or strengthen the institutions of the state" (Call and Cousens 2008: 4). The aim of such interventions is foremost to replace informal wartime governance structures – rebel groups, paramilitaries and black-market networks

7

– with formal institutions – justice systems, legislatures, security forces and civil services – that are assumed to be more efficient, accountable and better at preventing renewed warfare (Barnett 2006: 91; Doyle and Sambanis 2006: 335; Mac Ginty 2011). In this literature, particular focus is often given to institutional designs and reforms that are expected to improve democratic governance. This includes mechanisms such as setting up independent electoral commissions, creating electoral systems that include elements of proportional representation, ensuring judicial independence, supporting a separation of power and interim/peace commissions that can oversee the implementation of peace accords (see e.g. Lyons 2005; Reilly 2008; Zürcher 2011). The underlying assumption is that such mechanisms will increase transparency, ensure more broad-based legislative representation and prevent governmental abuse and, by extension, reduce the risk of violence. A central premise in this school of thought is often the need to delay the holding of elections until strong, formal institutions are constructed (Paris 2004; Doyle and Sambanis 2006). Paris (2004), for instance, argues that without strong institutions, political liberalization is unlikely to generate democracy and risks sowing the seeds of new violence. For some, power-sharing agreements – whereby the former belligerents divide cabinet posts, legislative seats and ministries amongst themselves (and at times non-warring parties) – is seen as one way to build confidence in the process and buy time until elections can be held (see e.g. Walter 2002, Hartzell and Hoddie 2003).

Meanwhile, the reason why peacemakers devote so much attention to supporting the construction of viable political parties is that they are commonly seen as "the agents of democratization" (Söderberg-Kovacs 2008: 139). In fact, such organizations are generally held as the "main intermediary organization of liberal democracy, linking citizens with the state" (Söderberg-Kovacs 2008: 139). As intermediaries, they are expected to perform a number of vital tasks. A first function is to aggregate and articulate the policy preferences of different social groups and interests. Parties thereby play a crucial role in ensuring political pluralism in the decision-making process (Lyons 2005: 123; Reilly 2008, 2013). Second, they also help to socialize new candidates for office (Reilly 2013: 89). Before most political leaders run for office, they first have to excel in intra-party politics: articulating policies, making compromises and being elected to various internal bodies and positions. Parties thereby ideally function as democratic nurseries, where candidates become acquainted with democratic principles and procedures. Finally, by binding elites to different political organizations, parties assist in "moving the exercise of power from individuals to institutions" (Chesterman et al. 2005: 367). Because post-war states tend to be characterized by widespread social marginalization, militant and authoritarian norms, and Big Man politics, party-building has the potential to ease tensions during democratization processes.

Due to the central role armed groups play in civil wars, particular emphasis is often given to transforming military organizations into viable political parties that renounce violence (see e.g. Zartman 1995; Manning 2004, 2007; Söderberg Kovacs 2007, 2008; Zeeuw 2007). For many armed actors, the prospect of taking part in, and possibly winning, future elections is a key reason for accepting peace. However, militant organizations are often ill-equipped to take part in electoral politics. First, wartime leaders – who have often been promoted due to their military cunning and authoritarian leadership styles – may have a difficult time operating in a context that tends to reward compromise, alliance-building and more moderate discourses. Second, it may be difficult for political parties which have evolved from armed groups to discard militant norms overnight. Such norms – in conjunction with continued access to arms and (informal) command structures – may make it tempting for them to resort to violence and different forms of harassment when challenged by political opponents. Finally, many armed groups have a rather narrow support base and may have employed exclusionary and even xenophobic discourses during the war. If the militant organizations' successor parties are not able develop more moderate and inclusionary policies, they may struggle to win at the polls. To ensure that armed actors do not fear the arrival of electoral politics – and ultimately renege on their commitment to peace – scholars and practitioners have stressed the need to support so-called rebel-to-party transitions. Such assistance can range from providing security guarantees and political recognition, to giving economic and material assistance.

Formal structures and informal realities

There are, however, problems associated with confining the analysis of, and the work towards attaining, post-war democracy to institution- and party-building. The reason for this is that in the short to intermediate term these social goods are often unattainable. In the aftermath of war, state institutions tend to be weak or non-existent. Armed opposition groups often target institutions of the state to undermine the ability of the regime to wage war or to signal their refusal to recognize its authority to rule. Meanwhile, in some instances governing elites purposefully destroy their own institutions during war; by dismantling official structures, and taking personal control over state patronage, government leaders can not only force local communities to award loyalty to them as persons rather than the institutions they serve, but also engage in the systematic plundering of resources and collective goods that would not be tolerated during normal peacetime conditions (see e.g. Reno 2000). Of course, in some instances the very origins of civil wars can – at least partially – be traced back to fragile or faltering institutions that are unable to uphold law and order and deliver crucial services (Gurr 2000). Once peace arrives, these institutional deficiencies are seldom alleviated by externally

9

driven statebuilding interventions. In fact, more often than not such initiatives generate façade institutions where much governance and power continues to be concentrated in and implemented through informal structures; ranging from systems of patronage, regional or ethnic bonds, to old political and military ties (Kahler 2009; Hameiri 2011; Mac Ginty 2011; Utas 2012; Zürcher et al. 2013).[5] Rather than being strong, neutral and transparent, post-war state structures are therefore often characterized by clientelism and elite predation (Mac Ginty 2011: 86; Richmond and Mitchell 2012: 3). One reason why statebuilding has proven so elusive is that it often results in the weakening of bonds between the state and local communities. This is because the structures set in place tend to answer to foreign, not local demands (de Guevara 2008). In addition, governing elites often have incentives to hinder or distort efforts at institutional reforms: by too enthusiastically bowing to international pressures for change they risk undermining the very patronage networks that brought them to and keep them in power (Zürcher et al. 2013).

Efforts to build strong, viable and democratic political parties have proven to be just as challenging as constructing formal and functioning institutions. There are multiple reasons for this. First, in developing countries in general and transitional environments in particular, parties are often poorly institutionalized and tend to be organized around narrow identity markers or personal relations. Commonly they only come to life during elections, and are seldom based on a clear ideology or political agenda (Reilly 2013). "As a result, politics tends to be both highly personalized and strongly identity-based around whatever cleavages [sic] – tribe, language, regional or religion – is most salient" (Reilly 2013: 90). These tendencies are often reinforced in war-torn societies, where authority is unclear and suspicion and fear permeate communities. Under such circumstances people are even more inclined to attach themselves to like-minded individuals or people who share similar traits (Burt 2005; Lyons 2005). As a consequence the "prospect of meaningful and properly functioning party politics is ... very remote" in many post-war countries (Berdal and Ucko 2009: 6). In fact, in such settings political party organizations tend to be non-existent, weak or fragmented (Jarstad and Sisk 2008: 32). Sadly, efforts by peacemakers to remedy such deficiencies are often counterproductive. In fact, by favoring models of proportional representation and unconstrained party formation, custodians of peace often undermine the possibility of creating large political parties that can span different social groups. Instead such policies favor the creation of small parties that de facto function as political platforms of one or several Big Men (Reilly 2013: 90).

A second reason for the weakness of political parties in war-ridden societies is that the organizational structures of armed groups seldom function as a base conducive to building parties. In many civil wars, especially in an African context, militant organizations are created around the interest of one or several elites and their networks of dependents. Such organizations can best be likened to warlord enterprises, whose raison d'être is to further the political and economic interests of their leaders. Political parties organized around warlord figures not only tend to be unstable – as there are few formal structures holding them together – they are usually just façades geared towards providing political legitimacy for their leaders (Duffield 1998; Reno 1998; Anders 2012; Utas 2012). In other instances, the pressures of peace may fractionalize armed movements that were previously united and organizationally strong. In a first phase, intra-elite disputes may arise over the necessity of ending the violence and making painful compromises, as well as establishing who is a valid spokesperson for the group (Zartman 1995; Stedman 1997; Darby and Mac Ginty 2000: 233). In a second phase, tensions often arise over the division of peacetime spoils. For instance, by gaining access to material benefits, external recognition and positions in the government or bureaucracy, some leaders increase their power vis-à-vis others (Pearlman 2008/2009). Such tensions often continue as former armed groups engage in electoral politics; individuals that enter parliament may, for instance, gain access to resources and a new power-base unavailable to party leaders standing outside the legislature (Manning 2002). These intra-party conflicts can result in anything from internal bickering to formal splits and even armed violence (Pearlman 2008/2009). Irrespective of the course such conflicts take, they put constraints on the ability of armed groups to transform themselves into viable political parties. Other armed movements are able to withstand similar centrifugal pressures and participate in electoral politics as strong and unified organizational entities. This is, for instance, true for liberation movements such as the People's Movement for the Liberation of Angola (MPLA) and the Zimbabwe African National Union (ZANU), and well-organized rebel groups such as the National Resistance Army (NRA, Uganda) and the Rwandan Patriotic Front (RPF). The resilience and unity of such political parties is, however, not necessarily a function of a clear political ideology, internal democratic procedures and a transparent and efficient party bureaucracy; characteristics often associated with functioning political parties. Rather they tend to be headed by strong leaders who run their organizations by relying on personalistic and clientelistic mechanisms of internal control (Söderberg Kovacs 2008: 146). Put differently, the ex-militaries heading such organizations are the ultimate Big Men who not only stand above party politics, but sometimes the state itself. The personal power that such elites possess has the potential to impede efforts to employ ex-armed movements as agents of change.

Warlord democrats as electoral navigators

Due to the difficulties of constructing viable and democratic political parties and institutions, post-civil war societies are often dominated by Big Men. In such societies, political outcomes have less to do with institutional procedures, bureaucratic principles of good governance and electoral competition between strong political parties than with alliance-building between networks of elites representing different economic, political and military interests (Nugent 1995; Daloz 2003; Utas 2012). Power is personalized and upward mobility occurs when a Big Man connects other men and women, and their followers, to his faction (Utas 2012). In this context elections are characterized by intense negotiations between Big Men seeking to convince potential opponents, as well as local elites, to mobilize clients on their behalf. Due to the personal nature of such interactions, there is often sudden and abrupt side-switching where elites declare their intention to carry their followers to other leaders in order to get a better deal.

When such Big Man politics are carried out in post-civil war societies, WDs often have a competitive advantage over other elites seeking to carve out a political space for themselves. There are several reasons for this. First, many WDs have greater economic resources at their disposal. During war military elites often accumulate vast personal resources through pillage, racketeering, contraband and land-grabbing. The rents generated from these activities can provide economic security in the post-war period (Spear 2006; Brancati and Snyder 2013). In fact, it is not uncommon for military leaders to invest resources acquired during war in peacetime business enterprises. Furthermore, many peace accords award ex-militaries control over certain government portfolios or positions within the administration, allowing them to engage in further rent-seeking behaviors (Hartzell and Hoddie 2003; Spear 2006; Englebert and Tull 2008). Ex-militaries seeking to launch a political career are therefore, economically speaking, well positioned to successfully compete in electoral politics. This is particularly true since patronage politics tends to reward candidates who are known, or at least assumed, to possess great wealth. Due to the risk of betting on the "wrong" candidate, voters tend to reject political newcomers in favor of candidates – such as WDs – who can more credibly call upon substantial resources (Daloz 2003).

Second, many former military leaders have a popular following in local communities. This may be particularly true for ex-militaries that have played an active role in defending civilian populations against the abuses and predatory behavior of other armed groups and where post-war insecurity is still rife (Lyons 2005; Biró 2007). During elections ex-military elites can play on these feelings of wartime solidarity and security fears to rally support. Under such circumstances "[c]ivilian candidates and those who do not have a convincing answer to the issue of post-election security are unlikely to prevail" (Lyons 2005: 61).

Third, WDs often control (in)formal military structures – unavailable to many other Big Men – that can be used to mobilize supporters, intimidate voters or attack political opponents. For instance, despite efforts to demobilize and disarm armed groups, WDs often continue to control their former command structures, giving them a reliable pool of ex-fighters who can be mobilized for various political, military and economic purposes (Hoffman 2007; Christensen and Utas 2008; Themnér 2015). WDs who have positioned themselves as heads of states, or other influential official capacities, as a result of the war may also have access to the state's security forces. Irrespective of how weak or strong the armed forces, police and secret services may be, they do provide WDs with additional leverage against political opponents. However, even such state-bearing WDs often go to great lengths to keep ex-command structures alive as they are often superior at carrying out shady activities such as organizing illicit economic enterprises or engaging in covert violence (Utas 2012).

The main reason why ex-military leaders possess these advantages is not necessarily because of long and loyal service to an armed group, but is rather a function of their personal abilities to acquire resources, followers and status through violent means. In fact, many military leaders can be described as opportunists: even if armed movements use their services to attain certain political goals, they similarly use armed groups as a route to personal empowerment. For instance, according to Anders (2012: 159), leaders of armed factions in Africa should be seen as:

> Self-made men, entrepreneurs who rely solely on their personal skills as military organizers, political leaders and charismatic orators [who] use war as a resource to benefit from personally, to accumulate prestige and wealth. After the cessation of hostilities they try to convert their gains made during war into material security and social status.

As entrepreneurs, such military leaders can easily switch loyalties between different armed groups, bringing their followers with them in the process. For instance, Idrissa Kamara – renowned rebel commander from Sierra Leone, also known as "Leatherboot" – started his military career as an officer in the Sierra Leone Army (SLA). After a 1997 coup that ousted the democratically elected government, he joined the African Forces Revolutionary Council (AFRC) junta, thereafter switching over to the Revolutionary United Front (RUF) in 1999. Finally, he became head of the personal bodyguard of Ernest Koroma, leader of the All People's Congress (APC) and president since 2007. Throughout this process Kamara was able to carry a good number of (ex-)fighters with him (Christensen and Utas 2008).

When navigating in the context of electoral politics, WDs have several strategies at their disposal. They can – together with their military comrades – transform their armed groups into political parties. After the ending of the civil war in El Salvador in 1992, for instance, the highest leadership of the rebel movement Farabundo Martí Front for National Liberation (FMLN) dismantled its military structures in order to form a political party with the same name (Söderberg Kovacs 2007). Some ex-militaries may, however, prefer to join established political parties, if such exist, rather than take the risk of running for office under the banner of political movements whose electoral capacity is uncertain. The former are often more than willing to welcome such political refugees, who may be able to bring not only resources and potential voters but also ex-combatants who can be employed as "armed thugs" during political showdowns. This is what happened in Sierra Leone. Even if the interim leader of the RUF, Issa Sesay, spearheaded the launch of the Revolutionary United Front Party (RUFP) for the upcoming 2002 elections, several ex-commanders preferred to campaign on behalf of one of the country's two historically dominant parties: APC and Sierra Leone People's Party (SLPP) (Themnér 2011). An alternative strategy is to run as an independent in national or local elections. Such a strategy can be especially useful for former military leaders whose constituency is concentrated in a specific electoral district. Under such circumstances there may be less need to be part of an official party, as it is enough to have one name on the "ticket". For instance, during the 2005 national elections in Liberia, the ex-general Prince Johnson was elected as an independent into the senate for Nimba County. Due to his strong support amongst the Gio and Mano ethnic groups in the county – many of which saw Johnson as having protected them during the war – he could run a local campaign without the backing of a party (see e.g. Chapter 3). A final type of electoral strategy is to form a completely new political organization, with no ties to a former armed group or an existing party. This can be beneficial for WDs who want to set their own political agenda, but have higher political ambitions than just being an independent; using a party platform they can attempt to get loyalists elected into the legislature and increase their bargaining power vis-à-vis political opponents. This was a strategy employed by Sekou Conneh during the run-up to Liberia's 2005 elections. Instead of seeking to transform his Liberians United for Reconciliation and Democracy (LURD) into a political party, Conneh launched his own movement – Progressive Democratic Party (PRODEM) – that de facto functioned as his own political enterprise (see e.g. Chapter 3).

Hence, for former military leaders, electoral politics is not merely a question of transforming their armed groups into political parties; thanks to their resources and skills they are often well versed at navigating within the confines of post-war democratization contexts, at times even switching between different electoral strategies. The abovementioned Johnson, for instance, abandoned his 2005 tactic of running as an independent during the 2011 elections (see e.g. Chapter 3). In order to have a more national appeal and increase his chances of being elected president, he founded the National Union for Democratic

Progress (NUDP). Not only did this put him in third place in the first round of the presidential elections, he became the king – or rather queen – maker by helping the incumbent President Ellen Johnson-Sirleaf win in the second round. After falling out with his NUDP colleagues he eventually abandoned the party and once again ran successfully as an independent in the 2014 senatorial elections. During the run-up to the 2017 presidential elections, it was reported that Johnson was conducting far-reaching negotiations with a number of political leaders about the possibility of running on a common presidential/vice-presidential ticket.

In sum, while previous research on post-civil war democratization and peacebuilding has highlighted the difficulties of building institutions and political parties that are both viable and democratic, and described how such shortcomings create fertile ground for Big Men in general and WDs in particular, it has not drawn the logical conclusion of this finding: to truly understand post-war electoral politics it is necessary to employ WDs as the unit of analysis. In fact, when studying war-ridden politics, most scholars continue to be constrained by Weberian straitjackets limiting their analysis to organized actors such as state institutions, political parties, civil society organizations and armed groups, explaining what ought to be, rather than what is.[6] This is, however, problematic since such explanations "offer no theoretical explanation for the preferences of key actors" (Boone 2003: 12). There are, more specifically, two problems associated with not acknowledging the agency of individual WDs. First, there is a risk that crucial security dynamics are overlooked, and even if such behavior is observed, it may not be possible to understand its causes. Second, it is difficult to understand the outcome of electoral politics. In fact, the electoral maneuvering of WDs can substantially affect who succeeds at the polls, who is included in the structure of government and how post-war governance is conducted.

Warlord democrats in an African context

There are three reasons for why we, in this edited volume, focus on WDs operating in a Sub-Saharan African context. First, states in Africa tend to be institutionally weaker than in most other parts of the world (Spears 2013: 43). According to Jackson and Rosberg (1985: 424–425), since independence African states have had "abstract political institutions, but they do not have them in the concrete or realized sense. Institutional rules do not effectively govern the behavior of most leaders most of the time". The general weakness of the African state, in conjunction with the destruction caused by civil war, has severely constrained the possibility of building strong and viable institutions in war-ridden societies. Second, Big Man politics is particularly widespread in Africa (Bratton and van de Walle 1997; Chabal and Daloz 1999; Utas 2012; Spears 2013: 43). In fact, Chabal and Daloz (1999: 16) have described the African state as "a décor, a pseudo-Western façade masking the realities of deeply personalized political relations". In this context politics is often organized around the notion of a "neo-patrimonial marketplace", where rulers engage in continuous negotiations with local elites to purchase their and their followers' loyalty (de Waal 2009). The personalized nature of African politics has made it difficult to build inclusive and viable political parties. Finally, armed groups organized around the economic and political interest of one or a few key individuals – sometimes referred to as warlords – is especially prominent in Africa (Reno 1998; Anders 2012; Utas 2012; Day and Reno 2014). The "glue" holding such armed entities together is military leaders' ability to distribute patronage (or credible promises of future rewards) and build personal relations with key commanders, rather than well-articulated political ideologies and formalized political-bureaucratic structures. Due to these characteristics African armed groups are often organizationally unstable, with commanders frequently switching sides or creating their own military outfits depending on shifts in military fortunes or flows of patronage. As has already been touched upon, such armed groups are often unfit to be transformed into political parties. In addition, the weakness of the African post-civil war state, the centrality of Big Man politics and the difficulties of transforming African armed groups into viable political parties mean that the challenge posed by WDs should be particularly prevalent on the African continent. Even if this volume focuses on African WDs in the post-Cold War era, it is crucial to stress that it is not a new phenomenon on the continent. In fact, before 1989 WDs played an important role in countries such as Nigeria and Zimbabwe.

Having said this, it is important to mention that the presence of WDs is not confined to Sub-Saharan Africa. On the contrary, it is a global phenomenon that occurs in a wide variety of post-civil war societies. In countries such as Afghanistan (e.g. Burhanuddin Rabbani), Indonesia/Aceh (e.g. Muzakir Manaf and Irwandi Yusuf), Kosovo (e.g. Hashim Thaçi) and Timor-Leste (e.g. Xanana Gusmão) ex-military turned politicians have played an influential – and at times controversial – role in electoral politics. The global reach of the question at hand has a number of important implications. The findings generated from this study cannot, for instance, be viewed through a purely Africanist lens, particularly since weak states, Big Men and fluid armed groups also exist in other parts of the world (although to a lesser extent). In fact, we believe that we can learn important aspects about African WDs by bringing in examples from other parts of the world (something which we do in this chapter), especially when considering how understudied the topic at hand is. We are therefore critical of the view that Africa is somehow unique, something that is common amongst Africanist scholars. However, this does not mean that we can – based on this book's findings – make outright generalizations to non-African cases. Before this can be done, it is first necessary to conduct similar studies outside of Africa.

Lords of peace or instigators of insecurity

What happens to democracies' capacity to deliver post-war security when electoral politics are dominated by WDs rather than strong institutions and consolidated, democratic political parties? Is there a heightened risk of insecurity or can we expect WDs to shepherd their followers towards long-term peace? We can gain an initial understanding of the range of possible security outcomes by referring to previous research – such as the literature on causes of war, peacebuilding and post-civil war democratization – that has investigated the propensity of elites to either support peace or engage in violence.

Warlord democrats as peacelords A central objective of conflict resolution is to create the necessary incentives, and sometimes deterrents, to convince military leaders to "buy into" peace. For some leaders, understanding the hopelessness of continued fighting – due to damaging stalemates or a sense of impending military doom – is enough to invest in such war-to-peace transitions (see e.g. Zartman 1989; Stedman 1991). Other elites may, however, need more tangible inducements to lay down their arms, ranging from security guarantees, amnesties, minority rights, regional autonomy and democratic reforms, to power-sharing agreements and government employment giving them access to state patronage (Gurr 2000; Walter 2002; Hartzell and Hoddie 2003; Jarstad and Sisk 2008; Melander 2009; Spears 2013). Whichever form such concessions take, peacemakers hope that they will be enough to convince military leaders to become allies as they tread the troublesome road towards sustainable peace and democracy.

Experience has also shown that such expectations are not held in vain; in fact, ex-military elites often play a constructive role in peace processes. Initially such leadership is crucial in order to deliver followers. Ex-military leaders can do this by convincing the latter of the necessity of making painful concessions, to end the violence and to disarm and demobilize (Zartman 1995: 19; Darby and Mac Ginty 2000: 239; Jarstad and Sisk 2008: 23). In many post-civil war societies, the latter has proven to be particularly crucial. Giving up arms is often a traumatic event for fighters. Having looked after their own security during the war, they are suddenly expected to trust the security forces – who may be their former opponents – to protect them. The qualms associated with disarmament and demobilization may therefore require that military leaders conduct tours in their fiefdoms to convince their subordinates that they have nothing to fear by becoming civilians (Themnér 2011). As peace progresses, the same leaders can play a crucial role in reconciling war-affected communities. They can do this by verbal and symbolic acknowledgement of

17

their own side's misdeeds, as well as recognizing the other side's wartime suffering (Kaufman 2006; Brounéus 2008). Such efforts should preferably not be one-time events. It is crucial that ex-military leaders "develop tools for gathering support without extreme nationalist appeals" (Kaufman 2006: 209) and "reconstruct their nationalist discourses to emphasize the strands that justify peace and reconciliation, sidelining the hostile discourses that lead back into the symbolic politics trap" (Kaufman 2006: 215). The leadership style most closely associated with these peace-striving virtues is "transformational", where leaders seek to look beyond prevailing circumstances and provide alternative ideas, aspirations and hopes to followers (Burns 1978).

It can be argued that if ex-military leaders have played a positive role in initiating and building peace – by for instance convincing their followers to stop fighting and to disarm, and engaging in reconciliation initiatives – they should also have incentives to play an equally productive role in an electoral context. This is particularly true if electoral participation provides an actual opportunity to transform military might into post-war influence, rather than a process seeking to ensure their political-economic marginalization.

It is important to stress that peacelords – WDs who invest in the new peace order being built – come in many stripes and colors. At one extreme one finds ex-militaries who can best be described as transformational; WDs who actively seek to address the root causes of the war, employ inclusive discourses or seek to depoliticize communal tensions. Through his efforts to build an inclusive South Africa in the aftermath of Apartheid, Nelson Mandela is probably the WD that came closest to embodying these qualities. At the other extreme of the peacelord continuum are WDs who do not undermine post-war security, but at the same time do not actively seek to address the structural conditions that may generate renewed violence. Such WDs are essentially conservative, preferring to retain the status quo rather than risk unleashing societal changes that may undermine their own positions of power.

Warlord democrats as instigators of insecurity Even if we can assume that some WDs will, under certain circumstances, embrace their role as peace-lords, there are reasons to believe that the opposite may also be true. In fact, the interplay between a volatile post-war transitional environment and WDs' militant background may push or entice the latter to resort to aggression. Concerning the former, post-civil war societies are – especially during the first years following the cessation of hostilities – extremely challenging environments that put immense pressure on WDs. With the arrival of peace, wartime structures – such as command structures, logistical support systems and illicit economic networks – are either dismantled or reconfigured, as political pacts are renegotiated and patronage networks realigned. During such transitions wartime actors seek to maintain their power, while new actors hope to carve out a political space for themselves. Due to the fluidity of this process, it is extremely difficult for elites to assess their relative differences in power and who is most likely to prevail in upcoming elections. This uncertainty – in conjuncture with fears of being targeted by opponents, arrested for war crimes and the prevalence of rumors (reliable media outlets are notoriously scarce in many war-ridden countries) – often creates anxieties about what the future has in store (see e.g. Anders 2012). A particular problem for WDs is that – unless they control the reins of power or extensive business enterprises – time is not on their side. Coming out of war and participating in the first post-civil war elections, WDs often have, as previously touched upon, an economic advantage over other candidates. However, being a Big Man is an extremely expensive affair. Not only do the latter have to distribute substantial amounts of patronage to retain their Big Men positions, they are also expected to parade their wealth by flaunting costly prestige goods and organizing impressive social events (Daloz 2003: 281). According to Daloz (2003: 281):

> Supporters expect their respective leader to display external signs of wealth with regard to those representing other networks. They revel in the idea that he possesses more prestigious and impressive goods for these are in some way a credit to the whole community or of the faction which identifies with it ... the effect of ostentatious display is the manifestation of a certain kind of prosperity and power, but also somehow reassures the followers of a particular Big Man about his capacity to supply and satisfy the network of dependents.

For WDs this entails that they must invest substantial amounts of resources if they are to have a chance at the polls. In fact, if they lose the first post-war elections they may never get another chance. Having spent a large portion of their wealth, they may lack the resources to credibly run for office a second time. This is particularly true when considering that WDs' wartime capacity to extract resources and instill fear generally diminishes over time. In addition, once new actors gain access to public office – and the economic resources associated with it – they are likely to outspend any WD seeking to defeat them at the ballots. The costs of being a Big Man and the need to gain quick returns on Big Man investments therefore puts additional pressures on WDs.

When faced with such transitional pressures, it is not uncommon for elites to react violently. For some leaders, such violence is largely opportunistic. When regimes fall or there is a transition between governments, some elites utilize political or security vacuums to address old grievances through violent mobilization. Other leaders may engage in aggression for more defensive reasons. Incumbents who fear losing power can, for instance, employ violence to fend off opponents or stall the implementation of further political reforms. Meanwhile, fearing that institutions can no longer ensure the security of their ethnic or religious communities, minority leaders sometimes arm their followers when state structures fall apart (Brown 1996; Figueiredo and Weingast 1999; Gurr 2000).

There are reasons to suspect that the militant background of WDs make them particularly prone to respond aggressively to the pressures inherent in war-to-peace transitions. Research has, for instance, shown that military experience has a negative effect on agreeableness; a concept employed to capture qualities such as kindness, sympathy, warmth, consideration and willingness to cooperate. This entails that WDs should, for example, be more likely to act aggressively towards others and have difficulty in getting along with people (Jackson et al. 2012). In addition, it has been argued that the "sheer familiarity with the instruments of armed coercion create conditions that may predispose military leaders in favor of using force" and "officers see the world through unique lenses that impact their choices about the use of force in specific, predictable ways" (Sechser 2004: 750). This is because military elites are not trained to make cautious and introspective decisions; in fact, during war lengthy deliberations are dangerous and may result in defeat. In addition, due to their military training generals and officers have a tendency to employ military solutions even in situations which may call for alternative responses (Sechser 2004). Furthermore, because WDs are less likely than non-military leaders to trust political adversaries, we can expect them to shun risky agreements and not see the long-term advantages of sustained relationships (Jervis 2013: 164). Hence, this school of thought teaches us that once a military, always a military; there are, in other words, few prospects of socializing WDs into becoming peacelords.

Given that some WDs may react aggressively while navigating in a transitional electoral environment, how is this behavior likely to manifest itself? We argue that WDs are particularly likely to support different forms of organized violence, securitize wartime identities, criminalize politics or foster human rights abuses.[7]

SUPPORTING ORGANIZED VIOLENCE When engaged in elite power struggles, it is reasonable to suspect that WDs may order or sponsor different forms of organized violence – held as armed force employed against political or military rivals, their supporters or property. In fact, several scholars have pointed to the danger of elites who feel threatened by ongoing democratization processes initiating different types of violence (Höglund 2008; Jarstad and Sisk 2008). By employing such forms of aggression leaders may hope to disrupt the transition process, overthrow election results, disrupt political rallies or hinder voters from going to the polls (Jarstad and Sisk 2008: 25). In the Republic of Congo, for instance, former Cobra warlords who were members of the cabinet ordered army units loyal to them to attack former rebels during the run-up to the 2002 national elections. They thereby hoped to provoke a conflict with the ex-rebels and force the president to postpone the elections – elections which they feared would result in their political and economic marginalization (Themnér 2011). However, the violence that WDs initiate does not have to take the form of warfare. In fact, WDs may choose to incite their supporters to engage in rioting[8] or attack opposition leaders or supporters, as well as party headquarters or government buildings. If ex-military turned politicians incite, order or finance such forms of organized violence there is a heightened risk that the credibility of political institutions to function as a conflict resolution mechanism will be compromised. From experience, violence is particularly likely to take place during the first post-war elections, when fears generally run higher, former wartime actors wield more power and power structures are more fluid (Jarstad and Sisk 2008; Brancati and Snyder 2013). Irrespective of the exact form the violence takes, mobilization is often facilitated by WDs' access to different kinds of military networks. It is, for instance, not uncommon for WDs to have cordial relations with their former mid-level commanders (ex-MiLCs) long after the war has ended. In turn, such broker figures often retain a substantial amount of influence over their ex-fighters, making it relatively easy for ex-MiLCs to recreate militia units, set up military task forces or orchestrate riots on behalf of WDs (Themnér 2012).

SECURITIZING WARTIME IDENTITIES During war leaders often play on the collective fears of communities to mobilize support for the war effort. According to Brown (1996) many elites competing for power in weak states play the ethnic card. While blaming economic and political shortcomings on members of other communal groups, elites may seek to present themselves as "the champions of ethnic groups" (Brown 1996: 586). In the wake of such agitation, feelings of insecurity appear, increasing ethnic solidarity and convincing men and women to rally behind their leaders (Brown 1996: 585-590; Lyons 2005: 43-47). In this process many military leaders can make use of their rhetorical skills; studies have, for instance, shown that one of the reasons why warlords are able to mobilize popular support is because of their charismatic qualities (Reno 1998). The net result of this is that civil wars tend to polarize group identities by creating inter-group stereotypes, removing complexities and cementing perceived differences between in- and outgroups (Bar-Tal 2000).

With the arrival of peace and electoral politics it is crucial to change the ethos of war into one of peace (Bar-Tal 2000). As previously touched upon, elites have the potential to play a decisive role in this process. By publicly acknowledging wartime transgressions and employing inclusive discourses of peace and justice, they can support efforts to reconcile war-afflicted groups (Kaufman 2006; Brounéus 2008). A central problem is, however, that societal reconciliation may not be in the interest of WDs. In fact, the latter may want to keep fears and hatred alive by continuing to securitize wartime identities – portraying members of other groups as hostile, claiming that members of their own group are in jeopardy, describing ex-combatants as a menace to peace or threatening to use violence. Under such circumstances former military leaders can play on their wartime credentials and attract votes by arguing that only they can protect their constituencies from parties of other groups or control the violent agency of ex-fighters (see e.g. Paris 2004; Lyons 2005; Kaufman 2006; Papagianni 2008: 66–67; Brancati and Snyder 2013). According to Lyons (2005: 62), this may mean that "[l]eaders who have the most violent pasts may make the most convincing claim that a vote for them is a vote for peace". This is what happened during the first post-conflict elections in Bosnia-Herzegovina, where moderate and multi-ethnic parties fared poorly due to ethnic outbidding by more radical parties (Lyons 2005: 62).

Aggressive discursive practices by WDs can put immense pressure on state institutions and risks undermining their capacity to mitigate conflicts. When communities continue to be engulfed in fear and mobilized along wartime cleavages, even seemingly minor events – from a macro perspective – can trigger outbursts of organized violence. In 2010 the killing of a teenage girl from the Loma ethnic group in Lofa County, Liberia, set off riots between Lomas and Mandingos – two communities that had supported opposite sides during the previous civil wars – that left four dead and at least eighteen injured (Reeve and Speare 2010). If there are no institutions constraining the effects of such communal fears – such as a strong and neutral police force and judiciary that is under democratic control – there is a risk that ex-militaries will manipulate wartime identities to remobilize for war (see e.g. Chowdhury and Krebs 2009: 382).

CRIMINALIZING POLITICS The power and influence of military leaders is partly a function of their ability to set up illicit economic networks – used to engage in racketeering or to smuggle arms, drugs, valuable natural resources, as well as plundered goods – that can finance their armed activities. As previously touched upon, these networks often also function as a route to personal enrichment for many military elites. With the cessation of hostilities and holding of elections it can therefore be tempting for ex-militaries to seek to retain control over these structures (Zürcher 2011: 74; Zürcher et al. 2013: 23). At worst, this can result in the criminalization of politics – here referred to as situations where WDs run, order or sponsor international smuggling, drug dealing or racketeering. Such processes are facilitated by the ease with which wartime economic structures are transformed into peacetime organized criminal networks (Höglund 2008: 89). Hashim Thaçi, former head of the Kosovo Liberation Army (KLA) and President of Kosovo, for instance, has been accused of personally leading a criminal network responsible for

trafficking arms, drugs and organs (Lewis 2010). In fact, the resources generated from criminal activities can be used to finance electoral campaigns and
distribute patronage amongst potential voters. Experiences from several
African countries have even shown that it is often necessary for Big Men
to incorporate criminal elements within their networks; elites lacking such
connections risk forfeiting incomes generated from illicit enterprises, which is
major source of financing in many developing countries (Utas 2012). In some
instances, the very rationale for entering politics is to protect and expand
one's criminal enterprises by gaining access to the official structures of the
state (Manning 2007: 257).

Irrespective of the reason, the intermarriage of crime and politics is likely
to have serious consequences for post-war societies. Running or sponsoring
such outfits generally necessitates the use or threat of violence to fend off
potential competitors. In several post-civil war countries, such as El Salvador,
turf wars between criminal gangs have resulted in a sharp increase in crime
and more casualties per year than during the previous civil war (Höglund
and Söderberg Kovacs 2010). If ex-militaries running for or holding office
engage in similar criminal activities, then "democracy" has arguably failed in
its efforts to mitigate conflicts peacefully: rather than entrenching the notion
that economic redistribution should be attained via electoral politics, it can
incite citizens to use criminal means to attain social mobility. This can, at worst,
create a culture of impunity, which glorifies violence as a tool to resolve societal
disputes (Höglund and Söderberg Kovacs 2010; Themnér and Ohlson 2014).

FOSTERING HUMAN RIGHTS ABUSES During civil wars military leaders often
order their forces to abuse or kill both external and internal opponents, as
well as civilians. By utilizing such tactics, there is always a risk that military leaders become caught in a mindset where they believe it is acceptable and even legitimate to physically abuse political opponents. In fact, it
is not uncommon that human rights abuses continue after the cessation of
hostilities. Often the perpetrators of such misdeeds are government officials or
other actors who played a key role in the previous armed conflict (Höglund
2008: 94). For instance, after being elected president in 1997, the ex-warlord
Charles Taylor ordered his former militiamen to attack supporters of United
Liberation Movement of Liberia – Johnson faction (ULIMO-J) (ICG 2002).
If ex-militaries engage in human rights abuses such as beatings, torture or
extrajudicial killings, or arrest political opponents or critics under the guise of
democracy, there is a risk that the legitimacy of the electoral process will come
into question (Kumar 1997: 9). At worst such misdeeds have the potential to
trigger renewed hostilities. The violations orchestrated by Taylor (see above)
resulted in an exodus of opposition elites into exile, where they eventually
regrouped under the guise of LURD. Having experienced the harshness of

Taylor's regime, LURD leaders refused to stop fighting unless Taylor stepped down as president (Themnér 2011).

Why warlord democrats further peace or foster insecurity

Why do some WDs choose to sponsor organized violence, foster human rights abuses, criminalize politics or securitize wartime identities while others act more benevolently? To address this question, the chapter authors trace the war- and peacetime trajectories of the selected WDs. Even though this is foremost done through inductive process tracing, it can, at this point, be useful to say something about possible factors that may push or entice WDs to either support peace or undermine post-war security. Here we identify four such clusters of explanatory factors: electoral constraints, capacity to misbehave, cost of misbehaving and personality traits.

Electoral constraints A first set of variables relates to the chances of being elected. A central aspect in this category concerns how "democratic" the political system is. If WDs perceive that they will not be given a fair chance at the polls, they may resort to bullying behavior. This could, for instance, be the case when opponents engage in electoral fraud or harassment of supporters, or when central state institutions such as electoral commissions, judiciaries or bureaucracies are biased towards the incumbent regime (Zeeuw 2007: 20, 251; Jarstad and Sisk 2008: 25). The latter is a particular problem in many African states, which tend to be dominated by one political party (Manning 2007: 268). Similar problems may arise due to how electoral systems are constructed. For instance, majoritarian systems and high barriers to enter the legislature (i.e. requirements that political parties need to receive a large percentage of the vote to be represented in the legislature) can frustrate WDs' efforts to become elected (Zeeuw 2007: 21, 237). Equally important is the size of WDs' potential electorate; in fact, without a large support base WDs may struggle to attract votes (Zeeuw 2007: 20–21; Themnér 2012). The potential electorate is likely to be large when WDs' armed groups did not engage in systematic large-scale abuses during the war, WDs command loyalties in multiple and large social groups, there are few other political actors competing for the same vote and old wartime incompatibilities still dominate political discourses (Manning 2007: 255; Söderberg Kovacs 2007: 33, 199).

Another type of electoral constraint concerns the strength of WDs' patronage networks. In order to successfully compete in elections, WDs – like most Big Men – need access to substantial economic resources. Without such assets, it is difficult for WDs to fund electoral campaigns and distribute patronage to clients and potential voters (Lindberg 2003). WDs are most likely to accumulate substantial resources when they have acquired multiple leadership positions, such as official state positions and heads of business enterprises, religious communities or criminal networks, which allow them to draw resources from numerous sources (Utas 2012). A particular problem is when WDs are dislodged from such positions or when less patronage can be extracted from these sources. With fewer benefits to distribute, WDs risk being defeated in upcoming elections. Experiences have shown that leaders – particularly incumbents – are prone to use violence, and disrupt elections, under such circumstances (Southhall and Melber 2006; Jarstad and Sisk 2008: 25).

To some extent, international actors have – besides putting pressure on governing elites to democratize post-war societies – the capacity to offset some of the electoral constraints that WDs experience. It is, for instance, not uncommon that international donors provide economic resources and democratic/political training to former wartime actors in order to help them compete in upcoming elections (Söderberg Kovacs 2007: 37; Zeeuw 2007: 27). In addition, foreign powers can confer legitimacy on certain elites, while withholding it from others, thereby enhancing the bargaining power of the former (Barnett and Zürcher 2009: 32).

The capacity to misbehave A second cluster of variables concerns the ability of WDs to engage in belligerent acts. In this context, WDs' access to men and women who can quickly be mobilized for violent enterprises – irrespective of whether they are for political or criminal purposes – is of particular importance. This is of course easiest if WDs have access to the security forces, or at least parts of them. Even if such WDs, often heads of state, do not always enjoy a monopoly on violence, they can at least relatively quickly field forces when challenged by protesters or armed groups. Habitually oppositional WDs do not have access to similar armed units, since they are often expected to disband and demobilize their armed groups with the arrival of peace (Berdal 1996). However, at times oppositional WDs are allowed to keep smaller armed units intact, often designated as bodyguards. Such armed entities can be valuable if tensions escalate. In fact, they can function as a core to build an armed group around or be used for small-scale attacks (Themnér 2011). Lacking such units, WDs become dependent on informal command structures that bind them to their ex-commanders and fighters. Even if WDs generally have access to such networks, there is often great variation in how many ex-fighters the former can mobilize at any given time. The size and strength of ex-command structures usually varies depending on how many years have passed since the war ended and the amount of resources and time WDs have invested in ensuring the loyalty of their former followers (Themnér 2015). Access to armed followers is, however, not the only type of capacity that matters. Here it is important to mention aspects such as the availability of arms and ammunition, as well as access to illicit trade networks and regional or international sponsors who are willing to promote belligerent acts (Berdal

1996; Stedman et al. 2002; Nilsson 2005; Zeeuw 2007: 22-23). If these three factors are not present, threats by WDs that they will employ violence may ring hollow, and it would be difficult for them to sustain armed actions once initiated. In addition, it should be difficult for WDs to criminalize politics without having access to actors who specialize in moving contraband, arms, drugs or valuable natural resources over regional and international borders.

The cost of misbehaving A third set of variables is structural conditions that increase the cost of being belligerent. The most obvious of these factors is the ability of and commitment by the ruling elite to uphold law and order. For instance, if the security forces are weak or non-existent it may be tempting for WDs to challenge the new peace order (Zeeuw 2007: 251; Cramer 2009: 136). Because of the fragility of police and armed forces in many war-ridden countries, international support for the peace process may in many instances be of even greater importance (Greenhill and Major 2006/2007). Such assistance can range from having peacekeepers on the ground to providing security guarantees promising military support in case any actors seek to re-engage in violence (Walter 2002; Fortna 2008). Strong international commitment is presumably particularly crucial when WDs control the reins of power; without such constraints WDs may employ security forces against their domestic enemies. These factors are not only likely to affect the willingness of WDs to support organized violence. In fact, it can be argued that WDs will also think twice before fostering human rights abuses, securitizing wartime identities and even criminalizing politics if security forces are strong and the international commitment to uphold the new peace order is undisputable. Furthermore, when it comes to criminalizing politics, a decisive factor may be how effective and accountable state institutions are. If they are permeated by corruption and lack of transparency, it should facilitate efforts by WDs to manipulate state structures for their own criminal purposes (Cramer 2009: 133-134).

Personality traits A final set of factors concerns WDs' personality traits. As previously touched upon, research has shown that there is a correlation between military experience and aggression. This does not, however, mean that all WDs are likely to exhibit the same levels of militarism and authoritarianism. In fact, there are reasons to believe that there is great variation depending on the duration and intensity of the war, how engaged the WDs were in the actual planning and implementation of the hostilities, and to what degree the WDs were able to centralize the power of their armed movements during the war; WDs who succeeded in doing the latter are likely to possess more authoritarian peacetime leadership styles (Zeeuw 2007: 14). Studies have also shown that leaders who have experienced defeats or loss are more likely to engage in atrocities (Kim 2010: 239). Militant norms are not merely a function of what happened during the war though. They can also be an effect of WDs' personal background and traits and values acquired before the war. Jervis (2013: 164), for instance, holds that there is a link "between a more closed intellectual style and a predisposition toward tough measures and the use of force". The militant traits of WDs can, however, be mitigated by other, more positive experiences. For instance, if a wartime leader has "some experience with democratic politics, possesses some governance and political expertise" they are more likely to act benevolently (Zeeuw 2007: 232). Aspects relating to learning thereby become important, allowing former military leaders to acquire a new set of norms or worldview (Levy 1994; Ohlson 1998).

Trying to detect nuances in WDs' personality types can be likened to Stedman's (1997) efforts to construct a typology of different kinds of spoilers. True, some WDs may be close to what Stedman refers to as total spoilers "who pursue total power and exclusive recognition of authority and hold immutable preferences" and "see the world in all-or-nothing terms and often suffer from pathological tendencies that prevent the pragmatism necessary for compromise settlements of conflicts" (Stedman 1997: 10-11). Yet, when taking a closer look at what appear to be total spoilers, it may become apparent that peacemakers are actually confronted by greedy or limited ones, whose mental frames are not defined in "all-or-nothing" terms. From a peacemaking perspective it makes all the difference if WDs are examples of the two latter, rather than the former; if WDs resemble Stedman's greedy or limited spoilers there is a possibility that they can be induced or coaxed into behaving benevolently.

Probing the cases

In order to answer the research questions guiding this book (does the electoral participation of WDs tend to have a positive or negative effect on post-civil war security; and if there are negative implications, how do they manifest themselves?) subsequent chapters will trace the war- and peacetime trajectories of ten WDs in seven countries: DRC, Guinea-Bissau, Liberia, Mozambique, Rwanda, Sierra Leone and South Sudan. The chapter authors differ when it comes to the number of ex-military leaders that they analyze – anything from one to three – and the extent to which their inquiries have a deductive theoretical or a more inductive empirical approach. The chapters do, however, have two essential aspects in common. First, the cases and points of comparison are individual WDs rather than the states they operate in. Hence, even if country-specific factors can play a role in determining security outcomes, the WDs' actions can only be understood by taking into account the set of resources at WDs' disposal and the personality traits that define them. Second, a set of common questions are used to steer the analysis of each chapter. This will facilitate efforts to draw more general conclusions about when and why WDs seek to further peace, rather than foster insecurity, and what strategies peacemakers can employ when faced with different kinds of ex-military turned democrats.

The first set of questions concern the maneuverings of WDs during their electoral careers and the effect on larger political outcomes:

- Which electoral strategy did the ex-militaries choose?
  - Did they seek to transform their former armed group into a political party, join other political parties, form a completely new political party, or run as independents?
  - What explains their choice of strategy?
  - Did they use different electoral strategies and switch over time?
  - If they switched, what explains their shift in strategies?
- How did the WDs' electoral maneuverings affect the political dynamics in their respective countries?

As previously noted, there are reasons to believe that when WDs engage in electoral politics some may play a positive role by investing in the peace process, while others may engage in more detrimental and aggressive behaviors (e.g. sponsoring organized violence, securitizing wartime identities, criminal-izing politics and fostering human rights abuses). To establish whether and how the studied ex-militaries did this, the following questions will be posed:

- Did the WDs in question play a positive role in consolidating the peace process?
  - If so, did they do this by merely refraining from engaging in aggressive behaviors (sponsoring organized violence, securitizing wartime identities, criminalizing politics and fostering human rights abuses)?
  - Or did they take more direct steps to further long-term peace (e.g. symbolic and public measures to further societal reconciliation or democracy-building, or take steps to address the root causes of war)?
- Did the WDs in question support, order or finance organized violence (armed force employed against political or military rivals, their supporters or property)?
- Did they seek to securitize wartime identities (portray members of other groups as hostile, claim that members of their own group were in jeopardy, describe ex-combatants as a menace to peace or threaten to use violence)?
- Did they run, order or sponsor criminal activities (international smuggling, drug dealing or racketeering)?
- Did they commit or were they responsible for any human rights abuses (beatings, torture or extrajudicial executions, or arrest political opponents or critics)?
- Did they switch between the abovementioned strategies (seeking to consolidate the peace process; support, order or finance organized violence; secu-

ritize wartime identities; run, order or sponsor criminal activities; foster human rights abuses) over time?

To gain a better understanding of which trajectories ex-military democrats can use to either function as peacelords that support the consolidation of peace or undermine post-civil war security (sponsoring organized violence, securitizing wartime identities, criminalizing politics and fostering human rights abuses), a number of additional questions will be posed to each case:

- What factors explain the WDs' choice to either help to consolidate the peace process or foster insecurity (sponsor organized violence, securitize wartime identities, criminalize politics, fostered human rights abuses)?
  - Did these factors predominately concern electoral constraints, capacity to misbehave, cost of misbehaving or personality traits?
  - Were any other set of factors important?
- If the ex-militaries switched between being benevolent leaders and sponsoring organized violence, securitizing wartime identities, criminalizing politics and fostering human rights abuses, what explains these switches in strategy?

Finally, to develop more efficient strategies for how peacemakers can deal with ex-military turned politicians, the following set of queries will be addressed in each case:

- What strategies or policies (if any) did national or international peacemakers or governments employ to convince WDs to support the consolidation of the peace process?
  - If the WDs did sponsor organized violence, securitize wartime identities, criminalize politics or foster human rights abuses, what were the reactions of national or international peacemakers or governments?
  - Were these actions successful in constraining the belligerency of the WDs?
  - What lessons can be drawn from these experiences?

Chapter breakdown

In Chapter 1 Judith Verweijen traces the post-war trajectories of Antipas Mbusa Nyamwisi, former leader of the Congolese Rally for Democracy/Kisangani-Liberation Movement (Rassemblement Congolais pour la Démocratie/ Kisangani-Mouvement de Libération, RCD/K-ML). After the 2002 Pretoria Accord, which ended the war in the Democratic Republic of Congo, Mbusa spearheaded the transformation of RCD/K-ML into a political party and ran as its standard-bearer in two successive presidential elections (2006 and 2011). After having initially supported the regime of President Joseph Kabila, Mbusa increasingly fell out of favor with the latter. This constituted a serious threat to Mbusa's political survival – with less access to state patronage he risked losing his position of influence. Verweijen lucidly highlights how this development not only pushed Mbusa to drift towards the opposition, but also to fan rumors about his influence over a number of opposition armed groups. In this sense, Mbusa hoped to regain political leverage by deploying conflict narratives as a mobilizing resource. Even if it is difficult to verify to what extent Mbusa actually supported different forms of organized violence, his *pompier-pyromane* (firefighter-pyromaniac) strategy did ensure a certain amount of continued political relevance. The chapter illustrates how the semblance of continued military influence may be just as crucial for WDs as actual armed capacity.

Chapter 2 by Lars Waldorf focuses on the efforts of Paul Kagame – leader of RPF – to centralize power in post-genocide Rwanda. Even if Kagame de facto controlled the reins of government after RPF's military victory in 1994, it was not until 2000 that he became Rwanda's president. In two successive presidential elections (2003 and 2010) Kagame reconfirmed his and RPF's hold on power. Kagame's time in office highlights a central dilemma of post-war reconstruction: militaristic leadership styles can, on the one hand, facilitate impressive economic and developmental achievements (which has presumably had a stabilizing effect on Rwanda's post-war security), but can, on the other hand, generate systematic human rights abuses. Waldorf argues that the regime's choice to target real and suspected political opponents was a function of Kagame's personality and the fact that ethnic Tutsis (Kagame's main supporters) merely constitute a small minority of Rwanda's population.

In Chapter 3, Carrie Manning and Anders Themnér analyze the electoral navigations of two Liberian former military leaders – Sekou Conneh (ex-LURD) and Prince Johnson (ex-Independent National Patriotic Front of Liberia (INPFL)). While Conneh failed to convince the electorate to make him president (as a standard-bearer of the PRODEM) in 2005, Johnson succeeded in being elected senator in both 2005 and 2014 (both times as an independent) and came in third place in the 2011 presidential elections (as leader of NUDP). A cornerstone of both WDs' electoral strategies was to securitize wartime identities. By reminding potential voters of the fragility of the peace process and instilling fear amongst the former, they were able to make their old military credentials relevant in a democratic context. This was a rational strategy; as increasingly marginal figures in post-civil war Liberia, aggressive discourses provided Conneh and Johnson with much-needed public attention. In fact, faced with a strong UN peacekeeping force, the securitization of wartime identities constituted a form of "spoiling on the cheap". However, Conneh and Johnson mixed such discourses of fear with reconciliatory statements emphasizing their commitment to peace. Hence, by pointing to the "rhetorical ambivalence" (Chowdhury and Krebs 2009: 379) of Conneh and Johnson, Manning and Themnér highlight the chameleonic behavior of WDs.

By portraying themselves as both villains and saviors, WDs can increase their bargaining range vis-à-vis political opponents.

Afonso Dhlakama, former leader of the Mozambican National Resistance (Resistência Nacional Moçambicana, RENAMO), is the focus of Chapter 4. In this chapter, Alex Vines traces Dhlakama's efforts to ensure continued political relevance during Mozambique's war-to-peace transition. Having shepherded RENAMO's transformation into a political party and participation in electoral politics, Dhlakama became leader of one of Africa's largest opposition parties in the 1990s. In fact, during the 1999 national elections, Dhlakama came close to winning the presidential elections. However, from the early 2000s and onwards Dhlakama became increasingly belligerent. Electoral constraints – due to electoral tampering by the Mozambique Liberation Front (Frente de Libertação de Moçambique, FRELIMO) regime and a faltering patronage network – pushed Dhlakama to seek to securitize wartime identities by threatening to engage in organized violence. A contributing factor in this transformation may also have been his insecure personality. After riot police began arresting RENAMO supporters in 2012, Dhlakama delivered on his promise and eventually took to arms. The return to violence was facilitated by the failure to demobilize Dhlakama's Presidential Guard. For Dhlakama the main objective for escalating the hostilities was to coerce the government into making economic and political concessions and subsequently solidify his networks of dependents. Through a detailed empirical analysis, Vines displays how a relatively benign and democratic WD can become "socialized" into belligerency when operating in a semi-autocratic context. The example of Dhlakama also teaches us that winning at the polls may not necessarily be the main objective of WDs. In flawed democracies, WDs can have more to gain by seeking to coerce the regime – through threats, demonstrations and violence – into cutting political and economic deals, allowing them to sustain their networks of patronage.

In Chapter 5, Henrik Vigh tells the story of one of Africa's most resilient and innovative WDs, Guinea-Bissau's João Bernardo Vieira. Throughout his political career Vieira had a canny ability to reinvent himself; from celebrated freedom fighter, to Marxist dictator, two-time president elect (in 1994 as standard-bearer for PAIGC and in 2005 as an independent), and finally feared drug kingpin. Interestingly, as head of state in the early 1990s Vieira spearheaded the country's democratic process and organized relatively free and fair elections. However, after being reinstated in office in 1994, and after the 2005 elections, Vieira fell back on old authoritarian and militaristic patterns; not only were political opponents attacked and killed, there was a general obstruction of the press. Furthermore, Vieira was only able to make a political comeback in 2005 (he had been ousted from power in 1999) by promising key elites a cut of a cocaine smuggling enterprise that he planned to build if elected. Once in office, Vieira delivered on his promise and transformed Guinea-Bissau into a conduit for international drug smuggling. Through his detailed narrative, Vigh provides two central insights concerning the nature of WDs. First, even if some WDs may be good at initiating democratic transitions, they are likely to be bad at sustaining and entrenching them. Second, there is a risk that if elected, WDs may employ their informal military and economic networks to criminalize the state and politics. This is particularly true if the WDs in question have few alternative economic resources to sustain their patronage networks.

In Chapter 6, Mimmi Söderberg Kovacs and Ibrahim Bangura compare the post-civil war experiences of three Sierra Leonean WDs – Julius Maada Bio (former head of the junta National Provisional Ruling Council, NPRC), Eldred Collins (ex-spokesperson of the RUF), and Samuel Hinga Norman (ex-leader of the Kamajor militia). Bio, Collins and Norman employed different strategies to maximize their chances of carving out a political space for themselves in post-war Sierra Leone: Norman was a key electoral mobilizer for the SLPP, Collins supported the transformation of his rebel group into a political party (RUFP), and Bio eventually positioned himself as the head of SLPP. The electoral machinations of both Bio and Norman were to some extent successful; while the latter was made minister of internal affairs in 2002, Bio ensured that SLPP (which had lost the 2007 elections) continued to be Sierra Leone's main opposition party after the 2012 elections. It was only Collins who struggled to retain some semblance of political influence, coming fifth in the 2012 elections as RUFP's presidential candidate.

Interestingly, the security effects of the three WDs' electoral participation were very different. Norman, who was initially a stout supporter of the peace process, began to securitize wartime identities and possibly even encourage armed violence after his indictment by the Special Court for Sierra Leone in 2003. Even if there is limited evidence that Bio ordered the violence committed by SLPP supporters during the 2012 elections, he undoubtedly benefited from it. Having built his political career on his youthfulness, militancy and a promise to stand up against the aggressiveness of the APC regime, Bio had little interest in stopping local outbursts of violence. Meanwhile, as a representative of a political movement that had inflicted mass atrocities during the previous war, had been military defeated, and had a limited following, it was strategic for Collins to embrace a reconciliatory discourse and not upset the public by engaging in further belligerency. Söderberg Kovacs and Bangura's comparative analysis illustrates two general observations about WDs. First, even when WDs have incentives to undermine post-civil war security, they are often acutely aware of what domestic audiences and international actors deem "acceptable" behavior. Under such circumstances, they may prefer to securitize wartime identities or indirectly associate themselves with violent acts, rather than openly support armed aggression. Second, counterintuitively it may be WDs linked to the most appalling atrocities that are most willing to embrace a peaceful and reconciliatory political discourse. This is particularly true if they have limited domestic support.

Johan Brosché and Kristine Höglund's Chapter 7 investigates the political maneuverings of Riek Machar. As a key figure of the Sudan People's Liberation Movement/Army (SPLM/A), Machar played a pivotal role in cementing the party's dominance over South Sudan's political and economic life after the signing of the 2005 Comprehensive Peace Agreement (CPA). In fact, in 2005 Machar became vice-president, a position that he retained after the 2010 national elections and South Sudan's 2011 declaration of independence. However, in 2013 Machar fell out with President Salva Kiir, when the former declared his intention to challenge Kiir for the leadership of SPLM and by extension who would rule South Sudan. In response, Kiir sacked Machar as vice-president. The rupture between Machar and Kiir had far-reaching implications; not only did Machar begin to securitize wartime identities by accusing Kiir of promoting "Dinkocracy", but by December 2013 the leaders were embroiled in a bloody civil war. Machar's growing belligerency can be explained by the risk of losing his patronage networks (due to his ousting from the government) and President Kiir's increasingly autocratic leadership style. Meanwhile, had it not been for Machar's continued armed capacity – loyal cadres within the armed forces and a thoroughly militarized Nuer community (from which Machar hailed) – it would have been difficult for him to challenge Kiir militarily. A key takeaway from Brosché and Höglund's analysis (and to a large extent Vines' Chapter 4) is that when entangled in political disputes, WDs are reluctant to quickly escalate hostilities. In fact, evidence suggests that they only engage in organized violence after having first securitized wartime identities.

In the concluding chapter, Anders Themnér compares the post-war experiences of the ten WDs analyzed in this volume. The focus is on providing an answer to the book's two main research questions: does the electoral participation of WDs tend to have a positive or negative effect on post-civil war security; and if there are negative implications, how do they manifest themselves? Drawing on the chapter authors' main findings, Themnér also teases out factors that appear to either increase or decrease WDs' belligerency. At first glance, the prospect of WDs becoming "peacelords" appears disheartening. In fact, nine out of ten WDs engaged in some form of behavior – ranging from supporting organized violence and securitizing wartime identities, to fostering human rights abuses and criminalizing politics – that constituted a challenge to the peace in their respective countries. However, on closer scrutiny the trend is not as gloomy as it may first appear. First, it was relatively rare that the WDs sponsored organized violence. In fact, it was only Dhlakama and Machar that engaged in such activities. It was more common that ex-military turned politicians employed less "risky" forms of aggression, such as playing on the ambiguity of their involvement in violent incidences or seeking to securitize wartime identities. Such acts were often combined with reconciliatory statements and discourses of peace. This form of "rhetorical ambivalence" was often a key ingredient of what can best be described as a "chameleonic leadership" style (Chowdhury and Krebs 2009: 379; Gormley-Heenan 2006). For the WDs the ultimate goal of such a strategy was to increase their bargaining range by alluding to their capacity to disrupt peace, while at the same time promising to prevent such events from unfolding if they were elected or attached to the state in some other way. Second, many of the volume's WDs commenced their electoral careers as rather benevolent leaders, only later switching to confrontational tactics. Since personality traits tend to evolve slowly, it is likely that any shift in WD behavior is a function of contextual dynamics. Put differently, given the right circumstances it should be possible for warlords to become peacelords.

How, more specifically, can we explain when and why WDs choose to challenge rather than foster peace? Based on the empirical evidence provided by the chapter authors, it appears as if electoral constraints – in the form of democratic deficiencies, limited electorates or waning patronage networks – create an initial desire to engage in belligerency. In most instances, this will take the form of WDs securitizing wartime identities or indirectly associating themselves with acts of violence. In this process, the weakening of patronage networks appears to play a particularly crucial role. Many oppositional WDs seek to position themselves as peacetime brokers, funneling resources from the state to their networks of supporters. However, if WDs' broker position is threatened – whereby their ability to sustain clients decreases – they may have incentives to engage in aggression to oblige the regime to respect their broker status. Whether WDs choose to escalate to violence is largely a function of their capacity to misbehave (access to non-demobilized armed units or militarized communities) and the cost of misbehaving (the strength of the security forces, presence of strong peacekeeping troops and the international community's commitment to enforce peace). Meanwhile, experiences from Rwanda and Guinea-Bissau also indicate that electoral constraints – either in the form of a limited electorate and restricted patronage networks – can play a role in determining whether WDs seek to foster human rights abuses or criminalize politics. Finally, as Collins' post-war navigations highlight, it may be the WDs with the most violent and abusive pasts that are most likely to act benevolently.

A central message from this edited volume is that WDs are not a priori reckless, irrational actors bent on spoiling peace processes and democratization efforts. In fact, except in the case of Kagame, there is little evidence suggesting that personality traits predetermined ex-military turned politicians engaging in aggression. On the contrary, most WDs only act belligerently under very specific conditions. In this context, socialization processes play a vital role, but not in the manner commonly anticipated. In the democratization literature, democratic participation is often assumed to moderate radical, formerly armed actors. The problem is that few war-ridden societies are mature democracies. In Africa, most WDs operate in a semi-democratic context where fears, threats, abuse and democratic tampering is rife. In such a context, socialization is not so much about schooling democrats as about tutoring autocrats.

Notes

1 In this chapter, I will use the generic term Big Men to depict elites, irrespectively if they are men or women. This also makes empirical sense due to the fact that women often struggle to acquire leadership positions in post-civil war societies.

2 The ultimate goal of post-war democratization efforts is to construct stable and viable democratic systems of governance. However, in the short to medium perspective most post-war societies can best be described as semi-democratic and suffer from deficiencies such as electoral fraud, harassment of political opponents and biased electoral commissions and judiciaries (for more information see, for instance, Jarstad and Sisk 2008).

3 Even though there is a growing literature that seeks to theorize about the role of elites in war- and peacemaking (see e.g. Brosché 2014; Kalyvas 2006; Stedman 1997; Utas 2012), we are of the opinion that Brown's assertion still largely holds.

4 Even if internal armed conflicts are less common in strong democracies, studies have shown that states going through democratization processes are more prone to experience armed rebellions (see e.g. Mansfield and Snyder 1995).

5 The weakness of state institutions does not mean that state elites do not govern post-war societies. On the contrary, studies have shown that they instead develop informal modes of ruling by, for instance, outsourcing key governance functions to broker figures such as chiefs,

youth leaders and former mid-level commanders (see e.g. Themnér 2015; Bøås 2015).

6 An important exception is Utas (2012), who analyzes the political, economic and military influence of Big Men – and their networks – in a number of civil war and post-civil war contexts.

7 In this volume we confine the analysis to security outcomes in the WDs' home countries. It is true that the belligerency of WDs – for instance supporting organized violence, fostering human rights abuses and criminalizing politics – may also be operating on a regional level. However, such regional acts of aggression are less likely to be associated with the dynamics of electoral politics, which is the focus of this study.

8 Studies have shown that even seemingly less structured forms of violence, such as riots, involve a high level of organization and often necessitate elite involvement (see e.g. Varshney 2002).

Bibliography

Anders, G. 2012. "Bigmanity and International Criminal Justice in Sierra Leone." In *African Conflicts and Informal Power: Big Men and Networks*, ed. M. Utas. London and New York: Zed Books.

Bar-Tal, D. 2000. *Shared Beliefs in a Society: Social Psychological Analysis*. Thousand Oaks, CA: Sage.

Barnett, M. N. 2006. "Building a Republican Peace." *International Security* 30 (4): 87-112.

Barnett, M. N. and C. Zürcher. 2009. "The Peacebuilder's Contract: How External Statebuilding Reinforces Weak Statehood." In *The Dilemmas of Statebuilding: Confronting the Contradictions of Postwar Peace Operations*, ed. R. Paris and T. D. Sisk. London and New York: Routledge.

Berdal, M. 1996. "Disarmament and Demobilisation after Civil Wars." *Adelphi Paper* (303): 1-88.

Berdal, M. and D. H. Ucko. 2009. *Reintegrating Armed Groups After Conflict: Politics, Violence and Transition.* London and New York: Routledge.

Biró, D. 2007. "The (Un)bearable Lightness of… Violence: Warlordism as an Alternative Form of Governance in the 'Westphalian Periphery'?" In *State Failure Revisited II: Actors of Violence and Alternative Forms of Governance*, ed. T. Debile and D. Lambach. Duisburg: INEF Report no. 89.

Bøås, M. 2015. *The Politics of Conflict Economies: Miners, Merchants and Warriors in the African Borderland.* London and New York: Routledge.

Boone, C. 2003. *Political Topographies of the African State: Territorial Authority and Institutional Choice.* Cambridge et al.: Cambridge University Press.

Bourdieu, P. 1986. "The Forms of Capital." In *Handbook of Theory of Research for the Sociology of Education*, ed. J. E. Richardson. Westport, CT: Greenwood Press.

Brancati, D. and J. Snyder. 2013. "Time to Kill: The Impact of Election Timing on Postconflict Stability." *Journal of Conflict Resolution* 57 (5): 822–853.

Bratton, M. and N. van de Walle. 1997. *Democratic Experiments in Africa – Regime Transitions in Comparative Perspective.* Cambridge: Cambridge University Press.

Brounéus, K. 2008. *Rethinking Reconciliation: Concepts, Methods, and an Empirical Study of Truth Telling and Psychological Health in Rwanda.* Uppsala: Department of Peace and Conflict Research, Uppsala University.

Brosché, J. 2014. *Masters of War: The Role of Elites in Sudan's Communal Conflicts.* Uppsala: Uppsala University Press.

Brown, M. E., Ed. 1996. *The International Dimensions of Internal Conflict.* Cambridge, MA: The MIT Press.

Brown, M. E. 2001. "Ethnic and Internal Conflicts: Causes and Implications." In *Turbulent Peace: The Challenges of Managing International Conflict*, ed. C. A. Crocker, F. O. Hampson and P. Aall. Washington, DC: United States Institute of Peace.

Burns, J. M. 1978. *Leadership.* London and New York: Harper and Row.

Burt, R. S. 2005. *Brokerage and Closure: An Introduction to Social Capital.* Oxford: Oxford University Press.

Call, C. T., Ed. 2008. *Building States to Build Peace.* Boulder and London: Lynne Rienner Publishers.

Call, C. T. and E. M. Cousens 2008. "Ending Wars and Building Peace: International Responses to War-Torn Societies." *International Studies Perspective* 9: 1–21.

Chabal, P. and J.-P. Daloz. 1999. *Africa Works: Disorder as Political Instrument.* Oxford and Bloomington: James Currey and Indiana University Press.

Chesterman, S., M. Ignatieff and R. Takur, eds. 2005. *Making States Work: State Failure and the Crisis of Governance.* Tokyo, New York and Paris: United Nations University Press.

Chowdhury, A. and R. R. Krebs. 2009. "Making and Mobilizing Moderates: Rhetorical Strategy, Political Networks, and Counterterrorism." *Security Studies* 18 (3): 371–399.

Christensen, M. M. and M. Utas. 2008. "Mercenaries of Democracy: The 'Politricks' of Remobilized Combatants in the 2007 General Elections, Sierra Leone." *African Affairs* 107 (429): 515–539.

CIJ (Coalition for International Justice). 2005. "Following Taylor's Money: A Path of War and Destruction."

Coalition for International Justice (May): 1-33.

Clapham, C. and J. A. Wiseman. 1995. "Assessing the Prospects for the Consolidation of Democracy in Africa." In *Democracy and Political Change in Sub-Saharan Africa*, ed. J. A. Wiseman. New York: Routledge.

Cramer, C. 2009. "Trajectories of Accumulation through War and Peace." In *The Dilemmas of Statebuilding: Confronting the Contradictions of Postwar Peace Operations*, ed. R. Paris and T. D. Sisk. London and New York: Routledge.

Daloz, J.-P. 2003. "'Big-Men' in Sub-Saharan Africa: How Elites Accumulate Positions and Resources." *Comparative Sociology* 2 (1): 271-285.

Darby, J. and R. Mac Ginty, eds. 2000. *The Management of Peace Processes*. Basingstoke: Macmillan Press.

Day, C. R. and W. S. Reno. 2014. "In Harm's Way: African Counter-Insurgency and Patronage Politics." *Civil Wars* 16 (2): 105-126.

De Guevara, B. B. 2008. "The State in Times of Statebuilding." *Civil Wars* 10 (4): 348-368.

De Waal, A. 2009. "Mission Without and End? Peacekeeping in the African Political Marketplace." *International Affairs* 85 (1): 99-113.

Doyle, M. W. and N. Sambanis 2006. *Making War and Building Peace: United Nations Peace Operations*. Princeton, NJ and Oxford: Princeton University Press.

Duffield, M. 1998. "Post-Modern Conflict: Warlords, Post-Adjustment States and Private Protection." *Civil Wars* 1 (1): 65-102.

Englebert, P. and D. Tull. 2008. "Postconflict Reconstruction in Africa: Flawed Ideas about Failed States." *International Security* 32 (4): 106-139.

Figueiredo Jr., R. J. P. d. and B. R. Weingast. 1999. "The Rationality of Fear: Political Opportunism and Ethnic Conflict." In *Civil Wars, Insecurity, and Intervention*, ed. B. F. Walter and J.

Snyder. New York: Columbia University Press.

Fortna, V. P. 2008. *Does Peacekeeping Work: Shaping Belligerents' Choices after Civil War*. Princeton, NJ: Princeton University Press.

Gormley-Heenan, C. 2006. "Chameleonic Leadership: Towards a New Understanding of the Northern Ireland Peace Process." *Leadership* 2 (1): 53-75.

Greenhill, K. M. and S. Major. 2006/2007. "The Perils of Profiling: Civil War Spoilers and the Collapse of Intrastate Peace Accords." *International Security* 31 (3): 7-40.

Gurr, T. R. 2000. *Peoples Versus States: Minorities at Risk in the New Century*. Washington, DC: United States Institute of Peace Press.

Hameiri, S. 2011. "A Reality Check for the Critique of the Liberal Peace." In *A Liberal Peace? The Problems and Practices of Peacebuilding*, ed. S. Campbell, D. Chandler and M. Sabaratnam. London and New York: Zed Books.

Hartzell, C. and M. Hoddie. 2003. "Institutionalizing Peace: Power Sharing and Post-Civil War Conflict Management." *American Journal of Political Science* 47 (2): 318-332.

Hoffman, D. 2007. "The City as Barracks: Freetown, Monrovia, and the Organization of Violence in Postcolonial African Cities." *Cultural Anthropology* 22 (3): 400-428.

Höglund, K. 2008. "Violence in War-to-Democracy Transitions." In *From War to Democracy: Dilemmas of Peacebuilding*, ed. A. K. Jarstad and T. D. Sisk. Cambridge: Cambridge University Press.

Höglund, K. and M. Söderberg Kovacs. 2010. "Beyond the Absence of War: The Diversity of Peace in Post-Settlement Societies." *Review of International Studies* 36: 367-390.

ICG (International Crisis Group). 2002. "Liberia: The Key to Ending Regional Instability." International Crisis Group, Report No. 43, Africa, 24 April.

Inquirer 2005. "Adolpus Dolo Petitioned for Senetorial Seat." *Inquirer*, 7 February.

Jackson, J. J., F. Thoemmes, K. Jonkmann, O. Lüdtke and U. Trautwein. 2012. "Military Training and Personality Trait Development: Does the Military Make the Man, or Does the Man Make the Military?" *Psychological Science* 23 (3): 270-277.

Jackson, R. H. and C. G. Rosberg. 1985. "Personal Rule: Theory and Practice in Africa." *Comparative Politics* 16 (4): 421-442.

Jarstad, A. K. and T. D. Sisk, eds. 2008. *From War to Democracy: Dilemmas to Peacebuilding.* Cambridge: Cambridge University Press.

Jervis, R. 2013. "Do Leaders Matter and How Would We Know?" *Security Studies* 22 (2): 153-179.

Kahler, M. 2009. "Statebuilding after Afghanistan and Iraq." In *The Dilemmas of Statebuilding: Confronting the Contradictions of Postwar Peace Operation*, ed. R. Paris and T. D. Sisk. London and New York: Routledge.

Kalyvas, S. N. 2006. *The Logic of Violence in Civil War.* Cambridge: Cambridge University Press.

Kaufman, S. J. 2006. "Escaping the Symbolic Political Traps: Reconciliation Initiatives and Conflict Resolution in Ethnic Wars." *Journal of Peace Research* 43 (2): 201-218.

Kim, D. 2010. "What Makes State Leaders Brutal? Examining Grievances and Mass Killing During Civil War." *Civil Wars* 12 (3): 237-260.

Kumar, K., Ed. (1997). *Rebuilding Societies after Civil War: Critical Roles for International Assistance.* Boulder and London: Lynne Rienner Publishers.

Lewis, P. 2010. "Kosovo PM is Head of Human Organ and Arms Ring, Council of Europe Reports." *The Guardian.* 14 December.

Levy, J. 1994. "Learning and Foreign Policy: Sweeping a Conceptual Minefield." *International Organization* 48 (2): 279-312.

Lindberg, S. I. 2003. "'It's Our Time to "Chop"': Do Elections in Africa Feed Neo-Patrimonialism rather than Counteract it?" *Democratization* 10 (2): 121-140.

Lyons, T. 2005. *Demilitarizing Politics: Elections on the Uncertain Road to Peace.* Boulder and London: Lynne Rienner Publishers.

Mac Ginty, R. 2006. *No War, No Peace: The Rejuvenation of Stalled Peace Processes and Peace Accords.* Basingstoke and New York: Palgrave MacMillan.

Mac Ginty, R. 2011. *International Peacebuilding and Local Resistance: Hybrid Forms of Peace.* Houndmills and New York: Palgrave Macmillan.

Manning, C. 2002. "Elite Habituation to Democracy in Mozambique: The View from Parliament, 1994-2000." *Commonwealth & Comparative Politics* 40 (1): 61-80.

Manning, C. 2004. "Armed Opposition Groups into Political Parties: Comparing Bosnia, Kosovo, and Mozambique." *Studies in Comparative International Development* 39 (1): 54-76.

Manning, C. 2007. "Party-Building in the Heels of War: El Salvador, Bosnia, Kosovo and Mozambique." *Democratization* 14 (2): 253-272.

Mansfield, E. D. and J. Snyder. 1995. "Democratization and the Danger of War." *International Security* 20 (1): 5-38.

Melander, E. 2009. "Justice or Peace? A Statistical Study of the Relationship between Amnesties and Durable Peace." *JAD-PbP Working Paper Series.* Lund: Lund University.

Menezes, G. 2005. "Liberia Readies for Presidential Run-Off." *Voice of America*, 18 October.

Michels, R. 1962. *Political Parties: A Sociological Study of the Oligarchical Tendencies of Modern Democracy.* New York: The Free Press.

Moran, M. 2006. *Liberia: The Violence of Democracy.* Philadelphia: University of Pennsylvania Press.

Nilsson, A. 2005. *Reintegrating Ex-Combatants in Post-Conflict Societies.* Stockholm: SIDA (Swedish

International Development
Cooperation Agency).

Nugent, P. 1995. *Big Men, Small Boys and Politics in Ghana*. London and New York: Pinter.

Ohlson, T. 1998. *Power Politics and Peace Policies. Intra-State Conflict Resolution in Southern Africa*. Uppsala: Uppsala University Press.

Ottaway, M. 1997. "From Political Opening to Democratization?" In *Democracy in Africa: The Hard Road Ahead*, ed. M. Ottaway. Boulder: Lynne Rienner Publishers.

Papagianni, K. 2008. "Participation and State Legitimation." In *Building States to Build Peace*, ed. C. T. Call. Boulder and London: Lynne Rienner Publishers.

Paris, R. 2004. *At War's End: Building Peace After Civil Conflict*. Cambridge: Cambridge University Press.

Paris, R. and T. D. Sisk, eds. 2009. *The Dilemmas of Statebuilding: Confronting the Contradictions of Postwar Peace Operations*. London and New York: Routledge.

Pearlman, W. 2008/2009. "Spoiling Inside and Out: Internal Political Contestation and the Middle East Peace Process." *International Security* 33 (3): 79-109.

Reeve, R. and J. Speare. 2010. *Security and Justice from a County Perspective*. International Alert and Initiative for Peacebuilding. Available from http://www.international-alert.org/sites/default/files/publications/201011IFPlofasecurity.pdf.

Reilly, B. 2008. "Post-War Elections: Uncertain Turning Points of Transition." In *From War to Democracy: Dilemmas of Peacebuilding*, ed. A. K. Jarstad and T. D. Sisk. Cambridge: Cambridge University Press.

Reilly, B. 2013. "Political Parties and Post-Conflict Peacebuilding." *Civil Wars* 15 (S1): 88-104.

Reno, W. 1998. *Warlord Politics and African States*. Boulder and London: Lynne Rienner Publishers.

Reno, W. 2000. "Shadow States and the Political Economy of Civil Wars."

In *Greed and Grievance. Economic Agendas in Civil Wars*, ed. M. Berdal and D. M. Malone. Boulder and London: Lynne Rienner Publishers.

Richards, P. 2005. *No Peace No War: An Anthropology of Contemporary Armed Conflicts*. Athens, OH and Oxford: Ohio University Press and James Currey.

Richmond, O. P. and A. Mitchell, eds. 2012. *Hybrid Forms of Peace: From Everyday Agency to Post-Liberalism*. Basingstoke: Palgrave Macmillan.

Sechser, T. S. 2004. "Are Soldiers Less War-Prone than Statesmen?" *Journal of Conflict Resolution* 48 (5): 746-774.

Söderberg Kovacs, M. 2007. *From Rebellion to Politics: The Transformation of Rebel Groups to Political Parties in Civil War Peace Processes*. Uppsala: Department of Peace and Conflict Research, Uppsala University.

Söderberg Kovacs, M. 2008. "When Rebels Change Their Stripes: Armed Insurgents in Post-War Politics." In *From War to Democracy: Dilemmas to Peacebuilding*, ed. A. K. Jarstad and T. D. Sisk. Cambridge: Cambridge University Press.

Southhall, R. and H. Melber, eds. 2006. *Legacies of Power: Leadership Change and Former Presidents in African Politics*. Uppsala: The Nordic Africa Institute.

Spear, J. 2006. "Disarmament, Demobilization, Reinsertion and Reintegration in Africa." In *Ending Africa's Wars: Progressing to Peace*, ed. O. Furley and R. May. Aldershot: Ashgate Publishing.

Spears, I. A. 2013. "Africa's Informal Power-Sharing and the Prospects for Peace." *Civil Wars* 15 (1): 37-53.

Stedman, S. J. 1991. *Peacemaking in Civil War: International Mediation in Zimbabwe 1974-1980*. Boulder and London, Lynne Rienner Publishers.

Stedman, S. J. 1997. "Spoiler Problems in Peace Processes." *International Security* 22 (2): 5-53.

Stedman, S. J., D. Rothchild and E. M. Cousens, eds. 2002. *Ending Civil Wars: The Implementation of Peace Agreements.* Boulder and London: Lynne Rienner Publishers.

The Analyst. 2005. "I'm Not a Monster – Adolphus Dolo Opens Up." *The Analyst,* 16 February.

Themnér, A. 2011. *Violence in Post-Conflict Societies: Remarginalisation, Remobilisers and Relationships.* New York and London: Routledge.

Themnér, A. 2012. "Former Mid-Level Commanders in Big Man Networks." In *African Conflicts and Informal Power: Big Men and Networks,* ed. M. Utas. London: Zed Books.

Themnér, A. 2015. "Former Military Networks and the Micro-Politics of Violence and Statebuilding in Liberia." *Journal of Comparative Politics* 47 (3): 334‑353.

Themnér, A. and T. Ohlson 2014. "Legitimate Peace in Post-Civil War States: Towards Attaining the Unattainable." *Conflict, Security & Development* 14 (1): 61‑87.

Toweh, A. 2005. "Infamous Liberia Warlords Seek Rebirth as Senators." *Reuters News,* 13 October.

TRC (Truth and Reconciliation Commission). 2009. *Volume II: Consolidated Final Report.* Monrovia: Truth and Reconciliation Commission of Liberia.

Utas, M., Ed. 2012. *African Conflicts and Informal Regimes of Power: Big Men and Networks.* London: Zed Books.

Walter, B. F. 2002. *Committing to Peace: The Successful Settlement of Civil Wars.* Princeton, NJ and Oxford: Princeton University Press.

Varshney, A. 2002. *Ethnic Conflict and Civil Life.* New Haven, CT: Yale University Press.

Zartman, W. I. 1989. *Ripe for Resolution: Conflict and Intervention in Africa.* New York and Oxford: Council on Foreign Relations.

Zartman, W. I., Ed. 1995. *Elusive Peace: Negotiating an End to Civil Wars.* Washington, DC: The Brookings Institution.

Zeeuw, D., Ed. 2007. *From Soldiers to Politicians: Transforming Rebel Movements after Civil War.* Boulder: Lynne Rienner Publishers.

Zürcher, C. 2011. "The Liberal Peace: A Tough Sell?" In *A Liberal Peace? The Problems and Practices of Peacebuilding,* ed. S. Campbell, D. Chandler and M. Sabaratnam. London and New York: Zed Books.

Zürcher, C., C. Manning, K. Evenson, R. Hayman, S. Riese and N. Roehner. 2013. *Costly Democracy: Peacebuilding and Democratization after War.* Stanford, CA: Stanford University Press.

1 | *Pompier-pyromanocracy:* Mbusa Nyamwisi and the DR Congo's inflammable post-settlement political order

Judith Verweijen

Introduction

In April 2003, the belligerents of the Second Congo War (1998–2003) adopted a peace accord, signed in December 2002, that was bombastically dubbed the "Global and All-Inclusive Agreement". This inaugurated a transitional period that would last up to the organization of general elections in 2006. The accord paved the way for a double political and military power-sharing deal, implying that the breed of violent actors that had gained dominance during the war were officially entitled to a part of the "national cake". Positions in the politico-administrative apparatus were divided among the signatories of the peace deal, including the political representatives of former insurgent outfits, which were transformed into political parties. This form of power-sharing was mirrored in the military domain. New national armed forces were cobbled together from troops and officers of most of the ex-belligerent factions, leading to the creation of mixed units placed under an integrated command chain.

The political order that developed out of this power-sharing exercise is characterized by intense and sometimes violent power competition, in particular in the eastern part of the country, where violence at various levels of intensity is ongoing. In the immediate post-settlement period, politico-military entrepreneurs struggled to maintain and extend the political, economic and military spheres of influence they had carved out during the wars, both within and outside the state apparatus. At the same time, the various competing factions tried to take advantage of the new political constellation by repositioning themselves in the national and sometimes also regional political and military arenas. A common method of such repositioning was participation in electoral politics, notably the 2006 and 2011 presidential and parliamentary elections. However, the electoral and wider political inclusion of former warlords is generally believed to have contributed to the ongoing violence in the east, in part by creating incentives among those with poor electoral prospects and results to take up arms. Furthermore, by reinforcing ethnic outbidding, it is said to have provided an impetus to armed mobilization along ethnic lines (Stearns et al. 2013).

Without contradicting these observations, this chapter intends to refine the analysis of how the electoral and wider political inclusion of ex-belligerents has contributed to the militarization of the eastern Democratic Republic of the Congo (henceforth the Congo). By exploring the post-settlement trajectory of one particular politico-military entrepreneur, Antipas Mbusa Nyamwisi, it shows how even political actors with relatively good electoral prospects and results, and who do not explicitly draw upon antagonistic ethnic discourses, have contributed to ongoing violence. During the Second Congo War, Mbusa was the president of the insurgent movement Congolese Rally for Democracy/Kisangani-Liberation Movement (Rassemblement Congolais pour la Démocratie/Kisangani-Mouvement de Libération, RCD/K-ML), the main stronghold of which was the Grand Nord area, encompassing Beni and Lubero territories in the north of North Kivu province. After the signing of the final peace accord, the RCD/K-ML was transformed into a political party, of which Mbusa became the president. Mbusa was subsequently appointed minister in the transitional and first post-transitional governments, and stood for president in both the 2006 and 2011 elections. In 2011, he also ran for election as a member of parliament (MP). However, whereas in 2006 the RCD/K-ML participated as part of a platform of pro-government parties, in 2011 it ran on an opposition ticket, reflecting the growing rift between Mbusa and Congo's President Joseph Kabila.

This switch to the opposition can be attributed both to the changing position of Mbusa Nyamwisi in the national and provincial political landscape and the strategies he devised for navigating these arenas. Mbusa reigned supreme over the RCD/K-ML and therefore had preponderant influence in determining the party's course. In continuity with the war era, his strategies largely followed the logics of "brokerage" and "multi-positioning": he maintained contacts with nominally opposed factions, whether in the political or military domain, which enabled him to reinforce his negotiation position by threatening to intensify links to other factions' enemies. Furthermore, Mbusa positioned himself at once locally (in the Grand Nord, and subareas thereof), provincially (North Kivu), nationally (Congo) and regionally (Great Lakes area). This multi-positioning allowed him to play a role as gatekeeper to and broker between different types of networks located at different levels.

Since Mbusa's strategy of multi-positioning and brokerage included maintaining ties with armed groups and military figures, his post-settlement quest for power had important security effects. But rather than manipulating armed groups directly, he mostly maintained low-key, secretive contacts, creating a veil of mystery surrounding his dealings. Yet in a climate awash with rumors, tensions and violence, mere suspicion of links to armed actors has direct security effects, for instance prompting opposing factions to militarily reinforce their position. Furthermore, in the militarized political-economic order of the eastern Congo, the ability to manipulate armed actors is a valued currency, as it often translates into enhanced negotiating power. By demonstrating the value of this currency, although with diminishing effectiveness, Mbusa's ways of navigating the post-settlement order have importantly contributed to its ongoing militarization, and therefore to the manifestations of organized violence that this militarization entails. As such, Mbusa's political dealings are reminiscent of the classic strategy of the *pompier-pyromane* (firefighter-pyromaniac), referring to the firefighter who lights fires in order to capitalize upon his or her own capacity to extinguish them.

While Mbusa's personal agency has been an important factor in determining his post-settlement trajectory, the latter has also been strongly shaped by the general political-military context. Therefore, the chapter sets out by sketching a number of general characteristics of the Congo's pre-war and post-settlement orders, and the two wars in between these periods. It then zooms in on Mbusa Nyamwisi, describing his personal career and the strategies he adopted both during the war and after the settlement, which are analyzed against the background of his position both in the RCD/K-ML and in the Grand Nord. The insights flowing from this analysis allow for a number of conclusions on the effects of the political participation of politico-military entrepreneurs on the nature of the post-settlement political order, in particular its violent character.

Two wars and two intransitive transitions

The violent nature of political competition in the post-2003 era is not a novel phenomenon in the Congo. At regular conjunctures in the country's history, various forms of violence have played a pronounced role in channeling power struggles. One such period followed Mobutu's announcement of a transition to multiparty democracy in 1990. The subsequent limited and imperfect opening of political space intensified ethnic and armed mobilization. At the root of this hardening of the political climate was a complex interplay between, on the one hand, local-level inter-community tensions, often surrounding land and local authority, and on the other hand, manipulation by national and provincial politicians. This manipulation was partly fed by the divide-and-rule politics that Mobutu embarked upon to thwart the nascent democratization process (Mamdani 1998). One manifestation of this was *géopolitique*, or an effort to balance political and administrative representation between different regional and ethnic groups. *Géopolitique* institutionalized competition between groups framed as "ethnic", and focused attention to the question of who was a "native" and could therefore represent a certain area, and who was not (Mararo 2005). A second strategy was the application of the *pompier-pyromane* scenario. This entailed stoking up animosities to the point that they turned violent, and then extinguishing them in order to reassert control, in this way reinforcing and demonstrating authority. The clearest application of this strategy was in the province of Shaba (now Katanga), where political manipulation fueled an ethnic cleansing campaign executed by radical youth militias that led to the expulsion of thousands of Kasaians, many of whom died, in 1992 and 1993 (Dibwe dia Mwembu 1999). While top-down manipulation was less evident in the case of the violence that flared up in North Kivu in 1993, which was strongly nourished by long-standing local tensions, the national political context did provide new incentives for armed mobilization, and the provincial politicians that played a key role as instigators were close allies of Mobutu (Mararo 2003).

Due to concerted efforts to derail the democratization process, not least by Mobutu, the announced introduction of a multiparty system heralded no more than an "intransitive transition" (de Villers and Omasombo 2002), which ultimately fostered exclusionary and violent politics. Yet despite managing to maintain the upper hand in this disorder, Mobutu was not to retain power for long. In 1997 he was ousted from power by an insurgent coalition backed by regional powers, the Alliance of Democratic Forces for the Liberation of Congo-Zaire (Alliance des Forces Démocratiques pour la Libération du Congo-Zaïre, AFDL). Within less than seven months, the insurgents managed to capture Kinshasa, thereby ending the First Congo War (1996–1997). However, the new regime that was installed under Laurent-Désiré Kabila soon fell out with its erstwhile backers, in particular Rwanda and Uganda. The latter therefore engineered yet another rebellion, that of the Congolese Rally for Democracy (Rassemblement Congolais pour la Démocratie, RCD), which erupted in August 1998. This inaugurated the Second Congo War (1998–2003), which grew to be a complex mixture of a regional war that drew in no fewer than seven African countries, a variety of civil wars that were fought on Congolese soil, and a myriad of local conflicts that turned violent. The Congo became a patchwork of political-military orders, having a government-held zone in the west, and a host of rebel-held areas in other parts, most of which were further fragmented due to the presence of dozens of small-scale armed groups, often labeled "Mai-Mai". The most important Congolese rebel movements were the Uganda-backed Movement for the Liberation of the Congo (Mouvement pour la Libération du Congo, MLC) in the northwest, and the RCD in the east. However, the RCD gradually fell apart into three factions due to power struggles and differences in political vision and strategic preferences, both between and among its foreign supporters and their Congolese clients. While the core group of the RCD, supported by Rwanda, controlled the province of South Kivu, and parts of the provinces of Maniema, Katanga and North Kivu, specifically its southern part, a Uganda-backed branch, which gradually morphed into the RCD/K-ML, had its fiefdom in the Grand Nord. A smaller faction called RCD-National, which was also sponsored by Uganda, operated to the north of that, in Orientale Province (Lanotte 2003; Stearns 2011).

The multitude of belligerents involved in the Second Congo War severely hampered the implementation of the final peace accord and related power-sharing arrangements. The signatories were a motley crew comprised of the following parties: the Congolese government, since 2001 headed by President Joseph Kabila in the wake of his father's assassination; the "unarmed political opposition" regrouping twenty-eight different political parties; the somewhat nebulous category of "civil society"; and finally five armed players, one of which, the so-called "Mai-Mai entity", consisted of a loose amalgam of myriad armed groups. All these factions vied for position not only between, but also among themselves, which both exacerbated existing internal divisions and generated new ones. This power competition compounded policy processes, not least because it polarized decision-making bodies. The transitional presidency, comprised of one president and no fewer than four vice-presidents from different factions, was no exception to this. This so-called "1 + 4" formula was emblematic of the entrenched factionalism, power grabbing and political paralysis that were a hallmark of this second transition, as epitomized by the widely circulating pun "1 + 4 = 0" (Willame 2007).

Aside from the power struggles, the transition was also hampered by the slow pace and problematic nature of the military integration process. In order to maintain their military spheres of influence, several belligerents withheld (a part of) their troops from integration. This was for instance the case with Mai-Mai groups that had only local spheres of influence and constituencies, and lacked connections and clout at the national level. Similar foot-dragging could be detected among larger groups that were marginalized in the presidential patronage network and stood little chance in the elections, but had relatively autonomous sources of revenue. For example they controlled trans-border trade networks or had direct outside support. To such groups, which included a part of the RCD, the main strategy of navigating the transition was to maintain a powerbase predominantly outside of the centrally controlled state apparatus. Consequently, they withheld a part of their troops from the military integration process. Other groups, by contrast, invested heavily in the political games played out in the new national political arena, and were more willing to send their troops into the national army. This did not imply, however, that they readily ceded control over their local strongholds or entirely gave up independent military capacities. Rather, they mostly changed the modalities of maintaining control, trying to manipulate the national and local state institutions, including the national armed forces. They maintained networks of loyal officers within the army, leading to parallel command chains and divided loyalties. For example, the MLC initially held on to a large separate security guard to protect its president. Some factions also resorted to non-state channels to retain a capacity for militarized maneuvering, such as liaising with foreign rebel groups or local militias (Verweijen 2014).

As will be further explained below, this was also the strategy followed by parts of the RCD/K-ML.

The ex-belligerents' half-hearted commitment to military integration importantly contributed to the ongoing militarization of politics, prompting competing factions to turn to (threats of) force or army disintegration to reinforce their political position. As this strategy was often successful, a system emerged in which political actors had incentives to take up arms (Eriksson Baaz and Verweijen 2013). The continued existence of (semi-)autonomous military forces both within and outside of the national military also perpetuated the militarization of the economy in the east, as these armed actors underpinned – either directly or indirectly – the coercion-based control of production and trade networks. Electoral politics added significant volatility to this toxic mix. The post-settlement Congo became a competitive-authoritarian order (Matti 2010), where those linked to the presidential patronage network have preferential access to coveted positions in the state apparatus. This confines the opposition to positions of lesser influence, mainly in the toothless parliament. The result is a zero-sum game political environment, where access to the government and presidential patronage network is the highest price. In the militarized context of the eastern Congo, such a political environment incentivizes those faced with bleak electoral prospects or results to manipulate armed actors. This could most clearly be observed among the RCD, whose poor electoral prospects contributed to the group's disintegration, prompting a dissident faction to launch a new rebellion, the National Congress for the Defense of the People (Congrès National pour la Défense du Peuple, CNDP) (Stearns 2013a).

The potential for electoral processes to have destabilizing effects is further reinforced by the strong ethnic and regional identity-based character of political mobilization in the Congo (Ngoy-Kangoy 2007). On occasion, this translates into ethnic outbidding, which may include the manipulation of non-state armed groups formed along ethnic lines. Electoral politics also contributes to volatility by fostering the severe fragmentation of the political landscape, which intensifies power competition. Based on proportional representation with open-list, multi-member constituencies,[1] the electoral system promotes a focus on candidates rather than programs. This focus is further reinforced by the personalization of politics and the absence of a tradition of party politics with parties grounded in well-articulated political visions (Ngoy-Kangoy 2006). No fewer than 9,709 candidates stood for the 2006 elections, a large part of whom ran as independents. Furthermore, from the around 269 parties registered at that time, sixty-seven entered the 500-seat legislature (Carter Center 2007). The first legislative elections organized after the transition, in 2011, were characterized by an even more pronounced fragmentation: while 18,386 candidates participated, ninety-eight of the registered 417 political parties entered the national assembly, of which seventy-six had five seats or less (Carter Center 2011). A similar fragmentation is visible in the military sphere, at least in the eastern Congo, home to several dozens of domestic and foreign armed groups of all stripes. This multifaceted fragmentation has created a climate in which forging and changing political and military alliances have become important power strategies.

It can be concluded that the 2003–2006 period has largely turned out to be yet another "intransitive transition", not having induced a significant transformation of the patronage- and violence-based political order of the pre-settlement era (Vlassenroot and Raeymaekers 2008). Although operating in a different context and with a different style than Mobutu, President Joseph Kabila similarly relies on a combination of coercion and doling out patronage-related benefits via personal networks, even while his control over the coercive apparatus is tenuous. Yet, as the post-settlement trajectory of Mbusa Nyamwisi clearly demonstrates, the presidential patronage network has sufficient weight to heavily shape political actors' position in the political landscape, and those who are marginalized by this network suffer serious losses of influence. Militarized maneuvering can only partly undo such marginalization.

The trajectory of Antipas Mbusa Nyamwisi: champion of double-dealing

As an amalgamation of elites with different political visions and interests, the RCD rebellion was never a coherent movement. In March 1999, then leader Ernest Wamba dia Wamba, a former university professor who was strongly backed by Ugandan President Yoweri Museveni, was ousted from the movement. He established himself in the city of Kisangani, where he engineered his own branch of the RCD with the help of Uganda, eventually called the RCD-Liberation Movement (RCD-Mouvement de Libération, RCD-ML). Soon after, a definite falling out between Uganda and Rwanda, leading to heavy clashes in the city of Kisangani, forced the movement to set up its headquarters in the town of Bunia (in Orientale Province) to the east. It was here that a vicious and at times violent leadership struggle started that would end in Mbusa Nyamwisi taking over the presidency of the movement in November 2000, in what has generally been described as a coup d'état that triggered fierce fighting (International Crisis Group 2000). Mbusa is a politician of Nande origins, representing the single largest ethnic group in the province of North Kivu. The Nande are concentrated in the Grand Nord, but also have a substantial presence in Orientale. Reflecting the ethno-regional character of his primary support base, Mbusa decided to establish the headquarters of the movement, which now came to be known as RCD/K-ML, in Beni, an important trade center in the Grand Nord close to the Ugandan border.

The bumpy road to prominence Mbusa had started his political career in the shadow of his brother Enoch Muvingi, who had been a ministerial adviser and minister in various governments under Mobutu. Enoch was also one of the founders of the political party Federalist Christian Democracy (Démocratie Chrétienne Fédéraliste, DCF), which was formed after the opening of political space in 1990. He led the DCF/Nyamwisi, which had a mostly Nande constituency, but was a member of the wider Christian Democrat political family. Muvingi reached the apex of his power during the transition, when *géopolitique* led to the marginalization of the Banyarwanda in the provincial and national political institutions. The term "Banyarwanda" refers to Hutu and Tutsi, and both groups are "Rwandophones" or speakers of Kinyarwanda language.[2] The Banyarwanda, an amalgam of heterogeneous groups, are the second largest category in North Kivu, and have been involved in a long-standing struggle with the Nande for political and economic preponderance at the provincial level (Mararo 2003). Muvingi tried to capitalize upon this struggle, hoping to draw popular support by propagating antagonism against the Banyarwanda. He also supported a variety of militias to reinforce his power, thereby constituting an early example of a politico-military entrepreneur. These included the Kasindiens, located in the home base of the Nyamwisi family, the Rwenzori region, and the Bangilima, which operated as a type of youth militia of the DCF/Nyamwisi (Mararo 2003). Discovering the political and economic leverage obtained through contacts with armed actors, Muvingi volunteered to become a broker between Mobutu and the Ugandan rebels of the National Army for the Liberation of Uganda (NALU) based in the Ruwenzori mountains. Mobutu intended to employ this group to weaken Ugandan President Museveni, a political leader he profoundly disliked (Raeymaekers 2009). This shows that the militarization of politics in the eastern Congo had already started before the outbreak of the wars.

When Enoch Muvingi was assassinated in 1993, Mbusa became his political heir, assuming the position of secretary general of the DCF/Nyamwisi. Although he lacked the charisma and rhetorical skills of his brother, he took direct inspiration from the militarized strategies of power politics and multi-positioning the latter had pioneered. However, Mbusa did not immediately embark upon a political career, being initially more active in the long-distance trade with East and Southeast Asia. His political star first started to rise after he allied himself with the AFDL, the regional-domestic insurgent coalition that toppled Mobutu in 1997, of whose plans he was informed during a meeting with Museveni in Uganda in 1996. When learning of Uganda's intention to get involved in the second insurgency that started in 1998, he again seized the opportunity and became one of the RCD's founding members (Omasomba et al. 2009). While his exact motives for this move are unknown, it seems that personal ambitions and the opportunities that unfolded due to his regional contacts played an important role.

The splits and power struggles within the RCD and its offshoots subsequently offered Mbusa yet more possibilities for advancing his career. The strong dominance of Banyarwanda in the Rwanda-backed RCD wing established in Goma allowed him to play upon fears among the Nande population about the growing power of this group. Mbusa was also well positioned within the powerful Nande business community, which has traditionally thrived on forms of cross-border trade under favorable tax regimes resulting from the manipulation of rules and regulations. Additionally, he could draw on the networks and reputation of his deceased brother, the politician Enoch Muvingi. What further consolidated his power was that he managed to build up close ties with key figures in the militarized trans-boundary economic networks that developed in the course of the war, often building on pre-existing economic configurations. Thus, he maintained friendly relations with certain Ugandan businesspeople and officers of the Ugandan armed forces, like General James Kazini and Museveni's half-brother Salim Saleh (International Crisis Group 2003). In combination with aggressive political maneuvering, this powerbase allowed him to eventually take over the leadership of the RCD/K-ML. Although Ugandan President Yoweri Museveni disliked Mbusa and the form of ethnicized politics that he represented, clearly favoring the more ideologically oriented Wamba dia Wamba, he eventually accepted the power takeover largely for pragmatic reasons (International Crisis Group 2000).

Multi-positioning and brokerage In comparison to the much bigger RCD to the south, the RCD/K-ML was a second-tier politico-military movement. It exercised weak and contested control over the Nande-dominated territories of Beni and Lubero, not least due to strong divisions among the Nande and between the Nande and minority groups, while also having a zone of varying influence in Orientale Province. Its military wing, the Congolese Popular Army (Armée Populaire Congolaise, APC), numbered around 3,000–5,000 troops, and functioned as a conventional army with a core of partly Uganda-educated officers (International Crisis Group 2006). It was placed under the control of the political executive, which was presided over by Mbusa Nyamwisi and two vice-presidents, who directed a number of *commissaires* or ministers with various portfolios. However, these ministers had little influence, as Nyamwisi and a small clique around him had preponderant power over the movement. Similarly, the congress of the RCD/K-ML, formally erected to represent the base, had a mostly symbolic character (Raeymaekers 2007).

Rather than creating entirely new administrative structures, the RCD/K-ML administered the Grand Nord by means of influencing existing agencies via a combination of patronage politics, coercion and evasion, or the bypassing of the administration by seeking new channels, notably in the business sector. While this allowed the movement to have a reasonable degree of influence, it diminished its chances of gaining widespread support and legitimacy, focused as it was on co-opting business and administrative elites. Overall, the movement had limited popularity outside the circle of those directly benefiting from its economic governance. It was, for example, strongly contested by players like the influential Catholic Church and the Mai-Mai militias that mushroomed in the countryside (Raeymaekers 2007). This situation strongly shaped Mbusa's strategies and paths of action, both during the war and in the post-settlement era.

In order to ensure the support and tap into the resources of the Nande business community, a crucial constituency that was however not particularly keen on getting involved in insurgent politics, the RCD/K-ML administration seized upon the existing system of pre-financing that had been pioneered by customs agencies. Under this system, economic operators were granted tax exemptions in return for fixed pre-payments on customs duties in cash. Engaging in such arrangements was mutually beneficial, as it gave the RCD/K-ML income and allowed traders to continue their business activities in a beneficial tax and security climate. Since the income of the RCD/K-ML thus came to depend directly on the flourishing of the business community, the movement had vested interests in guaranteeing property rights and the safety of important trade routes. At the same time, its dependence on economic operators allowed the latter to remain relatively autonomous vis-à-vis the insurgents, which enabled them to play a growing role in the provision of public goods like infrastructure (Raeymaekers 2007). The resulting business-friendly climate led to significant prosperity for some, generating a construction boom in the Grand Nord's main towns of Beni and Butembo, for instance. This boom was further promoted by the RCD/K-ML's policy of exempting building materials like cement from import duties, a measure that was partly intended to win popularity. A similar rationality motivated other tax cuts, fostering an overall beneficial fiscal climate.[3] However, large parts of the population of the Grand Nord were excluded from the spoils, or even saw their income drop drastically, as rampant insecurity in the countryside hampered agricultural production and trade (Raeymaekers 2004). Furthermore, much prosperity was generated via economic networks that engaged in coercive and illegal strategies of accumulation, such as theft, tax fraud, manipulation of the money supply and the instrumentalization of local militias to control resource-rich areas. Much of the benefit accrued to Ugandan economic operators, most of whom were exempted from tax payments, leading to accusations of resources plunder (UNSC 2002).

Insecurity in the countryside was partly the result of the activities of numerous Mai-Mai groups, which mobilized around narratives of resistance against foreign influence. These groups were often instrumentalized by local strongmen, like economic operators and customary chiefs, to reinforce their position in local conflicts and the economy. Certain groups also received support from figures in the Catholic Church, which had tense relations with the Protestant Nyamwisi. While many Mai-Mai groups, like Muhola and Vurundo, occasionally clashed with Mbusa's forces, some would at times also collaborate with them, following the complex pattern of ever-changing alliances between a multitude of domestic and foreign armed actors that characterized the Second Congo War (Belaid 2015). In the RCD/K-ML's area of influence, foreign forces did not only include the Ugandan military, but also the remnants of the NALU, which had by then fused with another Ugandan rebel group named Allied Democratic Forces (ADF) (Titeca and Vlassenroot 2012). Despite numerous counterinsurgency operations by the Ugandan military, this group continued to retain substantial capacity for nuisance, including within Uganda.

While changes of alliances were ongoing, some were more important than others. One of the most significant shakeups of the political-military landscape occurred at the end of the year 2000, when Uganda tried to reunite the three major insurgent movements it sponsored in the Congo (the MLC, RCD/K-ML and RCD-N), proposing Jean-Pierre Bemba, the leader of the MLC, as the president of the united movement. Experiencing this as a direct threat to his leadership, Mbusa decided to sabotage the reunification attempt, leading to intense fighting in the course of 2001 (International Crisis Group 2003). Realizing he would be in a weak position if the other two movements formed a common front against him with the support of an increasingly hostile Kampala, he decided to play a new card and approached Kinshasa.[4] The same repositioning prompted the RCD/K-ML to reinforce contacts with the ADF-NALU (International Crisis Group 2007), which helped to gain further leverage vis-à-vis Uganda. This shows how Mbusa's war-era strategy consisted essentially of two components. First, "multi-positioning", or flexibly maintaining contacts with numerous often nominally opposed factions, and then gaining leverage by changing or threatening to change alliances. Second, "brokerage", or deriving political capital from having and controlling access to different networks and groups located in various arenas and at various scales (local, provincial, national, regional).[5] These strategies were partly born out of weakness, with the RCD/K-ML lacking comprehensive political and military control, while enjoying only limited popularity (Raeymaekers 2004).

Transitional dealings and electoral posturing: sort of running for president Mbusa's 2001 rapprochement with Kabila was not only the product of the changing strategies of Kampala. It was also related to the new dynamics generated by an acceleration of the peace process and the looming of a negotiated settlement based on the principle of power-sharing. By placing his bets on an alliance with Kinshasa, Mbusa hoped to entrench his rather tenuous grip over his fiefdom and secure his place in the transitional order.

This strategy was largely successful: Mbusa became well positioned in the presidential patronage network, allowing the RCD/K-ML to obtain a significant number of posts in the transitional institutions. The party was granted two ministerial and two vice-ministerial posts, important appointments in the public enterprises, fifteen out of 500 seats in the general assembly, and considerable weight in the provincial administration of North Kivu. Mbusa Nyamwisi became minister of regional cooperation, allowing him to build on and extend his network of regional contacts.[6] He also capitalized on his privileged access to the presidential circle, which enabled him to play a role as broker between his local networks in the Grand Nord and politicians at the national level. In continuity with the personalized and patronage-based politics that had been a hallmark of the RCD/K-ML in its insurgent years, it was mostly Mbusa who decided on appointments in the national institutions, a discretionary power that significantly reinforced his position among his local constituency.[7] At the same time, this intermediary role meant that Kinshasa had to go through him to exercise influence over the Grand Nord, rendering him an indispensable ally in the reunification process.

Kinshasa's dependency on Mbusa's brokerage granted the RCD/K-ML and its wider networks a relatively high level of autonomy, which allowed them to maintain a predominant influence over the customs, border control and intelligence agencies in the Grand Nord, in particular at the border post of Kasindi. In this manner, Mbusa was able to guarantee the continuation of a favorable fiscal climate, and thereby to secure the support of the trans-border trade networks that were at the heart of the RCD/K-ML's powerbase. However, since these networks thrived on protection agreements and locally negotiated tax reductions, they deprived the political center of important sources of revenue. Kinshasa's position was however too fragile to seek an immediate showdown, not least since the RCD/K-ML's position of relative autonomy was backed up by continuing coercive control. Throughout the transition, the Grand Nord was controlled by the 88th and 89th brigades, which were predominantly composed of APC troops, although these were now formally part of the new national armed forces, the Armed Forces of the Democratic Republic of the Congo (Forces Armées de la République Démocratique du Congo, FARDC) (Meece 2006a). It was only after the 2006 elections that a part of these troops departed in order to participate in the military integration process, leading to their replacement by FARDC Integrated Brigades, composed of soldiers of various ex-belligerent factions (Dougherty 2006). However, many ex-APC troops remained quasi-demobilized in the Grand Nord, guarding their uniforms and arms,[8] while others were sent into the forest to form a new group (UNSC 2016). This "reserve force" was in contact with ex-APC officers who had integrated into the FARDC, but continued to further factional interests.

The transition allowed Mbusa to consolidate his position not only vis-à-vis Kinshasa, but also within the Grand Nord, capitalizing upon his control over the RCD/K-ML's access to the national political-administrative arena. He had even started to gain somewhat in popularity, being applauded as a "pioneer of national reunification". He was also credited with having reinforced the Nande's political representation and influence at the national level, as exemplified by the elevation of Beni and Butembo to the status of city during the transition, a long-standing demand of the Nande.[9] Emboldened by his strengthened position, Mbusa decided to stand for president during the 2006 elections, despite his limited popularity outside the Grand Nord. This decision is likely to have been influenced by his expectation to run on the ticket of a broad electoral alliance under the name of Forces du Renouveau (Forces for Renewal). This strategy, however, largely fell through, as certain key factions declined to join the alliance. Crucially, Mbusa's main partner, Olivier Kamitatu of the Alliance for the Renewal of the Congo (Alliance pour le Renouveau du Congo, ARC), rallied to the electoral platform linked to the incumbent, the Alliance for the Presidential Majority (Alliance pour la Majorité Présidentielle, AMP). Realizing he had few other options, Mbusa decided just before the elections not to compete with the incumbent, encouraging his constituency to vote for Kabila, while campaigning with the Forces du Renouveau as part of the AMP (Meece 2006b).

Post-transitional waxing and waning While implemented last-minute, this altered electoral strategy paid off: the Forces du Renouveau, which also regrouped the DCF/Nyamwisi, closely allied to the RCD/K-ML, obtained three ministerial and three vice-ministerial positions in the new government, and twenty-eight out of 500 seats in the national assembly. Mbusa was rewarded for his move to the Kabila camp with a ministerial post of vital importance, that of Foreign Affairs and International Cooperation.[10] Provincially, too, the RCD/K-ML managed to hold on to its influence. This became particularly clear in the battle for the position of governor of North Kivu, who is elected by the provincial assembly. Aside from giving access to power, the position of governor has a high symbolic value, reflecting who has predominant influence at the provincial level. It had therefore been a thorn in the Nande's flesh that during the transition the position had been occupied by a Hutu issuing from the Rwanda-backed wing of the RCD. These high political and symbolic stakes prompted the RCD/K-ML to engage in concerted efforts to push through its own candidate, despite the fact that the AMP supported another Nande politician, Jean-Chrysostome Vahamwiti Mukesyayira. Wary to let this crucial position slip out of its hands, the RCD/K-ML mobilized its contacts in the Nande business community to gather the funds and harness the pressure needed for a favorable outcome of the gubernatorial elections.[11]

On 27 January 2007, Julien Paluku Kahongya, member of RCD/K-ML and protégé of Mbusa Nyamwisi, was elected with twenty-five out of forty-two votes.[12] These results indicate that although linked to the ruling platform of the AMP, the RCD/K-ML had managed to maintain an autonomous powerbase at the level of North Kivu.

This base would soon start to erode. At the end of 2008, after a government reshuffle following the demission of Prime Minister Antoine Gizenga, Mbusa lost his prestigious job as minister of foreign affairs, being appointed to the much less influential post of minister of Decentralization and Spatial Planning. The reasons for this demotion are difficult to fathom, but could well be linked to the general tendency in patronage-based systems to ensure regular rotations of office with an eye to avoiding clients building up too much autonomy (see Bayart, [1989] 2006). In this case, it is possible that Kinshasa hoped that weakening Mbusa, already seen as dissident by pushing through his own candidate for governor, would allow them to reinforce their grip over the political-economic networks in the Grand Nord that continued to deprive it of important revenues. Mbusa, however, was unwilling to allow the political center to encroach upon his sphere of influence, adopting an increasingly antagonistic stance vis-à-vis the Kabila government, which he accused of corruption and opportunism. Having less to distribute to his networks in terms of influence and access to positions at the national level, he gradually started to lose standing both within his party and among his wider constituency in the Grand Nord (Brock 2009). Increasingly distributing the scarce available resources among his inner circle only, criticism of his leadership grew, as it highlighted his penchant for clientelism and autocratic tendencies.[13] These developments caused certain groups in the party, like the *boyomais* (referring to inhabitants of Orientale Province) political cadres and party membership, to feel increasingly marginalized. Although the majority of the RCD/K-ML's national MPs had been elected in Orientale Province, it was predominantly Nande from the Grand Nord who were granted access to positions of importance at the national level. These exclusionary tendencies eventually caused certain politicians to leave, thus undermining the party by weakening its base (Jokanko no date).

Mbusa's popularity among his electorate in the Grand Nord was similarly on the wane, fed by growing dissatisfaction about his mediocre efforts to improve the quality of governance and the weak performance of the Kabila government more generally. Insecurity in the Grand Nord remained rampant, as multiple Mai-Mai and foreign armed groups, notably the ADF, continued to operate, often with the support of political and economic actors who appealed to these groups to reinforce their position. Mbusa was not immune to that logic, allegedly maintaining contacts with certain armed group commanders and ex-APC officers in the FARDC who were linked to the ex-APC "reserve force".[14] This militarized power complex, in turn, reinforced the mobilization of competing groups, such as the Mai-Mai led by Kakule Sikuli Lafontaine. However, like many other Mai-Mai groups, Lafontaine claimed to be in the bush to counter the influence of the CNDP, an important Tutsi-led armed group operating in the southern part of North Kivu (Belaid 2015). In the face of the operational weaknesses of the FARDC, the specter of the CNDP induced an informal policy of encouraging or tolerating secret alliances with other armed groups (Stearns 2013b). This policy is likely also one of the reasons why few steps were undertaken to investigate allegations of continuing contacts between parts of Mbusa's network and the ADF, reported to run via Mbusa's brother Edouard Nyamwisi, the chief of Ruwenzori sector (Mwanawavene et al. 2006). While there were several indications that these links existed, Kinshasa undertook no action, in part because it believed that the ADF could function as a bulwark of last resort against CNDP influence (Titeca and Vlassenroot 2012). Whether real or imagined, these presumed contacts with armed groups gave Mbusa Nyamwisi political leverage both in Kinshasa and in Kampala, which still feared the ADF. Believing that Mbusa could ultimately muster a certain influence over these groups, he continued to be seen as indispensable for maintaining regime security, in spite of his diminishing weight in formal political institutions.[15]

In sum, similar to other important political figures with a rebel background, Mbusa Nyamwisi's post-settlement strategies have remained firmly marked by a militarized logic, leading him to maintain contacts of a varying nature with different armed actors. While not hesitating to feed into and instrumentalize divisions, Mbusa has, however, largely refrained from stoking up ethnic antagonisms by employing extremist rhetoric. Certainly, as an important incarnation of the Nande's aspirations, he regularly appealed to their competition with and dislike for Rwandophones, not hesitating to characterize the latter in stereotypes and ascribe them evil intentions (see for example Brock 2009). However, he has employed such narratives generally more in internal power competition, accusing fellow Nande of being complicit with Rwandophones, than to directly target Rwandophones themselves.[16] Hence, especially in comparison with more radical voices, he has been relatively moderate, and is not known for grounding his influence in fueling ethnic tensions. Yet this moderation has done little to assure him popularity, and might have even undermined it.

Slipping toward the opposition With his influence and popularity steadily on the wane, and feeling increasingly hostile towards Kabila, Mbusa embarked upon a dangerous move. On 24 May 2010 he created a political platform called Liberal and Patriotic Center (Centre Libéral et Patriotique, CLP) together with three other ambitious and outspoken politicians who were also linked to the

AMP (pro-government alliance).[17] While interpretations of the reasons behind this initiative vary, it is generally believed that it was born out of dissatisfaction with the performance of Prime Minister Muzito and the government in general, and the desire to influence the appointment of his successor, not least out of personal ambition. At the same time, it was a way of political repositioning in the face of the upcoming general elections, including for Mbusa, who hoped it would help counter his marginalization. Enraged by the initiative, which posed a clear threat to his power, President Kabila abruptly broke off a journey to Egypt and called an emergency meeting at Kingakati, his private ranch east of Kinshasa, on 26 May 2011. Not holding back his anger, he gave what the media called "the gang of four" an ultimatum to end what he saw as a secessionist attempt within the AMP, a threat that was sufficiently serious to prompt "the gang" to immediately withdraw (Le Potentiel 2010; La Prosperité 2010). In the case of Mbusa, the damage done to his relations with Kabila appeared irreparable, leading him to quit the AMP. Not surprisingly, in the next cabinet reshuffle in September 2011, he was not reappointed as minister. Aside from destroying his relations with Kabila, the CLP adventure caused further dissension and divisions within the RCD/K-ML, as Mbusa had embarked upon the initiative without consulting the party.[18]

A similar controversy was sparked by Mbusa's rather unexpected and last-minute decision to run for president in the 2011 elections. As in 2006, this plan seems to have been informed by his anticipation of a great electoral coalition, this time of all opposition candidates. However, as with previous strategic moves, he failed to consult the party, some factions of which doubted the wisdom of his candidacy given the lack of time and resources for campaigning.[19] Hence, this electoral adventure further illustrates how the RCD/K-ML served to a large extent as a vehicle for Mbusa's interests, with his powerbase being ultimately grounded more in economic networks in the Grand Nord than in the party. As in 2006, Mbusa's expectations concerning the possibilities to forge an electoral coalition proved too optimistic, and the opposition eventually failed to unite. In combination with his own lack of preparation, this made him decide to advise his electorate to vote for the opposition figure Étienne Tshisekedi, although he did stand as a presidential candidate himself. In the Grand Nord his advice was overwhelming followed, although a fair share of the electorate still voted for Mbusa himself,[20] allegedly as a result of a last-ditch effort by the Butembo business community to mobilize voters.[21] This support also helped him draw a large number of votes in the legislative elections, allowing him to become MP for the constituency of the city of Butembo. In general, the RCD/K-ML did relatively well in the 2011 legislative elections, obtaining six seats in the national assembly, while sister party DCF/Nyamwisi managed to get three (CENI 2012). At the root of this relative success was a general disappointment with the Kabila government in the Grand Nord, causing the electorate to overwhelmingly support the RCD/K-ML's move to the opposition.

However, in light of the zero-sum nature of politics in the Congo, where the government camp virtually monopolizes power, the move to the opposition created hardship for the party and Mbusa's personal networks. Barred from access to positions of importance, they experienced a steep decline in influence and income, making it increasingly attractive to switch sides. The possibilities to do so were greatly enhanced when governor Julien Paluku, who had been elected to the national assembly in 2011 on an RCD/K-ML ticket, announced the creation of his own party shortly after the elections, the United Bloc for the Renaissance and Emergence of the Congo (Bloc Uni pour la Renaissance et l'Émergence du Congo, BUREC). Due to his function of governor, and his favorable position in the presidential patronage network, it was henceforth Paluku who controlled the Nande's access to the state apparatus, albeit more at the provincial than the national level. This was a desirable scenario for Kabila, allowing him to gradually weaken the RCD/K-ML, and therefore the quasi-autonomous economic networks depriving Kinshasa of income. Compared to Mbusa, Paluku has less influential connections in the Nande business community and at the regional (Great Lakes) level, and fewer capabilities for mobilizing (threats of) force, since he lacks connections to ex-APC officers or armed groups. Consequently, he depends to a large extent on Kabila's patronage for the exercise of power, rendering him a loyal client.

With political mobilization in the Congo continuing to follow regional-ethnic lines, it was clear that Paluku depended on the same constituency as the RCD/K-ML. In an effort to rally its cadres to his own party, he employed a strategy of carrots and sticks, including threats to purge the administrative apparatus of those who would not change political color. This led to what is generally called the *burecation* of the provincial and local institutions.[22] That this strategy was successful is powerfully evidenced by the decision of the mayors of Beni and Butembo to change political camps, since both these cities used to be important strongholds of Mbusa. *Burecation* also touched upon the posts that guarantee the semi-autonomous functioning of Nande economic networks, such as the customs and import/export control agencies based in Kasindi or the provincial financial service of the Directorate-General for Revenue-North Kivu (Direction Générale des Recettes-Nord Kivu, DGR-NK). Hence the presidential patronage network has tried to seize upon the RCD/K-ML's waning influence to weaken the network's hold over the Kasindi border post, appointing loyalists either directly or via Paluku, who has a growing influence over appointments.[23] In this manner, the already heavily divided Nande community has become subject to further political rifts.

Misguided militarized posturing: flirting with the M23? Mbusa's efforts to deal with the waning influence of the RCD/K-ML have only reinforced political divisions among the Nande. In 2012, parts of the CNDP, which had integrated into the FARDC in 2009, mutinied and started a new rebellion, the Movement of 23 March (Mouvement du 23 Mars, M23). This movement was sponsored by Rwanda, but there were also indications of limited and more passive involvement by Uganda, believed to largely run via presidential military adviser General Salim Saleh (UNSC 2012). This involvement appears to have been more driven by Kampala's wish to have leverage over an insurgency which was close to its borders and implicated its powerful neighbor Rwanda than to actively promote it. Furthermore, getting involved would render Kinshasa partly dependent on Uganda for efforts to manage the insurgency, thus allowing Kampala to enhance its regional sphere of influence. One way to achieve the desired leverage, so it seems, was to motivate old allies of Uganda within the RCD/K-ML to join or liaise with the M23. Given his role as gatekeeper to this network, Mbusa Nyamwisi was an indispensable figure in these efforts. He willingly seized upon this opportunity to reposition himself at the national and regional level, fabricating the impression that he was an essential figure for the rebellion's expansion, which gave him renewed importance in both Kampala and Kinshasa. Following his familiar strategy of double dealings, he did not become openly allied to the M23 or actively involved in it, instead adopting a wait and see attitude and retaining a veil of mystery about his possible involvement. Thus he maintained a guarded silence from abroad, reportedly moving between South Africa and Tanzania after having gone into exile after leaving his post in parliament in 2012. His direct involvement in the M23 has therefore been difficult to prove, allowing his supporters to deny it and to ascribe the accusations to a smear campaign intended to crack down on the opposition (Nkole no date).

Yet several family members and former APC officers believed to be close to Mbusa did join the M23.[24] In December 2012, Mbusa's brother Edouard Nyamwisi was arrested in Butembo on allegations of maintaining contacts with M23-linked networks. Furthermore, there are indications that Mbusa was involved in engineering a new coalition of Nande armed groups under the leadership of Hilaire Kombi, an ex-APC officer who deserted from the FARDC in mid-2012. This group was reported to be in regular contact with M23, including via a liaison officer who also used to be in the APC (UNSC 2013). The mobilization of these military figures was relatively easy, given that many former ex-APC officers felt marginalized within the FARDC. These feelings were reinforced after the integration of the CNDP in 2009, which revived old resentments about Rwandophone domination of the command chain within the FARDC (Eriksson Baaz and Verweijen 2013). Furthermore, the large number of demobilized fighters in the Grand Nord, many of whom feel abandoned and disappointed with the post-settlement order, ensured that Hilaire and his coalition had no lack of recruits.[25]

Disappointment is not limited to military circles, but can also be found among the political cadres of the RCD/K-ML, who are in a dire position, being increasingly subject to the harassment and exclusion that befalls opposition parties in the Congo.[26] Such generalized resentment creates fertile ground for politico-military entrepreneurs and the manipulation of armed mobilization. In January 2014, the FARDC launched large-scale military operations against the ADF with the support of the United Nations Mission in the DRC, MONUSCO. This military shakeup has unleashed profound instability. In the course of 2014 and 2015, a string of attacks on civilians took place, which killed over 550 people and displaced hundreds of thousands. Only a part of these attacks are believed to have been perpetrated by the ADF, as a form of revenge killings and military strategy (UNSC 2016). The inability to identify the perpetrators of these massacres has created general confusion and generated a stream of rumors that competing factions among the Nande and other groups in the Grand Nord are trying to manipulate, including the personal networks of Mbusa Nyamwisi, other factions in the RCD/K-ML, and allies of Paluku linked to the presidential patronage network. This last camp alleged that Mbusa was behind the horrendous attacks, supposedly through his M23 connections, and used this as a pretext to crack down further on his networks, in particular those running the parallel economic system of the Grand Nord. A number of high-profile businesspeople were arrested, and numerous RCD/K-ML-affiliated urban authorities in the city of Beni were replaced by members of pro-government parties. Mbusa loyalists in the RCD/K-ML, for their part, have tried to capitalize upon the instability by presenting it as evidence for Mbusa's crucial role in stabilizing the Grand Nord. Furthermore, they have attempted to lay the blame on Paluku, accusing him of collaboration with the ADF via the army general in charge of military operations against this group (Sweet 2015). Mbusa also resurfaced in the media, claiming to have superior knowledge about the attacks, thereby again creating an aura of mystery that has been typical of his operations (Rolley 2014). However, the accusations against Mbusa also reinforced efforts by competitors within the RCD/K-ML to oust him from power. These opposing factions intensified publicity efforts to highlight that Mbusa had already been expelled from the presidency and the party by the national political council in November 2013, in the wake of allegations of his involvement with the M23. The fact that these earlier efforts to expel him had limited effects demonstrates the extent to which Mbusa continues to be seen as an incarnation of the party (Forum des As 2014).

The efforts to influence the framing of the instability and in this manner discredit opponents, or what Mbusa himself aptly described in a radio interview at the end of 2014 as "politique des boucs-émissaires" (scapegoat politics), shows that the manipulation of insecurity to reinforce one's position does not only take place in a direct manner, by sponsoring violence, but also in more subtle ways. In the absence of certainty about the facts, allegations, rumors and names are manipulated and instrumentalized, causing a semblance of maintaining links to armed groups, or allegations of being involved in massacres, to be almost as effective a power strategy as openly maintaining these links or perpetrating violence itself. This type of rumor economy also allows for linking unrelated conflicts and animosities, and thereby strategically deploying various conflict narratives as a mobilizing resource (Sweet 2015). Perversely, these smokescreen tactics seem to both lower the costs and enhance the effectiveness of the *pompier-pyromane* strategy, allowing growing numbers of political-military actors to reap its fruits.

Concluding remarks: the democratization of *pompier-pyromania*

The Global and All-Inclusive Accord, the adoption of which signaled a formal end to the Second Congo War in 2003, created a new architecture for the Congo's political and security landscape. Ex-belligerents transformed into political parties and, after a brief period of power-sharing, participated in electoral politics. This chapter has focused on the post-settlement trajectory of one of the politico-military entrepreneurs participating in these transformations, Antipas Mbusa Nyamwisi, the leader of the former insurgent movement RCD/K-ML, reconstituted in 2003 as a political party. Between 2003 and 2011, Mbusa held a ministerial portfolio, while also standing as a presidential candidate in both the 2006 and 2011 elections, although more for symbolic considerations than in the expectation of winning. Furthermore, in 2011 he successfully ran for office as a national MP in the city of Butembo, traditionally one of his strongholds. On both occasions, he anticipated running as part of a broader platform, but each time this strategy fell through. Therefore, in 2006, he eventually took part in a pro-government alliance and in 2011 he went ahead as a standalone part of a fragmented opposition.

This shift towards the opposition at once reflected and further promoted his changing position in the political landscape, characterized by a growing marginalization within and eventual falling out of grace with the presidential patronage network. Furthermore, it appears to be in part an outcome of the continuation of his war-era strategies of "multi-positioning" and "brokerage". These strategies consisted of forging links to multiple factions, including those nominally opposed, in various arenas, allowing him to serve as a gatekeeper and to gain leverage by constantly threatening to switch sides. Crucially, Mbusa served as an intermediary between Kinshasa and powerful Nande business networks in the Grand Nord, his main powerbase. In exchange for loyalty, he shielded this constituency from central state regulation and taxation. While this underpinned his power in the immediate post-settlement era, it became a source of frustration to the presidential patronage network in the medium term, as these networks deprived it of significant tax revenues and influence. Consequently, the president and his entourage stepped up efforts to break into the quasi-autonomous power complex of the Grand Nord. An important way to accomplish this was to weaken Mbusa's position in the national political arena, which would increase his dependency on presidential patronage. When these efforts failed to have the desired effects, the presidential patronage network engineered and co-opted a competitor to divide the Grand Nord power complex.

Mbusa responded to his growing marginalization by employing the same tried-and-tested strategies as he had relied on during the war, which had prompted him at the time to maintain links with various armed actors, including Mai-Mai groups, the Ugandan rebels of the ADF, and figures in the Ugandan military establishment. In the post-settlement era, some of these links continued, although not in so overt a fashion or always with the purpose of direct manipulation. Rather, these contacts served as a way of hedging, of continuing to be of relevance to various regimes and factions eager to ward off potential threats, and allowed him to enlarge his room for maneuver by keeping a potential for armed mobilization and side-switching. In so far as maintaining these contacts and pursuing these strategies have contributed to the eastern Congo's ongoing militarization, the fostering of organized violence can be seen as the main security outcome of Mbusa's post-settlement political participation, although this outcome has often been achieved in a more indirect than a direct manner.

The reasons for Mbusa's continuing to covertly play the rebel card lie both within his individual agency, being heir to a form of militarized political strategizing that had been pioneered by his brother Enoch Muvingi, and the nature of the Congo's post-settlement political order. This order contains incentive structures that promote employing armed posturing as a way of political positioning (Stearns et al. 2013). The periodic organization of elections further feeds into this. Not only do elections widen the space for political competition, drawing in large numbers of actors and thereby intensifying competition, they also raise the stakes, due to the zero-sum game nature of the political environment. Furthermore, elections fuel ethnic outbidding, which may lead to the increased mobilization of armed groups formed along ethnic lines. The politico-military entrepreneurs that populate the eastern Congo's political landscape combine electoral politics with various forms of military manipulation, as evidenced by the large number of provincial and national MPs and candidates who harness armed groups to influence electoral processes or compensate for their disappointing outcomes (UNSC 2011). In comparison to the pre-war order, these politico-military entrepreneurs have become more numerous, more independent of the political center, and more active also at lower levels of the power pyramid. As such, the post-settlement order seems to be characterized by a type of "democratization" of the strategy of the *pompier-pyromane*, with politico-military entrepreneurs proliferating at all levels of the system. This democratization unleashes a dynamic that often acquires a momentum of its own, due to the multiplicity of the involved factions and their complex and ever-changing alliances. As a result, not everyone who divides is still able to rule, and not everyone who ignites is still able to extinguish.

Yet, as the political trajectory of Mbusa Nyamwisi and the RCD/K-ML shows, it is not only electoral participation and outcomes that create incentives for political positioning via real or suspected recourse to arms. It was to a large extent Mbusa's efforts to maintain or regain a position in the presidential patronage network that pushed him to continue links with armed actors. Therefore, when analyzing the causes of the militarization of the current order, it is difficult to disaggregate the specific effects of politico-military entrepreneurs' electoral participation from those related to their general inclusion in the political arena, including their integration in the state apparatus and presidential patronage network. At the same time, Mbusa's trajectory illustrates that there are clear limitations to translating control over militarized networks into political capital. Importantly, his power has been increasingly undermined by the rising fortunes of Julien Paluku, who has only limited influence over armed actors. However, even Paluku has benefited from armed mobilization, although in a very indirect manner, trying to capitalize upon the massacres that took place in the course of 2014 and 2015 by engaging in scapegoat politics.

The tragic episode of the massacres demonstrates how, due to the multitude of armed factions that are present in the Grand Nord, as in the eastern Congo as a whole, participation in *pompier-pyromania* is widening, even though sometimes primarily through smokescreen tactics. By generating profound confusion and uncertainty over perpetrators and alliances, this opaque multitude allows political actors of all stripes to accuse their opponents of engaging in manipulation and violence, regardless of the evidence. These complexities highlight that while the Congo's post-settlement order is militarized, this militarization has become of an increasingly diffuse nature, with covert and suspected alliances with armed groups being as important as the direct and open sponsoring of violence. However, real violence continues to be the engine of this economy of rumors and posturing, and capitalizing upon suspected links to armed groups is only possible when these groups actually exist.

While the described militarization of the post-settlement order is to a large extent an outcome of the wars and the subsequent transition, it draws on developments that started in the pre-war period. At the start of the 1990s, Mbusa's brother Enoch Muvingi pioneered liaising with armed groups as a political strategy. These continuities show how strongly the Congo's post-settlement order is shaped by institutional configurations that developed in the Mobutu era, putting the effects of politico-military entrepreneurs' post-settlement political participation in that order into perspective. Hence, the roots of the current system of *pompier-pyromanocracy* run much deeper than the post-settlement period, although the dynamics in this period, as shaped by the practices of politico-military entrepreneurs like Antipas Mbusa Nyamwisi, have played an important role in its further expansion and democratization.

The fragmentation, volatility and opacity of the political-military landscape fostered by the rise of *pompier-pyromanocracy* have become increasingly difficult to manage, for the political center and external actors alike. Failing to get a grip on the complex political dynamics, the latter have largely resorted to either purely military or technocratic interventions. Meanwhile, *pompier-pyromanes*, especially those that are not dressed in fatigues but don the cloaks of respectable politicians, have been able to light their fires quite openly. In fact, despite the reigning confusion, there are often substantial indications which politico-military entrepreneurs are involved in what blaze. Yet the Congolese government has mostly attempted to make use of such allegations for its own benefit, such as by discrediting political opponents. International actors, for their part, have been hesitant to get involved in the messy and risky business of addressing "rebels in suits" (Verweijen 2013). However, while indeed entailing a risk of being burnt, getting to the source of the fire seems the only viable way for the eastern Congo to rise out of its smoldering ashes.

Notes

1 Open lists imply that voters can choose any candidate from the political party lists they vote for. A multimember constituency means that each constituency has more than one elected representative, which tends to entrench fragmentation in divided systems.

2 The Banyarwanda encompass a range of groups with different historical trajectories, including communities present on the soil of the Congo Free State when its boundaries were fixed; colonial-era labor migrants from Rwanda; and waves of Rwandan refugees arriving on the eve of and at various stages after the Congo's independence (Mamdani 1998).

3 Interview with former RCD/K-ML cadre, Goma, 5 April 2014.

4 Interview with former secretary-general RCD/K-ML, Goma, 6 April 2014.

5 I am indebted to Mehdi Belaid for this qualification of Mbusa Nyamwisi's strategies.

6 Interview with former secretary-general RCD/K-ML, Goma, 6 April 2014.

7 Interview with RCD/K-ML party cadres, Goma, 6 and 7 April 2014.

8 Information obtained from multiple sources during field research in Beni territory, April 2010.

9 Granting Beni and Butembo the statute of city concerns a war-era policy decision of the RCD/K-ML that was formalized during the transition. Interviews with civil society members, Butembo, 28 April 2010.

10 Interview with RCD/K-ML party cadres, Goma, 6/7 April 2014.

11 Interview with RCD/K-ML party cadres, Goma, 7 April 2014.

12 "Julien Paluku Kahongya", https://fr.wikipedia.org/wiki/Julien_Paluku_Kahongya.

13 Interview with former RCD/K-ML cadre, Goma, 6 April 2014.

14 Information obtained during field research in Beni territory, April 2010.

15 Interview with political analyst, Goma, 7 April 2014.

16 I am grateful to Rachel Sweet for bringing up this point. Personal communication, 12 December 2014.

17 It concerned the ministers José Endundo and Olivier Kamitatu as well as the MP Modeste Bahati Lukwebo.

18 Interview with political cadres RCD/K-ML, Goma, 6 and 7 April 2014.

19 Ibid.

20 With the presidential elections, Mbusa came in fourth at the level of North Kivu with 12.74% of the votes. In three districts of the Grand Nord, he was the most voted-for presidential candidate: Beni (36.93%), Beni ville (32.98%) and Butembo (44.73%). Résultats présidentielle par territoires et villes [Results of the presidential elections per territory and per city], http://www.congoforum.be/upldocs/res_pres_territoires_villes_2011.pdf.

21 Personal communication with Rachel Sweet, 12 December 2014.

22 Interview with sub-federal president RCD/K-ML, Goma, 5 April 2014.

23 Interviews with journalists working in the Grand Nord, Goma, 6 April 2014.

24 See for example the list of M23 officers exempted from reintegration into the FARDC published by the DRC government (Radio Kivu 1 Goma 2013).

25 Interviews with ex-Mai Mai Vurundo officers, Butembo, 27 April 2010.

26 Interview with RCD/K-ML cadres, Goma, 6 April 2014.

Bibliography

Bayart, J.-F. [1989] 2006. *L'Etat en Afrique: La Politique du Ventre* [The State in Africa. The Politics of the Belly]. 2nd edition. Paris: Fayard.

Belaid, M. 2015. *"Après la Forêt." Guérilla et Politiques de Sortie de Guerre. Les Combattants Maï-Maï, l'Etat et la Reproduction de la Violence en République Démocratique du Congo* ["After the Forest". Guerilla and Peacebuilding Politics. Mai-Mai Combatants, the State and the Reproduction of Violence in the Democratic Republic of the Congo]. PhD Diss., Université Paris 1 Pantheon, Sorbonne.

Brock, S. 2009. *DRC: Mbusa Nyamwisi – Yesterday's Man?* US Embassy in Kinshasa, 19 June, 09KINSHASA578. http://cables.mrkva.eu/cable.php?id=213003.

Carter Center. 2007. *International Election Observation Mission to Democratic Republic of Congo 2006*. Presidential and Legislative Elections Final Report, Atlanta, GA.

Carter Center. 2011. *Presidential and Legislative Elections in the Democratic Republic of the Congo*. Final Report, Atlanta, GA.

CENI (Commission Electorale Nationale Indépendante). 2012. *Elections de Députés Nationaux de 2011* [The 2011 Elections of National Members of Parliament]. Commission Electorale Nationale Indépendante – Republique Democratique de Congo. http://www.ceni.gouv.cd/deputes/ETAT_Depute2011BParListe.PDF.

De Villers, G. and J. Omasombo. 2002. "An Intransitive Transition." *Review of African Political Economy* 29 (93/94): 399-410.

Dibwe dia Mwembu, D. 1999. "L'épuration ethnique au Katanga et l'éthique du redressement des torts du passé" [Ethnic Cleansing in Katanga and the Ethics of Redressing the Wrongs of the Past]. *Canadian Journal of African Studies/La Revue canadienne des études africaines* 33 (2-3): 483-499.

Dougherty. 2006. *FARDC Building Up Force Levels in North Kivu*. US embassy in Kinshasa, cable 06KINSHASA1870_a, 18 December. https://www.wikileaks.org/plusd/cables/06KINSHASA1870_a.html.

Eriksson Baaz, M. and J. Verweijen. 2013. "The Volatility of a Half-Cooked Bouillabaisse. Rebel-Military Integration and Conflict Dynamics in Eastern DRC." *African Affairs* 112 (449): 563-582.

Forum des As. 2014. "Le RCD/K-ML désavoue Mbusa Nyamwisi" [The RCD/K-ML Repudiates Mbusa Nyamwisi]. *DigitalCongo*, 14 November. http://www.digitalcongo.net/article/103837.

International Crisis Group. 2000. *Scramble for the Congo. Anatomy of an Ugly War.* Brussels: International Crisis Group.

International Crisis Group. 2003. *The Kivus: The Forgotten Crucible of the Congo Conflict.* Brussels: International Crisis Group.

International Crisis Group. 2006. *Security Sector Reform in the Congo.* Brussels: International Crisis Group.

International Crisis Group. 2007. *Congo: Bringing Peace to North Kivu.* Brussels: International Crisis Group.

Jokanko. No date. "Pourquoi Joseph Bangakya a quitté Mbusa Nyamwisi?" [Why has Joseph Bangakay Left Mbusa Nyamwisi?]. *Le Millénaire.* http://lemillenaireinfoplus.e-monsite.com/pages/politique/pourquoi-joseph-bangakya-a-quitte-mbusa-nyamwisi.html.

Lanotte, O. 2003. *République Démocratique du Congo. Guerres sans Frontières. De Joseph-Désiré Mobutu à Joseph Kabila* [Democratic Republic of the Congo. War without Borders. From Joseph-Désiré Mobutu to Joseph Kabila]. Brussels: GRIP and Editions Complexe.

La Prosperité. 2010. "Fini la blague à l'AMP. Kabila menace de frapper Kamitatu et consorts!" [Over with the Joke to the AMP. Kabila Threatens to Strike Kamitatu and Company!]. *La Prosperité*, 27 May. http://www.congoforum.be/fr/nieuwsdetail.asp?subitem=1&newsid=167823&Actualiteit=selected.

Le Potentiel. 2010. "Reconfiguration de l'Amp: Un nouveau regroupement politique dénommé 'Centre Libéral et Patriotique' voit le jour." [Reconfiguration of the AMP. Creation of a New Political Group Named 'Liberal and Patriotic Center']. *Le Potentiel*, 26 May. http://www.digitalcongo.net/article/67207.

Mararo, B. S. 2003. "Le Nord-Kivu au Cœur de la Crise Congolaise" [North Kivu at the Heart of the Congolese Crisis]. In *L'Afrique des Grands Lacs, Annuaire 2001-2002*, ed. S. Marysse and F. Reyntjens. Paris: Karthala.

Mararo, B. S. 2005. "Kinshasa et le Kivu depuis 1987: Une Histoire Ambigue" [Kinshasa and Kivu since 1987: An Ambiguous History]. In *L'Afrique des Grands Lacs, Annuaire 2004-2005*, ed. S. Marysse and F. Reyntjens. Paris: L'Harmattan.

Mamdani, M. 1998. *Understanding the Crisis in Kivu: Report of the CODESRIA Mission to the Democratic Republic of Congo September, 1997.* Centre for African Studies, University of Cape Town.

Matti, S. 2010. "The Democratic Republic of the Congo? Corruption, Patronage, and Competitive Authoritarianism in the DRC." *Africa Today* 56 (4): 42-61.

Meece, R. 2006a. *FARDC in Eastern DRC Often Undermining Security.* US embassy in Kinshasa, cable 06KINSHASA859_a, 31 May 2006. https://www.wikileaks.org/plusd/cables/06KINSHASA859_a.html.

Meece, R. 2006b. *Presidential Hopeful Nyamwisi Throws Votes To Kabila.* US Embassy in Kinshasa, 25 July 2006, 06KINSHASA1179. http://www.cablegatesearch.net/cable.php?id=06KINSHASA1179.

Mwanawavene, R. K., N. B. Bahete and C. N. Bilali. 2006. *Trafic d'Armes. Enquete du Terrain au Kivu (RDC)* [Arms Traffic. Field Enquiry in Kivu (DRC)]. Brussels: GRIP.

Ngoy-Kangoy, K. H. 2007. "The Political Role of the Ethnic Factor around Elections in the Democratic Republic of the Congo." *African Journal on Conflict Resolution* 7 (2): 219-238.

Ngoy-Kangoy, K. H. 2006. *Parties and Political Transition in the Democratic Republic of the Congo.* EISA Research report No. 20. Johannesburg: EISA (Electoral Institute for Sustainable Democracy in Africa).

Nkole, J. K. No date. "M23 et Mbusa Nyamwisi: la crainte de la répétition de l'histoire?" [M23 and Mbusa Nyamwisi: Fear for a Repetition of History?]. *Le Millénaire*. http://lemillenaireinfoplus.e-monsite.com/pages/est-de-la-rdc/m23-et-mbusa-nyamwisi-la-crainte-de-la-repetition-de-l-histoire.html.

Omasomba, J. et al. 2009. *Biographies des Acteurs de la Troisième République* [Biographies of Key Figures of the Third Republic]. Tervuren: Musée Royal de l'Afrique Centrale.

Radio Kivu 1 Goma. 2013. "Liste complète de commandants du M23 non eligibles a l'intégration dans les FARDC" [Complete List of M23 Commanders Non-eligible for Integration into the FARDC]. *Radio Kivu 1 Goma*, 27 September. http://bukavuonline.com/2013/09/liste-complete-commandants-du-eligibles-lintegration-les-fardc/#sthash.06JxEwkE.dpuf.

Raeymaekers, T. 2004. "The Political Economy of Beni-Lubero." In *Conflict and Social Transformation in Eastern DR Congo*, ed. K. Vlassenroot and T. Raeymaekers. Ghent: Academia Press Scientific Publishers.

Raeymaekers, T. 2007. *The Power of Protection. Governance and Transborder Trade on the Congo-Ugandan Frontier*. PhD Diss, Ghent University.

Raeymaekers, T. 2009. "The Silent Encroachment of the Frontier: A Politics of Transborder Trade in the Semliki Valley (Congo–Uganda)." *Political Geography* 28 (1): 55-65.

Rolley, S. 2014. "ADF-Nalu: Un ancien ministre Congolais met en cause un haut gradé" [ADF-NALU: A Former Minister of the Congo Warns against a Superior Officer]. *Radio France Internationale*, 25 October. http://www.rfi.fr/afrique/20141025-adf-nalu-ancien-ministre-congolais-met-cause-haut-grade/.

Stearns, J. 2011. *Dancing in the Glory of Monsters: the Collapse of the Congo and the Great War of Africa*. New York: PublicAffairs.

Stearns, J. 2013a. *From CNDP to M23. The Evolution of an Armed Movement in Eastern Congo*. London: Rift Valley Institute.

Stearns, J. 2013b. *PARECO. Land, Local Strongmen and the Roots of Militia Politics in North Kivu*. London: Rift Valley Institute.

Stearns, J., J. Verweijen and M. Eriksson Baaz. 2013. *The National Army and Armed Groups in the Eastern Congo. Untangling the Gordian Knot of Insecurity*. London: Rift Valley Institute.

Sweet, R. 2015. "Guest Blog: Politics and Business Intersect in String of North Kivu Killings." *Congo Siasa*, 6 January. http://congosiasa.blogspot.be/2015/01/guest-blog-politics-and-business.html.

Titeca, K. and K. Vlassenroot. 2012. "Rebels without Borders in the Rwenzori Borderland? A Biography of the Allied Democratic Forces." *Journal of Eastern African Studies* 6 (1): 154-176.

UNSC (United Nations Security Council). 2002. *Final Report of the Panel of Experts on the Illegal Exploitation of Natural Resources and Other Forms of Wealth of the Democratic Republic of the Congo. S/2002/1146*. New York: United Nations Security Council.

UNSC (United Nations Security Council). 2011. *Final Report of the Group of Experts on the Democratic Republic of the Congo, S/2011/738*. New York: United Nations Security Council.

UNSC (United Nations Security Council). 2012. *Final Report of the Group of Experts on the Democratic Republic of Congo, S/2012/843*. New York: United Nations Security Council.

UNSC (United Nations Security Council). 2013. *Mid-term Report of the UN Group of Experts on the DRC S/2013/433*. New York: United Nations Security Council.

UNSC (United Nations Security Council). 2016. *Final Report of the Group of Experts on the Democratic Republic of the Congo, S/2016/466*. New York: United Nations Security Council.

Verweijen, J. 2013. "Rebels in Suits. Tackling Civilian Support networks of Armed Groups in the Eastern DR Congo." Amani Itakuya

#8, *Christophvogel.net.* http://
christophvogel.net/2013/10/31/
amani-itakuya-rebels-in-suits-tackling-
civilian-support-networks-of-armed-
groups-in-the-eastern-dr-congo/.

Verweijen, J. 2014. "Half-Brewed: the
Lukewarm Results of Creating an
Integrated Congolese Military." In *New
Armies from Old. Merging Competing
Military Forces after Civil Wars*,
ed. R. Licklider. Washington, DC:
Georgetown University Press.

Vlassenroot, K. and T. Raeymaekers. 2008.
"New Political Order in the DR Congo?
The Transformation of Regulation."
Afrika Focus 21 (2): 39-52.

Willame, J.-C. 2007. *Les "Faiseurs de
Paix" au Congo. Gestion d'une Crise
Internationale dans un État sous
Tutelle* ["Peacebuilders" in the Congo.
Management of an International Crisis
in a State under Tutelage]. Brussels:
GRIP and Éditions Complexe.

2 | Apotheosis of a warlord: Paul Kagame

Lars Waldorf

> If Kagame can achieve half of what he has set out to do, he will go down
> in African history. If he can achieve it all, leaders of every poor country
> on earth will look to Rwanda for lessons, and bands of angels will sing in
> heaven. (Kinzer 2008: 338)

Introduction

From 1994 to 2010, President Paul Kagame was easily the most celebrated
warlord democrat on the world stage. The *Financial Times* and *Time* magazine
named him one of the fifty most influential people of the new millennium for
transforming a nation devastated by genocide into a showcase of post-conflict
reconstruction. Politicians, religious dignitaries and journalists championed
his visionary leadership and his moral rectitude. Donors and businessmen
rewarded his stewardship of a growing economy with large infusions of aid
and investment.

Rick Warren, the influential American preacher, praised Kagame in a 2009
Time profile for having "successfully modeled the transition from soldier to
statesman" and for "his willingness to listen to and learn from those who
oppose him". A very different side of Kagame was on display just a year later
during his re-election campaign when he labeled political opponents "hooli-
gans" and "useless people" (Kagame 2010a). Even after winning an unbelievable
93% of the vote, Kagame (2010b) continued to attack his opponents:

> Those who deal in rumours and falsehoods – the likes of Rusesabagina,
> Kayumba, Karegeya, Rudasingwa, Gahima – these are all useless characters.
> They don't represent anyone among our more than 11 million Rwandans.
>
> Those trading in falsehoods and their foreign backers – like some human
> rights organisations and foreign media practitioners – should know that
> nobody loves Rwanda and Rwandans more than we do. ...
>
> If you declare war on Rwanda with intention to destabilise the country,
> the people and their property, never complain if you get a beating.

When one of those "useless characters" – former intelligence chief Patrick
Karegeya – was brutally murdered in 2014, Kagame sent an unmistakable
message to his other political opponents: "Whoever betrays the country will
pay the price" (Birrell 2014).

As that suggests, you can take the democrat out of Kagame, but not the warlord. This chapter describes how Kagame transformed his rebel army into an electoral party (the Rwandan Patriotic Front or RPF) and himself from victorious warlord to elected president (in 2003 and again in 2010), while retaining his authoritarian ways. De Zeeuw (2008: 12) defines a "successful" rebel-to-party transformation as requiring two structural changes – demilitarization and party organization – and two attitudinal changes – democratized decision-making and adapted political goals. He sets out five factors that influence transformation: rebel leadership; conflict settlement; domestic context; regional stability; and international support (De Zeeuw 2008: 19-23). All those factors worked against the RPF's "successful" transformation. First, Kagame's authoritarian leadership style and the RPF's centralized structure prevented internal democratization and power-sharing. Second, the RPF's military victory gave it control of the state and the monopoly of legitimate (and illegitimate) violence. Third, the RPF started off with a very narrow base of support and was unlikely to win over the Hutu majority. Fourth, the RPF uses the threat from unrepentant *génocidaires* in the eastern Democratic Republic of Congo to justify militarism at home and abroad. Finally, a guilty international community went through the motions of democracy promotion while turning a blind eye to the RPF's suppression of democracy. Overall, the RPF did not become "a normal – that is, unarmed – political party" (De Zeeuw 2008: 16). Rather, it became a political party with an army and a state at its command (Reyntjens 2009a: 4).

The chapter begins by tracing Rwanda's political trajectory through snapshots of Kagame's life history. It then explores how Kagame turned the RPF into an electoral party, focusing on the structural and attitudinal changes identified by de Zeeuw. Finally, it examines two security outcomes of Kagame's participation in electoral politics: domestic human rights abuses and consolidation of the peace process. Those security outcomes can be explained by agency (Kagame's personality and vision) and structure (the Tutsi as a permanent minority).

Background: Kagame's avatars

Kagame's personal and political journey is fatefully intertwined with the tragic history of ethnic politics between the majority Hutu and minority Tutsi in Rwanda and the wider Great Lakes region. Hutu and Tutsi are complicated, socially constructed ethnic identities: both groups speak the same language, share the same culture, practice the same religion, live together and often intermarry.[1] In pre-colonial times, Hutu and Tutsi were somewhat fluid identities based largely on socio-political status and economic activity. The German and then the Belgian colonialists treated Hutu and Tutsi as fixed racial identities and viewed the Tutsi as racially superior "Hamites" who supposedly came from Ethiopia. The Belgians imposed a system of ethnic identity cards and favored the Tutsi elite who had governed the pre-colonial kingdom. In 1959, the Belgians suddenly switched allegiance from the Tutsi elite to the Hutu majority and supported the 1959 "social revolution" that led to an independent Hutu republic in 1962.

The post-colonial Hutu regimes further instrumentalized ethnic identities. Despite claims to represent the Hutu majority, the post-independence, neo-patrimonial regimes discriminated among Hutu: Grégoire Kayibanda's First Republic favored Hutu from central and southern Rwanda, while Juvénal Habyarimana's Second Republic benefited Hutu in the northwest. Both regimes discriminated against Tutsi and occasionally incited violence against them to serve their own political interests.

Ethnic violence in Rwanda is a modern, sporadic and mostly state-initiated phenomenon: Hutu political elites whipped up violence against the Tutsi minority in the face of intra-Hutu and Tutsi political challenges in several distinct periods (Des Forges 1999: 41-49; Straus 2006: 175-200). The first major round of ethnic violence between Hutu and Tutsi occurred in the context of the independence struggle from 1959 to 1963 and was partly instigated by the Belgian colonialists. Approximately 400,000 Tutsi fled the violence and became refugees in neighboring countries (Prunier 1998: 119, 121 n. 11). Under Kayibanda's First Republic (1962-1973), the regime engaged in periodic pogroms against Tutsi, often in response to incursions from Tutsi guerrillas seeking to reinstate the Tutsi monarchy. Habyarimana came to power in a 1973 military coup, promising to end the violence between Hutu and Tutsi that Kayibanda had fomented that year to shore up his slipping power. Habyarimana created a one-party dictatorship, in which all Rwandans, both Hutu and Tutsi, were members of the single party from birth. Despite widespread, institutionalized discrimination against Tutsi, there was no ethnic violence against Tutsi until 1990, when Kagame's RPF invaded the country.

Refugee-warrior Kagame was born into the Tutsi elite in 1956 just as their power and privileges were being challenged by Hutu populists and Belgian colonial administrators. Three years later, the Hutu "Social Revolution" was launched amidst ethnic violence against the Tutsi. Kagame remembered his family fleeing from a mob that was killing people and burning houses (Kinzer 2008: 9). In 1961, Rwanda gained its independence from Belgium under the leadership of Kayibanda, who claimed to rule in the name of the Hutu majority. That same year, Kagame's family crossed into Uganda, joining some 400,000 Tutsi who sought safety in exile.

Kagame grew up in a refugee camp in Uganda where he first met many of his future military and political colleagues, including Fred Rwigyema (Dorsey 2000: 328-329). Kagame and Rwigyema threw in their lot with Yoweri Museveni in 1978, helping him and the Tanzanians to overthrow Idi Amin. Then, in 1981, they were the first Rwandans to sign up to Museveni's National Resistance

Army (NRA). Eventually, some 3,500 Rwandans joined the NRA's ranks in response to the Ugandan government's persecution of Tutsi refugees. In 1986, the NRA arguably became "the first insurgent movement effectively to take over power from an incumbent African government" (Ngoga 1998: 91). Museveni reestablished a strong, central state and rewarded his Rwandan allies, making Rwigyema army chief of staff and Kagame deputy chief of intelligence.

Rebel Museveni's victory prompted the creation of the RPF in Kampala in 1987. The RPF's Eight Point Plan called for democracy, national unity and refugee return, though "[t]he specifics of how these goals would be translated into practical public policies were side-stepped to maintain unity" (Reed 1996: 486). While Kagame joined the RPF early on, Rwigyema only did so after Museveni dismissed him in 1989. Rwigyema's dismissal sent a signal that Rwandan refugees would never be fully integrated into Ugandan politics and so more "decided to turn to the RPF and its radical project of reconquest" of Rwanda (Prunier 1998: 127).

By late 1990, the RPF was being marginalized by developments inside Rwanda. Under pressure from France and internal opponents, President Habyarimana started a hesitant process of democratization. More crucially, Habyarimana began discussing the partial repatriation of Tutsi refugees. To assert its relevance, the RPF invaded Rwanda in October 1990 with some 2,000 Rwandan NRA soldiers who had deserted their posts. Instead of a quick victory, the RPF met with disaster (see Rudasingwa 2013: 93–94). Rwigyema was killed on the second day and both his replacements were killed within a month. Kagame left a military training course in the US to take command of the rebel forces in November 1990. He quickly shifted the RPF's military strategy from fighting conventional battles to guerrilla warfare.

In August 1992, the RPF and Rwandan government[2] signed the first of several peace agreements (collectively known as the Arusha Accords). After massacres of Tutsi civilians in February 1993, the RPF violated the ceasefire, making a large-scale attack in northwest Rwanda that displaced hundreds of thousands. Habyarimana's army was only able to halt the RPF advance on the capital with French military support. Peace talks resumed and a final peace agreement was signed in August 1993. The Arusha Accords created a broad-based transitional government that left Habyarimana in place, but sharing power with the RPF and internal opposition parties. It also established a small and ineffectual UN peacekeeping mission.

Savior On 6 April 1994, unknown assailants shot down Habyarimana's plane, killing all on board.[3] Hutu extremists seized control of the state, restarted the civil war and launched an extermination campaign against the Tutsi. Using hate media, they portrayed all Tutsi civilians as a "fifth column" of the RPF.

71

During the genocide, the RPF placed military objectives ahead of rescuing Tutsi. When Lieutenant-General Roméo Dallaire, head of the beleaguered UN peacekeeping mission, asked for more help in saving Tutsi, Kagame responded: "If the [Tutsi] refugees have to be killed for the cause, they will be considered as having been part of the sacrifice" (Dallaire 2003: 358). The RPF also publicly opposed efforts to send in new UN peacekeeping forces to protect Tutsi (Des Forges 1999: 699-701; Rudasingwa 2013: 159). The RPF's military victory in July 1994 ended the genocide but, by then, at least half a million Tutsi, as well as thousands of Hutu, had been slaughtered.

The 1994 genocide was the making of Kagame. His defeat of the genocidal forces gave him the moral authority, political power and military means to refashion Rwanda. The political parties, civil society organizations and religious institutions that might have stood in his way were devastated or compromised by the genocide. Kagame's victory owed nothing to the international community and he repeatedly shamed the UN and Western countries for their failure to halt the genocide.

Soldier In July 1994, the RPF installed a "Government of National Unity" that grouped together all the non-extremist political parties, while ensuring it held the balance of power in the presidency, cabinet and parliament. General Kagame took the posts of vice-president and defense minister, through which he controlled the army and, with it, the state.

Between 1994 and 2000, Kagame led two counterinsurgency campaigns inside Rwanda and two invasions of Congo. The most infamous episode of the first counterinsurgency (July 1994–September 1995) was the killing of approximately 4,000 internally displaced persons (IDPs) at Kibeho in April 1995 in full view of UN peacekeepers and humanitarian workers (Prunier 1997: 360-363). The First Congo War (1996–1997) began as an effort to stop *génocidaires* from using Hutu refugee camps in Congo to launch attacks into Rwanda but ended with the deposing of Congo's long-time dictator, Mobutu Sese Seko, and his replacement with Rwanda's ally, Laurent Kabila. The RPF killed tens of thousands of Hutu and Congolese civilians (UN High Commissioner for Human Rights 2010). The repatriation of Hutu refugees imported the civil war back into Rwanda and the RPF found itself fighting a second, bloodier counterinsurgency (1997–1999) in northwest Rwanda. The Second Congo War (1998–2003) started when Kabila turned on his Rwandan allies and they attempted to replace him. This time, the war drew in eight other African countries and left an estimated 5 million dead (mostly from starvation and disease).

Party leader Kagame became first vice-chairman of the RPF shortly after the death of Rwigyema. From the start, he had more power than the party's other top officials. The chairman (Colonel Alexis Kanyarengwe), a prominent opponent of Habyarimana, was little more than a Hutu figurehead (Reyntjens 2013: 80; Rudasingwa 2013: 97, 403). The second vice-chairman (Patrick Mazimpaka), third vice-chairman (Denis Polisi) and secretary general (Theoneste Rudasingwa) were all Tutsi but none were military men.

Kanyarengwe was removed in 1998 after protesting at massacres of Hutu civilians during the second counterinsurgency (Reyntjens 2009b: 184-185). Kagame then assumed the party chairmanship and Pasteur Bizimungu, the Hutu president, became vice-chairman. This effectively meant "the vice president was acting as the president's boss" (Sebarenzi 2009: 141). At that point, Bizimungu was the only Hutu on the RPF's executive committee (Reyntjens 2013: 19).

President Kagame assumed the presidency in 2000 after Bizimungu was pressured to resign (Reyntjens 2013: 15-16). At the urging of donors, Rwanda held its first national elections in 2003. Before announcing his candidacy, Kagame resigned from the army. He won the presidency in 2003 with 95% and in 2010 with 93%. As president, Kagame has presided over a highly ambitious policy of state-building and social engineering (Straus and Waldorf 2011). The RPF has undertaken a series of dramatic political, economic and social projects, including the world's boldest experiment in transitional justice, comprehensive land tenure and agricultural reform, forced villagization, and the systematic redrawing and renaming of Rwanda's territory. These projects not only aim to alter Rwanda's governance and economic structures, they also seek to change social identities, cultural norms and individual behavior.

CEO Kagame has been hailed as CEO of Rwanda, Inc. (Crisafulli and Redmond 2012: 3). He has adopted a developmental state agenda that aims to make Rwanda a lower middle-income country by 2020. This involves replacing small-scale and subsistence agriculture with larger agribusiness and ranching ventures, while also building up the service industry, particularly in information technology. The government has attracted foreign investment by reducing bureaucratic red tape, lowering corporate tax rates and combating corruption. The World Bank ranks the country as the forty-fifth easiest place in the world to do business. The annual growth rate averaged 8% between 2007 and 2012. Per capita GDP rose from $202 in 2003 to $620 in 2012 and inequality has declined since 2006. The country has largely met the Millennium Development Goals on maternal health and universal primary education.

Kagame is also the de facto CEO of a shadowy set of holding companies – Tri-Star Investments/Crystal Ventures Ltd. and Horizon Group – that are controlled by the RPF and military respectively (Booth and Golooba-Mutebi 2012: 396-399; Rudasingwa 2013: 436-437). Those entities have dominated or monopolized certain sectors – including telecommunications, private security and food processing – during various periods.

Warlord Since the Second Congo War officially ended in 2003, Kagame has supported proxy militias in eastern Congo to fight Hutu rebels and exploit natural resources. In 2012, the UN Group of Experts reported that Rwanda was providing weapons, recruits and financing to M23 (Movement of 23 March), a Congolese Tutsi rebel group, in violation of a UN arms embargo. It also found that the Rwandan army had intervened directly in Congo to assist those rebels (United Nations 2012). The US Ambassador-at-Large for War Crimes warned Rwanda's leaders that they could be prosecuted for aiding and abetting crimes against humanity (McGreal 2012). Germany, Sweden, the Netherlands, the US and eventually the UK suspended, delayed or redirected development assistance.

Peacekeeper Despite Kagame's blatant warmongering in the Congo, he has paradoxically become one of Africa's indispensable peacekeepers. The Rwandan army has contributed thousands of troops to United Nations and African Union peacekeeping missions in Darfur, Mali, South Sudan and Central African Republic (Jowell 2014: 288). Kagame has several motives for peacekeeping, some altruistic and some political. For one thing, it keeps his soldiers busy outside Rwanda. For another, it reinforces the RPF's moral authority in preventing genocide and provides a counternarrative to the army's depredations in Congo (Beswick 2010). Peacekeeping also gives Kagame leverage over the UN as well as Western powers.[4]

"A very strange" man Kagame ended a lengthy interview with *New York Times* bureau chief Jeffrey Gettleman (2013) saying "God created me in a very strange way". Gettleman's profile depicts Kagame as a Jekyll-and-Hyde character: austere and charming, imperious and friendly, cerebral and impassioned, fastidious and brutal. Gettleman details Kagame's fearsome reputation for beating his staff. To his surprise, Kagame did not deny being physically abusive:

> "It's my nature," Kagame said. "I can be very tough, I can make mistakes like that." But when I pressed him on other violent outbursts, he responded irritably, "Do we really need to go into every name, every incident?" He said that hitting people is not "sustainable," which struck me as a strange word to use, as if the only issue with beating your underlings was whether such behavior was effective over the long term. (Gettleman 2013)

Kagame certainly comes off as an authoritarian personality with a penchant for violence. As Gettleman observes, "Kagame is not the only African leader who is both impressive and repressive, though he may be the *most* impressive and among the *most* repressive" (Gettleman 2013).

Transforming the RPF from rebel movement to electoral party

Kagame's personal transformation from rebel to statesman parallels a similar shift in the RPF from vanguard movement to ruling party. The RPF started as a "reform insurgency" to replace a Hutu elite (ruling in the name of the Hutu majority) with a non-ethnic elite promoting national unity.[5] While the RPF was formed by civilian refugees in the late 1980s, it was forged by Kagame and his armed rebels during the civil war. Under Kagame's leadership, the RPF became a hierarchical, disciplined and effective fighting force. Still, it could not have succeeded without external support from the Tutsi diaspora and covert support from Museveni and former colleagues in the NRM (Prunier 1998: 131). Prunier (1998: 119) describes the RPF as "an oddity among guerrilla movements":

> It was created outside the country where it intended to operate, its members were initially recruited among the armed forces of a foreign power, most of its combatants had never set foot in the land where they were going to fight, and they never managed to get any support from the masses of the population in whose name they were struggling.

The RPF resembled an army more than a guerrilla force (Prunier 1998: 132; Jones 2012: 233). Still, there are key similarities between the RPF and other reform insurgencies in Ethiopia, Eritrea and Uganda: discipline, effectiveness and inclusive nation-building agendas (Clapham 1998: 13).

The RPF began transitioning to a political party during the peace negotiations so it could take up ministerial posts and legislative seats in the transitional government promised by the Arusha Accords (Rudasingwa 2013: 140-141; Prunier 1997: 115-116). Yet Kagame's high command continued to dominate the party's executive committee (Dorsey 2000: 337). The RPF's former secretary general described the RPF at that time as "a highly centralized organization, with a bare minimum of internal democracy" (Rudasingwa 2013: 169). After military victory, Kagame set about remaking the RPF into a ruling political party but this did not entail meaningful demilitarization, democratized party organization and decision-making, or adapted political goals (i.e. real power-sharing) (see de Zeeuw 2008).

Outward demilitarization The RPF was understandably loath to demilitarize given its position as an occupying power over "a mostly hostile, mostly Hutu country" (Prunier 1998: 133). It also faced very real military threats from the genocidal forces that had regrouped in Congo and from insurgencies inside Rwanda. Furthermore, the RPF's soldiers helped assure the party's political dominance in the Government of National Unity and in the countryside (Dorsey 2000: 319-320). As the party's former secretary general recalled, "Essentially, what we had was a military government, with civilians working under this authority" (Rudasingwa 2013: 175; see Prunier 1997: 370).

Kagame's forces, which numbered perhaps 25,000 at the end of the genocide (Prunier 1997: 117), became the backbone of a new national army that took the same name as the RPF's military wing: the Rwandan Patriotic Army (RPA). Between late 1994 and 2001, the RPA reeducated and reintegrated 15,000 Hutu soldiers from the defeated army, but did not follow the Arusha Accords formula for sharing posts with Habyarimana's former army. As the RPA's spokesman told me, "Already, the Arusha Accords had been violated. What did not die was the principles of the Arusha Accords ... a force that actually reflected Rwanda and Rwandans, a force that wasn't sectarian, that didn't belong to one ethnic group."[6] In 2008, a leaked US Embassy cable observed that the chiefs of defense staff, army and air force, the military district commanders, and heads of the Rwanda National Police and the National Security Service were all Anglophone Tutsi who had grown up in Uganda. Today, most of the rank and file is Hutu, while the senior leadership is predominantly Tutsi who fought with the NRA and RPF (Jowell 2014: 279-280).

The RPF partly demilitarized through a disarmament, demobilization and reintegration (DDR) program that ran between 1997 and 2001. Many of the 19,000 fighters who went through DDR were privates who had swelled the RPF's ranks during and after the genocide. Those fighters were less committed, experienced and disciplined than the NRA and civil war recruits (Prunier 1997: 322).

The advent of electoral politics in 2003 prompted further, albeit symbolic, demilitarization of the RPF. The RPA was renamed the Rwandan Defense Forces, thus rhetorically distancing the army from the RPF. The 2003 Constitution defined the army's role as professional and non-partisan. It also required Kagame to resign from the army to compete for the presidency. This had no real effect on his control of the army as the president is commander-in-chief.

While the RPF has been outwardly demilitarized, the key players around Kagame are all military and intelligence men (Rudasingwa 2013: 431-432; Verhoeven 2012: 265). As one scholar points out, "The army remains the institution which is, firstly, the core institution for the implementation of state policy, secondly, the key space for the socialization of the elites and, thirdly, a link to the citizenry" (Jones 2012: 240). It also plays a key, if opaque, role in the economy through financial institutions, companies and resource exploitation in Congo (Jowell 2014: 285; Booth and Golooba-Mutebi 2012).

Party organization and decision-making The RPF's internal decision-making has not become more democratic as it changed into an electoral party.[7] This is not to say the RPF is monolithic. At times, Kagame and the party have tolerated divergent views on certain policy issues.[8] If the RPF now seems to speak with one voice that reflects Kagame's increased consolidation of power within the party. Indeed, Rwanda's shift to competitive authoritarianism has been accompanied by Kagame becoming an ever more personalistic leader.

The RPF's political and military leadership is dominated by Anglophone Tutsi from Uganda (Prunier 1997: 115-116; Dorsey 2000: 331; US Embassy 2008; Rudasingwa 2013: 431-432). They are closely linked by shared exile and family ties. Most came from two refugee camps in Uganda and many went to school or university together (Dorsey 2000: 328-329). While tensions have periodically surfaced among different returnee factions (i.e. Ugandan, Burundian, Congolese, Tanzanian, European and American), these have never threatened the Ugandan Tutsi's control of the party.

The RPF leadership has narrowed dramatically over the years. In July 1994, the RPF's three most prominent Hutu members were given highly visible posts: Pasteur Bizimungu as president, Seth Sendashonga as minister of interior, and Alphonse Marie Nkubito as justice minister. Sendashonga and Nkubito were fired in August 1995 (Prunier 1997: 367-368; Reyntjens 2013: 8-9). Bizimungu was pressured to resign in 2000 and later imprisoned after trying to form a new party. President Kagame not only sidelined prominent Hutu in the RPF, he also turned on longstanding Tutsi allies in the party and military. Several fled Rwanda in 2000 and 2001 (Reyntjens 2013: 17, 87-88). Gerald Gahima, who was on the RPF's executive committee and who had served as prosecutor general and Supreme Court judge, left Rwanda in early 2004 after being accused of corruption. His brother, Theoneste Rudasingwa, a former RPF secretary general and former adviser to Kagame, went into exile in 2005 after being acquitted of fraud in a military tribunal (Rudasingwa 2013: 295-319). Colonel Patrick Karegeya, the former intelligence chief, fled to South Africa in 2007 after serving an eighteen-month sentence for insubordination.

Some donors and scholars have attempted to identify "progressive champions of change" within the RPF (see DFID 2004: 6). For example, Clark (2010) argued that "the divides within the RPF have widened and more moderate voices ... have challenged Kagame over a host of issues, including the openness of political and media space and the question of presidential succession".[9] He further claimed that "RPF moderates have substantial clout within the government and have scored major political successes in the past" (Clark 2010). Clark named several RPF elites whom he considered moderate: Richard Sezibera (health minister), Tharcisse Karugarama (justice minister), Lieutenant General Charles Muhire (air force chief of staff), Major General Emmanuel Karenzi Karake (intelligence chief) and General Faustin Kayumba Nyamwasa (former army chief of staff). Leaving aside whether these RPF elites could truly be called "moderate", it is worth looking at where they were by the end of 2015. Sezibera became secretary general of the East African Community in 2011 while Karugarama was sacked in 2013. Generals Muhire and Karake were both arrested in 2010 on charges of corruption and immoral conduct, respectively.[10] General Nyamwasa fled to South Africa in 2010, where he has escaped three attempted assassinations. Clark's supposed "moderates" were purged by Kagame, contradicting his assertion that "Kagame does not always get his way" (Clark 2010).

The absence of democracy within the RPF is best demonstrated by the succession issue. Under the 2003 Constitution's term limits, Kagame could not run again in 2017. After hearing in mid-2013 that Justice Minister Karugarama – one of Clark's "reformists" – had said he should step down in 2017, Kagame responded:

> Why don't you tell him to step down himself? All those years he's been there, he's not the only one who can be the justice minister ... In the end we should come to a view that serves us all.
>
> I'm sure if the RPF went on for 40 years it would be a crime, but for the Liberal party in Japan it's not a crime. This is what disturbs me. Sometimes you feel like doing things just to challenge that – that somebody is entitled to do something, but says when you do it you are wrong. ... If it happens elsewhere and people think it's OK, why do people say it's not OK when it happens in Rwanda? I just don't accept this sort of thing. We have many struggles to keep fighting. Some of the things are like racism: "These are Africans, we must herd them like cows." No! Just refuse it. (McGreal 2013)

Less than a week later, Kagame sacked Karugarama.[11] In mid-April 2014, Kagame left open the possibility of a third term, stating "we need to leave countries and people to decide their own affairs" (Smith 2014). In October, the leadership of three small parties allied to the RPF proposed amending the constitution. One party president, who also serves as the minister of internal security, stated "We do not accept the idea of limiting the number of mandates because this is not democracy" (Agence France Presse 2014). In July 2015, parliament voted to amend the constitution to allow Kagame to stand for a third term. The December 2015 referendum produced predictably lopsided results, with 98% of all eligible voters approving constitutional changes that permit Kagame to stand for election until 2034 (when he will be seventy-five). Casting his vote in the referendum, Kagame insisted that "What is happening is [the] people's choice" (McVeigh 2015).

Adapted political goals? Winning elections As a rebel movement, the RPF had difficulty attracting Hutu recruits despite its inclusive ideology and its prominent Hutu spokesmen. The RPF conducted an electoral campaign for mayors in the demilitarized north in 1993 but Habyarimana's party took all the posts. "The RPF realized then that it stood no chance in an open political contest" (Reyntjens 2013: 7, n.16).

Under the Arusha Accords, the transitional government was supposed to last only twenty-two months and then be followed by elections. When the RPF formed the Government of National Unity in July 1994, it declared the transition period would run for five years, thereby giving it time to prepare for electoral victory. In 1999, as the deadline approached, the RPF extended the transition for another four years. International donors eventually pressured the RPF to hold national elections in 2003.

To prepare for those elections, the RPF began transforming itself from a vanguard party to a mass party without changing its undemocratic centralism. Emulating the NRA's "Movement", the RPF describes itself as a "family" (umuryango), with Kagame as the father figure. Although political campaigning was prohibited during the transition period, the RPF circumvented that restriction. It used local-level elections in 1999 and 2001 "to begin to develop a new RPF 'cadre' in the countryside and to build the party's political base ahead of presidential and parliamentary elections in 2003" (International Crisis Group 2001: 35). The party expanded its base through aggressive recruitment of members. Local officials held meetings where people, particularly influential community members like teachers, were pressured to become RPF members (Human Rights Watch 2003: 2–3). Before the 2008 parliamentary elections, a Rwandan associate told me how local officials repeatedly visited her home to persuade her to switch parties. The party also offers patronage. For example, local officials throw "celebrations" (ubusubane) where community residents are given free beer and reminded to vote "well" – that is, for Kagame and the RPF (European Union Electoral Observation Mission 2003: 2). Many believe that party membership will provide benefits in accessing government services. But party membership also comes with a price tag: members are expected to remit 10% of their incomes to the party (Habamenshi 2009: 133).

The problem with such mass recruitment drives is that it becomes difficult to distinguish opportunists from believers. The party leadership does not trust its new Hutu recruits to actually vote for the RPF in free and fair elections. Fearing a reenactment of the 1993 Burundi elections, when a Hutu majority voted a Tutsi president out of office (Human Rights Watch 2003: 4), the RPF has taken several measures to ensure electoral victory.

First, it co-opted, undermined or banned other political parties (Reyntjens 2013: 37–55; Longman 2011: 31–34; Sebarenzi 2011). Two key examples will suffice. In 2000, the RPF weakened the Liberal Party, which was largely supported by Tutsi genocide survivors.[12] It accused the party's most prominent figure, Speaker of Parliament Joseph Sebarenzi, of corruption and plotting the return of the Tutsi king from exile. Members of the Liberal Party, especially those close to the RPF, turned against him. Sebarenzi (2009: 176) later described how Kagame personally forced his resignation. Soon after, he fled into exile and the Liberal Party became closely aligned with the RPF. In early 2003, the

RPF destroyed the main Hutu opposition party, the Democratic Republican Movement (MDR). It established a parliamentary commission that accused the MDR of fomenting ethnic divisions and promoting genocidal ideology. Parliament voted to ban the party and the cabinet approved the decision (Human Rights Watch 2003: 4-8; Reyntjens 2013: 26-27, 30-32). In this way, the RPF effectively neutered its only significant opponents in advance of the 2003 elections.

Second, the RPF introduced a new constitution in 2003 that created a complicated mix of directly elected, indirectly elected and appointed seats for parliament. Only fifty-three of the eighty deputies in the lower house are directly elected. The rest – twenty-four women deputies, two youth deputies and one disabled deputy – are elected by organizations controlled by the RPF. Of the twenty-six senators in the upper house, twelve are elected by members of local government, eight are appointed by the president, four are designated by the Forum of Political Parties, and two are academics elected from private and public universities. Given RPF dominance over local government, the Forum and the universities, this guarantees RPF control over the Senate and over the twenty-six indirectly elected seats in the Chamber of Deputies (Reyntjens 2013: 39-40).

Third, the RPF ensures that elections are neither free nor fair. It uses state resources to mount its campaigns. It restricts campaigning by other parties. It dominates the state and private media. It arrests, harasses and intimidates non-RPF campaign workers and election observers. It stacks the National Election Commission. It also practices widespread fraud, including ballot-box stuffing (European Union Electoral Observation Mission 2004; European Union 2009; Reyntjens 2013: 37-39, 45-47, 50-55). The RPF's results pretty much speak for themselves. It won parliamentary elections with 76% in 2003, 78% in 2008 and 76% in 2013. In fact, the RPF actually won 96-98% in 2008 but then did "reverse-rigging" to lower its vote count to a more credible 78% and to give a handful of parliamentary seats to two "competing" parties (the Liberal Party and Social Democratic Party) – to preserve the fiction of power-sharing (Reyntjens 2009b).

Adapted political goals? Power-sharing without sharing power Several observers make much of the RPF's power-sharing with other political parties. They emphasize the RPF's decision to form a "Government of National Unity" based on the power-sharing formula in the Arusha Accords despite its overwhelming military advantage. They point to the 2003 Constitution which institutionalized power-sharing in parliament and the cabinet.[13] They note the number of government ministers who belong to other parties. Golooba-Mutebi and Booth (2013: 13), in particular, insist on the "robust inclusiveness" of the political settlement (elite bargain) that has existed since 2003. Not surprisingly, their claims are based on interviews with members of the RPF and its satellite parties.

The RPF capped its military victory in 1994 with a unilateral declaration establishing a unity government.[14] Why didn't the RPF just seize power for itself? The party recognized that a show of commitment to the Arusha Accords would enhance its legitimacy with a restive Hutu populace and with the international donor community. Yet, as the RPF's former secretary general later explained: "If you have to share power after seizing the state, it has to be done on your own terms. This is what the RPF leaders and RPA officers, while in Uganda's NRA, had seen, preached and experienced" (Rudasingwa 2013: 142). Thus, the RPF awarded itself the presidency and newly created vice-presidency as well as all the cabinet posts that would have gone to Habyarimana's party. It justified that power-play arguing that the RPF's "special role in the struggle against fascism confer [sic] upon it an historical responsibility to ensure that the process of pacification, of national reconciliation, and of reconstruction are *not hindered by political maneuvering*" (RPF 1994: para. 3, emphasis added). This gave the RPF effective control of the cabinet.[15] The subsequent Protocol of Agreement between all the parties in the Government of National Unity gave the RPF the same number of parliamentary seats (thirteen) as the three other major parties (Liberal Party, Social Democratic Party and Democratic Republican Movement) combined, but it also gave the RPF-controlled army six seats.

As Prunier (1997: 369) recognized early on, the RPF's power-sharing was "largely a make-believe exercise". First, the RPF ran a shadow government which had more power than the official government (International Crisis Group 2002: 7, 22). As the RPF secretary general later confirmed, "Where we had a Minister or any other official who was not RPF or a Tutsi, an assistant (almost in all cases, a Tutsi) was deployed. It was another unwritten yet very much known rule about how RPF was to govern" (Rudasingwa 2013: 176). A leaked US Embassy cable (2008) confirmed that: "Some major positions are held by Hutus, but their actual authority often appears limited, and they are widely perceived to be 'twinned' with more powerful Tutsi colleagues" (see also International Crisis Group 2002: 11; Prunier 1997: 369; Reyntjens 2013: 81). Second, "the former opposition parties have been so damaged that they tend to be simple clubs of Hutu 'big men' who broker among themselves the shares of quasi-power the Tutsi are willing to leave to them" (Prunier 1997: 371). Over time, these parties were infiltrated, undermined or, in the case of the MDR, erased.

In 1999, the RPF created the Forum of Political Parties, which it chairs, to regulate the activities of all parties.[16] As the former Speaker of Parliament recalled:

Creating the Forum of Political Parties was a way for Kagame to remove members of parliament who stood in his way. ...

Even my own party [the Liberal Party] supported it! It demonstrated how greatly the RPF had weakened the political parties. Also, most of the parties' leaders … were cabinet ministers, which would mean that the forum would allow them to exert power over members of parliament who could investigate and censure them. …

If there was any doubt who was in control, the forum did not vote out members of parliament who belonged to the RPF or the military – those members were simply told to leave by RPF officials. Also, if one of the other parties wanted someone out whom the RPF supported, the RPF always won. (Sebarenzi 2009: 147, 147-148, 150-151)

The Forum plays several other roles. It disciplines political parties. It also elects four senators. Finally, it channels the state funding that all the parties – except the RPF – depend on for their continued existence (European Union 2009: 27). By 2002, it was clear that the remaining political parties "are only tolerated if they agree not to question the definition of political life drawn up by the RPF" (International Crisis Group 2002: 2).

Security outcomes of Kagame's and the RPF's electoral participation

Kagame and the RPF decided to participate in electoral politics from 2003 on – even though it was unlikely they could win free and fair elections. By that point, they had alienated the Hutu majority through massacres of Hutu civilians in Rwanda and Congo and through mass arrests of Hutu genocide suspects in Rwanda. In addition, they had lost support among their core base (Tutsi returnees) and natural allies (Tutsi genocide survivors and Hutu democrats). Given these constraints and dangers, why bother to hold elections at all?

The RPF entered electoral politics for several reasons. First, international donors, such as the US and UK, pressured Kagame to hold elections, partly to justify increasing development assistance to Rwanda for their own domestic constituencies. At the same time, donors signaled to Kagame that they were not expecting (or demanding) free and fair elections. As one donor representative told me just before the 2003 presidential elections, "After having pushed Rwanda to hold elections before they were ready to do so, it wouldn't be fair to now threaten to cut off funding for those elections [because of human rights abuses]."[17] Second, and relatedly, Kagame understood that elections would give his regime procedural legitimacy both domestically and internationally. Elections bring "attention, approval, and money" from Western powers (Carothers 1997: 90-91). Nearly 50% of the Rwanda government's budget comes from development assistance. Third, elections (and other nominally democratic institutions) can strengthen – and lengthen – hegemonic authoritarian regimes. As Gandhi and Przeworski (2006: 21) state, "Elections are intended to show that the dictatorship can make the dog perform tricks, that it can intimidate a substantial part of the population, so that any opposition is futile." Similarly, Simpser (2013: xv) points out how "[m]anipulating elections excessively and blatantly [i.e. beyond what is necessary to win] can make the manipulating party appear stronger". This helps explain Kagame winning more than 90% and the RPF more than 75% of the vote. Such vote tallies are not meant to be convincing; rather, they are meant to signal to potential opponents and the populace that Kagame and the RPF are in full control.

Electoral participation influences the regime's policy choices, which then result in a range of outcomes for post-war security: domestic human rights abuses but also domestic peace-building.[18] Regime critics focus on the first, while regime supporters emphasize the latter. In fact, they are inextricably linked in Kagame and the RPF's version of illiberal peace-building.

Fostering human rights abuses Rwanda's human rights situation usually worsens around elections (see Front Line 2005; Longman 2011; Sebarenzi 2011). Political opponents are imprisoned and their parties prevented from competing. Independent journalists are arrested and their newspapers closed. Human rights organizations are often refused permission to monitor elections. Such legalized repression is fairly commonplace in hegemonic electoral regimes. What is more surprising is the way the regime also resorts to crude, extra-legal violence. Assassinations and disappearances are a throwback to an earlier way of settling scores and intimidating opponents.[19] One scholar who interviewed high-ranking RPF officials observes that "years of forced secrecy, distrust of the outside world and an embrace of the transformative power of force have formed the RPF character" (Verhoeven 2012: 270).

After former President Bizimungu formed a new political party to challenge the RPF in 2001, one of the founding members, Gratien Munyarubaga, was shot and killed on a busy street in the capital at midday. After a parliamentary committee accused the MDR of fomenting ethnic division and genocide ideology in April 2003, two high-profile figures were "disappeared": Dr. Leonard Hitimana, the MDR parliamentarian who had been tasked with rebutting those accusations because he was well known for saving Tutsi during the genocide; and Lieutenant Colonel Augustin Cyiza, the former vice-president of the Supreme Court (Human Rights Watch 2003).

Whereas those earlier disappearances and killings were directed at Hutu opponents, recent violence has been aimed at Anglophone Tutsi returnees who have broken with the RPF. Frank Habineza, a Tutsi returnee from Uganda, founded the Democratic Green Party in 2009 to challenge Kagame in the 2010 elections. The party was not allowed to register and the Hutu vice-president, André Kagwa Rwisereka, was found decapitated in July 2010.[20]

After former army chief of staff General Nyamwasa fled to South Africa in 2010, he joined up with three high-profile RPF colleagues who had gone into exile earlier: former external intelligence chief Colonel Karegeya, former Prosecutor General Gahima, and former RPF Secretary General Rudasingwa. Together, they issued a political tract that labeled Kagame a corrupt dictator and Rwanda "a hard-line, one-party, secretive police state with a façade of democracy" (Nyamwasa et al. 2010). They followed that up by creating an exiled opposition movement, the Rwandan National Congress (Rudasingwa 2013: 390–411).

RNC members have been targeted by legal and especially extra-legal measures. General Nyamwasa was nearly killed by two assassination attempts in June 2010.[21] In January 2011, the RNC's four founding members were tried *in absentia* by a military court and found guilty of endangering state security, destabilizing public order, divisionism, defamation and forming a criminal enterprise. They each received sentences of twenty years or more. A former RPF soldier and RNC member, Jonathan Musonera, received a warning from the London Metropolitan Police in May 2011 that "the Rwandan Government poses an immediate threat to your life". Charles Ingabire, a Tutsi genocide survivor and journalist, was murdered in November 2011 in Uganda, where he was living in exile. In August 2012, Frank Ntwali, General Nyamwasa's brother-in-law, was nearly assassinated before he was due to testify in a South African trial against six people (including three Rwandans) accused of the attack on Nyamwasa. Karegeya was murdered in South Africa in January 2014. Kagame denied involvement in Karegeya's murder while, at the same time, threatening other opponents: "Whoever betrays the country will pay the price. I assure you. … Whoever it is, it is a matter of time" (Birrell 2014).[22] Two months later, a third assassination attempt was made on Nyamwasa. The South African government expelled three Rwandan diplomats for "sustained and organized efforts to kill some of the refugees living in the Republic".[23] In August 2014, a South African magistrate convicted four men for the 2010 attempted murder of Nyamwasa, stating that it was politically motivated and was orchestrated by "a certain group of people in Rwanda" (Birrell 2014).[24]

Consolidating the domestic peace process Kagame has been widely hailed for building peace in Rwanda. The country boasts stability and security. It also appears safely out of the danger zone for relapsing into civil war. But Kagame and the RPF are after something much more ambitious: "national unity and reconciliation". This means winning over the Hutu majority's hearts and minds with a two-prong strategy: forcible re-education and public goods. The party recognizes it has little chance of success with the generation that lived through the civil war, Congo refugee camps and northwest insurgency, so it is focusing on youth (Pells 2011). Overall, Kagame is aiming for a more "positive peace", though one that is decidedly illiberal (see Soares de Oliveira et al. 2013; Waldorf 2015).

So how do elections help Kagame consolidate this peace process? First, the staggered election cycles for presidential, parliamentary and local elections mean that the RPF is engaged in near-continuous campaigning. This allows for constant reiteration and reinforcement of the party's ideological and policy messages. Second, the RPF's outsized electoral wins enable Kagame to demonstrate his personal appeal to a non-ethnic majority. This helps him legitimate his personalistic rule to domestic audiences within the RPF and the country at large, as well as to the international community. Third, elections are the only real way that Kagame can measure progress in achieving "national unity and reconciliation". Even if the public results are false, the RPF leadership has to know just how much falsification was required. Finally, it can be argued that the RPF's unfair elections help consolidate the peace by preventing the sort of ethnic appeals and ethnic violence that characterized Rwanda's multiparty elections in 1993. The RPF certainly sees majoritarian democracy with free elections not just as a recipe for political defeat but also for murderous violence.[25]

DE-SECURITIZING WARTIME IDENTITIES Re-education seeks to transform Hutu and Tutsi into Rwandans who will no longer think or act – or vote – along ethnic lines. Kagame (2004) declares, "We are inculcating a new outlook that is Rwandan, and not ethnic". A high-ranking party leader once put it more cynically: "the ordinary citizens are like babies" who "will need to be completely educated if we want to move towards democracy" (quoted in Reyntjens 2013: 82). There are three components to this re-education. The first is the inventing of a harmonious past. Kagame invokes this "imagined community" repeatedly in his speeches:

[T]he most characteristic feature of Rwanda and Rwandans is that, before colonialism, we had always been a united people for over five centuries. ... This harmonious coexistence was disrupted by the advent of the colonialists, who deliberately chose to divide us ... In Rwanda, this policy had a devastating effect because, for the first time, the notion of one nation was shattered, as the idea of ethnic groups was introduced.[26]

The second component is the dissemination of an ideology of "national unity and reconciliation" (ubumwe n'ubwiyunge). The final one involves criminalizing ethnic discourse as ethnic divisionism or genocidal ideology.

Re-education takes several forms. Since the late 1990s, the RPF has required certain segments of the population – initially demobilized soldiers and former insurgents, and later university-bound youth – to go through political and historical indoctrination in ingando (solidarity camps) (Mgbako 2005: 201–224). With the advent of electoral politics in 2003, re-education became more urgent. The National Unity and Reconciliation Commission, which runs ingando, launched *intorero* (civic education training) for teachers, health workers and youth in 2007. After a lengthy moratorium, teaching of Rwandan history resumed in primary and secondary schools but this is very much the RPF's version of history (Buckley-Zistel 2009). The RPF launched a public education campaign of de-ethnicization in 2013 called *Ndi Umanyarwanda* ("I Am Rwandan") (Mbaraga 2013).

However, these efforts to erase ethnic identity are undercut by other policies. First, the regime practices "forced memorialization" of the genocide (Vidal 2004) in ways that reinforce ethnic divisions (Eltringham 2011). For example, the constitution was amended in 2007 to replace "genocide" with "the 1994 Tutsi genocide". Second, the regime's prosecution of approximately a million Hutu for genocide-related crimes through the *gacaca* community courts had the effect of imposing collective guilt on Hutu (Waldorf 2010: 200). Third, the regime's prosecutions of two Hutu presidential contenders (Victoire Ingabire and Bernard Ntaganda) for genocidal ideology during the 2010 elections invariably reinforced ethnic divisions (Waldorf 2011). Indeed, Kagame frequently uses ethnic language in attacking Hutu electoral opponents. Even after his overwhelming election victory in 2003, Kagame played "the race card" against his main Hutu challenger, Faustin Twagiramungu:

> He was living in Belgium and the Belgians sponsored him to come. When he came, the diplomats here took him up. So he really became a foreigner's candidate … I knew Twagiramungu was being brought to say, well, you man, go there after all you are a Hutu and Hutus need a leader; just go and tell them you are Hutu and they will support you against Kagame.
> (*The Monitor* 2008)

Kagame used very similar ethnic language in 2010 to attack another Hutu presidential contender, Victoire Ingabire: "Some foreigners say there is a woman who is fighting for Hutu rights and they want us to listen to that woman because she represents the majority, but which majority is that?" (Cappa 2010).[27] Such language invokes the threat of ethnic divisions and ethnic violence, particularly for his Tutsi constituency. It also reminds Hutu voters that they cannot vote for Hutu candidates without the regime seeing them as voting along ethnic lines (i.e. insufficiently re-educated).

Overall, it is far from clear whether the regime's efforts to create a non-ethnic national identity are working – and not just because of the regime's mixed messages. In contemporary Rwanda, it is not permissible to use survey instruments that ask ordinary Rwandans about their ethnic identification. Even if that was possible, Rwandans would be extremely reluctant to respond truthfully given the criminalization of ethnic discourse.

PROVIDING PUBLIC GOODS Kagame not only seeks to re-educate the Hutu but also to win them over with economic growth, poverty reduction and public goods. Instead of "providing private goods selectively to members of the coalition, as the cheapest and most reliable means of political survival … the RPF and its allies are gambling on the 'expensive' option of building support on a broad base by demonstrating an ability to provide more and better public goods" (Booth and Golooba-Mutebi 2012: 391). To that end, Kagame adopted a developmental state agenda that envisions Rwanda becoming a lower middle-income country by 2020. The country has made an impressive economic recovery since the genocide, with an average annual growth rate of 6% in the past several years.[28] Since 2005, the government has turned its attention to reducing poverty and inequality.

Economic growth enables Kagame to provide public goods from universal primary school enrollment to near-universal health insurance. Results in the health sector have been particularly impressive. The maternal mortality rate declined dramatically between 2000 and 2010 thanks in large part to the impressive increase in births at health facilities over that period (Chambers 2012: 2). This success is partly the result of policy coherence and performance discipline (Chambers 2012: 2–3), but it also owes much to threats and coercion (Chambers and Golooba-Mutebi 2012: 39). In his second inaugural speech, Kagame (2010c) rejected such concerns: "when we do what every government is expected to do – deliver services; instill accountability, transparency and efficiency; build social and economic infrastructure; and raise living standards – the goalposts change, and we are then accused of forcing progress on the people and of being repressive". Still, it remains to be seen whether output legitimacy (i.e. improved services) can make up for the lack of procedural input legitimacy (i.e. coerced participation) (see Zuercher et al. 2009: 25).

Conclusion

This chapter has explored how Kagame transformed his armed rebel group into an electoral party and then used the party's apparatus to win presidential elections in 2003 and 2010. This transformation does not meet de Zeeuw's (2008) criteria for "success". Structurally, the party did not fully demilitarize and only partly reorganized. Attitudinally, the party adapted its political goals to appeal to the Hutu majority but did not democratize its decision-making. And yet it is precisely this unsuccessful transformation that partly explains the party's extraordinary ability to monopolize power, re-educate the population, deliver public goods, and attract donors and investors.[29]

Kagame's and the RPF's shift to electoral politics contributed to two security outcomes: human rights abuses and consolidation of the peace process. The factors that explain these outcomes are two-fold: Kagame's personality and narrow base of political support among the Tutsi minority. Kagame's self-transformation from warlord to warlord democrat has only limited value for understanding how to move "from war to democracy" (Jarstad and Sisk 2008). For one thing, Rwanda is one of only a handful of cases where rebels became the ruling party through an outright military victory.[30] For another, Kagame's electoral participation does not represent a move to democracy. The literature on war-to-democracy transitions often seems to assume a degree of good faith on the part of rebels-turned-parties (and the international community) to play by the democratic rules of the game. This is evident in Anna K. Jarstad's (2008: 35) approach:

> Appreciation of the particular dilemmas that arise in each post-war situation is necessary for the design of proper means to advance synchronized democratization and peacebuilding. Ideally, such analysis makes it possible to avoid several of the dilemmas and properly design means to support peace and democracy simultaneously. However, at particular points in time the inevitable choice arises between promoting efforts to democracy or peace. … This is why … sequencing, timing, and design of peace missions are vital.

What is absent from such technocratic prescriptions is the agency of warlord democrats, like Kagame, who see democracy and peace as mutually opposing. From that perspective, peace-building requires illiberal democracy. What this chapter points up is the need to explain a subset of warlord democrats (such as José Eduardo Dos Santos, Paul Kagame and Meles Zenawi) who became highly successful, if highly illiberal, presidents and peace-builders feted by international donors or investors (see Soares de Oliveira et al. 2013). Of course, the big question for Rwanda's illiberal peace is whether it can follow Ethiopia's example and outlast its warlord democrat.

Notes

1 It is commonly estimated that Hutu make up 85%, Tutsi 14% and the indigenous Twa forest people less than 0.5% of Rwanda's population. Since the genocide, the census has not recorded ethnicity.

2 By this point, the government represented an unstable coalition between Habyarimana's ruling party and several newly formed opposition parties (Prunier 1998: 145–146).

3 The former RPF secretary general, who now leads an exiled opposition movement, claims Kagame ordered that attack (Rudasingwa 2013: 413–426).

Accusations and counteraccusations have swirled around the plane crash for years. In November 2006, a French investigating magistrate accused Kagame and several top-ranking RPF officers of shooting down Habyarimana's plane (Tribunal de grande instance, Nov. 17, 2006). In response, the Rwandan government set up its own investigating commission, which exonerated the RPF and found Habyarimana's forces responsible (Independent Committee of Experts, 2010).

4 Kagame threatened withdrawal of 3300 peacekeepers from Darfur in 2010

over a leaked UN report that documented Rwanda's crimes in the Congo.

5 According to Clapham (1998: 7), a "reform insurgency" is "directed towards the creation of a new kind of state," while a "warlord insurgency" seeks "a change of leadership which does not entail the creation of a state any different from that which it seeks to overthrow." I use the term warlord throughout the chapter to be consistent with this book's title.

6 Interview with Major Jill Rutaremara, Spokesman and Director of Planning, Policy and Capacity-Building, Ministry of Defense, Kigali, 13 June 2006.

7 In truth, we know very little about the party's structure or internal debates – other than from a few RPF insiders who fell out with Kagame (see e.g. Habemenshi 2009; Rudasingwa 2013). If the former RPF secretary general is right, then the real locus of power rests with Kagame and his securocrats rather than the party:

> The third layer in Rwanda's power pyramid after the President and his wife are a core of high ranking military officers who formerly worked as President Kagame's bodyguards during the civil war; intelligence and close protection personnel of the elite Republican Guard. (Rudasingwa 2013: 431)

He describes the successive lower layers as composed of the 3,000-strong Republican Guard, Brigadier General Jack Nziza's informal security networks, the formal intelligence services, the Rwanda Defense Forces, and then finally the RPF (Rudasingwa 2013: 432-435).

8 This was most clearly reflected during former President Bizimungu's "reflection meetings" with political, military and economic elites between May 1998 and March 1999. The official summary of those meetings presents a fascinating, if sanitized, view into RPF policy debates (Republic of Rwanda 1999).

9 As Verhoeven (2012: 266) points out, "It is a commonly trumpeted myth that the main intra-RPF fault-line runs between 'reformers' and 'security hawks'; in reality, generals and business interests agree on most substantive issues."

10 While General Muhire was retired in 2014, General Karake was later reinstated and made head of external security.

11 In late 2013, Golooba-Mutebi and Booth (2013: 15) were still insisting that there was "collective leadership" within the ruling party. That ignores the crucial distinction between contested and established autocrats: "Contested autocrats can be credibly threatened with a removal; established autocrats have effectively monopolized power" (Svolik 2012: 55). As an established autocrat, Kagame is freer to act on his personal preferences: "Just as personalist leaders are freer to fight, they are also freer to compromise, innovate, and implement bold initiatives" (Weeks 2014: 174).

12 The RPF leadership has an uneasy relationship with the Tutsi survivor community. Early on, survivors' organizations criticized the RPF's reintegration of suspected génocidaires into the government and army, its manner of commemorating the genocide, and its failure to provide reparations to genocide survivors. In 2000, the RPF engineered a coup of those organizations and installed a member of its executive committee as head of the largest organization, IBUKA (see International Crisis Group 2002: 13; Reyntjens 2013: 11-14, 16).

13 For example, the Constitution does not allow the party with the majority of seats in the lower house to have more than fifty percent of the cabinet posts. For the RPF's violation of that provision, see Reyntjens (2013: 43).

14 The other parties only endorsed that four months later.

15 Subsequent cabinet reshuffles strengthened the RPF's control (Reyntjens 2013: 18).

16 The Forum only gained a constitutional and legal basis in 2003.

17 Interview with donor representative, London, 1 July 2003.

18 This article does not examine the regime's sponsoring of organized violence and looting of natural resources in the DRC because those activities preceded Kagame's electoral participation and do not seem to correlate to subsequent election cycles.

19 While it is difficult to assign responsibility for most of these killings, it is certainly telling that all the victims were RPF opponents and that little effort has been made investigate or prosecute these crimes.

20 Habineza fled the country but returned in late 2012. He was finally permitted to register his party just before the 2013 parliamentary elections.

21 Independent journalist Jean-Leonard Rugambage was shot and killed outside his house in June 2010 after his newspaper published a story linking senior government officials to that assassination attempt.

22 For earlier statements by Kagame condoning attacks on his opponents, see Reyntjens (2013: 90 n. 157, 93 n. 176). Defense Minister James Kabarebe also justified Karegeya's murder: "When you choose to be a dog, you die like a dog … Actually such consequences are faced by those who have chosen such a path" (News of Rwanda 2014).

23 The facts in this paragraph are largely drawn from Human Rights Watch (2014), Reyntjens (2013: 88-96) and Wrong (2014).

24 Two Rwandans allege they were hired by Rwandan intelligence to assassinate Kagame's enemies (York and Rever 2014).

25 This view is also shared by academics (see e.g. Paris 2004, 78), as well as a number of Rwanda's donors (see Hayman 2011).

26 The historian Jan Vansina has shown that the Rwandan nation is a twentieth-century creation and that the split between Hutu and Tutsi occurred before the arrival of Europeans (Vansina 2004: 198-199).

27 Kagame used such ethnic discourse only to then denounce it: "Which majority are they talking about because the majority is you people and Rwanda doesn't belong to Hutu, Tutsi or Twa – it belongs to Rwandans" (Rwanda News Agency 2010).

28 This growth, however, is partly dependent on illegal resource exploitation from the Congo and on overseas development assistance.

29 Golooba-Mutebi and Booth (2013) explicitly credit Rwanda's authoritarian developmentalism for much of its success.

30 Not surprisingly, much of the literature focuses on the more typical case of rebels transforming themselves into opposition parties under peace agreements and/or UN administrations (see e.g. Kovacs 2008; Manning 2007; Manning 2004; Reilly 2013).

Bibliography

Agence France Presse. 2014. "Rwandan Leader's Allies Seek Vote to Allow Him a Third Term." *Agence France Presse*, 17 April.

Beswick, D. 2010. "Peacekeeping, Regime Security and 'African Solutions to African Problems': Exploring Motivations for Rwanda's Involvement in Dafur." *Third World Quarterly* 31 (5): 739-754.

Birrell, I. 2014. "Assassins Linked to Kagame Regime." *The Independent*, 29 August.

Booth, D. and F. Golooba-Mutebi. 2012. "Developmental Patrimonialism? The Case of Rwanda." *African Affairs* 111 (444): 379-403.

Buckley-Zistel, S. 2009. "Nation, Narration, Unification? The Politics of History Teaching after the Rwandan Genocide." *Journal of Genocide Research* 11 (1): 31-53.

Cappa, M.. 2010. "Rwanda doesn't Belong to Hutu, Tutsi or Twa – Says Kagame." *Rwanda News Agency*. 4 August. Available at http://www.rnanews.com/ele-2010/3949-rwanda-doesnt-belong-to-hutu-tutsi-or-twa-says-kagame.

Carothers, T. 1997. "Democracy Assistance: The Question of Strategy." *Democratization* 4 (3): 109-132.

Chambers, V. 2012. *Improving Maternal Health When Resources Are Limited: Safe Motherhood in Rural Rwanda*. London: Overseas Development Institute.

Chambers, V. and F. Golooba-Mutebi. 2012. *Is the Bride Too Beautiful? Safe Motherhood in Rural Rwanda*. London: Overseas Development Institute.

Clapham, C. 1998. "Introduction: Analysing African Insurgencies." In *African Guerrillas*, ed. C. Clapham. Oxford: James Currey.

Clark, P. 2010." Rwanda: Kagame's Power Struggle." *The Guardian*, 5 August.

Crisafulli, P. and A. Redmond. 2012. *Rwanda, Inc.: How a Devastated Nation Became An Economic Model for the Developing World*. Basingstoke: Palgrave Macmillan.

Dallaire, R. 2003. *Shake Hands with the Devil*. Toronto: Random House Canada.

Des Forges, A. 1999. *Leave None to Tell the Story*. New York: Human Rights Watch.

De Zeeuw, J. 2008. "Understanding the Political Transformation of Rebel Movements." In *From Soldiers to Politicians: Transforming Rebel Movements after Civil War*, ed. J. de Zeeuw. Boulder: Lynne Rienner Publishers.

DFID (Department for International Development). 2004. "Rwanda: Country Assistance Plan 2003-2006." Available at www.eldis.org/vfile/upload/1/document/0708/DOC14126.pdf.

Dorsey, M. 2000. "Violence and Power-building in Post-genocide Rwanda." In *Politics of Identity and Economics of Conflict in the Great Lakes Region*, ed. R. Doom and J. Gorus. Brussels: VUB Press.

Eltringham, N. 2011. "The Past is Elsewhere: The Paradoxes of Prescribing Ethnicity in Post-Genocide Rwanda." In *Remaking Rwanda: State Building and Human Rights after Mass Violence*, ed. S. Straus and L. Waldorf. Madison: University of Wisconsin Press.

European Union Electoral Observation Mission. 2003. "Déclaration préliminaire" [Preliminary Declaration]. DV\506164FR.doc. 27 August. Available at http://www.europarl.europa.eu/meetdocs/committees/deve/20030909/506164FR.pdf.

European Union Electoral Observation Mission. 2004. "Rapport Final" [Final Report]. Available at http://aceproject.org/ero-en/regions/africa/RW/Rwanda%20-%20moe_ue_final_2003.pdf.

European Union. 2009. *Republic of Rwanda: Final Report: Legislative Elections to the Chamber of Deputies, 15-18 September 2008, 26 January*.

Front Line Defenders. 2005. *Front Line Rwanda: Disappearances, Arrests, Threats, Intimidation and Co-option of Human Rights Defenders, 2001–2004*. Dublin: Front Line.

Gandhi, J. and A. Przeworski. 2006. "Cooperation, Cooptation and Rebellion under Dictatorships." *Economics & Politics* 18 (1): 1-26.

Gettleman, J. 2013. "The Global Elite's Favorite Strongman." *The New York Times Magazine*, 4 September.

Golooba-Mutebi, F. and D. Booth. 2013. *Bilateral Cooperation and Local Power Dynamics: The Case of Rwanda*. London: Overseas Development Institute.

Habamenshi, P. 2009. *Rwanda: Where Souls Turn to Dust*. New York: iUniverse.

Hayman, R. 2011. "Funding Fraud? Donors and Democracy in Rwanda." In *Remaking Rwanda: State Building and Human Rights after Mass Violence*, ed. S. Straus and L. Waldorf. Madison: University of Wisconsin Press.

Human Rights Watch. 2003. *Preparing for Elections: Tightening Control in the Name of Unity*. Human Rights Watch Briefing Paper.

Human Rights Watch. 2014. *Rwanda: Repression Across Borders*, 28 January.

International Crisis Group. 2001. *Consensual Democracy in Post-Genocide*

Rwanda: Evaluating the March 2001 District Elections, 9 October.

International Crisis Group. 2002. *Rwanda at the End of the Transition: A Necessary Political Liberalisation*, 13 November.

Jarstad, A. K. 2008. "Dilemmas of War-to-Democracy Transitions: Theories and Concepts." In *From War to Democracy: Dilemmas of Peacebuilding*, ed. A. K. Jarstad and T. D. Sisk. Cambridge: Cambridge University Press.

Jarstad, A. K. and T. D. Sisk, eds. 2008. *From War to Democracy: Dilemmas of Peacebuilding*. Cambridge: Cambridge University Press.

Jones, W. 2012. "Between Pyongyang and Singapore: The Rwandan State, Its Rulers, and the Military." In *Rwanda Fast Forward*, ed. M. Campioni and P. Noack. Basingstoke: Palgrave Macmillan.

Jowell, M. 2014. "Cohesion through Socialization: Liberation, Tradition, and Modernity in the Forging of the Rwanda Defence Force." *Journal of Eastern African Studies* 8 (2): 278-293.

Kagame, P. 2010a. *Speech by H.E. Paul Kagame, President of the Republic of Rwanda at 16th Commemoration of the Genocide*, Kigali, 7 April.

Kagame, P. 2010b. *Speech by H.E. Paul Kagame, President of the Republic of Rwanda, during the opening ceremony of 8th National Dialogue (Umushyikirano)*, Kigali, 20 December.

Kagame, P. 2010c. *Speech by H. E. Paul Kagame, President of the Republic of Rwanda, on Inauguration Day*, Kigali, 6 September.

Kagame, P. 2004. *Speech by His Excellency President Paul Kagame at the University of Washington*, 22 April.

Kinzer, S. 2008. *A Thousand Hills: Rwanda's Rebirth and the Man Who Dreamed It*. Hoboken: John Wiley.

Kovacs, M. S. 2008. "When Rebels Change Their Stripes: Armed Insurgents in Post-War Politics." In *From War to Democracy: Dilemmas of Peacebuilding*, ed. A. K. Jarstad and T. D. Sisk. Cambridge: Cambridge University Press.

Longman, T. 2011. "Limitations to Political Reform: The Undemocratic Nature of Transition in Rwanda." In *Remaking Rwanda: State Building and Human Rights after Mass Violence*, ed. S. Straus and L. Waldorf. Madison: University of Wisconsin Press.

Manning, C. 2007. "Party-Building on the Heels of War: El Salvador, Bosnia, Kosovo, and Mozambique." *Democratization*, 14 (2): 253-272.

Manning, C. 2004. "Armed Opposition Groups into Political Parties: Comparing Bosnia, Kosovo, and Mozambique." *Studies in Comparative International Development* 39 (1): 54-76.

Mbaraga, R. 2013. "State Pushes Campaign that Critics Say it is Ethnically Divisive." *The East African*, 16 November.

McGreal, C. 2012. "Rwanda's Paul Kagame Warned He May Be Charged with Aiding War Crimes." *The Guardian*, 25 July.

McGreal, C. 2013. "Is Kagame Africa's Lincoln or a Tyrant Exploiting Rwanda's Tragic History?" *The Observer*, 19 May.

McVeigh, T. 2015. "Rwanda Votes to Give President Paul Kagame Right to Rule until 2034." *The Observer*, 20 December.

Mgbako, Chi. 2005. "Ingando Solidarity Camps: Reconciliation and Political Indoctrination in Post-Genocide Rwanda." *Harvard Human Rights Journal* 18: 201-24.

The Monitor. 2008. "Twagiramungu Tried to Reap where he did not Sow, Says Kagame." *The Monitor*, 28 August.

News of Rwanda. 2014. "Gen Kabarebe on Karegeya: 'When you Choose to be a Dog, you die like a Dog.'" *News of Rwanda*, 11 January.

Ngoga, P. 1998. "Uganda: The National Resistance Army." In *African Guerrillas*, ed. C. Clapham. Oxford: James Currey.

Nyamwasa, K., P. Karegeya, T. Rudasingwa and G. Gahima. 2010. *Rwanda Briefing*. Available at http://rwandinfo.com/documents/Rwanda_Briefing_August2010_nyamwasa-et-al.pdf.

Paris, R. 2004. *At War's End: Building Peace after Civil Conflict*. Cambridge: Cambridge University Press.

Pells, K. 2011. "Building a Rwanda 'Fit for Children.'" In *Remaking Rwanda: State Building and Human Rights after Mass Violence*, ed. S. Straus and L. Waldorf. Madison: University of Wisconsin Press.

Prunier, G. 1997. *The Rwanda Crisis: History of a Genocide*. New York: Columbia University Press.

Prunier, G. 1998. "The Rwandan Patriotic Front." In *African Guerrillas*, ed. C. Clapham. Oxford: James Currey.

Reed, W. C. 1996. "Exile, Reform, and the Rise of the Rwandan Patriotic Front." *Journal of Modern African Studies*, 34 (3): 479–501.

Reilly, B. 2013. "Political Parties and Post-Conflict Peacebuilding." *Civil Wars* 15 (s1): 88–104.

Republic of Rwanda. 1999. *Report on the Reflection Meetings Held in the Office of the President of the Republic from May 1998 to March 1999*. Office of the President of the Republic, Kigali, August.

Reyntjens, F. 2013. *Political Governance in Post-Genocide Rwanda*. Cambridge: Cambridge University Press.

Reyntjens, F. 2009a. *The Great African War: Congo and Regional Geopolitics, 1996–2006*. Cambridge: Cambridge University Press.

Reyntjens, F. 2009b. *Rwanda: A Fake Report on Fake Elections*. Available from: http://hungryoftruth.blogspot.com/2009/01/rwanda-fake-report-on-fake-elections.html.

Rudasingwa, T. 2013. *Healing a Nation: A Testimony*. North Charleston, SC: Create Space Independent Publishing Platform.

Sebarenzi, J. 2009. *God Sleeps in Rwanda*. New York: Simon and Schuster.

Sebarenzi, J. 2011. "Justice and Human Rights for All Rwandans." In *Remaking Rwanda: State Building and Human Rights after Mass Violence*, ed. S. Straus and L. Waldorf. Madison: University of Wisconsin Press.

Simpser, A. 2013. *Why Governments and Parties Manipulate Elections: Theory, Practice, and Implications*. Cambridge: Cambridge University Press.

Smith, D. 2014. "Paul Kagame Hints at Seeking Third Term as Rwandan President." *The Guardian*, 23 April.

Soares de Oliveira, R., W. Jones and H. Verhoeven. 2013. *Africa's Illiberal State-Builders*. Oxford: Oxford Refugee Studies Centre, Working Paper No. 89.

Straus, S. 2006. *The Order of Genocide: Race, Power, and War in Rwanda*. Ithaca, NY: Cornell University Press.

Straus, S. and L. Waldorf. 2011. "Introduction: Seeing Like a Post-Conflict State." In *Remaking Rwanda: State Building and Human Rights after Mass Violence*, ed. S. Straus and L. Waldorf. Madison: University of Wisconsin Press.

Svolik, M. W. 2012. *The Politics of Authoritarian Rule*. Cambridge: Cambridge University Press.

UN High Commissioner for Human Rights. 2010. *Democratic Republic of the Congo, 1993–2003: Report of the Mapping Exercise Documenting the Most Serious Violations of Human Rights and International Humanitarian Law Committed within the Territory of the Democratic Republic of Congo between March 1993 and June 2003*. Available at http://www.ohchr.org/Documents/Countries/CD/DRC_MAPPING_REPORT_FINAL_EN.pdf.

United Nations. 2012. *Addendum to the Interim Report of the Group of Experts on the Democratic Republic of the Congo (S/2012/348) Concerning Violations of the Arms Embargo and Sanctions Regime by the Government of Rwanda*, UN Doc. S/2012/348 /Add. 1, 27 June.

US Embassy Kigali. 2008. "Ethnicity in Rwanda – Who Governs the Country?" 5 August. Available at https://wikileaks.org/plusd/cables/08KIGALI525_a.html.

Vansina, J. 2004. *Antecedents to Modern Rwanda: The Nyiginya Kingdom*. Madison: University of Wisconsin Press.

Verhoeven, H. 2012. "Nurturing Democracy or into the Danger Zone? The Rwandan Patriotic Front, Elite Fragmentation, and Post-Liberation Politics." In *Rwanda Fast Forward*, ed. M. Campioni and P. Noack. Basingstoke: Palgrave Macmillan.

Vidal, C. 2004. "La Commémoration du Génocide au Rwanda: Violence Symbolique, Mémorisation Forcée et Histoire Officielle" [The Commemoration of Genocide in Rwanda: Symbolic Violence, Forced Memorization, and Official History]. *Cahiers d'études africaines* 64 (175): 575-592.

Waldorf, L. 2010. "'Like Jews Waiting for Jesus': Posthumous Justice in Post-Genocide Rwanda." In *Localizing Transitional Justice*, ed. R. Shaw and L. Waldorf. Stanford, CA: Stanford University Press.

Waldorf, L. 2011. "Instrumentalizing Genocide: The RPF's Campaign Against 'Genocide Ideology.'" In *Remaking Rwanda: State Building and Human Rights after Mass Violence*, ed. S. Straus and L. Waldorf. Madison: University of Wisconsin Press.

Waldorf, L. 2015. "Rwanda's Illiberal Peacebuilding." *Afriche et Orienti* 3/2014: 21-34.

Warren, R. 2009. "Paul Kagame." *Time*, 24 May.

Weeks, J. L. P. 2014. *Dictators at War and Peace*. Ithaca, NY: Cornell University Press.

Wrong, M. 2014. "Leave None to Tell the Other Story." *Foreign Policy*, 1 April.

York, G. and J. Rever. 2014. "Assassination in Africa: Inside the Plots to Kill Rwanda's Dissidents." *The [Toronto] Globe and Mail*, 2 May.

Zuercher, C., N. Roehner, and S. Riese. 2009. "External Democracy Promotion in Post-Conflict Zones: A Comparative-Analytical Framework." *Taiwan Journal of Democracy* 5 (1): 1-26.

3 | Discourses of peace and fear: the electoral navigations of Sekou Conneh and Prince Johnson in post-war Liberia

Carrie Manning and Anders Themnér

Introduction

Liberia is often portrayed as the archetype of warlord politics (Duffield 1998; Reno 1998). Between 1989 and 1996, rebel and militia leaders divided the country into personal fiefdoms and engaged in the systematic exploitation and plunder of valuable natural resources. The main objective of the 1997 elections was to once and for all settle the leadership question and decide which warlord should control the reins of power. Thanks to the following and wealth that he had amassed during the war, Charles Taylor and his National Patriotic Party (NPP) won a landslide victory. Perhaps more importantly, the elections made the armed actors' political parties the main political contenders and solidified the notion that power was attained through the barrel of the gun. In addition, due to the authoritarian nature of Taylor's rule (1997–2003) and his continued ruthless exploitation of the country's resources, his tenure in office was largely a continuation of warlordism under the guise of normal politics (Adebajo 2002b: 231–239).

In contrast, the period following the second civil war (1999–2003) – in which a new set of rebels succeeded in forcing Taylor into exile in 2003 – is often depicted as the end of warlord politics. Such portrayals only tell part of the story, however. Even if "civilian" leaders and parties – with no or limited links to the two civil wars – became the main political contenders (particularly after the 2005 elections), warlord politics merely took a new form. With the fragmentation of the armed groups and their failure to transform into political parties, there was a proliferation of "warlord democrats" – such as Sekou Conneh, Adolphus Dolo, Prince Johnson and Isaac Nyenabo – acting as political free agents. Many of these ex-military turned politicians held weak political loyalties, joined other parties than those associated with their ex-warring factions and sometimes ran as independents. Even if these individuals were not true contenders for the presidency, they were often successful in winning seats in the Senate or House of Representatives. Due to their position in the legislature and the influence they had in their local communities, other actors had to take them into consideration when, for instance, building political alliances during presidential elections.

While the consequences of Taylor's ascent to power in 1997 is well known – gross human rights violations and a subsequent return to war – there is a lack of studies analyzing the security effects of the reconfiguration of warlord politics in the post-2003 era. For instance, did the dual process of marginalization and proliferation of individualistic warlord democrats constrain or escalate the belligerency of the latter? To what degree did the ex-military leaders use their electoral platform to foster peace and reconciliation? And if the warlord democrats undermined the new peace order, what form did such aggression take? This chapter aims to address these questions by conducting a systematic comparison between Sekou Conneh and Prince Johnson; two influential warlord democrats whose electoral maneuverings have received much domestic and international attention. As leader of the main rebel movement that forced Taylor to leave power – Liberians United for Reconciliation and Democracy (LURD) – Conneh was initially well placed to shape developments in post-civil war Liberia. In order to contend in the 2005 presidential elections Conneh launched a new political party, Progressive Democratic Party (PRODEM), which only had limited links to LURD. Even if Conneh received much media attention during his campaigns, he fared badly. Conneh's failure at the polls prompted him to leave politics and recommence his career as a businessman. Initially Johnson, former leader of Independent National Patriotic Front of Liberia (INPFL), faced a more uphill battle. After having captured and executed President Samuel Doe in 1990, Johnson was eventually forced to flee to Nigeria in 1993. Upon his return in 2004, Johnson was a political outsider. Despite this, he ran a successful campaign and was, as an independent, elected as senator for Nimba County in 2005. Five years later Johnson launched a new political party, National Union for Democratic Progress (NUDP), to help him contend the presidency the following year. In the elections, Johnson not only came in third place, but also acted as a "queenmaker", helping the incumbent President Ellen Johnson-Sirleaf to win in the second round. Johnson was later one of the few warlord democrats to successfully defend his senate seat in the 2014 elections – again running as an independent – and is currently positioning himself for the upcoming 2017 presidential elections.

To some extent both Conneh and Johnson built their electoral careers on securitizing wartime identities. The former systematically securitized the ex-combatant issue, presenting himself as the only candidate who could control the violent agency of ex-fighters. Meanwhile, the latter sought to attract voters by reminding his audience of the fragility of the peace process and made veiled threats about the consequences should he be arrested for war crimes. Conneh and Johnson did, however, often mix such aggressive rhetoric with messages of peace and reconciliation, underlining their ambiguous attitude to the new peace order. Evidence suggests that their decisions to securitize wartime identities were largely a function of the electoral constraints they faced. During the run-up to the 2005 elections both warlord democrats had a marginal support base. It therefore made sense to instill fear amongst the electorate and remind the latter of their wartime power. Such a strategy promised to once again make Conneh and Johnson's military credentials relevant. After Johnson established himself as a senator in 2005, his continued belligerency was increasingly a response to the activities of the Truth and Reconciliation Commission (TRC) and its recommendations that he, and other wartime elites, should face prosecution.

Warlord politics in Liberia

On 12 April 1980 a Master Sergeant of the Armed Forces of Liberia (AFL), Samuel Doe, ended Americo-Liberian rule in Liberia when he ousted President William Tolbert from power. Since Liberia's independence in 1847 American-Liberians – descendants of freed African-American slaves – had controlled the political, economic and social life of Liberia. As the first "indigenous" Liberian president, Doe sough to dismantle the Americo-Liberian elite. Not only did he publicly execute a number of top officials from the Tolbert regime, he also appointed members of his own ethnic group, the Krahn, to top positions. This strategy was, however, only partially successful, as some Liberian-American Big Men continued to control strategic commercial sectors – with its connections to international trade networks – and occupy key positions in the state bureaucracy. The influence of such strongmen increased as the government lost access to foreign aid in the late 1980s (Reno 1998: 91).

Overlaying the bonds of clientelist politics and commercial networks was a complex pattern of ethnic relations. In addition to filling top military and security positions with his Krahn co-ethnics, Mandingos – another ethnic group with historical commercial ties of their own in the region, particularly in Guinea – "provided Doe with a counterbalance to strongmen whose local power and commerce were out of his direct control" (Reno 1998: 91–92). Mandingos were viewed by other Liberians as "foreigners" and were willing to accept security from Doe in exchange for a share of their regional trade.

In response to international pressure, particularly from the United States, which had become a key backer of Doe, the regime adopted a new constitution and organized national elections in 1985. The latter were generally seen as fraudulent and were heavily criticized by the international community. Unable to harness domestic legitimacy through political liberalization, Doe's rule was increasingly characterized by elite-centered patronage networks. Rather than building a state, Doe built a network of clients that undermined the establishment of impersonal state institutions or the rule of law (Ellis 1999; Reno 1998).

The first civil war: 1989–1996 Liberia's first civil war began on 24 December 1989 when Charles Taylor led the invasion of the country by the National

Patriotic Front of Liberia (NPFL). As Reno points out, "Taylor's arrival was the catalyst that toppled Doe's dual patronage system, as his capture of Doe's commercial networks encouraged strongmen to desert the president and seek security in cooperation with Taylor's organization" (Reno 1998: 91). The Taylor-led NPFL immediately gained control of areas of the country that cut Liberia in two. NPFL was able to take over the majority of the country, excluding Monrovia, by April 1990.

Taylor's NPFL also played on ethnic divisions. Gio and Mano had been singled out for abuse under Doe, thus Nimba County, their historic heartland, provided fertile recruiting ground for Taylor. Doe had offered land and government positions to the Mandingo community, in Nimba County especially, to build an alliance to counter his political opponents, who relied on support from the Gio and Mano communities. Once the war began, Doe used his mostly Krahn army to attack Gio and Mano villages. As Bøås and Hatløy (2008: 46) point out, "this created a lasting pattern, in which the Gio and Mano communities – particularly in Nimba – became Taylor's most faithful allies, while the Krahn and the Mandingo formed their own militias after Doe's murder in September 1990".

The dynamics of the war changed dramatically in July 1990. Under the leadership of Nigeria, the Economic Community of West African States (ECOWAS) assembled a military monitoring group (ECOMOG) that intervened in the country and frustrated Taylor's hopes of capturing Monrovia. In the same month, Prince Johnson broke away from NPFL and formed the INPFL. Originally numbering 500 fighters, INPFL was able to militarily outmaneuver Taylor's NPFL and ultimately capture Doe in September. The latter's execution by Johnson on 9 September constituted a blow to Taylor's prestige.

In November 1990, the three warring parties – AFL, NPFL and INPFL – signed an agreement that produced an Interim Government of National Unity (IGNU), led by an academic, Amos Sawyer. Unlike the interim governments to follow, IGNU explicitly excluded representatives of warring factions. The agreement soon fell apart with renewed fighting. Subsequent agreements were reached in Banjul (December 1990) and Lome (February 1991), but neither lasted. Still more warring factions soon emerged. United Liberation Movement for Democracy (ULIMO), the first enduring opposition to NPFL, was launched in 1992 in Lofa County by "Mandingo intellectual and former Doe deputy minister for information, Alhaji Kromah" (Reno 1998: 102). ULIMO also attracted a large number ex-AFL Krahn soldiers (Adebajo 2002b).

For the next year and a half, fierce fighting continued between AFL, NPFL, ULIMO and ECOMOG, with the latter taking a clear anti-Taylor stance. INPFL's strength had progressively diminished, and by October 1992 the group disbanded. On 25 July 1993, the warring parties signed the Cotonou Accord. The Accord put an end to the so-called "civil state" and placed the future of the Liberia directly in the hands of the warring factions. It created the Liberian National Transitional Government (LNTG), which consisted of an executive Council of State, run by the warlords, and a Transitional Legislative Assembly in which the signatories were each given a share of power (UN Security Council 1994).

Rather than putting an end to Liberia's conflict, however, the accord gave rise to more armed groups over the next year, including the Liberian Peace Council (LPC), headed by a former minister in the Doe administration, George Boley, and drawing support from the Krahn ethnic group. For its part, ULIMO divided in the wake of the accord. In March 1994, Roosevelt Johnson formed the ULIMO – Johnson faction (ULIMO-J), which was majority Krahn, while Kromah led the ULIMO – Kromah faction (ULIMO-K) with its predominantly Mandingo fighters. The Lofa Defense Force (LDF), a faction with close ties to NPFL, emerged in 1994 and was led by Francois Massaquoi.

At this point, the war degenerated into a scramble to consolidate control over valuable resources, such as timber, rubber and diamonds. Taylor's NPFL was the most profitable of the factions, charging rents from various international firms operating in the region and exporting timber and rubber (Reno 1998). It was, for instance, able to make a profit of $75 million each year from exporting resources, $10 million a month from their collection of rents from international mining corporations, and $300,000 a month from other international actors dealing with timber (Ismail 2008: 267). But others also fought for and gained control over economic resources, including LPC and ULIMO-J (Adebajo 2002b: 175).

After several failed initiatives in 1995–1996, peace efforts finally bore fruit in the second Abuja Agreement. The accord produced a ceasefire and called for disarmament, a roadmap to elections and an enlarged (six-seat) executive Council of State. A powerful precedent was set, in which participation in politics allowed warring factions to secure and perhaps increase their access to economic spoils, while also gaining access to legitimized repressive power of the state.

Post-war politics: the 1997 elections Interestingly, in contrast to the wartime interim governments that were inclusive of the most powerful warring factions, the 1997 elections were seen by many as an attempt to "settle Liberia's leadership question" (Kieh 2011: 85). Elections offered winners the promise of freedom from the pretense of power-sharing between rival groups. This made participation in elections both indispensable for the major warring factions and also created an extremely high-stakes competition. Ex-warlords could, under these circumstances, be expected to follow any strategy that promised to secure them elected office, with control of the executive being the primary prize.

Three of the warlords sitting on the Council of State resigned to form political parties and run in the elections. They were Taylor, under the banner of his newly created NPP; Boley, heading the National Democratic Party of Liberia (NDPL, Samuel Doe's former party); and Kromah, who transformed his ULIMO-K into the All-Liberia Coalition Party (ALCOP). Ellen Johnson-Sirleaf returned from exile and left her position at United Nations Development Program to run for president as the candidate of Unity Party (UP). She was backed by three other parties with historical roots in Liberia – True Whig Party, Liberia Unification Party (LUP) and Liberia People's Party (LPP).

The elections were largely peaceful. Taylor won 75.3% of the presidential vote, compared to 9.6% for Johnson-Sirleaf, the second-place candidate. Both Boley and Kromah fared poorly. Taylor's NPP also took twenty-one of twenty-six seats in the Senate and forty-nine of sixty-four seats in the House of Representatives. Taylor and his NPP thus came away from the elections dominant at all political levels. As many observers have noted, Taylor enjoyed disproportionate economic and organizational advantages. He ascended to the presidency with an estimated annual income of $450 million in natural resource exports to his name (Adebajo 2002a: 65). He "had a countrywide institutional infrastructure that had a presence in nearly every village and the resources to distribute rice to displaced [sic] camps and to run a wide-ranging humanitarian operation" (Lyons 1999: 45). Taylor also controlled national media and his campaign led voters to believe that "Taylor was already president and the election was designed merely to ratify his power" (Lyons 1999: 45). Others have suggested that Liberian voters feared that if he was not elected, Taylor would simply return the country to the chaos from which it had only recently emerged (Adebayo 2002a: 64–67).

The road to war President Taylor did not cease to be a warlord after the war. Instead, the presidency "merely gave him the political, legal, and military cover to pursue looting by other means" (Adebajo 2002b: 231). These actions laid the groundwork for the second Liberian war, from 1999 to 2003.

As all of the warlords had sought to do during the earlier transitional governments, Taylor used executive power to monopolize economic resources and disable his rivals. But this time he did not have to keep up the pretense of sharing power. "Most of Taylor's opponents view the state apparatus as an extension of his personal power; justice is not perceived to be neutral" (Adebajo 2002b: 235). Taylor would not have disagreed. Adebajo quotes him as saying, "Once you are in [power], because of the chaos created from outside, you become undemocratic in the preservation of power. It is almost like the survival of the fittest" (Adebajo 2002b: 236).

Upon assuming the presidency, Taylor "demobilized" his own NPFL fighters directly into the new Liberian army and created a praetorian guard in the guise of an "anti-terrorist unit" (Adebajo 2002b: 235). He spent the interwar years looking for ways to undermine or eliminate his political and former military rivals. Radios and newspapers were closed and civil society critics harassed or sent into exile. In 1998 Taylor accused his chief political opponents, including Kromah, Johnson, Boley and Johnson-Sirleaf of attempting to overthrow the government. Some were imprisoned, while others who had already left the country were tried and convicted in absentia (Adebajo 2002b: 236).

President Taylor failed to pay civil service salaries for more than a year, sought to give himself sole legal control of all contracts for strategic commodities, and generally ran roughshod over any semblance of institutional governing structure (Adebajo 2002a: 67–73). In sum, as one observer put it at the time, "the situation in postwar Liberia parallels that in prewar Liberia: widespread insecurity, a weak economy, patronage-fueled corruption, government harassment of the press and civic groups, interethnic clashes, trumped up coup plots, and external financial sanctions" (Adebajo 2002a: 73).

The second war: 1999–2003 The response from his rivals was not long in coming. The succession of interim governments had reinforced the notion that armed conflict helped one ascend to political power, which in turn provided one with both physical security and economic power. In mid-1999 a rebel movement – that would later assume the name LURD – entered Liberia from Guinea, carrying out attacks in Lofa County. The group was primarily composed of Mandingo and Krahn fighters who had previously fought under in ULIMO-K and ULIMO-J and was eventually led by a Mandingo businessman, Sekou Conneh (Nilsson and Söderberg Kovacs 2005: 400).

Taylor responded by sponsoring Revolutionary United Front (RUF) rebels from Sierra Leone to make incursions into Guinea to go after them (Adebajo 2002b: 234). Guinea's president, Lansana Conté, then increased his support for the LURD rebels. By early 2002, LURD forces were attacking areas close to Monrovia. Later that year (September), Taylor supported a coup attempt against Ivorian President Laurent Gbagbo, who then joined Conté in supporting LURD. In 2003 a new armed faction, Movement for Democracy in Liberia (MODEL), supported by President Gbagbo, appeared. The group was primarily composed of Krahns who were either based in Ivory Coast, or had left LURD. International sanctions, resulting from Taylor's adventurism in neighboring countries, as well as his domestic attacks on rivals, began to bite in 2003 and allowed the rebels to gain ground. By May 2003, according to the UN Security Council (2003), "the two rebel movements had gained control of nearly two thirds of the country and were threatening to seize Monrovia".

The second peace process: spoils or politics? In response to international pressure, the warring factions were brought to the negotiating table in Accra,

Ghana in June 2003 and subsequently agreed to a ceasefire. Unfortunately, this coincided with the announcement of an International Criminal Court indictment against Taylor, precipitating renewed violence in Monrovia as Taylor now rejected the ceasefire. However, by August Taylor had decided to accept an offer of asylum from Nigeria and he stepped down from power. A few days later, the three parties signed a Comprehensive Peace Agreement (CPA). The peace was overseen by a sizable UN peace operation. In September 2003, United Nations Mission in Liberia (UNMIL) arrived with a Chapter VII mandate that provided for multidimensional peace operations as well as powers over a transitional administration. With a combined military, civilian police and civilian staff of 19,000, of which 15,000 were soldiers, UNMIL was the largest peacekeeping force in the world to date.

The CPA once again called for the formation of a transitional government (National Transitional Government of Liberia, NTGL), gave extensive representation in the executive to the warring factions and also divided key public sector companies among them. Twenty-three ministerial positions were designated for representatives of the signatories of CPA; twenty-one of these went to the warring factions. The chair and vice-chair of NTGL could be held only by representatives of non-military parties and civil society organizations. The agreement also created a Transitional National Assembly, which included twelve members from each of the warring parties, eighteen members of political parties, seven civil society members and one representative from each of the fifteen counties of Liberia. Each of the warring groups was also given control of public corporations and autonomous economic agencies, ensuring an income stream for each of the groups.

The NTGL was to be responsible for implementation of CPA and preparation for October 2005 elections, with the help of UNMIL. In addition, provisions were made for the creation of a Truth and Reconciliation Commission. Finally, a newly elected government was to take power in January 2006. Gyude Bryant, head of the Liberia Action Party (LAP) and a businessman in Monrovia, was appointed chair of the transitional government, with Wesley Johnson, opposition politician and university lecturer, as vice-chair.

One of the most enduring effects of the transitional period was the visible disintegration of the warring parties as united political actors. For instance, after the end of the demobilization process in November 2004, both LURD and MODEL ceased to exist as organizational entities and neither of the factions succeeded in transforming into a political party. In addition, NPP struggled to uphold its previously dominant position. This was in sharp contrast to the first peace process (1996–1997), when ex-warlords and their armed groups were the dominant actors. How can these divergent dynamics be explained?

A first explanation concerns the lack of a clearly articulated political agenda, especially within LURD and MODEL. The common denominator that united most LURD members was the slogan that Taylor must go (Käihko 2015). Once this had been achieved, there was little uniting the armed movement. Having been created in early 2003, MODEL had not organizationally matured by the time the war ended in August, undermining subsequent efforts to create a peacetime organization. In addition, MODEL was largely a creation of Ivory Coast's desire to punish Taylor for his support to Ivorian rebels. Hence, once Taylor left Liberia, President Gbagbo had few reasons to continue his support to the MODEL leadership.

A second reason can be found in NTGL itself. Leaders who took part in the transitional government were barred from taking part in the 2005 national elections. This restriction forced ex-warlords to take a tough decision on whether to enter the government, with all its opportunities for immediate personal enrichment, or bide their time in the hope of winning office in 2005. This put immense pressure on the unity of the armed groups. Knowing that they only had two years to amass enough resources to ensure their Big Man status, ex-warlords within NTGL engaged in what can only be described as peacetime plunder. In this sense the transitional governing arrangements were a continuation of warlord politics. International auditors and an incipient press and civil society were able to document gross economic mismanagement and describe how ex-military leaders in charge of state ministries and autonomous agencies had treated these positions as opportunities for personal enrichment (ICG 2005). However, the economic plundering did not benefit the armed groups as a whole. In fact, it was only the ex-military leaders in power, and their closest aides, that benefited. It was particularly the armed group's ex-commanders and fighters who were left out when the spoils of peace were divided (Chaudhary 2012: 252). The failure of NTGL representatives to distribute their patronage more widely caused immense internal divisions within LURD, MODEL and NPP, and contributed to their disintegration.

A final explanation for why at least NPP was weakened during 2003–2005 was the removal of Taylor from the political scene. Taylor had been the "godfather" of NPFL and NPP. Through this position Taylor had centralized political and economic control over NPFL and the NPP government in his hands. Even if Taylor tried to control his NPP allies from his Nigerian exile this largely failed (Nilsson and Söderberg Kovacs 2005). With no apparent heir and NPP leaders striking deals with political opponents, NPP became a shadow of its former self.

The proliferation and weakening of warlord democrats What was perhaps the most striking aspect of the first post-war election, held in October and November 2005, was the absence of ex-warlords as the leading contenders for executive power. Sawyer (2008: 177) notes that these elections "were held at a critical historical juncture when, for the first time in a quarter century,

Liberia was not dominated by a warlord, or shaken by the threat of being taken over by one". In fact, the second round of the presidential elections was a run-off between two "civilian" candidates – Johnson-Sirleaf of UP and George Weah, standard bearer of the newly formed Congress for Democratic Change (CDC). In the end Johnson-Sirleaf triumphed, receiving 59.4% of the votes.

Ex-military leaders were not absent from the political scene, however. On the contrary, many ex-warlords contested and won seats in the Senate and House of Representatives. What was unique was that so many ran under the banner of parties other than those of their ex-warring factions or as independents. This was, for instance, true for Richard Devine (ex-MODEL, Coalition for the Transformation of Liberia (COTOL)), Adolphus Dolo (ex-NPFL, COTOL), Kia Farley (ex-MODEL, CDC), Malliam Jallabah (ex-LURD, ALCOP), Prince Johnson (ex-INPFL, independent), Roland Kaine (ex-NPFL, CDC), Isaac Nyenabo (ex-LURD, NDPL) and Zoe Pennue (ex-LURD, independent), who were all elected into office. In addition, Conneh preferred to form his own party, PRODEM, coming fifteenth in the presidential race. In fact, Abel Massaley (NPP) and Kromah (ALCOP) were among the few who contested the elections on behalf of their military successor parties; Massaley won a senate seat and Kromah came in eighth place in the presidential race.

This development was in sharp contrast to 1997, when the electoral process was wholly dominated by ex-warlords and their political parties. How should we understand the tendency of civilian politicians to become the main electoral contenders and warlord democrats only playing a secondary role? First, the ex-military leaders who may have had the economic patronage needed to mobilize voters on a more national scale – members of NTGL – were, as already touched upon, barred from taking part in the elections. This, together with the divisions within the ex-armed movements, meant that there were few ex-warlords with the national presence and visibility to be serious contenders for the presidency. In addition, the peacetime plundering of NTGL representatives also appear to have tarnished the appeal of electing ex-warlords in general. The only true chance ex-militaries had of being elected was therefore to run for the Senate or House of Representatives, whereby they could employ their personal appeal in counties where they had enjoyed the greatest wartime influence. In addition, "civilian" parties like CDC and UP, with more national infrastructure and presence, were extremely efficient at co-opting warlord figures. Not only did Johnson-Sirleaf convince Conneh's former wife Aisha Conneh – a key leader in LURD – to support her presidential bid, NPP threw in their lot with the UP standard-bearer. Weah and CDC also had some success in mobilizing warlord democrats for their cause; Farley and Kaine became members of CDC, while Conneh, Johnson and Kromah all declared their allegiance to Weah during the second round of the presidential elections.

The centrifugal tendencies continued after 2005. The 2011 (presidential, House of Representatives, Senate) and 2014 (Senate) elections constituted a disappointment for many warlord democrats. Many of those who had entered the legislature in 2006 were not given renewed confidence by the voters. In addition, during these elections a number of ex-warlords, who had either been barred from the 2005 elections due to their participation in NTGL or only recently returned from exile, attempted to make a political comeback. These efforts were, however, thwarted as figures such as Thomas Nimely (ex-MODEL, Liberty Party (LP)) and Boley (ex-LPC, People's Unification Party (PUP)) were rejected at the polls. The only real exception was Johnson. Not only did he make a spectacular entrance on the national political scene by coming third in the 2011 presidential elections (as standard-bearer of the newly formed NUDP), he also defended his seat – as an independent – in the senate in 2014. The growing political marginalization of ex-warlords also put economic pressure on them. With decreasing access to state patronage, many struggled to hold up their Big Man status and networks of clients. An additional challenge was the prospect of being arrested for war crimes. One of the main recommendations of TRC – the final report was published in December 2009 – was the establishment of an "Extraordinary Criminal Court for Liberia" to try a total of 116 ex-warlords and generals (Truth and Reconciliation Commission 2009). Even if this recommendation has not yet been implemented, it has created a sense of urgency amongst many warlord democrats (see section on Johnson below).

Sekou Conneh: securitizing the ex-combatant issue

Sekou Conneh was born into a prosperous Mandingo family in Gbarnga in 1960. After graduating from the Gbarnga Methodist School in 1985, Conneh commenced his professional life working as a tax collector for the Doe regime. With the outbreak of the civil war, Conneh fled to Guinea where he established himself as a local businessman selling used cars. It was only after the end of the war and the 1997 elections that Conneh dared to return to Liberia. After a short stint with his old employer at the Ministry of Finance, Conneh returned to Guinea. This time he focused his business activities on exporting used cars from Guinea to Liberia. However, he was soon arrested by Liberian officials accused of having smuggled cars into the country. He was only released after the personal intervention of Taylor. In fact, Conneh's wife, Aisha Conneh, was a spiritual adviser and adoptive daughter of President Conté of Guinea (Brabazon 2003; IRIN 2003).

Conneh was propelled into the international spotlight after the Taylor-sponsored invasion of Guinea in 2000. In order to push back the attack and punish Taylor, Conté – who initially held lukewarm feelings towards the Liberian insurgents – decided to fully support the rebels, providing them with arms and a safe haven inside Guinea. In order to facilitate interactions with their sponsors, the LURD National Executive Council elected Conneh as the rebel group's new national chairman and commander in chief in 2001. Via Conneh and his wife Aisha, LURD had direct access to Conté. However, despite Conneh's close relations with the Guinean president, the former's position was precarious throughout the war. Other LURD leaders generally saw him as a weak compromise candidate who could easily be replaced once Taylor had been ousted. In addition, Conneh's relationship with senior commanders was, at times, uneasy due to the former's inability to provide them with supplies (Brabazon 2003, 2010: 48, 53, 207; Melville 2004a; Reno 2007).

After the signing of CPA in August 2003, Conneh decided not take part in NTGL. Hoping to have a shot at the presidency in 2005, he instead attempted to run LURD from outside the government. This strategy soon faltered, as Conneh's already precarious hold over the movement deteriorated into open factionalism. Conneh was accused of selling government positions, which had been allotted to LURD by CPA, to individuals with only weak links to the movement. This criticism was particularly strong amongst ex-commanders and fighters who had not received the peacetime benefits promised to them. Things took a turn for the worse in January 2004, when forty ex-LURD commanders called for the replacement of Conneh by his wife Aisha, a move that was supported by the latter. Aisha had apparently been infuriated by Conneh's decision to award Losone Kamara – the brother of a former wife – the position of finance minister (ICG 2004; Paye-Layleh 2004a). Conneh's estrangement from his wife constituted a serious conundrum for the LURD leader; without Aisha, Conneh lost access to the Guinean president's economic and military support. Conneh could initially count on the backing of National Executive Council in his power struggle with Aisha, which on several occasions turned violent (ICG 2004; Sesay 2004). However, in June 2004 the council declared Conneh suspended as LURD leader, instead electing Cheyee Doe (Samuel Doe's younger brother) as national chairman. The stated reason for Conneh's removal was an alleged deal between Kamara and Conneh, where the former agreed to pay the latter US$300,000 per month. When Doe died only two days after assuming power, the Council threw in their lot with Justice Minister Kabineh Janneh, who in July declared himself to be the new LURD national chairman (The Analyst 2005a; BBC Monitoring Africa 2004; Jarkloh 2004; Melville 2004b). Conneh declared the move illegal, insisting that he was still head of the movement.

During Conneh's struggle to control the reins of LURD, he consistently sought support from the international community, presenting himself as the only leader who could deliver on LURD's promise to support the peace process and referring to his opponents as criminal impersonators fostering insecurity

(The Analyst 2004a, 2004c). In this sense, he employed a "discourse of peace" in his efforts to marginalize internal dissent. However, despite similar appeals and declarations that he was the only legitimate leader of LURD, Conneh was never able to regain full control over the movement. By the time LURD was officially disbanded in November 2004 the leadership question had still not been settled.

Later efforts to reconcile the different ex-LURD factions, in order to transform the movement into a political party, failed. Evidence suggests that Conneh was reluctant to associate himself with NTGL (and its ex-LURD members), which was widely unpopular due to the corruption accusations lodged against it (The Analyst 2005a). Instead Conneh opted to launch his own political party, PRODEM, in April 2005, and publicly declared his intention to run for president as its standard bearer (IRIN 2005a). When confronted by critics about the wisdom of electing yet another ex-warlord as president, Conneh loftily proclaimed "[w]hen elected president, I am not going to be like Taylor and people should be appreciative that I Sekou Damate Conneh am transforming from being a factional leader to a political leader" (IRIN 2005a).

As PRODEM's leader, Conneh promised health empowerment, equal wealth distribution, free education, more jobs, an end to ethnocentrism, regional development for peace and security, as well as judicial reform to ensure the rule of law (Dennis 2005), and his official campaign slogan was "reconciliation, unity, rule of law, development, freedom for all" (Blair 2005). Conneh also took some concrete steps towards fostering reconciliation. In July 2005, Conneh apologized for any unintentional destruction caused by LURD military actions (Borteh 2005). One reason why Conneh put so much emphasis on developmental issues and reconciliation was the small size of the Mandingo electorate and the general unpopularity of the latter amongst other ethnic groups, due to their economic strength and their position as "latecomers" to Liberia. By avoiding ethnic appeals, and focusing on more universal aspects such as healthcare and education, Conneh hoped to attract voters from across the ethnic spectrum. However, in the end most followers appear to have been Mandingos (Reuters 2005). To entice internally displaced persons to vote for him, Conneh reportedly distributed rice in the camps of the latter (The Analyst 2005b). One group that Conneh gave particular public attention to was ex-combatants – not only of his own faction, but of all armed groups. This was not a new strategy. In fact, after the launch of the DDR (disarmament, demobilization and reintegration) process in 2004 Conneh had already taken on the role as an unofficial spokesperson for struggling ex-fighters and a critic of the DDR program's shortcomings (IRIN 2004).

Even if Conneh emphasized messages of reconciliation, peace and forgiveness in his speeches and media statements, he often alluded to his military background and wartime credentials. In an interview in May 2005 he declared that:

We [LURD] are not warlords. We are liberators [...] I don't feel any
responsibility. Everything that has happened in this country, Taylor is
responsible. He kept our people hostages in this country. Though we regret
the incident, that Taylor even had to be president, we regret that. Even
for taking arms, we regret it. But we were forced to do so. There was no
way that we could advocate. No other means but to resist the government.
(Voice of America 2005a)

Meanwhile, during his main political rally at Monrovia's football stadium
in September, he reminded his followers that "we are the liberators, make no
mistake" (Reuters 2005).

When analyzing Conneh's speeches it also becomes clear that he made
a concerted effort to securitize wartime identities. In fact, a cornerstone of
Conneh's presidential bid was to present himself as the only candidate who
could control the violent agency of ex-combatants in Liberia. For instance,
in an interview in October 2005, he stressed that:

Somebody who comes into the presidency, who has not been to this
country in over 10, 20 years, do[es] not even know how to talk to fighters,
do[es] not even know how to approach the issue of ex-fighters. And they
come to head this government. You know there will be problems here every
day. (Bavier 2005)

The significance of such statements was clear; Conneh deliberately
constructed an image of the ex-combatants as one of the most acute threats
to post-war stability in Liberia, and himself as the most suitable candidate
to handle this threat. Put differently, without his leadership peace would not
prevail. To drive home the point, Conneh stressed that he was the preferred
candidate of ex-combatants of all factions. Not only did he claim that the
latter had petitioned him to run for office, he also said that he would rely
on the ex-fighters to "canvass" his political message across the country (AFP
2005a; Bavier 2005).

Why did Conneh, whose previous post-war rhetoric had been characterized
by messages of peace, employ a more belligerent discourse during the election
campaign? This was presumably caused by the severe electoral constraints that
he faced. After his power struggle with Aisha he could no longer count on
any substantial ex-LURD support. In fact, his former wife actively campaigned
for Johnson-Sirleaf and UP. In an interview in May 2005 Aisha even attacked
Conneh and taunted him for not being able to control his "home":

Look, let me tell you something. Damate Conneh is not capable of
becoming president in this country. It is not time for warlord. Let him go
back to school and prepare himself for the future. Damate cannot settle his
home, then he wants to become president. Is he joking? (Jabateh 2005)

Thanks to her influence over ex-LURD commanders, Aisha was able to convince many of them to mobilize voters on behalf of Johnson-Sirleaf, rather than for Conneh.[1] Conneh also faced an uphill battle due to his ethnicity. As already touched upon, Mandingos are often resented by members of other communities. In addition, Mandingos only constitute approximately 3% of the population.[2] To make things worse, Conneh faced fierce competition from other political actors who were also vying for the Mandingo vote. Kromah and his ALCOP were largely dependent on the Mandingos and UP had always had a strong support amongst them. With limited and waning domestic and, as we have seen, regional support, it made sense for him to remind the voters of his presence and wartime power. Even if such a strategy was not certain to win him the presidency, it could at least provide seats in the legislature for his PRODEM or force a new future government or uneasy international peacemakers to offer him a government position or employment. The amount of international and media interest that Conneh received because of his aggressive rhetoric is also witness to the efficiency of his strategy; it gave him a political platform that he otherwise would not have had (IRIN 2005a, 2005b; Sieh 2005; Melville 2005; Reuters 2005; Voice of America 2005a, 2005b).

However, in the end, Conneh's efforts to securitize wartime identities did not pay off. He only received 0.6% of the vote and PRODEM did not win a single seat in the Senate or House of Representatives. During the second round of the presidential elections, Conneh tried to win back some political leverage by throwing his lot behind Weah. His efforts at playing kingmaker failed when Johnson-Sirleaf prevailed. Conneh was, however, gracious in defeat and acted in a statesmanlike manner when he called on the supporters of the opposition to accept the results and uphold peace. In a last effort to salvage some political influence, he called on UP to create a government of inclusion to erase the fears of the opposition (The Analyst 2005c). However, no offers were forthcoming from the new government. After his electoral defeat Conneh left the political scene and went back to being a businessman.[3]

Prince Johnson: preacher of fear

Prince Johnson, a Gio from Nimba County, was born in 1952. After having been raised by his uncle in Monrovia, Johnson entered the armed forces in 1971. Once in AFL he received military training in the United States and was by the early 1980s a junior officer and aide-de-camp to AFL's Commander General Thomas Quiwonkpa. In the wake of increased persecution of non-Krahns and a move by Doe to marginalize Quiwonkpa (a Gio), Johnson followed the latter into exile in 1983. Two years later Johnson participated in a failed attempt to oust Doe from power. This resulted in the death of Quiwonkpa – the coup plot's mastermind – and prompted Johnson to join other Liberian dissidents, such as Charles Taylor, who were organizing a new rebel movement in Burkina

Faso. Due to his military credentials and experiences, Johnson became the chief military instructor of NPFL – as the group would later be called – during their stay in Libya (Ellis 1999).

With the launch of the NPFL insurrection in December 1989, Johnson headed one of two NPFL units that invaded Liberia. From the onset there were severe tensions between Johnson and Taylor. In fact, by January 1990 Johnson's unit was acting independently, refusing to take orders from Taylor. The conflict between Johnson and Taylor was not new; it was part of a larger leadership struggle that had originated during NPFL's stay in Libya, when Johnson is said to have sought Taylor's removal as head of the movement. By May, these tensions escalated into open clashes. Due to the military experience of his troops, which were largely composed of ex-AFL soldiers from Nimba, Johnson's faction made quick advances, approaching Monrovia by early July (Ellis 1999; Gerdes 2013: 35; Huband 1998: 61). That same month, Johnson formalized the split within NPFL by publicly declaring the existence of INPFL.

After Johnson's capture and execution of Doe, he declared himself Acting President of Liberia (Ellis 1999: 11). Despite hopes that his ECOMOG backers would support the move, Johnson and INPFL became increasingly marginalized. Johnson had initially had close relations with ECOMOG; not only had ECOMOG troops been allowed to land and set up base in areas controlled by INPFL, the latter also provided the peacekeepers with valuable intelligence. However, with the creation of the interim government – headed by Sawyer as president – in November 1990 ECOMOG decided to throw in its lot with the new government. ECOMOG troops, under Nigerian leadership, subsequently took steps to reign in INPFL troops in their vicinity (Ellis 1999: 2, 15; Gerdes 2013: 34, 116). What made things worse was that Johnson did not possess the domestic political backing and economic resources to sustain a prolonged military campaign. As a result, INPFL had lost most of its political and military relevance by 1992. In a last effort to turn the tide, Johnson switched sides and supported a bid by Taylor to conquer Monrovia in October. However, fearing deceit, Johnson renounced the deal at the last minute. The ensuing turmoil resulted in infighting within INPFL and Taylor loyalists conquering areas remaining under Johnson's control. The latter was only saved by the timely intervention of ECOMOG troops. By late 1992 INPFL had ceased to exist as an armed entity and Johnson was relocated to Nigeria where the authorities provided him with a villa in Lagos (Ellis 1999: 99; Gerdes 2013: 34, 116; Huband 1998: 213).

During his exile in Nigeria, Johnson engaged in a much-publicized metamorphosis, which – according to himself – shed him of his militant past. After having attended a theological seminary, Johnson found God and supported himself as an evangelist pastor (Ellis 1999: 26; Gerdes 2013: 117, 208). As a born-again Christian Johnson presented himself as an agent of reconciliation;

not only did he come to terms with the Doe family, he also preached and wrote about the need for forgiveness and reconstruction in Liberia (Johnson 2003; The Analyst 2006). A central tenet in Johnson's new philosophy was that "the guns that liberate should not rule", pointing to the dangers of allowing ex-warlords, such as Taylor, to control the reins of power (Huband 1998: 213; Johnson 2003). It can be argued that this personal transformation was one of the few avenues available for Johnson to recreate himself as a Big Man and return to Liberia; with negligible political-military influence and barred from participating in peace talks, he could at least build up a new following through his religious work (Johnson 2003).

Upon returning to Liberia in March 2004, Johnson soon waived his principle that "the guns that liberate should not rule". He proclaimed his intention to join LAP of Interim President Bryant and announced that he would run for one of the senate seats allotted to Nimba County (Giardino 2004; Dukulé 2004). To convince Liberians that he was a changed man, Johnson continuously stressed his new Christian identity and asked for forgiveness. In one interview he declared that "I have asked all Liberians to forgive me for whatever wrong I may have committed; and I equally stand ready to forgive all those who have offended me" (Paye-Layleh 2004b). However, in April Johnson's political comeback came to an abrupt end. Claiming that Cheyee Doe had threated to kill him, Johnson called on his ex-fighters to protect him. After they failed to respond, Johnson went into hiding and eventually made his way back to Nigeria (Giardino 2004; Dukulé, 2004).

It was only five months later that Johnson dared to return to Liberia and resume his political campaign. After abandoning the idea of running on a LAP ticket and being defeated in the UP primary to become the party's senatorial candidate, Johnson settled for running as an independent (The Analyst 2005d). To convince Nimbians to vote for him, Johnson promised to eradicate corruption, promote health and education, and work for a fairer distribution of resources (Sendolo 2005). In his efforts to mobilize supporters, Johnson received crucial assistance from networks of Nimba businessmen and local chiefs whom he convinced to support his candidacy (Gerdes 2013: 207–208). Johnson's speech acts often included pleas for peace and reconciliation. For instance, in September 2004 he called Liberians to rid their "[h]earts of hatred, grudges, and evils in order for us have permanent peace. Let us spiritually disarm our hearts so that Liberia will know lasting peace and rebuild" (Seakor 2004). In addition, he often stressed the need for Krahns, Mandingos, Gios and Manos to put the past behind them and work together (Kwanue 2004).

However, while Johnson was employing a discourse of peace, he had a habit of simultaneously boasting about his military credentials. In interviews Johnson described himself as a "revolutionary" and "freedom fighter" who had defended his people against the evils of Doe (Colomban 2005; Sendolo 2005).

111

Such statements were not only meant to evoke the electorate's appreciation, but also to remind the people of Nimba about the fragility of the peace process and their continued vulnerability. According to Sawyer (2008: 195), Johnson "constantly reminded voters of his role as leader of an armed group and assured them of his commitment to their defense should there be another war" and "voters seemed to have responded more to fears of future insecurity than to a sense of gratitude for past services" (Sawyer 2008: 195). In fact, a central pillar of Johnson's electoral strategy was to promise to protect Nimba County from further Krahn aggression (Gerdes 2013: 207-208). It can therefore be argued that Johnson made an orchestrated effort to securitize wartime identities during his campaign. To remind the voters of his military strength Johnson often made use of videos and written accounts about the war in his speeches. This included showing a video of how Johnson and his fighters tortured Doe in 1990 to crowds before he engaged the audience (O'Mahony and Fair 2012).

What prompted Johnson, who had gone to such lengths to present himself as an agent of change and man of God, to stir up ethnic fears? The answer can presumably be found in the weakness of Johnson's support base. After twelve years in exile Johnson was a marginal figure by the time of his return in 2004. To some extent he had attempted to recreate networks of clients during his stay in Nigeria by, for instance, assisting Liberian refugees in the country to return home (The Analyst 2004b). However, Johnson's precarious following became clear in April 2004 when he failed to mobilize his ex-fighters to protect him from the alleged death threat by Cheyee Doe. For Johnson it therefore made sense to remind Gio and Manos about his role in "liberating" them from Doe's autocratic regime and to stress his commitment to defend them in the future. By instilling fear amongst Nimbians, Johnson's military past became an asset rather than a liability.

Johnson's belligerent strategy was successful. Receiving 32% of the vote – as compared to the 17% mustered by the runner-up – Johnson clinched the senate seat. During the second round of the presidential election Johnson lent his support to Weah, whose candidacy he claimed "crossed ethnic lines" and constituted the best hope for peace (AFP 2005b). However, Johnson's effort to become kingmaker failed when Johnson-Sirleaf defeated Weah. Despite his previous criticism of UP and Johnson-Sirleaf, Johnson later called on opposition demonstrators to accept the results and give peace a chance (Sieh 2005).

After the 2005 elections, the actions and implications of TRC took up much of Johnson's attention. In fact, the prospect of being arrested for war crimes pushed Johnson to escalate his belligerency – at least in the media. For instance, in March 2006 he stated that:

When someone asks me, "What about the war-crimes tribunal?" I say, "It's not going to be a good thing." Not that I feel guilty about something that

I've done, that I'm afraid to appear – no! But if you start arresting a few
people for war crimes the others who wouldn't want to be arrested will go
to the bush. Don't forget that the arms may not have been totally given to
the peacekeepers. (Anderson 2006)

Meanwhile, in January 2008 Johnson asked TRC to stop calling him as a
witness. As a "liberator" Johnson proclaimed that he did not want to have
anything to do with TRC, since most testifying witnesses were liars with fake
allegations (BBC Monitoring Africa 2008; Saywah 2008). Later he proclaimed
that "[m]y people, the Nimba people, will resist any attempt by the TRC to
forcibly have me appear before it [TRC] to explain circumstances in connection
with Doe's death" (The Analyst 2008).

Even if Johnson eventually agreed to testify, in August 2008, he continued
to question the TRC's actions and legitimacy and made it perfectly clear what
would happen if he was detained. For instance, in January 2009 Johnson
warned that "[w]e former faction leaders, we revolutionaries, we are for peace
in this country. But no one should witch hunt us; no one should try to arrest
me, because there will be resistance" (AFP 2009). Hence, through his speeches,
Johnson deliberately constructed a daunting scenario in which armed actors
would plunge Liberia into new civil strife due to the actions and recommendations of TRC. By defining the source of this threat as TRC, he could, rather
ingeniously, send a message of impending doom without incriminating himself.

In January 2010 Johnson made media headlines after declaring his intention to contest the presidential elections the following year (New Democrat
2010). To bolster his chances at the polls, and give his campaign a more
national appeal, Johnson launched a new political party, NUDP. Johnson's
political agenda was based on promises of greater legislative and economic
autonomy for Liberia's counties and harsher punishment for perpetrators of
rape and corruption. In fact, Johnson proclaimed that if elected president he
would endorse laws that would execute those convicted of corruption (ICG
2011; Swaray 2010). With limited support outside Nimba, Johnson needed to
appeal to non-Gios and Manos to become a true contender for the presidency.
For this reason, in his campaign Johnson targeted ex-combatants at large,
a constituency that was particularly prominent in Monrovia. Not only did
Johnson provide economic assistance to many ex-fighters, he also promised
them employment and improved housing.[4] In addition, he selected a former
NPFL commander and Grand Cape Mount Senator, Abel Massaley, as his
vice-presidential candidate (New Democrat 2010).

During the campaign Johnson continued to emphasize his religious transformation to muster support. In an interview in August 2010 Johnson described how:

No-one who accepts Christ remains the same. You are a new creature,
a new person [...] That person of General Johnson in the wartime is

not the Johnson now. The Johnson now is the diplomat, the senator and pastor. It's wonderful! [...] I believe if God can touch that sort of person there are many more God is touching, and I think there is hope for Liberia [...] Reconciliation is not about ourselves, it's firstly with God. (The Informer 2010)

However, just as during the 2005 elections, Johnson combined calls for reconciliation and personal change with a rhetoric aimed at instilling fear amongst the electorate. For instance, when Johnson explained why he was running for office in February 2010 he stated that "we are seeking the presidency to properly address the security situation of this country. The Liberian peace process is still fragile because of insecurity. Armed robberies, etc., are giving our people sleepless nights" (Paye-Layleh 2010). According to Massaley and Johnson, this security deficit could only be solved by electing strong leaders with a solid military background (BBC Monitoring Africa 2010). Hence, by reminding Liberians how easily fresh violence could erupt, Johnson once again made his military credentials relevant. In addition, by talking about the challenge posed by criminals – a problem that many Liberians could relate to – Johnson could compensate for his lack of political support amongst non-Gios and Manos and reach out to voters outside of Nimba.

In the first round of the October 2011 presidential elections, Johnson surprised observers by coming in third place with 11% of the vote. Johnson's success was largely due to the massive backing that he received from the Gio and Mano communities in Nimba. In addition, NUDP won six seats in the House of Representatives and one in the Senate. In the run-up to the second round – in which President Johnson-Sirleaf faced the CDC standard-bearer Winston Tubman – Johnson called on his supporters to vote for Johnson-Sirleaf as "the lesser of two evils" (ICG 2012: 12-13). Johnson thereby de facto functioned as "queenmaker" and contributed to the president's re-election. Evidence suggests that there were three main reasons why Johnson rallied to the incumbent's side. First, CDC had previously committed itself to implementing the TRC's recommendations, including setting up a war crimes tribunal, a move that estranged the former warlord. Second, by supporting Tubman and CDC, Johnson feared alienating his Nimba supporters; the latter have historically been wary of CDC's strong links to the Krahn community (ICG 2012: 12-13). Third, rumors hold that Johnson received a substantial amount of money to throw his lot in with Johnson-Sirleaf (The New Dispensation 2011).

For Johnson, the period after the 2011 elections was characterized by intra-NUDP struggles, continuous belligerency and positioning for the 2014 senatorial and 2017 presidential elections.[5] In February 2012 NUDP declared that it had expelled Johnson as head of the party, due to his unilateral decision to support President Johnson-Sirleaf in the 2011 elections. Initially Johnson disputed the decision and questioned its legality. However, by mid-2013 he had accepted the move and proclaimed his intention to once again run as an independent to defend his senatorial seat. The strategy paid off. With the backing of UP, key members of the Nimba elite and many of the county's ex-combatants, Johnson won a landslide victory, tallying 67% of the vote (David 2014; Lomax 2014). Meanwhile, on several occasions Johnson made statements indicating his continued determination to keep wartime fears alive. For instance, in May 2012 he relaunched his attack against a possible war crimes tribunal, warning that any "illegal implementation" of the TRC report would cause "instability" in the country (Heritage 2012). Furthermore, in a church sermon in July 2015, Johnson warned that those in power should be wary of the moment that UNMIL leaves; without the protection of peacekeepers, the economically marginalized may take their revenge (The New Republic Liberia 2015). Finally, during the run-up to the 2017 presidential elections, the ex-warlord continued doing what he was best at: electoral maneuvering to maximize his political leverage. In fact, it was reported that Johnson was negotiating with numerous politicians concerning the prospects of running on a common president/vice-president ticket, including Joseph Boakai (UP), Charles Brumskine (LP) and George Weah (CDC) (Genoway 2013; Karmo 2015; Daygbor 2015).

Concluding discussion

The aftermath of the 2003 CPA agreement, which ended the second Liberian civil war, saw the proliferation of warlord democrats acting as political free agents. However, even if these actors were well represented in both chambers of congress, they only played a secondary political role. In fact, civilian politicians and parties came to dominate post-2003 politics. This was in sharp contrast to Liberia's first post-war democratic experiment (1996–2003), in which warlord democrats and the political heirs of their armed groups dominated the political scene. This chapter has sought to analyze what effect this shift in warlord politics has had on Liberia's post-war security. More specifically, we systematically compared the trajectories of two influential warlord democrats – Sekou Conneh (ex-LURD) and Prince Johnson (ex-INPFL). As standard bearer of PRODEM, a party that he had personally launched, Conneh failed to win the 2005 presidential elections. Meanwhile, Johnson ran for the senate in 2005 and 2014 and the presidency in 2011, the two former as an independent candidate and the latter as head of NUDP. Even if Johnson lost the 2011 presidential elections, he did win both senatorial races.

During their electoral careers both Conneh and Johnson employed mixed discourses, on the one hand preaching the merits of peace and reconciliation, and on the other hand making veiled threats and reminding the electorate of the fragility of the peace process. There may have been historical reasons for believing that attempting to securitize wartime identities could be an efficient way to increase their chances at the polls. During the 1997 elections, Taylor surprised many observers with his ability to mobilize voters amongst ethnic communities that had supported his opponents during the war. In fact, one of his main campaign slogans had been "He killed my ma, he killed my pa, I'll vote for him" (Polgreen 2006). Hence, by instilling fear amongst Liberians, Taylor reminded the voters that the country would only be at peace once he was elected president (Waugh, 2011). With limited electoral bases, Conneh and Johnson may have believed that similar threats would work to their advantage. Johnson's belligerency can also be explained by the activities of TRC and its recommendation to prosecute ex-military leaders for war crimes. This prompted Johnson to warn that there would be renewed violence if he and others were arrested.[6]

If Conneh and Johnson had misgivings about the new peace order being built, why did they not attempt to spoil it by engaging in organized violence? Their lack of interest in employing violence can probably be explained by two factors. First, neither of the ex-warlords could count on the loyalty of their former fighters. In fact, by the 2005 elections they only had tenuous control over their previous command structures. Second, the presence of 15,000 peacekeeping troops made any moves to sponsor violence hazardous, to say the least. Hence, for Conneh and Johnson it therefore made sense to shy away from armed action and focus their attention on employing discourses of violence, a sort of "spoiling on the cheap".

What policy implications can be drawn from the chapter's findings? Oftentimes civil wars only reach a peaceful solution if transitional power-sharing arrangements are crafted, whereby the main belligerents are represented in the government (see e.g. Walter 2002). The problem with such provisions is that it provides ex-military leaders with the resources and political influence to dominate future elections. In Liberia, peacemakers addressed this problem by barring members of the transitional government from taking part in the 2005 elections. The dilemma of whether to enter the government or run in the elections generated ruptures within the armed movements, especially since many of those who became ministers were reluctant to share the economic spoils with their wartime colleagues. As a consequence, the warlord democrats who ran for office after 2003 not only failed to create strong national political parties, but also struggled to uphold their ex-combatant networks. This has undoubtedly been one of the main reasons for the relative success of the Liberian peace process. Hence, one way to control the violent agency of warlord democrats is to combine a strong peacekeeping mandate with restrictions exempting all individuals who have taken part in a transitional government from running for office.

Notes

1 This observation is based on fieldwork conducted by Anders Themnér in Liberia during November 2012.

2 GlobalSecurity.org: Liberia – People. Available at: http://www.globalsecurity.org/military/world/liberia/people.htm .

3 During the 2011 elections one PRODEM representative ran for one of Bong County's seats in the House of Representatives. Conneh, however, did not run for any office. From time to time, Conneh has continued to make headlines through his appearance in TRC, as well as comments concerning the continued threat of ex-combatant violence and the peace process.

4 This based on field research by Themnér in Liberia during 2010–2012 and O'Mahony and Fair (2012).

5 During 2013–2014 there were reports that Johnson supporters physically abused political opponents and journalists. However, it has not been confirmed whether Johnson ordered or knew about these attacks in advance.

6 It is important to note that it has not been possible to confirm or rule out a connection between Johnson's personal characteristics and his aggressive rhetoric. Ellis (1999: 4, 14–15) has, for instance, depicted the ex-warlord as a "psychopath", possessing a "notoriously violent temperament" and known for his "unpredictability and propensity for casual violence", while Gerdes (2013: 116) has described him as an "unstable character". Only further in-depth research can shed light on whether there is a causal link between his temperament and his belligerent statements.

Bibliography

Adebajo, A. 2002a. *Building Peace in West Africa: Liberia, Sierra Leone, and Guinea-Bissau.* Boulder, CO: Lynne Rienner.

Adebajo, A. 2002b. *Liberia's Civil War: Nigeria, ECOMOG, and Regional Security in West Africa.* Boulder, CO: Lynne Rienner.

AFP (Agence France Presse). 2005a. "Liberia Rebel Leader Sekou Conneh to Stand in Presidential Poll." *Agence France Presse*, 28 April.

AFP (Agence France Presse). 2005b. "Liberia Votes with Weah Still Leading Presidential Pack." *Agence France Presse*, 11 October.

AFP (Agence France Presse). 2009. "Liberian Ex-Warlord Claims War Crimes Indictments Pending: Report." *Agence France Presse*, 12 January.

Anderson, J. L. 2006. "After the Warlords: Letter from Liberia." *New Yorker* 82 (6): 58.

Bavier, J. 2005. "Liberian Ex-Rebel Campaigns for Rights of Former Combatants." *Voice of America*, 6 October.

BBC Monitoring Africa. 2004. "Liberia: Former Rebels LURD Leader Dismisses New Appointment." *BBC Monitoring Africa*, 28 July.

BBC Monitoring Africa. 2008. "Liberian Senator Prince Johnson Says Not Ready to Appear Before Truth Inquiry." *BBC Monitoring Africa*, 18 January.

BBC Monitoring Africa. 2010. "Liberian Senator Confirms Bid for 2011 Vice Presidential Post." *BBC Monitoring Africa*, 28 January.

Blair, D. 2005. "Liberians Queue up to Vote for a Lasting Peace." *The Daily Telegraph*, 12 October.

Bøås, M. and A. Hatløy. 2008. "'Getting In, Getting Out': Militia Membership and Prospects for Reintegration in Postwar Liberia." *Journal of Modern African Studies* 46 (1): 33–55.

Borteh, G. 2005. "Sekou Conneh Apologizes." *All Africa*, 29 July.

Brabazon, J. 2003. "Liberia: Liberians United for Reconciliation and Democracy (LURD)." *Armed Non-State Actors Project, Briefing Paper No. 1.* The Royal Institute of International Affairs, Africa Programme, February.

Brabazon, J. 2010. *My Friend the Mercenary.* New York: Grove Press.

Chaudhary, T. W. 2012. "The Political Economies of Violence in Post-War Liberia." In *The Peace in Between: Postwar Violence and Peacebuilding*, ed. A. Suhrke and M. Berdal. New York: Routledge.

Colomban, N. 2005. "VOA News: Liberia's Next Congress Will Be Fractured, Controversial." *Hindustan Times*, 3 November.

David, A. 2014. "UP Supports Prince Johnson Senatorial Bid." *The NEWS*, 29 July.

Daygbor, E. J. N. 2015. "PYJ Picks Boakai." *The New Dawn*, 5 August.

Dennis, J. E. 2005. "We Will Relax War Sekou Conneh Promises Liberians." *The Analyst*, 2 September.

Duffield, M. 1998. "Post-Modern Conflict: Warlords, Post-Adjustment States and Private Protection." *Civil Wars* 1 (1): 65–102.

Dukulé, A. W. 2004. "Prince Y. Johnson is Back to Nigeria." *The Perspective*, 12 April.

Ellis, S. 1999. *The Mask of Anarchy. The Destruction of Liberia and the Religious Dimension of an African Civil War*. New York: New York University Press.

Genoway, E. G. 2013. "PYJ Returning to CDC?" *The New Dawn*, 2 October.

Gerdes, F. 2013. *The Political Economy of War and Peace in Liberia*. Frankfurt and New York: Campus Verlag.

Giardino, C. 2004. "Liberia/Warlord (L-only)." Radio Scripts. *Voice of America*, 2 April.

Heritage. 2012. "Prince Johnson Decries Political Witch Hunt." *Heritage*, 28 May.

Huband, M. 1998. *The Liberian Civil War*. Abingdon and New York: Frank Cass Publishers.

ICG (International Crisis Group). 2004. "Rebuilding Liberia: Prospects and Perils." International Crisis Group. Report No. 75, Africa, 30 January.

ICG (International Crisis Group). 2005. "Liberia's Elections: Necessary but not Sufficient." International Crisis Group. Report No. 98, Africa, 7 September

ICG (International Crisis Group). 2011. "Liberia: How Sustainable Is the Recovery?" International Crisis Group Report No. 177, Africa, 19 August.

ICG (International Crisis Group). 2012. "Liberia: Time for Much-Delayed Reconciliation and Reform." International Crisis Group. Briefing No. 88, Africa, 12 June

IRIN. 2003. "Liberia: Profile of LURD Leader, Sekou Conneh." *IRIN Humanitarian News and Analysis*, 19 August.

IRIN. 2004. "Liberia: Rebels Back Down on Call for Bryant's Removal." *IRIN Humanitarian News and Analysis*, 27 January.

IRIN. 2005a. "Liberia: Former Rebel Leader to Run for President." *IRIN Humanitarian News and Analysis*, 27 April.

IRIN. 2005b. "Presidential Hopefuls for 11 October Polls." *IRIN Humanitarian News and Analysis*, 9 October.

Ismail, O. 2008. "Power Elites, War and Postwar Reconstruction in Africa: Continuities, Discontinuities and Paradoxes." *Journal of Contemporary African Studies* 26 (3): 259–278.

Jabateh, M. 2005 "Damate Must Go to School." *The Analyst*, 10 May.

Jarkloh, B. K. 2004. "Peace Process Rocks: LURD Pushes for Review, Says Bryant Is Incompetent." *The Analyst*, 18 June.

Johnson, P. 2003. *The Rise and Fall of President Samuel K. Doe: A Time to Heal and Rebuild Liberia*. Lagos: Soma Associates.

Käihko, I. 2015. "'Taylor Must Go': The Strategy of the Liberians United for Reconciliation and Democracy." *Small Wars & Insurgencies* 26 (2): 248–270.

Karmo, H. 2015. "'My Friend & Brother' - Weah, Brumskine Hold Tete-a-Tete." *FrontPageAfrica*, 8 July.

Kieh, G. K., Jr. 2011. "Warlords, Politicians and the Post-First Civil War Election in Liberia." *African & Asian Studies* 10 (2/3): 83–99.

Kwanue, C. Y. 2004. "Prince Johnson Cautions Liberians Against Tribalism." *The Inquirer*, 30 September.

Lomax, S. 2014. "Smooth Sailing PYJ? Incumbent Factor Favors Nimba Senator." *FrontPageAfrica*, 18 December.

Lyons, T. 1999. *Voting for Peace: Postconflict Elections in Liberia*. Washington, DC: The Brookings Institution.

Melville, C. 2004a. "Liberian Rebels Turn Guns on their Leader." *WMRC Daily Analysis*, 9 January.

Melville, C. 2004b. "New Twist in Endless Liberian Rebel Leadership Dispute." *World Markets Research Centre*, 10 June.

Melville, C. 2005. "Election 2005: Former Liberian Rebel Leader Announces Intention to Run for President." *Global Insight Daily Analysis*, 28 April.

New Democrat. 2010. "Scramble for Presidency Begins – Ex-Warlord "Throws Cap" in Race." *New Democrat*, 27 January.

Nilsson, D. and M. Söderberg Kovacs. 2005. "Breaking the Cycle of Violence? Promises and Pitfalls of the Liberian Peace Process." *Civil Wars* 7 (4): 396-414.

O'Mahony, G. and J. E. Fair. 2012. "From Lords of War to Leaders in Society: How Former Liberian Warlords Have Used 'Old' and 'New' Media to Self-Reframe." *Media, War and Conflict* 5 (1): 37-50.

Paye-Layleh, J. 2004a. "Liberian Rebel Leader's Wife Claims Leadership of Insurgency." *Associated Press*, 20 January.

Paye-Layleh, J. 2004b. "Liberia's Most Notorious Warlord after Taylor Returns Home, Asking Forgiveness." *The Associated Press*, 29 March.

Paye-Layleh, J. 2010. "One of Liberia's Most Infamous Warlords - Now a Senator - Says He Plans to Run for President." *The Associated Press*, 24 February.

Polgreen, K. 2006. "Master Plan Drawn in Blood." *The New York Times*, 2 April.

Reno, W. 1998. *Warlord Politics and African States*. Boulder, CO: Lynne Rienner.

Reno, W. S. 2007. "Liberia: The LURDs of the New Church." In *African Guerrillas: Raging Against the Machine*, ed. M. Bøås and K. C. Dunn. Boulder, CO: Lynne Rienner.

Reuters. 2005. "Liberian Ex-Rebel Leader Launches Presidential Bid." *Reuters*, 2 September.

Saywah, C. W. 2008. "Former Speaker Morkonmana Accused, But Denies Claims." *AllAfrica*, 23 January.

Sawyer, A. 2008. "Emerging Patterns in Liberia's Post-Conflict Politics: Observations from the 2005 Elections." *African Affairs* 107 (427): 177-199.

Seakor, S. 2004. "I Take Responsibility." *The Analyst*, 21 September.

Sendolo, J. 2005. "Prince Johnson Defends War Records." *Liberian Observer*, 30 September.

Sesay, T. 2004. "Rift Deepens over Command of Liberia's Main Rebel Group." *Agence France Presse*, 12 January.

Sieh, R. D. 2005. "Lack of 'Smoking Gun' Could Spell Embarrassment for Team Weah." *FrontPageAfrica*, 17 November.

Swaray, S. 2010. "We Will End Imperial Presidency." *The Analyst*, 10 May.

The Analyst. 2004a. "Dweh Threatens War, If – Gen. Opande Wheeled Sekou Away – Duala Residents Run Helter-Skelter – What Is Afoot." *The Analyst*, 5 August.

The Analyst. 2004b. "Prince Johnson Helps Liberian Refugees." *The Analyst*, 4 May.

The Analyst. 2004c. "Peace Process in Danger." *The Analyst*, 20 September.

The Analyst. 2005a. "LURD's Shadow Power - Loyalists Still Seek Impunity But Sekou Remains Circumspect." *The Analyst*, 4 January.

The Analyst. 2005b. "Vote Purchasing, A Vicious Virus." *The Analyst*, 14 September.

The Analyst. 2005c. "A Clarion Call!" *The Analyst*, 16 November.

The Analyst. 2005d. "G/Gedeans Are Not Fools." *The Analyst*, 24 October.

The Analyst. 2006. "Breaking Claws of Hatred." *The Analyst*, 9 February.

The Analyst. 2008. "If Tolbert's Killers Testify, I'll Testify About Doe's." *The Analyst*, 1 February.

The Informer. 2010. "Prince Johnson 'Finds God,' Seeks Presidency." *The Informer*, 16 August.

The New Dispensation. 2011. "Money Can Buy Votes: Ex-Warlord Prince Johnson Bought over for US$25 Million to Support Incumbent Prez Sirleaf in Run-off." *The New Dispensation*, 18 October.

The New Republic Liberia. 2015. "TRC Hits 'Rock.'" *The New Republic Liberia*, 28 July.

Truth and Reconciliation Commission. 2009. *Volume II: Consolidated Final Report*. 30 June. Monrovia: TRC of Liberia. Available from http://trcofliberia.org/reports/final-report.

UN Security Council. 1994. *Third Progress Report of the Secretary-General on the United Nations Observer Mission in Liberia*. Report No. S/1994/463. Secretary's General Reports. New York: United Nations.

UN Security Council. 2003. *Report of the Secretary-General to the Security Council on Liberia*. Rep. no. S/2003/875. Secretary's General Reports. New York: United Nations.

Voice of America. 2005a. "Liberia / Pol (L-O)." *Voice of America*, 28 May.

Voice of America. 2005b. "LIBERIA/POL (L-O)." *Voice of America*, 12 May.

Walter, B. F. 2002. *Committing to Peace. The Successful Settlement of Civil Wars*. Princeton, NJ and Oxford: Princeton University Press.

Waugh, C. 2011. *Charles Taylor and Liberia*. London: Zed Books.

4 | Afonso Dhlakama and RENAMO's return to armed conflict since 2013: the politics of reintegration in Mozambique

Alex Vines

Introduction[1]

Over two decades ago, in 1992, one of Africa's most brutal civil wars ended in Mozambique and until 2013 the country was regarded as having passed through a successful post-conflict transition. From April 2013 there was a return to limited armed conflict between fighters of the former rebel group Mozambican National Resistance (Resistência Nacional Moçambicana, RENAMO) and Mozambican government forces. A new agreement in September 2014 ended regular armed skirmishing in central Mozambique, but armed violence resumed in 2015.

This chapter examines how, from conducting a successful guerrilla campaign under its leader, Afonso Dhlakama, RENAMO's peacetime politics resulted in it becoming the largest opposition party in Africa until 2002 (even almost, or possibly, winning a presidential election in 1999) (Tavuyanago 2011) but why its fortunes went into steep decline between 2002 and 2014. According to Joaquim Chissano, Mozambique's second president, this has much to do with the tactics of RENAMO's leader: "He failed to transform his mentality from a guerrilla leader to post-war Mozambique. He has never reintegrated properly."[2] This chapter examines Dhlakama's leadership and RENAMO's strategy and traces the political navigations of Dhlakama (RENAMO's presidential candidate in five successive elections) up until late 2016. It highlights how Dhlakama – who initially played a positive role by ensuring RENAMO support for the country's peace and democratization process – became increasingly belligerent and eventually securitized wartime identities and engaged in organized violence.

RENAMO has been ignored by many academic comparative studies on the evolution of African rebel movements, such as *African Guerrillas* edited by Christopher Clapham in 1998 and *African Guerrillas: Raging Against the Machine* edited by Morten Bøås and Kevin Dunn in 2007. Clapham defined four broad categories: liberation insurgencies, separatist insurgencies, reform insurgencies and warlord insurgencies (Clapham 1998b: 7). He categorized the National Union for the Total Independence of Angola (União Nacional para a Independência Total de Angola, UNITA) after Angola's independence in 1975 and RENAMO on ideological grounds (pro-Western) to distinguish them from the governments they opposed (socialist), both of them offering pro-Western, capitalist and democratic credentials that were designed to attract external support. Clapham is wrong in arguing that this handicapped them. In 1992 UNITA won a significant number of votes and forced a presidential run-off to be arranged (though it never occurred) and RENAMO successfully fought to a stalemate and enjoyed good results in the 1994, 1999 and 2014 elections. In 1999 it came within a small margin of winning the presidential vote (some believe it actually won) and in 2014 it won a majority in five provinces.

It is true that UNITA was particularly good at using ideology to attract Western backers during the Cold War, buttressed by legitimate nationalist credentials and led by its charismatic leader Jonas Savimbi. Ideology was augmented or superseded by the role of charismatic leaders such as Jonas Savimbi for UNITA or Foday Sankoh of the Revolutionary United Front (RUF), as Bøås and Dunn (2007a: 29) have argued, but RENAMO's Dhlakama displays a completely different personality. His track record shows him to be a not particularly impressive public speaker: insecure, indecisive and frequently "flip-flopping", and influenced by the last person he met – although tactically he was undoubtedly an effective guerrilla commander. That said, during the 2014 election campaign Dhlakama's speeches and rallies showed significant improvement and may have contributed to RENAMO's improved electoral results.

Dhlakama and his leadership of the RENAMO party are not easily categorized and do not compare with some of the ex-militaries of West Africa or indeed even UNITA, which became a semi-conventional armed force. The limitations of Clapham's categories were examined in depth in Bøås and Dunn's edited volume, including acknowledging that there are different episodes and local, national, regional and international drivers. The same is true with the attempts at categorization in this book. Dhlakama and RENAMO do not sit comfortably within the unit of analysis and are not easily pigeon-holed.

Where Clapham is correct is that "insurgencies derive basically from blocked political aspirations and in some cases from reactive desperation" (Clapham 1998b: 5). This certainly is one of the drivers behind renewed support for RENAMO. RENAMO has never expected to capture the Mozambican state, but has always sought a military or political stalemate through which it can extract elite bargains from the dominant party, the Mozambique Liberation Front (Frente de Libertação de Moçambique, FRELIMO).

Independence and civil war

Mozambique obtained independence in June 1975, following a nationalist struggle against Portuguese colonialism by FRELIMO (Newitt 1995). In February 1977, FRELIMO formally declared its transformation from liberation movement into a Marxist-Leninist vanguard party. The decision came at a time when

Mozambique was beginning to skirmish with Rhodesia, and was seeking to attract military aid from Eastern Europe and the Soviet Union (Cann 1997).

Mozambique imposed sanctions against the neighboring white minority Rhodesian regime in 1976. The closure of the border with Rhodesia disrupted the Mozambican economy and deprived its ports of lucrative earnings. It also marked the start of hostile relations. The Rhodesians began to look at ways of arming and training a Mozambican opposition force – MNR (Mozambique National Resistance), later called RENAMO. RENAMO was created by the Rhodesian Central Intelligence Office (CIO) in retaliation for Mozambique's support for Zimbabwe nationalist guerrillas in 1977. André Matsangaissa was its first leader until death in action in 1979.[3] Following a power struggle that rumbled on into the early 1980s, at thirty years old Afonso Dhlakama became RENAMO's second leader in 1980 (Flower 1987).

Dhlakama did not initially inspire much confidence as a leader. "A weak character", according to Major Dudley Coventry, who led Rhodesian training of RENAMO (Emerson 2013). Ex-RENAMO representative Paulo Oliveira also observed that in the early 1980s Dhlakama was politically green, with a weakness for martial arts films, Coca-Cola and motor cycles (Oliveira 2006). Maybe it was these "weaknesses" that made Dhlakama attractive to the Rhodesian CIO and South Africa's Centre of Staff Intelligence? They certainly assisted his rise and protected him. RENAMO's first deputy Orlando Macomo disappeared in 1977, and the Rhodesians promoted Afonso Dhlakama in his place.[4] Following the death in military action inside Mozambique in October 1979 of André Matsangaissa, a leadership struggle erupted and contender Lucas Mhlanga also then disappeared by late 1980. Under orders from Dhlakama and others, MiG pilot Lieutenant Adriano Bomba, who had defected to South Africa, Bomba's brother and three others were executed in 1983 for the murder of RENAMO's first secretary general, Orlando Christina. At a hearing of the South African Truth and Reconciliation Commission (TRC) in 2000 it was revealed how South African intelligence arranged for transportation and a remote villa in Caprivi for the RENAMO leadership to try the five suspects and that South African intelligence subsequently dumped their bodies from a plane over the Atlantic Ocean off the coast of southwest Africa (Namibia) (Vines 2014).

What is not in doubt is that Rhodesian training, supplies and support and the offer of a safe haven were critical for RENAMO, which would have quickly disappeared without such support. RENAMO started small with only seventy-six fighters in 1977, growing to just over 20,000 by 1992. Over this period there were various episodes in RENAMO's evolution: the Rhodesian phase of 1977–1980; the overt South African phase of 1980–1984; the covert South African phase to 1988; the post-South African phase until 1990, by which time, according to the CIA (Central Intelligence Agency), RENAMO had become a self-sustaining fighting force; and a military stalemate and peace process phase (1990–1992) when both sides were exhausted and militarily spent.

According to Stephen Emerson, RENAMO became "addicted" to Rhodesian and later South African defense force support. He concludes that "RENAMO's military effectiveness for much of its existence was largely rooted in its Rhodesian and South African patrimony, adherence to a guerrilla warfare strategy, strong command and control and a steady source of war material" (Emerson 2013: 193).

For example, just before Zimbabwe gained independence in 1980, the management of RENAMO was turned over to South Africa's Directorate of Special Tasks (DST), which fell under the command of the Centre of Staff Intelligence. Some 45–60 tons of supplies were airlifted every month to Mozambique between 1980 and 1984 and by the mid-1980s RENAMO was getting R12–14 million in equipment. This ranged from pens and stationary to arms and ammunition – either of foreign origin or with South African identification marks removed prior to dispatch. An advanced British Racal frequency-hopping system, which the Mozambican and Zimbabwean governments could not intercept, gave RENAMO a command and control advantage until 1998 and helped it build up its own identity as it enabled RENAMO's leadership to communicate with its commanders long after apartheid South African support ended, although by 1989 the radio batteries and equipment had degenerated with significant impact on RENAMO's effectiveness.

The transfer of RENAMO to South Africa marked a turning point in the war, which soon began to escalate. The South African government used RENAMO as a tool for destabilizing Mozambique and as a counter to Mozambique's support for the African National Congress (ANC). Its aims were to destabilize Mozambique and bring FRELIMO to the negotiating table. RENAMO's strength increased between 1980 and 1982 from 1,000 to 8,000 fighters. The Rhodesians and South Africans sought to recruit discontented Mozambicans and dissidents, but RENAMO also forcibly abducted people to swell its ranks and forced recruits to commit human rights abuses as a method to buttress their loyalty.

The first combat areas were Manica and Sofala provinces, but RENAMO quickly expanded its military operations throughout most of the country. By 1982 fighting had spread to Gaza and Inhambane provinces and the country's richest province, Zambézia (Vines 1996: 22–25).

In the early 1980s, RENAMO acquired its reputation for savagery. It became particularly well known for its practice of mutilating civilian victims, including children, by cutting off ears, noses, lips and sexual organs. RENAMO also engaged in numerous attacks on civilian targets such as transportation links, health clinics and schools. A study of ex-combatants after the war in 1997 showed that 87% of RENAMO soldiers had been forced recruits, also supported by more recent studies and interviews with ex-RENAMO leaders (Dolan and Schafer 1997; Hultman 2009).

FRELIMO made a bid to end the war in 1984 when it signed the Nkomati non-aggression pact with South Africa, followed by proximity talks in 1985 with RENAMO, but both failed and the war continued. Indeed, RENAMO changed its military strategy as South Africa's DST significantly reduced its covert aid to the rebels, and prior to the Nkomati Accord had airlifted into Mozambique significant amounts of supplies to help RENAMO become more self-sustainable. Rather than relying on rear bases in South Africa, RENAMO would now have to provision itself from the local population and replenish its arms supplies from captured weaponry. RENAMO also moved away from attacking military targets in favor of attacking "soft" civilian targets. It also began to exercise greater control over populated areas and to engage in looting and pillaging on a wider scale (Vines 1996: 22–25).

By 1986, RENAMO units had pushed deep into Zambézia province. At one point it appeared as if RENAMO would capture the city of Quelimane, cutting the country into two (Manjate 2013: 250). More Tanzanian and Zimbabwean troops were brought in to help regain territory lost to RENAMO (Hall and Young 1997: 191–192). During this period, Mozambique's first president, Samora Machel, was killed in a mysterious plane crash and Joaquim Chissano, Mozambique's foreign minister since independence, became president. This led to a series of reforms, and ultimately peace negotiations with RENAMO that began in 1990.

Peace negotiations

By late 1988, it became clear that there could be no military solution to the war. President Chissano met South African President Botha at Songo in Tete province in September 1988 and secured a pledge that Pretoria would abide by the 1984 Nkomati Accord. Unlike the previous South African pledge, this one seems to have been largely honored. Chissano also gave senior church leaders permission to open direct contacts with RENAMO. A breakthrough came in February 1989 at a meeting in Nairobi and, following several failed initiatives and false starts, direct RENAMO-FRELIMO peace talks eventually began in Rome in July 1990 mediated by the Sant'Egidio Catholic lay community (Vines and Wilson 1997: 137–139).

Widespread famine injected a new urgency into the peace process in 1991 and 1992 as the war prevented provision of adequate relief to the needy population. As drought spread, RENAMO's ability to live off the land steadily collapsed and it became increasingly desperate in its search for food. During 1991 and 1992 negotiations between FRELIMO and RENAMO occurred intermittently while fighting continued across Mozambique. RENAMO was again on the offensive in the south, nightly attacking the suburbs of Maputo. After twelve often torturous rounds of negotiations, a ceasefire was eventually signed in Rome on 4 October 1992 between President Joaquim Chissano and RENAMO leader Afonso Dhlakama.

Paradoxically, climatic disaster provided a window of opportunity in the peace process. With RENAMO increasingly hungry and finding external supply sources drying up, peace looked increasingly attractive (Vines 1996: 142). FRELIMO too was exhausted militarily; both sides had reached a stalemate and needed an agreement.

In the only serious violation of the ceasefire, between 17 and 20 October 1992 RENAMO forces unexpectedly occupied four towns but the government retook them within a month. The then UN Special Representative Aldo Ajello recalled meeting RENAMO leader Dhlakama in Maringue and pointing out that there was little benefit from his aggressive approach, and that "Now Mozambican people want to know if you also have wisdom". At the end of the meeting Dhlakama concluded: "Wisdom, not muscle", and promised, "No more attacks. Even if I am provoked, and I know I will be, I will not react".[5] He kept his word up to 2013.

Under the terms of the General Peace Accord (GPA), demobilized RENAMO forces and government troops were to form a 30,000-strong army. Subsequently it was agreed that a United Nations Operation in Mozambique (ONUMOZ) force of up to 7,500 personnel would oversee the transition period. Multiparty elections were to follow once demobilization was complete and voters were registered.

According to the GPA this termination of armed conflict would consist of four phases: the ceasefire; the separation of forces; the concentration of forces for a new army; and demobilization. Disarmament would also be an integral part of this process. One week after the GPA was signed the UN Security Council approved ONUMOZ (Vines 1995: 17).

Demobilization and reintegration of ex-combatants

The implementation of most of the key provisions of the GPA was placed in the hands of the UN. According to UN Security Council Resolution 797, ONUMOZ was to perform a series of tasks including monitoring and verifying the implementation of the ceasefire, such as monitoring the retreat of Malawian and Zimbabwean units from Beira, Limpopo and Nacala transport corridors and protecting these corridors with its own forces.

In order to fulfil its mandate, ONUMOZ was provided with both civilian and military departments. ONUMOZ was mandated to monitor the cantonment, disarmament and demobilization of nearly 110,000 combatants from both sides, as well as the creation of the new army and the resettlement of 5–6 million refugees and displaced people. The cost was estimated to be US$331 million ($1 million per day) until 31 November 1993 (Synge 1997).

Demobilization and the new army The creation of a new Mozambican army, the Armed Forces for the Defense of Mozambique (FADM), was central to the peace process. It was intended that it should be in place before the elections and be an effective stabilizing force once the UN pulled out after the 1994 elections.

The question of how many soldiers would be part of the new army had been the main military point of discussion during the protracted peace negotiations in Rome. The government favored a larger army, RENAMO a smaller one. Both sides in Rome eventually agreed that the new FADM army would number 30,000, recruiting 15,000 from each side (McMullin 2004: 629).

The plan to have a 30,000-strong army on the ground before the October elections (thus putting into practice one of the lessons drawn from the failure of the Angola process) was not achieved. As the year progressed, discipline broke down in both armies, and a wave of mutinies struck government and RENAMO Assembly Areas (AA) alike. In the end 12,195 soldiers (8,533 from the FAM/FPLM and 3,662 from RENAMO) were selected for the FADM – about 5% of all soldiers in the AAs. But since this number included far too many mid-level officers, even some of the volunteers had to be demobilized, bringing the total initial troop strength of the FADM down to 11,579.

RENAMO soldiers appeared more willing to enlist into the new army than their government counterparts; for many it would be their first ever opportunity to earn a salary and their politicians had also promised them vastly improved conditions under a RENAMO government. Some simply lacked the qualifications. RENAMO sought funds in 1995 for driving lessons for its long-time military chief of staff General Faustino Adriano, to make him more employable.

Reintegration of ex-combatants Unlike demobilization, which ended in late August 1994, the social and economic reintegration of demobilized combatants was an open-ended process. To assist this, a reintegration support scheme (RSS) of monthly support for two years in cash, to be paid for six months by the government and eighteen months by the donor community, was instituted in early 1994. Demobilizing soldiers were given an introductory course about their rights and duties as civilians and were offered vocational training. They also had to choose the place they wanted to go and received a package of civilian clothing and transport to their chosen destination. The monthly sum was related to their last salary and paid into a local bank, although this was difficult for RENAMO. It was between $7 and $24 a month on average and a lump sum of $52 for all at the end. The RRS aimed to "pay them and scatter them" over a relatively short period to remove them from the conflict equation (McMullin 2004: 627–629).

By 1996, 87% of demobilized soldiers had been integrated into society; most of them had secured a food supply or small guaranteed income. Overall, ex-soldiers were reintegrating quickly. Many married, and depended on the income of their wives. This suggested that the RSS approach worked well, although there were some problems with implementation, especially delays in distribution and confusion over procedure. Training courses were less successful, and in some instances raised unrealistic expectations of employment prospects (McMullin 2004: 629).

The total reintegration budget was US$94.4 million; $35.5 million of this was allocated to support two years of cash for registered ex-combatants, of which $33.7 million went directly to demobilized soldiers. According to an evaluation for UNDP (United Nations Development Program), the overhead was low at 2.5% and cash and material benefits for all demobilized soldiers should be the base of all reintegration programs (Barnes 1997). In the end, some 92,000 soldiers benefited, about 71,000 from the government forces and 21,000 from RENAMO.

RENAMO combatants also complained at the time of exclusion from full reintegration benefits because they were not eligible for pensions as they had not had pension allowances deducted from their salaries like government troops. The Mozambican Demobilized Soldiers' Association (Associação Moçambicana dos Desmobilizados da Guerra, AMODEG), tried to assist, but its dependence on state funding made it less supportive of ex-RENAMO combatants in their efforts to reintegrate (Schafer 1998).

RENAMO proposed extending pension benefits to its soldiers as they had not been paid salaries during the war, but FRELIMO opposed it. FRELIMO used the pension debate to demonstrate its political strength. This issue resurfaced in the 2003 municipal elections and in the 2004 national elections but with little impact (McMullin 2004: 627–629). However, it became one of the triggers for renewed armed conflict by RENAMO in 2013.

Disarmament One of the surprises of the 2013 resumption of conflict between RENAMO and the government was the availability of arms for RENAMO. According to the Mozambican Force for Crime Investigation and Social Reinsertion (FOMICRES), 3–4 million weapons were circulating at the end of the war in 1992 (Reisman and Lalá 2012). During the 1992–1994 peace process the priority of the UN Operation in Mozambique was to help RENAMO transform itself into a political party and contest national elections. The UN priority was to dismantle RENAMO's command and control structures, and also disperse ex-combatants through a pay-and-scatter program. Disarmament was not a priority for the UN. After the withdrawal of ONUMOZ in 1995, and as crime rates increased in Mozambique and across the border in South Africa, two disarmament efforts got under way – Operation Rachel (a joint Mozambican-South African police initiative) and an Arms for Tools (TAE) program run by the Christian Council of Mozambique. Operation Rachel focused on the border regions of Gaza province and Mpumalanga. By 2003 several tons of weapons had been destroyed and the TAE reported it had collected 800,000 guns and other pieces of military equipment (Reisman and Lalá 2012).

An official mediator in the RENAMO and FRELIMO standoff, Bishop Dinis Sengulane, concluded that the failure to completely disarm in 1992–1994 resulted in many individuals retaining their weapons. The fact that the equipment used in the recent conflict is in much better condition than would be expected after so many years of disuse, and that some RENAMO fighters are younger than the ex-combatants would be, demonstrated how the possession of firearms attracted other gun owners to violence (Sengulane 2014). European Union election observers also concluded that the 2014 elections were impacted by failed disarmament (European Union Election Observation Mission 2014).

The process of demobilization, disarmament and integration of RENAMO into government forces has returned as a critical issue, with RENAMO alleging discrimination against its forces. The International Observer Military Team for the Cessation of Military Hostilities (EMOCHM) that was mandated by the September 2014 agreement between President Guebuza and Dhlakama ended in May 2015 (EMOCHM 2014). It was to have been made up of observers from Botswana, South Africa, Zimbabwe, Kenya, Cape Verde, Italy, Portugal, the United Kingdom and the United States. Headed by a brigadier from Botswana, after a ten-day installation period, it had been given 135 days to complete its task of monitoring the disarming and demobilizing of RENAMO's "residual forces" and their incorporation into the FADM and the police, or their return to civilian life.

The 135 days expired in February 2015, and a dispute followed over whether to renew the EMOCHM mandate. RENAMO sought an extension of 120 days, but the government insisted on sixty. EMOCHM's mandate eventually expired, unfulfilled, on 15 May 2015 (Botswana, Italy and the United Kingdom had recalled their observers earlier in 2015, while the United States never deployed its own).

By this time, RENAMO had not delivered a list of those it wished to see recruited into the FADM and the police, and the observers had little to observe – although the government said in October 2014 that it was prepared to incorporate into the armed forces and police 300 men from RENAMO's militia (200 and 100 respectively), a figure based on past contacts with Dhlakama.

RENAMO did not want to reintegrate its residual forces and finally disarm as this would reduce its leverage over the government in its continuing effort to extract political concessions. One conclusion drawn from RENAMO's strategy since 2013 is that maintaining armed men who are prepared to challenge the government has enhanced RENAMO's political standing in the short term and has resulted in a fresh effort to reach a new elite bargain.

Two other lessons can be drawn from the resumed violence of 2013–2014 and subsequent clashes. First, DDR (demobilization, disarmament and reintegration) efforts were not seen as an open-ended, long-term process that is not just technical and includes political inclusion. This meant that after a decade of peace, international donors concluded that Mozambique had undergone a successful post-conflict transition and that support for NGO (non-governmental organization) efforts in this field was no longer a priority.

A second lesson is that disarmament should not have been neglected and ONUMOZ missed an opportunity in this regard. After its withdrawal, the chance to disarm diminished and only a small percentage of weapons were given up through official and NGO efforts. We know today that RENAMO has maintained armed men and weapons stockpiles over twenty years. There was early warning of this, though. The NGO FOMICRES (Littlejohn 2015) located large arms caches in five districts in Sofala province, including heavy weapons, but politically it was not able to access them for destruction. RENAMO official Rahil Khan warned in January 2014 that RENAMO had arms caches across the country that it could draw upon (Agência Lusa 2014).

The origin of an armed RENAMO militia was a provision in the Rome General Peace Accords that the former rebels could maintain bodyguards (who would enjoy police status) as a "transitional guarantee" until elections in 1994. The objective was for the police then to take over these responsibilities, but Dhlakama's "bodyguards" could be given police training, if a list were provided. Although a list was eventually provided, the government insisted that once trained these men must obey police orders. In January 1998 Dhlakama, worried about losing authority over these men, categorically refused to allow his bodyguards to be incorporated into the police.

As a result, from 1994 to 2013 the Mozambican government reluctantly de facto accepted that there were several hundred armed RENAMO personnel resident in the Maringué and Cheringoma districts of Sofala province, who occasionally paraded with weapons and intimidated local FRELIMO activists (Xinhua News Agency 2005). A small group of them also escorted Dhlakama and provided security for his house in Nampula as his "presidential guard". They were poorly uniformed, with shoes falling apart and brandishing old weapons.[6] The government warned that it wished to disarm this "presidential guard" completely, and offered to integrate it with the national police force but, as mentioned, this offer was rejected. A further opening to reintegrate some of this RENAMO militia emerged from the September 2014 agreement which temporarily halted hostilities (as discussed above), but it depended on their fitness and the provision of a new list. That list was never forthcoming and again in 2016 "integration" of RENAMO members has been a key agenda item in the Joint Commission talks between the government and RENAMO.

Transformation into a political party

Transformation of RENAMO into a political party was supported by a UN Trust Fund which in the run-up to the 1994 election provided some $17 million to the former rebel movement. RENAMO and the government had quietly signed an agreement in December 1992 with Italy that it would provide RENAMO with $15 million and a further $17 million to be divided between all opposition parties. By March 1993 these funds had not appeared and funding and housing became a source of dispute right up to the elections with the private sector, the UN and governments contributing to the Trust Fund (Vines 1996: 152; 1998: 66-74).

As momentum towards peace negotiations increased, in 1989 RENAMO recruited between 100 and 200 secondary school students with the promise of scholarships abroad. This was an effort to increase the level of educated supporters, but backfired badly as RENAMO failed to deliver any scholarships to these recruits, who became disillusioned and felt they had been deceived. Nevertheless, despite its violent reputation during the war, RENAMO was able to attract new supporters quickly in 1993-1994, some anti-FRELIMO, many seeing opportunity. In 1995, only eighteen of RENAMO's 112 members of the National Assembly had been fighters. Even the commissions overseeing the peace process were mixed in composition, although the ex-guerrillas dominated three commissions that dealt with military issues. RENAMO's parliamentarians had few graduate educational qualifications in 1995; only 6% of RENAMO deputies have a university degree compared to 24% for FRELIMO. Eleven percent of RENAMO deputies have below a fourth grade qualification compared to 3% of FRELIMO deputies (Manning 1998: 185).

Tension between Dhlakama and ex-fighters and newer post-conflict RENAMO supporters looking for an alternative to FRELIMO has increased over time. As we will see below, this resulted in a serious of splits, with RENAMO parliamentarians at times ignoring the decrees of their leader and some newer members being more eager for conflict, having no experience of the realities of war.

Elections

RENAMO has contested all five presidential and parliamentary elections since the war ended in 1992. The October 1994 elections enjoyed high voter turnout, above 85%. The election campaign saw little violence and a low-key campaign, although there was some intimidation by both sides in their stronghold areas. The south and north voted mostly for Chissano and FRELIMO while the central provinces of Manica and Sofala were dominated by RENAMO, indicating that regional and ethnic politics played a role. The strategic provinces of Nampula and Zambézia, where 41% of the electorate were registered, gave RENAMO the advantage, but the results were close, neighboring villages often voting for opposing candidates.

Despite its handicaps, including its brutal military past, Mozambique's informal amnesty, traditional healing and forgiveness processes played a role, enabling RENAMO to compete against FRELIMO peacefully and did not appear to impact RENAMO's appeal to voters in central and northern Mozambique.

RENAMO was visibly weakened after the 2009 elections. The new parliament was dominated by FRELIMO, which had won 75% of the votes and had majorities in all former RENAMO strongholds. Positions in the National Assembly were allocated to parties in proportion to their number of parliamentary seats.

	1994	1999	2004	2009
J. Chissano (FRELIMO)	53.4%	52.4%	–	–
A. Guebuza (FRELIMO)	–	–	63.6%	75%
A. Dhlakama (RENAMO)	33.7%	47.7%	31.7%	16.41%

Table 4.1 Presidential elections in Mozambique, 1994–2009 (%)
Source: Boletins da República & Comissão Nacional de Eleições de Moçambique.

Candidate	Party	Votes received	Percentage
Afonso Dhlakama	RENAMO	1,800,448	36.60%
Filipe Nyusi	FRELIMO	2,803,536	57.00%
Daviz Simango	MDM	314,759	6.40%
Null votes		157,174	2.93%
Blank votes		300,412	5.59%

Table 4.2 2014 Presidential election results
Source: Conselho Constitucional (2014).

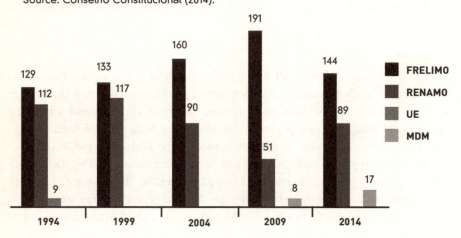

Figure 4.1 Parliamentary seats (1994–2014)
Source: Comissão Nacional de Eleições de Moçambique (2014).

For a while in the 1990s RENAMO became the largest opposition party in Africa, overtaken by Zimbabwe's Movement for Democratic Change (MDC) in 2002. RENAMO won the overall vote and the majority in five provinces in both the 1994 and 1999 elections. Its popularity at that time surprised many observers because of its atrocious record of human rights abuses during the war. Its support indicated discontent at continued domination by FRELIMO and that the country was still divided and the wounds of the civil war are yet to fully heal. Following the 1999 elections and up to 2014 RENAMO was declining as an opposition party, as Figure 4.1 shows, and it was not able to significantly challenge FRELIMO's hegemony.

Successful demobilization, poverty, lack of service delivery and conflict weariness contributed to an increasing disillusionment among grassroots RENAMO supporters and to protest against an increasingly distant leadership by Afonso Dhlakama.

After the 1994 and 1999 election results, where RENAMO's vote held up and Dhlakama came close to (or even beat) Chissano's support, FRELIMO concluded that RENAMO posed an electoral risk, as Tables 4.1 and 4.2 indicate.[7] The response was to more aggressively counter RENAMO, which at times included intimidation and harassment of its supporters, especially during electoral cycles. There have been electoral irregularities in the 1999, 2004, 2008 and 2014 elections. Indeed, the 2004 election was marred by misconduct including widespread ballot box stuffing which may have cost RENAMO at least two parliamentary seats.

RENAMO's task has not been helped by its lack of skilled cadres. Although it attracted fresh blood following the end of the conflict, this created tension, particularly among those who had remained loyal supporters during the years in the bush. RENAMO's poverty and inability to deliver on wartime promises contributed to a weakening support base. Carrie Manning noted that this decline was already visible in 1995. She observes that:

> However, it is important to note that the reintegration process proceeded
> haltingly in all areas, and was held up as much by government stiffening
> the requirements for entry into certain posts as it was by Renamo's inability
> to provide the government with accurate and timely data on its education,
> health, and administrative personnel. Government officials hung back while
> Renamo teachers and health workers blocked services to Renamo areas
> until local populations became impatient of Renamo. This strategy deprived
> Renamo of both patronage (in the form of civil service jobs) and of local
> popular support. By the end of 1995, Renamo was beginning to lose ground
> among formerly supportive populations by refusing to allow qualified
> government teachers and health personnel to come into its zones. For its
> part, Renamo was torn between not wanting to yield control of its areas and

its personnel, and the need for the patronage that state jobs represented. (Manning 1998: 185)

Between 1999 and 2004, RENAMO received about $1.4 million per year from the state, but almost half of this is unaccounted for (Carbone 2005: 431). Hardly any of these funds trickled down to the districts and with the fall in the number of RENAMO seats from ninety to fifty-one, the subsidy fell too, putting a severe financial squeeze on the party since it had never established effective collection of membership dues, and ran few businesses that could raise funds.

RENAMO's three peacetime national conferences, in Quelimane in February 1995 and in Nampula in October 2001 and July 2009, failed to modernize the party. Key appointments were still made by Dhlakama, not by free election (Manning 2002: 155–158). In 2001 Dhlakama, standing against Agostinho Murrial and Manuel Perreira, was overwhelmingly re-elected as party president by a Congress of some 700 delegates; the most significant outcome was a new National Council being elected, with its membership expanded from between ten and twelve up to sixty provincial delegates with an eye to improving RENAMO's electoral fortunes in the 2003 local elections. RENAMO's July 2009 Congress achieved even less, with Dhlakama re-elected as party leader until 2014 by 296 votes to ten for Rogério Francisco João Vicente, who appears to have been a symbolic contender with little profile even within the party (O País 2009). RENAMO did not boycott the 15 October 2014 national elections and in June 2014 its National Council met in Beira and was addressed by a twenty-two-minute phone call from Dhlakama (who was in hiding in central Mozambique at the time) and was unanimously voted in as RENAMO's leader and presidential candidate.

Although RENAMO has occasionally successfully organized protests such as the boycott of the 1998 municipal elections and public demonstrations against the 1999 election results, these did not result in concessions or a material improvement in its fortunes. In November 2000 RENAMO staged demonstrations throughout the country claiming that the 1999 election results were fraudulent. This led to violence, resulting in forty people killed and over a hundred injured during bloody clashes, particularly in Montepuez in the northern province of Cabo Delgado, although in some parts of the country, such as in the capital Maputo, demonstrations took place peacefully. This resulted in arrests, a crackdown and President Chissano cancelled an international trip in order to oversee efforts to calm the situation (AIM Reports 2000).

In 2003 RENAMO did contest the elections for control of thirty-three municipalities and successfully returned mayors in Beira, Ilha de Moçambique, Marromeu, Nacala and Angoche and won some 40% of the vote in Nampula, Quelimane and Chimoio.

However, in the 2008 municipal elections, RENAMO did not win control of a single municipality; four of its municipalities were won by FRELIMO and Beira was won by Daviz Simango (standing as an independent candidate). Dhlakama boasted at the time that he would swear the defeated RENAMO candidates into office to run parallel municipal administrations, but no such parallel administrations ever existed.

Province	2014			2009			
	FRELIMO	RENAMO	MDM	FRELIMO	RENAMO	MDM	PDD
Cabo Delgado	67	14	1	73	8	–	–
Gaza	69	–	1	80	–	–	–
Inhambane	58	11	1	80	–	–	–
Manica	40	39	1	61	19	–	–
Maputo -Provincia	59	12	9	75	5	–	–
Nampula	46	46	1	77	12	2	–
Niassa	42	34	4	66	2	2	–
Sofala	30	45	7	59	1	20	–
Tete	37	42	3	70	10	–	–
Zambézia	37	51	4	58	31	–	1

Table 4.3 Composition of provincial assemblies, number of seats (2009–2014)
Source: Conselho Constitucional (2014); Comissão Nacional de Eleições (2014).

After RENAMO's defeat in the 2009 presidential and parliamentary elections, Dhlakama regularly threatened to hold nationwide demonstrations against what he claimed were fraudulent election results but not a single RENAMO demonstration was staged. Dhlakama also announced that the RENAMO deputies elected in 2009 would boycott the new parliament, but all the RENAMO deputies including their secretary general defied him and took up their seats, anxious to claim their allowances.

Dhlakama's strategy between 1994 and 2014 was to regularly obstruct parliament or force decisions out of it and seek a high-level bilateral negotiation between both leaderships. There was little vision beyond oppositionist politics, and with RENAMO's electoral weakening until 2014 the bargaining power of Dhlakama was greatly reduced. FRELIMO and RENAMO delegations met in March 2011 and RENAMO raised concerns over the partisan nature of the police and the state, and the fight against electoral fraud. Dhlakama threatened that if he did not win concessions from these talks he planned to remove FRELIMO from power in just one day. However, FRELIMO said that there were no negotiations, merely a dialogue between the two parties, and clearly Dhlakama was unable to back up his threat.

RENAMO party networks are weak and the inability of Dhlakama to transform from an insecure, centralizing guerrilla leader contributed significantly to RENAMO's pre-2014 decline. Michel Cahen, who accompanied Dhlakama during his 1994 election campaign, noted soon afterwards, "Renamo's poor campaigning … was, in my opinion Renamo's greatest frailty and it comes in large part from the highly centralised and personalised aspect of the party" (Cahen 1998: 20). In 2011 Cahen further concluded that "Big men are not a guarantee. Renamo appeared and grew as a phenomenon used by part of the population as a tool to express their wish for another kind of state, far from Frelimo's authoritarian modernization process" (Cahen 2011: 12).

Between 1999 and 2013 the party was also marked by visible squabbling and internecine conflict. Fearful of being eclipsed by others, Dhlakama has moved against RENAMO officials that have become successful without his patronage. For example, after the December 1999 elections, Raúl Domingos suddenly lost his post as head of the parliamentary group, to be replaced by the unknown Ossufo Quitine (Slattery 2003: 129). Raúl Domingos had been a key guerrilla fighter since 1980 and became second-in-charge after Dhlakama and chief negotiator during the Rome peace talks. He was leader of the parliamentary group from 1994 to 1999, and made this one of the few relatively competent sections of RENAMO, overshadowing the chaotic party structure and weak presidency office headed by Dhlakama.

FRELIMO capitalized on these internal tensions. There followed, from February to May 2000, a series of contacts between Domingos and Transport Minister Tomás Salomão, which RENAMO presented as "negotiations" with the government over the 1999 election results. However, President Chissano claimed that Domingos had complained that he felt persecuted within RENAMO, and might need government protection; and that Domingos had asked for US$500,000 dollars to pay off a debt, $1 million for RENAMO, and a salary of $10,000 a month for Dhlakama. Domingos denied the president's version of events, but admitted he had been negotiating on behalf of RENAMO. He was suspended from RENAMO's National Council, from its Political Committee, and from the Standing Commission of the Mozambican parliament and in September 2000 he was expelled from the party (Carbone 2005: 129).

Raúl Domingos reflects the fact that Dhlakama had become increasingly out of touch with the politics of peacetime Mozambique:

> Dhlakama did not like that I was increasingly referred to as RENAMO's second in command by ambassadors and commentators because of my efforts in the National Assembly. His mistake was to refuse to engage in

parliamentary politics. He never stood for office and increasingly became jealous of me. During the war, he was never insecure in this way.[8]

Dhlakama quickly took the opportunity to get rid of his rival and his departure deprived the party of one of its most effective members, who had led its technocratic wing. Domingos subsequently launched his own political party, the Party for Peace, Democracy, and Development (Partido Para a Paz Democracia e Desenvolvimento, PDD) but has not won a seat in any election since 2004. He has said that if Dhlakama left RENAMO's leadership he might rejoin the party.[9]

There were demonstrations by demobilized RENAMO ex-combatants outside RENAMO's October 2001 Congress, which Dhlakama blamed on mischief-making by Raúl Domingos. Joaquim Vaz, the secretary general of the party, was also forced to resign in July 2002 after a year in the post because of his friendship with Raúl Domingos. Dhlakama took over as secretary general and combined it with that of party leader until RENAMO's National Council elected Viana Magalhaes as the party's new secretary general in November 2002. He was replaced by Ossufo Momade as secretary general in April 2005, followed by Manuel Bissopo, who was elected in July 2012. From May 2009 Dhlakama relocated permanently from Maputo to the northern city of Nampula. He defended his decision to move to the Nampula, saying:

> My move to Nampula is to be closer to the electorate. It is easier for me
> to lead RENAMO from Nampula and shows my authority as leader of the
> opposition. FRELIMO, even you have to come from London to see me here
> in Nampula. As you know I am the Father of Democracy in Mozambique,
> I brought peace and defeated the FRELIMO communists. They continue to
> want to deny democracy here using fraud; we will be planning nationwide
> protests they seriously negotiate with us. RENAMO is still strong despite
> these Marxist efforts to deny us. We are planning to train up our grass root,
> and will have a training course for them in March 2011. You asked me about
> Raúl [Domingos], he left RENAMO and has set up his own party and lost
> elections twice. In a democracy, splits happen, he has a different vision.
> MDM [Movimento Democrático de Moçambique] is not RENAMO, but
> some of our people have been confused and supported Simango. You know,
> when you are in intensive care and on life support, you do not rule in or out
> anything. We will consider any alliance that makes sense for us to continue
> our sacred role as the guardians of democracy in Mozambique.[10]

Dhlakama finally met President Guebuza in Nampula on 8 December 2011 for the first time since Guebuza's first-term inauguration as President of the Republic in 2005.[11] After this meeting Dhlakama said a working group would be established to examine RENAMO's concerns but he also continued to threaten anti-government demonstrations. Then on 8 March 2012 an armed confrontation erupted outside RENAMO's provincial offices in Nampula between government riot police, some 300 RENAMO ex-combatants and Dhlakama's armed "Presidential Guard", resulting in two deaths, injuries and thirty-four arrests. Some 400 former RENAMO guerrillas had assembled in Nampula in December 2011 after being called on by Dhlakama to take part in protests but had begun drifting home, some of them claiming they had been promised demobilization pay.

On 17 April 2012, President Guebuza met Dhlakama again for two hours in the Nampula provincial government. The men exchanged phone numbers and agreed to meet again. This meeting seemed to temporarily reduce tensions, but then in October 2012 Dhlakama left Nampula for Satunjira, Gorongosa, in central Mozambique, near Casa Banana, a guerrilla base that served as RENAMO's headquarters during the early 1980s. The date and place were significant: Satunjira was a former RENAMO military base and Dhlakama timed his arrival to commemorate the anniversary of the death of RENAMO's founder, André Matsangaissa, killed by FRELIMO during military action near Santunjira on 17 October 1979.

Armed attacks started in April 2013. Government riot police (FIR) raided RENAMO local headquarters in Muxúnguè and Gondola, Manica province and made arrests. RENAMO retaliated by attacking Muxungué police station, killing four members of the FIR and injuring at least nine; one RENAMO attacker was also killed. On 5 April 2013, RENAMO attacked traffic on the main north–south EN1 road for the first time. In June 2013 the government introduced military convoys along a 100 kilometer stretch of road between the River Save and Muxungué because of the number of attacks (these convoys continued until 28 August 2014).

Political tensions deepened on 21 October 2013, when FADM occupied the Satunjira base after RENAMO had again congregated there to commemorate the anniversary of the death of Matsangaissa. Dhlakama and his secretary general, Manuel Bissopo, escaped but Armindo Milaco, a member of parliament and RENAMO head of mobilization, was killed. Dhlakama fled to another base deep in the Serra da Gorongosa and the FADM moved on to occupy another RENAMO base, Maringué, which had remained a location for armed RENAMO men with tacit acceptance by the government since 1994.

After Satunjira RENAMO launched more attacks on traffic on the EN1 south of Muxungué and around Gorongosa and tried to open new fronts in Nampula, Inhambane and Tete provinces, resulting in deaths and injuries.[12] Much of the armed action remained in central Mozambique but in January 2014 RENAMO attempted to expand its operations by sending armed men into Homoine district, Inhambane province. In April 2014, attacks on the railway and trains carrying coal from Tete to Beira port was a major escalation and caught the attention of the international markets for the first time.

However, in early May, as peace talks progressed, RENAMO announced a ceasefire along EN1 to assist election registration efforts in central Mozambique for the October national elections. This included Dhlakama, who registered with a special mobile registration brigade near Gorongosa on 8 May. Fighting did take place between RENAMO and FADM near Mocuba in Zambézia on 15 May, and attacks by RENAMO along EN1 resumed on 2 June and lasted to 30 June 2014. The final RENAMO armed incident in 2014 was on 1 July in Condue, Mwanza, Sofala province along the railway (see Figure 4.2).

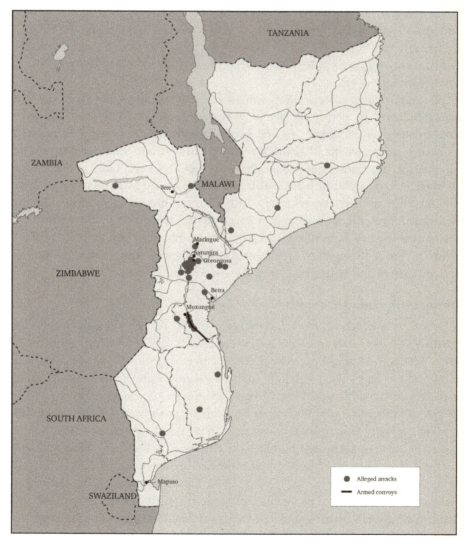

Figure 4.2 Armed clashes (April 2013 to July 2014)
Source: From @Verdade, AIM.

This was followed by RENAMO and the government agreeing a ceasefire at the seventy-fourth round of negotiations on 24 August 2014 in Maputo. Finally, Dhlakama agreed to leave his hiding place in central Mozambique and traveled to Maputo on 4 September; on 5 September President Guebuza and Dhlakama met in Maputo and formally signed the agreement ending the hostilities. During 2013 at least sixty people were killed and more than 300 injured in fighting. There are no accurate comparable figures for 2014, but observers believe the total was less than 100, mainly injured, while in 2015 the figure was some twenty killed and fifty injured.

In early 2015 RENAMO again threatened conflict if it did not obtain concessions from the government. On 2 April the FADM and RENAMO exchanged fire in Guija district, Gaza province. Dhlakama confirmed the incident, saying that 150 RENAMO troops had moved south (many of them aged forty and over).

Accurate figures of how many armed men Dhlakama remobilized are not available but they were probably only in the hundreds. Many of these were ex-combatants from central Mozambique, although some younger fighters seem to have been drawn to RENAMO by the fighting. Their tactics were repeats of classic low-intensity guerrilla ambushes that RENAMO had conducted up to 1992, such as ambush, hit and run and disruption of infrastructure such as digging large trenches across roads. RENAMO's ability to successfully disrupt was aided by weak government forces, unable to respond efficiently with counterinsurgency operations in central Mozambique. Although RENAMO tried to spread its military operations outside central Mozambique, this was less successful and better contained by government forces.

Drivers for renewed conflict

What many observers missed, however, is the post-war relationships between RENAMO's low- and mid-ranked veterans and its leadership. Studies in West Africa show that long after a conflict is over, military networks remain involved in a myriad of activities such as election campaigning, illicit trade, private security, mining and criminality (Thémner 2012). In Mozambique, with RENAMO's fortunes rapidly degrading, Dhlakama showed that he could still remobilize aging ex-combatants and arm them twenty years after the conflict ended because of patronage politics. The dependency between Dhlakama and core followers in central Mozambique was breaking down and in 2012 he moved back to shore up support (Wiegink 2015). A Dutch anthropologist who spent several years in this area estimates that some 3,000 RENAMO ex-combatants lived in Maringué district and that they had been "waiting" for the party to provide them benefits, although this estimate is in fact more likely for the whole of Sofala province (Wiegink 2013). This is a reminder of how Mozambique's politics can be localized, and that while RENAMO was unable to return to full conflict its structures remained intact enough in central Mozambique to return to limited violence.

The confrontation also grew out of RENAMO's rejection of electoral laws approved in parliament. During the extended debate on the electoral laws in 2012, RENAMO consistently demanded the right to have veto power in the National Elections Commission (CNE). Tensions had risen because of municipal elections in November 2013 and national presidential and parliamentary elections in October 2014.

Municipality	2013		2003	
	FRELIMO	MDM	FRELIMO	RENAMO
Lichinga	66.00%	34.00%	69%	31.30%
Pemba	74.10%	25.90%	66.9%	28.90%
Nampula City	46.80%	53.20%	57.1%	42.90%
Quelimane	31.80%	68.20%	52.6%	44.60%
Tete	65.70%	34.30%	75.1%	24.90%
Chimoio	53.10%	46.90%	60.2%	39.80%
Beira	29.50%	70.40%	42.2%	53.40%
Maxixe	73.20%	26.80%	87.9%	12.10%
Xai-Xai	80.10%	19.90%	95.4%	4.60%
Matola	56.50%	43.50%	88.5%	11.50%
Maputo City	58.40%	40.00%	75.2%	12.00%

Table 4.4 Municipal election results: 2013 compared with 2003 (%)
Source: Comissão Nacional de Eleições de Moçambique (2014).

RENAMO's boycott of the 20 November 2013 municipal elections backfired spectacularly, although at local level in Quelimane and Nampula RENAMO supporters tactically voted for the Mozambique Democratic Movement (MDM), a splinter party from RENAMO. FRELIMO won forty-nine mayoral seats and MDM four, including Beira, Quelimane and Nampula. MDM managed to secure 365 (30%) of 1,216 municipal assembly seats overall and its candidates took more than 40% of the vote in thirteen municipalities, including in the FRELIMO heartlands of Maputo and Matola, a feat never achieved by RENAMO, as Table 4.4 illustrates. This was the first time that the MDM contested municipal polls nationwide, and the results show that the party can campaign at the national level and attract support from urban areas outside Beira and Quelimane.[13]

There were only isolated violent incidents at the 2014 elections, demonstrating that RENAMO and FRELIMO remain the primary political players in Mozambique that can control their supporters (European Union Election Observation Mission 2014). Given that the elections followed eighteen months of targeted armed violence, this was an achievement and shows that peace can prevail when the leadership has political will. But electoral participation did not increase and was around 48.6% compared with 87% in 1994. Since then there has been a growing trend of indifference; more than half of registered voters (55.27%) ignored the 2009 elections.

Similarly, as after previous elections, the judiciary rejected opposition claims of irregularities on procedural grounds, such as vote counting and tabulation, but there were clearly irregularities and fraud. Although no significant evidence has been provided to conclude that it was on a scale that had affected the overall result of a FRELIMO presidential victory and parliamentary majority, fraud and incompetence by the electoral commission did occur. The opposition parties are also at fault for being unable to provide credible evidence of wide-spread fraud despite having deployed electoral observers across the country. The European Union Election Observation Mission concluded in their final report that the "opposition parties were unprepared and lacked organization and capable party structures to fully implement and benefit from the new [electoral] arrangement" (European Union Election Observation Mission 2014: 5) that RENAMO had pushed for. The result is suspicion, conspiracy and allegations, and this has contributed to deepening political suspicion between FRELIMO and opposition parties. Lessons from the 2014 elections are that the electoral legislation should be amended to provide a clear system of complaints and appeals and that judges, electoral managing bodies and political parties need training in how to use these procedures. There also needs to be efficient training on counting and tabulation procedures.

RENAMO has rejected all election results since 1994 but the 1999 and 2009 elections were particularly controversial. The perception of unfairness and irregularities in elections is not new, but on the latest occasion, due to the 2013–2014 outbreak of armed violence, it was important for reconciliation that the process was at least perceived to be better than in the past. This did not occur and stands in contrast with the credible presidential elections in 2014 and 2015 in neighboring Malawi and Zambia, where the electoral process and institutions were credible and showed independence.

RENAMO's strong performance, with Dhlakama winning a majority of the vote in five provinces (Nampula, Zambézia, Tete, Manica and Sofala), was surprising, not least because of his late start to campaigning.[14] Election campaigning began on 31 August 2014 and ran for forty-five days but Dhlakama did not begin until 16 September in Chimoio. Despite this, RENAMO rallies attracted large crowds and Dhlakama realized not only that targeted violence forced FRELIMO's hand into negotiations but also that its supporters rewarded it for this. Youth attended RENAMO rallies in large numbers and it seems they were attracted by the party offering an anti-establishment alternative, especially as FRELIMO officials are increasingly seen as self-enriching and not concerned with the poor. Media focus on Dhlakama also helped, especially as other parties such as MDM got little national coverage.

RENAMO's better showing has strengthened Dhlakama's position in the party and there are no longer calls for him to step down. RENAMO also believes that calculated armed violence has restored greater parity with FRELIMO, brought about concessions and marginalized the threat posed by MDM.

So some of the key drivers for resumed conflict from 2013 were:

- RENAMO veteran fighters: In 2011 the parliament approved FRELIMO-proposed legislation providing pensions for civil war veterans, although it did not win the support of RENAMO. Despite good intentions, the law raised unfulfilled expectations. The bureaucratic and lengthy process rekindled feelings of discrimination among RENAMO veterans, leading them to mobilize and pressure their leadership to do the same.
- Dhlakama: In 2016 Afonso Dhlakama, RENAMO leader since 1980, was sixty-three. His relative youth, by regional standards, means there is little discussion of a potential successor. Dissent against him can lead to expulsion, as with Raúl Domingos.[15] Dhlakama has also proved to be a poor negotiator, inconsistent and holding out for maximum concessions, using boycotts and threats.
- Guebuza: FRELIMO on several occasions "negotiated" with RENAMO concessions, resulting in financial compensation or electoral legislation amendments (Vines 2013). During Guebuza's tenure as president, he was less amenable to granting such concessions. It might also be that Guebuza wanted to extend his term in office by encouraging an armed standoff with RENAMO in 2013 and early 2014 until coming under internal and regional pressure to reach agreement in 2014.
- RENAMO's financial crisis and lack of accountability: Losing MPs in the 2009 election and being without local government representation further damaged RENAMO's already fragile finances. Leadership secrecy over party finances and patronage has been the norm since 1994. Dhlakama himself has faced allegations of misuse and greed, to which he replied that he never wanted to be an MP (Cahen 2011).
- The younger RENAMO generation: RENAMO does not have formal youth structures like FRELIMO and MDM but there are several important leaders who are not from the civil war generation, such as Manuel Bissopo, Ivone Soares, Saimon Macuiane and Eduardo Namburete. They are now in their thirties and forties, and some of them believe that FRELIMO will never be made to cede power without the use of force.
- Promise of riches: In 2012–2013 Mozambique's politicians but also private companies and the press talked up the prospects of Mozambique becoming rich on coal, oil and gas. This increased pressure on Dhlakama to act

radically and not just seek small cash handouts through an elite bargain. The political dangers of not managing the expectations of riches from natural resource endowments, highlighted by scholars such as Michael Ross, seem to be playing out now in Mozambique following the discovery of world-class gas fields (Ross 2012: 149–151).

During 114 rounds of talks with the government (between April 2013 and August 2015), RENAMO obtained concessions over politicization of the electoral system and additional jobs in the military. Some of the issues on the agenda, such as the politicization of the state and the electoral system were important. In early 2014, the delegations agreed on sweeping changes to the electoral legislation, which were then rubber-stamped by the parliament. The changes granted the parliamentary political parties absolute dominance of the electoral bodies and political appointees were inserted into the electoral apparatus.

During 2014, the dialogue concentrated on the second point on the agenda, defense and security, and this led to an agreement on a cessation of hostilities, signed by Guebuza and Dhlakama on 5 September 2014. As in 1992, RENAMO also obtained an amnesty approved by parliament for crimes committed since March 2012. However, as discussed above, RENAMO has refused to hand over a list of the members of its militia whom it wishes to join FADM and the police. The transfer of "residual forces of RENAMO" into the army and the police, funds for RENAMO and reducing FRELIMO party influence in the state remain unresolved.

In March 2015 RENAMO tabled its parliamentary bill for more autonomous provincial governments, expecting it to be debated in parliament. This proposal came after Dhlakama and President Nyusi held two rounds of bilateral talks in February 2015 aimed at improving relations. Nyusi successfully convinced Dhlakama to end his boycott of parliament and table the autonomous governments bill, promising that it would be taken seriously.

In the short term this provided hope of a modus vivendi between the government and RENAMO. But from late March 2015 Dhlakama and RENAMO were threatening that if the proposal was rejected, RENAMO would implement it in the provinces regardless; political tensions increased, resulting in some armed exchanges, and Dhlakama ended RENAMO's negotiations with the government in August 2015. On 30 April 2015 parliament rejected the RENAMO proposal by 138 votes to 98. All FRELIMO deputies voted against the bill, while MDM deputies voted with RENAMO in favor. On 31 July RENAMO submitted a constitutional amendment to the National Assembly proposing that provincial governors should be appointed by elected provincial authorities, but this was also rejected by all FRELIMO deputies during a vote on 7 December 2015. RENAMO's parliamentary chief whip, Ivone Soares, claimed the voting down of the amendment "is part of a strategy to push RENAMO into war".

The autonomous regions proposal sparked a national debate and FRELIMO responded to this debate by taking the issue to its grassroots, presenting it as an effort to divide the country. In fact, the proposal advocates a dual administration for elected municipal governments where there is a mayor and an elected assembly. Dhlakama would appoint five of six "council presidents" with the approval of the assemblies, and full elections would take place at the same time as the 2019 elections. There are two particularly controversial parts of the draft bill: heads of administrative posts and localities would be named by the new "council president" and provinces would be given half of all taxes paid on minerals, gas and oil extracted from the province. RENAMO would therefore draw revenue from Nampula, Zambézia, Tete, Manica and Sofala.

Dhlakama clearly understands that he is unlikely ever to win national power through the ballot box. It is also possibly recognition of a major tactical blunder in 2000 when he turned down the chance to nominate governors. In secret negotiations with the government, RENAMO was offered a deal which its then negotiator, Raúl Domingos, supported. This was overruled by Dhlakama, who demanded the right to name governors in the six provinces where RENAMO won a majority of the votes.

The proposal was for RENAMO and FRELIMO to submit a shortlist of three candidates for Manica, Sofala and Zambézia and President Chissano would agree to appoint one RENAMO candidate of the three. In the other three provinces, Nampula, Niassa and Tete, FRELIMO and RENAMO would nominate a shortlist of three candidates in each province, and President Chissano would choose one of the candidates supported by RENAMO. The deal collapsed because Dhlakama mentioned the negotiations to the press before the negotiations were finalized and President Chissano had obtained full support from within FRELIMO. Its hardliners having got wind of the deal immediately blocked it, saying it signaled weakness and could be read as acceptance that the 1999 presidential election results were not legitimate.[16]

Dhlakama has however calculated that if RENAMO is to survive in the long term it needs to build up long-term funding. Although not a true separatist, his autonomous regions proposal is an attempt to gain concessions that will put RENAMO in control of patronage positions to draw rents.

Increased political tensions and no progress saw increased renewed armed violence from May 2015. Sporadic armed clashes in parts of Tete province from June 2015 resulted in some dead and injured and up to 11,000 Mozambicans fled and registered as refugees in Malawi by mid-2016 (although the majority had returned home to Tete by September 2016).[17] Tensions also increased in last quarter of 2015, with sporadic armed clashes also in Zambézia and Sofala provinces and more broadly political kidnapping and killing that spread further to Nampula and Niassa in 2016. Dhlakama had on 21 August 2015 threatened violence if his demands were not met and suspended direct talks with the government after 114 sessions.

Dhlakama's own vulnerability became apparent when between 12 and 25 September his security escort was involved in two armed incidents in Manica province. The 12 September incident might not have been a genuine attack as one of the vehicles in Dhlakama's convoy had a high-speed tire blow-out on the outskirts of Chibata and his escort thought they were under armed attack and responded by opening fire. The second incident at Amatongas was certainly an armed attack and resulted in the killing of between fourteen and nineteen RENAMO combatants, destruction of ten RENAMO vehicles and the death of one civilian. As happened at Satunjira in 2013, described above, it seems that hardliners in FRELIMO wanted to humiliate RENAMO and had launched an ambush. The 25 September was also symbolic, being the Mozambican Armed Forces Day (and President Nyusi was out of the country). FRELIMO (and by extension, the security forces) remain divided between Nyusi's moderate allies and hardliners aligned to the former president Armando Guebuza, who has objected to a conciliatory approach to RENAMO.

After the 25 September incident Dhlakama again went into hiding in Gorongosa but mediators and journalists arranged to meet him in the bush and escort him to Beira on 8 October. He was then in effect placed under house arrest by armed riot police and a standoff ensued between police and Dhlakama's armed guards at his Beira house on 9 October 2015. The official reason for the siege was to reclaim police weapons that RENAMO had obtained at Amatongas. Due to mediation this standoff passed without violence as Dhlakama himself recognized that bloodshed needed to be avoided, but interviews with eyewitnesses by this author suggest that this standoff could easily have become violent and resulted in the death of Dhlakama as the security forces were receiving contradictory orders from different chains of command.[18] His guards handed over their weapons and in exchange the police released eight RENAMO supporters they had detained. The Beira disarmament deal also guaranteed that his armed guards would be retrained as government police. Shortly after this Beira standoff, Dhlakama left the city and returned to the safety of the area around Satunjira.

The armed clashes since October 2015 have escalated. According to the Confederation of Mozambique Business Associations (CTA), between October 2015 and June 2016 there were 107 RENAMO attacks in which forty people were killed and seventy-nine were seriously injured. The renewed conflict since early 2015 is more serious than the 2013–2014 insurrection but RENAMO's attacks seek to be low cost and high profile, intended to frighten people and show that the government is unable to guarantee security, especially of its officials. Soft targets such as on two hospitals and health clinics in 2016 are part of this objective, as are ambushes of road convoys, including once again digging trenches across major highways. The government response has been more violent than in 2013-2014, with civilians targeted in central Mozambique and Tete province, including reports of huts and property burnt, looting, killings. This is probably also reflective of splits in government military forces, different chains of command and mixed messages on how to respond to this renewed challenge by RENAMO.

Figure 4.3 shows how much more widespread these attacks have become since hostilities resumed in 2015, and the government has had to reintroduce

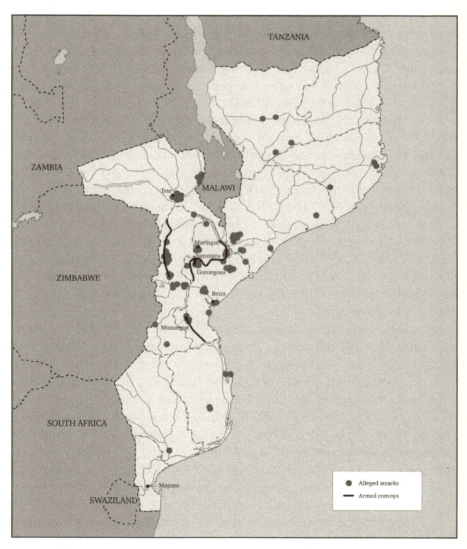

Figure 4.3 Armed incidents, July 2015–October 2016
Source: Armed Conflict Location and Event Data Project.

three armed convoy routes to protect traffic. There have also been renewed attacks on trains on the Sena line, disrupting the transport of coal from Moatize to Beira. By September 2016 violence in Manica province, along the Zimbabwe border, resulted in some 2,600 Mozambicans having fled to Zimbabwe to escape the violence.

These armed incidents and political killings, kidnappings and shootings, such as the January 2016 shooting by unidentified gunmen of RENAMO's Secretary General Bissopo in Beira, further eroded trust between the two sides. It has demonstrated RENAMO's vulnerabilities but also the splits within FRELIMO over what strategy it should adopt towards RENAMO. In October 2015 government officials announced that they would actively dismantle RENAMO's military bases and confiscate the group's weapons. It also outlined plans to accelerate the integration of RENAMO combatants into the police and military and offered wages and pensions to those individuals that disarmed voluntarily. Some RENAMO fighters responded to this and on 19 November 2015 the government suspended its forcible disarmament efforts and announced that going forward it would be voluntary. RENAMO claimed that the government's change of heart was due to its defeat of FRELIMO at the "Battle of Mathale" in Inhambane province, which might have been referring to a clash between the government's Defense and Security Forces (Forças de Defesa e Segurança, FDS) and RENAMO's armed men in Tsemane locality on 18 November 2015 which resulted in seven soldiers being injured. Meanwhile President Nyusi signaled that he still wanted a third round of direct talks with Dhlakama. Dhlakama subsequently threatened once more to take control of the six provinces where he claims RENAMO won majorities in the 2014 elections, but in June 2016 indicated that he had abandoned this plan as it would be misinterpreted.

Dhlakama had in fact responded to that in late May 2016. Discussions about talks between RENAMO and the government recommenced in Maputo and a Joint Commission was tasked with preparing a meeting between President Nyusi and himself. This resulted in two phone conversations between President Nyusi and Dhlakama in mid-June which endorsed a four-point agenda for the talks, two items from each side. RENAMO's agenda items were governing the six provinces won by RENAMO and integrating RENAMO military cadres into key positions in the armed forces, and the government's were an immediate ceasefire and the disarmament of RENAMO. The government also compromised on 7 July and agreed to international mediators (three chosen by RENAMO and three chosen by government).[19]

Since July 2016 the Joint Commission, along with the international mediators, has been working through the agenda items. The government and RENAMO have set up a sub-commission to work on constitutional amendments on decentralization. More decentralization seems inevitable and Dhlakama has demanded the power to appoint governors directly, which remains at heart a struggle for power and resources for RENAMO. Dhlakama told the press in August that the constitution must be changed to transfer power from FRELIMO governors to governors named by RENAMO, but he once again rejected suggestions for power-sharing, such as becoming vice president, because FRELIMO "is still Marxist".

Also in August the mediators also submitted a proposal for the creation of a demilitarized corridor for them to go to Gornogosa in central Mozambique to meet Dhlakama, which would require the withdrawal of government troops surrounding his base. The government rejected this, claiming that RENAMO would use the truce to reoccupy territory

The talks between the government and RENAMO are not helped by an ongoing struggle in FRELIMO over strategy. The two armed confrontations involving Afonso Dhlakama in September–October 2015 do not seem to have been mandated by the presidency, and highlight the divisions in FRELIMO, particularly between hardliners in the FRELIMO Political Commission and President Nyusi and his cabinet. The standoff outside Dhlakama's house in Beira was contrary to an agreement reached by peace mediators, who had guaranteed Dhlakama's safe passage as a buildup to a further meeting between President Nyusi and Dhlakama. It destroyed what trust was left.

Given the ongoing tussle within FRELIMO between hardliners and moderates, this process will progress slowly in fits and starts and Dhlakama has tried to moderate hardliners in RENAMO who call for direct military confrontation. Indeed, Dhlakama also faces challenges of maintaining unity over strategy and there are indications that some of his advisers have hoped to benefit from him miscalculating.

Meanwhile the security situation remains volatile, mostly driven by brinkmanship rather than brute force and mostly confined to the central provinces where RENAMO received most votes (Zambézia and Sofala), parity (Manica and Nampula) and near parity (Tete) in the October 2014 presidential and National Assembly elections. RENAMO has shown that it lacks the military capacity to sustain an insurgency across the country and there are signs of increasing fatigue among its mostly middle-aged combatants (forty- to sixty-year-olds), who want jobs and pensions and yearn for a lasting deal. It is significant that although Mozambique's youth vote for RENAMO in protest against FRELIMO, there is little evidence that significant numbers have become armed combatants. The renewed conflict since 2013 remains very much about RENAMO seeking to extract an elite bargain through violence, asserting that FRELIMO is increasingly unable to provide basic services while its leadership grows richer and inequality increases. The prospects for a durable peace settlement look at best to be a long-term prospect and will require compromise by FRELIMO and an acceptance that RENAMO has in the short term been able to capitalize on some of its shortcomings. A danger for RENAMO is that its armed militia is mostly middle-aged and that it will not be able to rely on them indefinitely to provide military backup. The party is also reliant on Dhlakama and there is no obvious successor to him as he maintains a culture of Big Man dominance and patronage over his supporters.[20]

Conclusion

RENAMO has made a remarkable journey. It was created by the Rhodesian CIO, foster-parented by apartheid South Africa and became a successful rebel movement. It limited a secure government presence to the towns, operated in all eleven provinces of Mozambique and accepted peace. The majority of RENAMO's fighters were initially forced into its service and it widely used violence and coercion in its operations. As a rebel force it was successful but ill-prepared for its transformation into a peacetime opposition political party.

Its military tactics up to the 1992 Rome GPA clearly helped bring about a negotiated settlement and introduced political pluralism to Mozambique. RENAMO also demobilized many of its ex-combatants and it would be impossible today to distinguish ex-RENAMO fighters from government troops in the new joint army, FADM. The RSS "pay them and scatter them" efforts worked well in Mozambique, especially because ex-combatants were tired of conflict and sought a civilian future. As leader of RENAMO, Dhlakama can therefore be credited with initiating this process, as well as throwing his support behind democratization. What's more, Dhlakama and RENAMO have now contested five post-conflict elections in 1994, 1999, 2004, 2009 and 2014. Remarkably, up to 2002 RENAMO was the largest opposition party in Africa, with over 100 seats in the National Assembly. This is unique in Africa and a remarkable success for a former rebel group, compared with the RUF of Sierra Leone for example.

Support for RENAMO has been in gradual decline since 1995, due to RENAMO's precarious financial situation and poor record in service delivery to the communities it represented. FRELIMO added to the difficulties, but RENAMO leader Dhlakama's inability to modernize and democratize his party in peacetime resulted in the party becoming simply oppositionist. Afonso Dhlakama continues to treat politics like combat and tries to run his party like a military movement. He became RENAMO's second leader in 1980 following a power struggle and has continued in that role for thirty-six years. In contrast there have been nine RENAMO secretary generals over the same period.[21] The militant leadership style of Dhlakama – in combination with the increased difficulties of sustaining the movement in peacetime – can thus help us understand why he went from being a supporter of the peace process, to securitizing wartime identities and eventually returning his RENAMO to armed conflict.

FRELIMO has effectively exploited this, encouraging division, such as over Raúl Domingos, and seeking to ensure that RENAMO is contained as a symbolic opposition party which poses no threat to its hegemony. For a few years it was the youthful and nimble MDM that preoccupied FRELIMO more, not RENAMO, but this changed in 2014 following RENAMO's improved showing in the elections and the armed threat it still poses in central Mozambique.

Some twenty years after the Mozambican conflict ended, although many RENAMO combatants have successfully reintegrated, a hardened core of ex-militaries remained mainly in central Mozambique and remobilized for armed conflict since 2013. The pay-and-scatter strategy and UN and other international efforts to dismantle the command and control structures of RENAMO have ensured that RENAMO could not reignite total civil war. Indeed, this remains a success story for DDR. However, this should be seen as a long-term process that is not just technical and includes political inclusion. International partners and the Mozambican government should also look at strategies to accommodate clusters of combatants that remain structured around mid- and low-level commanders.

Mozambique remains an example of mostly successful demobilization but poor elite reintegration. RENAMO's leader Afonso Dhlakama had failed to make the transition from guerrilla leader to democrat. His decision to return to targeted violence and seek concessions from that platform was rewarded by political concessions by FRELIMO and an increased number of seats in the 2014 elections. This has strengthened Afonso Dhlakama's leadership of the party in the short term.

Longer term, though, RENAMO still faces serious problems, including having held Dhlakama's leadership for thirty-six years. Mediators and negotiators to the peace talks complain that RENAMO speaks with many voices and flip-flops in its demands – a reflection of differing interests but also Dhlakama's long-established trait of indecision. It also shows a lack of vision. Dhlakama has hoped to replicate FRELIMO by setting up a neo-patrimonial system based on Big Man logic and redistribution. The gamble of targeted armed violence since 2013 was aimed at shoring up support in central Mozambique following an increased strategy of humiliation by FRELIMO under former president Guebuza. In 2015 Dhlakama also miscalculated through his absolutist tactics as these increased splits in FRELIMO over its RENAMO strategy and weakened President Nyusi's attempts to reach a lasting accommodation with him. The result by late 2015 was further direct armed confrontations including those aimed directly at the RENAMO leader and an increase in political kidnappings and killings.

FRELIMO's post-conflict strategy under Chissano was to weaken RENAMO's support base in central Mozambique through compromise, dialogue and patronage. This was abruptly ended by President Guebuza's zero-sum strategy of trying to impose total FRELIMO domination across Mozambique as RENAMO's election results in 1999 posed an existential threat to FRELIMO. Guebuza's strategy spectacularly backfired by humiliating Dhlakama and radicalizing RENAMO's ex-combatants, resulting in their pushing for a resumption of targeted armed violence. Isolated, and backed into a corner, Dhlakama felt he had nothing to lose by authorizing targeted violence.

This violence by RENAMO was rewarded in the 2014 elections, especially by voters in central Mozambique. The election results also strengthened Dhlakama's leadership position in RENAMO in the short term but it also again postponed long-needed party reform. The question still remains whether Dhlakama is able to move from being a military tactician to become a peacetime political strategist, especially if RENAMO obtains some provincial governorships. RENAMO does not promise any significant break from how FRELIMO conducts politics; in fact it is even more patrimonial in how it conducts politics and its main appeal is that it is not "the government". Dhlakama's strategy remains one of obtaining future elite bargains backed by armed violence or the threat of further violence. Comprehensive disarmament and reintegration of RENAMO's aging armed militia would end this strategy and Dhlakama is under pressure to reach a deal where he can provide patronage benefits to his supporters as most of RENAMO's armed men are middle-aged and do not to want a protracted conflict. Dhlakama clearly played an important role in bringing about the 1992 General Peace Accords but his track record since 1994 as a nimble peacetime politician, able to adapt after being an authoritarian guerrilla commander, is poor.

Notes

1 Research for this chapter benefited from a grant from the Department of War Studies, King's College London to support a visit Maputo and Nampula in September 2010. This chapter draws upon Vines (2013) and Vines et al. (2015).

2 Interview by author with Joaquim Chissano, London, 10 October 2011.

3 According to Máximo Dias, he and André Matsangaissa in Beira in late 1976 agreed to set up what became RENAMO. While André Matsangaissa in 1977 sought Rhodesian support, Dias, left for exile in Portugal and created MONAMO.

4 Dhlakama acknowledged some of the older RENAMO commanders objected to me being in the leadership (see Cabrita 2001).

5 Interview by author with Aldo Ajello, Rome, 17 October 2012.

6 Author witnessed them line up as guard of honour after his meeting with Dhlakama, Nampula, 23 September 2010.

7 Interviews by author with FRELIMO officials, Maputo, 22 September 2010.

8 Interview by author with Raúl Domingos, Rome, 17 October 2012.

9 On 4 October 2012 at a peace ceremony in Quelimane, Dhlakama effusively greeted Raúl Domingos for the first time in twelve years and both men agreed to stay in touch.

10 Interview by author with Afonso Dhlakama, Nampula, 23 September 2010. For an interview in 2009, see Reid and Wimpy (2013).

11 Dhlakama had boycotted an informal lunch that President Guebuza offered after the 2009 presidential elections. Only the second defeated

presidential candidate, Daviz Simango, leader of the MDM, accepted Geubuza's invitation.

12 According to residents of Tete province, RENAMO moved some of its armed men from central Mozambique to Tete in late 2012, to re-open armed bases with a small number of "sleeping" ex-combatants in Tete to prepare for armed action in addition to building up support networks. Interviews, Mozambique, March 2016. This pattern may also be the case in Inhambane and Dhlakama talked about "sleeping" bases in Nampula when this author interviewed him in 2010.

13 For an analysis of the impact of MDM on Dhlakama see Vines (2013: 388–389).

14 With FREELIMO's knowledge RENAMO was provided resources via the mediators to charter an aircraft to enable Dhlakama to campaign nationwide.

15 Other examples include Raimundo Samuge, Joaquim Vaz, David Aloni, Ossufu Quitine (see Diário Independente 2008).

16 Interviews with officials involved in these negotiations, Maputo, 18 March 2016.

17 Author interviews in 2016 with refugees, NGOs and officials who visited the refugees indicate that government forces violently abused communities but RENAMO also encouraged communities to flee, saying they would be safer in Malawi and would receive better food supplies. This also successfully humiliated the Mozambican government as it had demonstrated that the conflict had spread and it could not control its territory.

18 Interview with eyewitness observers, Maputo, 17 March 2016.

19 The mediators for the EU, South Africa; Vatican; Inter Mediate; Global Leadership Foundation; Tanzania

20 During interviews in Maputo in March 2016, a number of RENAMO supporters speculated that his niece, Ivone Soares, might be a possible successor. Several also mentioned that the son of RENAMO's first leader, André

Matsangaissa, was also being groomed for leadership.

21 Orlando Cristina (1981–1983); Evo Fernandes (1983–1986); post abolished (1986–1992); Vicente Ululu (1992–1995); Francisco Marcelino (1995–1998); João Alexandre (1999–2001); Joaquim Vaz (2001–2002); Viana Magalhaes (2002–2005); Ossufo Momade (2005–2012); Manuel Bissopo (2012–).

Bibliography

Agência Lusa. 2014. "Assesor da Renamo Garante Que Homens do Partido Têm Armas em Tudo o País." [Renamo Advisor Ensures that Party Men have Guns across the Country]. *Agência Lusa,* 10 January. Available from http://noticias.sapo.pt/internacional/artigo/assessor-da-renamo-garante-que-homens-do-partido-tem-armas-em-todo-o-pais_17143831.html.

AIM Reports. 2000. "Forty Dead as Renamo Clashes with Police." *AIM Reports*, No. 195, 13 November.

Armed Conflict Location and Event Data Project online database. Available from http://www.acleddata.com/.

Barnes, S. 1997. *The Socio-Economic Reintegration of Demobilised Soldiers in Mozambique.* Maputo: UNDP.

Bøås, M. and K. Dunn. 2007a. "African Guerrilla Politics: Raging Against the Machine?" In *African Guerrillas: Raging Against the Machine,* ed. M. Bøås and K. Dunn. Boulder, CO: Lynne Rienner.

Bøås, M. and K. Dunn, eds. 2007b. *African Guerrillas: Raging Against the Machine*: Boulder: Lynne Rienner.

Cabrita, J. 2001. *Mozambique: The Tortious Road to Democracy.* New York: Palgrave Macmillan.

Cahen, M. 1998. "'Dhlakama É Maningue Nice!' An Atypical Former Guerrilla in the Mozambican Electoral Campaign." *Transformation* 35: 1–48.

Cahen, M. 2011. *The Enemy as Model: Patronage as a Crisis Factor in Constructing Opposition in Mozambique.* OXPO Working Papers. Available from http://www.politics.ox.ac.uk/materials/centres/oxpo/working-papers/wp_10-11/OXPO_10-11f_Cahen.pdf.

Cann, J. P. 1997. *Counterinsurgency in Africa: The Portuguese War of War, 1961-1974*. Westport, CT: Greenwood Press.

Carbone, G. 2005. "Continuidade Na Renovação? Ten Years of Multiparty Politics in Mozambique: Roots, Evolution and Stabilisation of the Frelimo-Renamo Party System." *The Journal of Modern African Studies* 43 (3): 417-442.

Clapham, C. (ed.). 1998a. *African Guerrillas*. Oxford: James Currey.

Clapham, C. 1998b. "Introduction: Analysing African Insurgencies." In *African Guerrillas*, ed. C. Clapham. Oxford: James Currey.

Comissão Nacional de Eleições de Moçambique. 2014. "Publicação dos Resultados das Eleições Gerais e das Assembleias Provinciais." Unpublished document.

Conselho Constitucional. 2014. "Acórdão no. 21/CC/2014, de 29 de Dezembro." Maputo: Conselho Constitucional.

Diário Independente. 2008. "A Longa Lista das Vítimas do Ditador Dhlakama." [The Long List of Victims of the Dhlakama Dictator]. *Diário Independente*, 3 September. Available from http://www.open.ac.uk/technology/mozambique/sites/www.open.ac.uk.technology.mozambique/files/pics/d100061.pdf.

Dolan, C. and J. Schafer. 1997. *Reintegration of Ex-Combatants in Mozambique: Manica and Zambezia Provinces*. Refugee Studies Programme, University of Oxford.

Emerson, S. 2013. *The Battle for Mozambique: The Frelimo-Renamo Struggle, 1977-1992*, Pinetown: South Publishers.

EMOCHM (International Observer Military Team for the Cessation of Military Hostilities). 2014. *Termos de Referência da Equipa Militar de Observação Da Cessação Das Hostilidades Militares* [Terms of Reference for the Military Observation Team on the Cessation of Military Hostilities]. Available from http://www.open.ac.uk/technology/mozambique/sites/www.open.ac.uk.technology.mozambique/files/files/Renamo%20dialogo%20acordos.pdf.

European Union Election Observation Mission. 2014. *Mozambique: Final Report – General Elections, 15 October 2014*.

Flower, K. 1987. *Serving Secretly: An Intelligence Chief on the Record, Rhodesia into Zimbabwe, 1964-1981*. London: John Murray.

Hall, M. and T. Young. 1997. *Confronting Leviathan: Mozambique since Independence*. London: Hurst & Co.

Hultman, L. 2009. "The Power to Hurt in Civil War: The Strategic Aim of RENAMO Violence." *Journal of Southern African Studies* 35 (4): 821-834.

Littlejohn, G. 2015. *Secret Stockpiles, Arms Caches and Disarmament Efforts in Mozambique*. A Working Paper of the Small Arms Survey, 21 September. Available from http://www.smallarmssurvey.org/fileadmin/docs/F-Working-papers/SAS-WP21-Secret-Stockpiles.pdf.

Manjate, J. 2013. *Análise Estratégica da Liderança na Guerra em Moçambique: Unidade de Esforço na Batalha da Zambézia 1986-1992* [Strategic Analysis of Leadership in the War in Mozambique: Effort Unit in the Battle of Zambezia 1986-1992]. Maputo: Diname.

Manning, C. 1998. "Constructing Opposition in Mozambique: Renamo as Political Party." *Journal of Southern African Studies* 24 (1): 161-189.

Manning, C. 2002. *The Politics of Peace in Mozambique: Post-Conflict Democratization, 1992-2000*. Westport, CT: Praeger.

McMullin, J. 2004. "Reintegration of Combatants: Were the Right Lessons Learned in Mozambique?" *International Peacekeeping* 11 (4): 625-643.

Newitt, M. 1995. *A History of Mozambique.* London: Hurst & Co.

O País. 2009. "Ex-integrantes da Renamo Decepcionados com Eleição de Dhlakama" [Former Renamo Members Disappointed with Dhlakama Election]. *O País*, 23 July.

Oliveira, P. 2006. *Renamo, uma Descida ao Coração das Trevas: Dossier Makwakwa* [Renamo, a Descent to the Heart of Darkness: Makwakwa Dossier]. Lisbon: Europress.

Reid, I. D. and C. Wimpy. 2013. "Defining Opposition: An Interview with Afonso Dhlakama of RENAMO." *Ufahamu: A Journal of African Studies* 37 (1): 1-9.

Reisman, L. and A. Lalá. 2012. *Assessment of Crime and Violence in Mozambique & Recommendations for Violence Prevention and Reduction.* Open Society Foundations Crime and Violence Prevention Initiative & Open Society Initiative for Southern Africa.

Ross, M. L. 2012. *The Oil Curse: How Petroleum Wealth Shapes the Development of Nations.* Princeton, NJ: Princeton University Press.

Schafer, J. 1998. "'A Baby Who Does Not Cry Will Not Be Suckled': AMODEG and the Reintegration of Demobilised Soldiers." *Journal of Southern African Studies* 4 (1): 207-222.

Sengulane, D. D. 2014. Speech made at Chatham House, 14 July. Available from http://www.chathamhouse.org/event/restoring-peace-mozambique.

Slattery, B. 2003. "Development Without Equality: An Interview with Raúl Domingos." *Journal of International Affairs* 57 (1): 129-134.

Synge, R. 1997. *Mozambique: UN Peace-keeping in Action, 1992-1994.* Washington, DC: United States Institute of Peace.

Tavuyanago, B. 2011. "RENAMO: From Military Confrontation to Peaceful Democratic Engagement, 1976-2009." *African Journal of Political Science and International Relations* 5 (1): 42-51.

Themnér, A. 2012. "Former Mid-Level Commanders in Big Man Networks." In *African Conflicts and Informal Power: Big Men and Networks,* ed. M. Utas. London: Zed Books.

Vines, A. 1995. "Angola and Mozambique: The Aftermath of Conflict." *Conflict Studies* 280: 1-35.

Vines, A. 1996. *Renamo: From Terrorism to Democracy in Mozambique?* London: James Currey.

Vines, A. 1998. "The Business of Peace: 'Tiny' Rowland, Financial Incentives and the Mozambican Settlement." In *Accord: The Mozambican Peace Process in Perspective* (Issue 3), ed. J. Armon, D. Hendrickson and A. Vines. London: Conciliation Resources.

Vines, A. 2013. "Renamo's Rise and Decline: The Politics of Reintegration in Mozambique." *International Peacekeeping* 20 (3): 375-393.

Vines, A. 2014. "Review of Emerson, S. (2013), The Battle for Mozambique." *International Affairs* 90 (2): 46-47.

Vines, A. and K. Wilson. 1997. "Churches and the Peace Process in Mozambique." In *The Christian Churches and the Democratisation of Africa,* ed. P. Gifford. Leiden: Brill.

Vines A., H. Thompson, S. Kirk Jensen and E. Azevedo-Harman. 2015. *Mozambique to 2018: Managers, Mediators and Magnates.* London: Chatham House. Available from https://www.chathamhouse.org/publication/mozambique-2018.

Wiegink, N. 2013. "Why Did the Soldiers Not Go Home? Demobilized Combatants, Family Life, and Witchcraft in Post War Mozambique." *Anthropological Quarterly* 86 (1): 107-132.

Wiegink, N. 2015. "'It Will Be Our Time to Eat': Former Renamo Combatants and Big-Men Dynamics in Central Mozambique." *Journal of Southern African Studies* 41 (4): 1-17.

Xinhua News Agency. 2005. "Mozambican Opposition Leader Refuses to Disband 'Security Force.'" *Xinhua News Agency,* 7 October.

5 | From warlord to drug lord: the life of João Bernardo "Nino" Vieira

Henrik Vigh

Introduction

This chapter tells the story of the late João Bernardo "Nino" Vieira, the former president of the small West African country of Guinea-Bissau. It positions Vieira historically and socially, in pre- and post-independence Guinea-Bissau, clarifies his rise to power, and illuminates the intertwining of military and political skills and knowledge that enabled him to stay in power for over twenty years and eventually become the country's first democratically elected president. Vieira does not figure prominently in historical, political or anthropological work on the Upper Guinea Coast. The country in which he became president, Guinea-Bissau, is one of the smallest countries of the region, hemmed in between its two larger neighbors, Guinea Conakry and Senegal, and is not of major global or regional geo-political importance. As it is furthermore a place of few natural resources, limited military significance, and of scant interest to tourists, it remains relatively easily overlooked.

Yet, despite the fact that the country is little known, Guinea-Bissau is politically interesting in a number of ways. First of all, having played an important part in the supply of arms and soldiers to the Movement of Democratic Forces of Casamance (Mouvement des Forces Democratique de Casamance, MDFC) rebels in the Casamance region of neighboring Senegal,[1] Guinea-Bissau has been influential in the continued existence of the longest running civil war on the continent and, thus, one of the region's key destabilizing factors (Vigh 2006). Second, Guinea-Bissau has gained growing significance in relation to the cocaine trade that has increasingly tied the sub-region into the wider world. This small, impoverished country has become an important party in the transnational flow of illegal substances between Latin America and Europe, making its recent history an extraordinary example of the criminalization of politics. It provides a unique example of the manner in which a democratic state may be made to facilitate illegal enterprises (see Bayart et al. 1999). Not only is Guinea-Bissau a case of what we might term "the politics of poverty" – i.e. a system of governance that is both built upon and conducive to persistent scarcity (Vigh 2009) – the country's marginality also clarifies in this way some of the security issues of contemporary politics on the Upper Guinea Coast, in terms of civil war, cocaine economies and human rights abuse.

Central to all these security issues stands Nino Vieira, the warlord democrat in focus in this chapter. Vieira has twice been elected president during the country's short democratic history. He ran as a presidential candidate for the African Party for the Independence of Guinea and Cape Verde (Partido Africano da Independência da Guiné e Cabo Verde, PAIGC) in 1994 and as an independent candidate in 2005, both times successfully. In order to illuminate his pivotal role in the political and economic problems that have troubled Guinea-Bissau's recent history, the chapter will trace the military and political career of "Nino" Vieira, moving from his time as a soldier on the front lines of the war of independence, to his subsequent emergence as a famous freedom fighter, Marxist dictator, democrat and drug kingpin. Despite managing to gain democratic power by transforming a politico-military regime into a democratic one, and later running as an independent candidate, Vieira's story epitomizes the combination of militant power and political patronage in democratic disguise. It highlights how the move toward democratization may in itself be a tactical accommodation to external demands, creating not peace and increased prosperity but drastic security outcomes such as the criminalization of politics and the continuation of human rights abuses. As Vieira sought to maintain and regain power in the impoverished country, he used democratic pretexts and positions to intimidate the opposition and engage in large-scale illegal trade.

The criminalization of politics went hand in hand with human rights abuses. As Guinea-Bissau has only very little in terms of mineral resources, oil and gas, the country's revenue is minimal, profit meager and the contest over the country's few assets fierce. The criminalization of the Guinea-Bissauan state was driven by the need to channel funds into political networks and grease the patrimonial dynamics of the political scene (Vigh 2011). In such a context of scarcity, human rights violations appear merely as ruthless attempts to control competition and facilitate the flow of and access to resources. Guinea-Bissau is not a place of inter-ethnic or inter-religious animosity, but the pragmatics of control of a commodity as lucrative and explosive as cocaine entering into an environment as poor as Guinea-Bissau led to a surge in violations. However, as we shall see, Vieira was never a leader who worked to protect the rights of the country's population. He came of age in the battlefield and ruled as a warlord in times of peace or war. Yet before moving back in time to the making of Vieira as a military commander, I want to start with a more recent event, namely the demise of President Vieira and his last struggle for power in the country.

The end of an era

Guinea-Bissau's military headquarters exploded on 9 May 2009. Shattering the calm of the early evening, the explosion completely demolished one side

157

of the building, killing the chief of staff, General Batista Tagme Na Waie, in the process. Bissau is not unaccustomed to violence. The small capital has, over the last ten years, grown used to occasional coups and minor conflicts interrupting everyday life in the city. Yet these are normally indicated by the clatter of gunfire and the hollow booms of RPGs (rocket-propelled grenades), not by remote-controlled bombs, making the size, precision and high-tech nature of the device unusual. Whoever planted the bomb knew what they were doing and had the knowledge and skills necessary to do it expertly.

Seen from within Bissau, the advanced nature of the device indicated foreign influence, generating an abundance of rumors placing the blame on the Latin American or Asian cartels that are using the country as a transshipment point for the movement of drugs across the Atlantic (Vigh 2011).[2] While the actual culprit remains unknown, the local mastermind behind the assassination was quickly identified as President Vieira. Vieira had supposedly used his connections to the drug trade to get rid of a political problem. He had been caught in a power struggle with Na Waie, dating back to the independence struggle, and the old warlord, Vieira, had decided to solve it the way he knew best, namely by exterminating his opponent. He seems, however, to have underestimated his rival's ability to react. Na Waie had publicly stated that his eventual death would trigger the death of the president,[3] and the commotion following the blast had hardly settled before an "elite" unit of Na Waie's men[4] retaliated and attacked Vieira. Na Waie's death was mercifully swift – President Vieira's was anything but. The army unit that attacked his residence fired a grenade into the president's home. The ensuing blast severely injured Vieira, but failed to kill him, and as he stumbled from the debris Vieira was shot and repeatedly attacked with a machete until he finally succumbed to his attackers.[5]

The twin murders did not change much. In political terms the consequences were minor, and rather than clearing the way for more progressive forces, the assassinations merely created a political vacuum filled with more politicians of the same type, engaging in similar struggles over power and spoils. Yet the killings nonetheless marked the end of an era in Guinea-Bissau. First and foremost, it ended the reign of the veterans of the war of independence, who had been more or less permanently in power since the liberation of the country and constituted the bulk of the military and political elite. Second, it marked the final stages of a bitter rivalry that had dominated Guinea-Bissauan politics for decades. Vieira and Na Waie had fought together during the war of independence. They had both sacrificed their youth on the battlefield, become generals in the Guinea-Bissauan Armed Forces (FAG), and struggled for power within the post-independence state. However, while Na Waie's importance had been confined to the country's military, Vieira had become the embodiment of post-independence politics in Guinea-Bissau. He had, as a warlord and dictator, cultivated a political environment characterized by illegal and illicit trade, repression and violence, making his prolonged and brutal death in some ways a fitting reflection of his sad political legacy.

While Vieira ruled with brutality and insecurity, his regime being marked by oppression, corruption, organized crime and a blatant disregard for human rights, he was equally – and simultaneously – responsible for setting up a democratic political system in Guinea-Bissau and twice managed to become the country's democratically elected president. Vieira had ended his political career as a democrat. He had managed to access the meagre spoils that flow through the Guinea-Bissauan state, and distributed them within his interconnected military and political networks, with an air of democratic legitimacy – shadowing the patrimonial workings of his actual governance. He was not only a tyrant and the country's biggest drug kingpin but also a warlord democrat, and his presidency provides a showcase illustration of the way democracy can be manipulated in order to serve essentially non-democratic purposes.

Looking into his personal history, this is perhaps less surprising than it sounds. As he made the most out of a limited space of political and economic possibilities in Guinea-Bissau he survived and prospered by navigating the structures of power surrounding him, from the local military unit on the front lines of war, to national configurations of power, regional alliances, international politics and discourses of democracy (on social and political navigation see Vigh 2006, 2009).

Background: the making of a warlord

The truly remarkable thing about Vieira's life, besides his brutality and greed, was his ability to navigate the tumultuous waters of the independence, warring and post-independence states. He succeeded in skillfully making the most of minimal possibilities.

Vieira's point of departure was paltry. Born in Bissau, in 1939, in what was then Portuguese Guiné, he was raised by a single mother and grew up as one of the city's urban poor. Despite its relative proximity to Portugal, Guinea-Bissau was, during colonial times, one of the most marginal areas of the Portuguese empire. The territory was initially settled by the Portuguese in the sixteenth century through the establishment of a number of trading posts catering to the trans-Atlantic slave trade (Mark 1999). Yet, as the trans-Atlantic slave trade dwindled with the rise of the abolition movement, the Portuguese settlements on the upper Guinea coast lost their primary value and became mere points en route to the more profitable colonies of Brazil, Angola and Mozambique. Portuguese Guiné became a colony of minimal worth within the Portuguese empire, treasured primarily for its geographical location and agricultural produce. Being a colonial backwater, the territory was administered from Cape Verde, a group of islands a thousand kilometers into the Atlantic, and turned into a territory with Portuguese rulers, Cape Verdean administrators and destitute and marginalized local populations (Mark 1999, 2002). Portuguese Guiné grew in this manner increasingly economically and politically untenable. Despite the dwindling profits from its colonies, Portugal was unwilling to negotiate their status or autonomy. And as the first wave of liberation movements swept across Africa, in the decade following the Second World War, the country tightened its administrative and military grip on its colonies, and Guinea-Bissau became reclassified as an overseas Portuguese province in 1951.

However, dissatisfaction with Portuguese rule was increasing and started to take a more organized form. Five years after the official incorporation of Portuguese Guiné into Portugal proper, the liberation movement PAIGC was formed. Initially a peaceful, socialist movement working for the independence of Guinea-Bissau and Cape Verde, the PAIGC turned militant in 1959.[6] Once militant, the movement took shape as a tight-knit and well-organized guerrilla movement. It set up its headquarters in neighboring Guinea Conakry and turned, under the command of Amilcar Cabral, into an international icon of the later decolonization movements. Fighting against the colonial rulers from a NATO (North Atlantic Treaty Organization) country, the organization managed to secure military supplies and training from the Warsaw Pact countries, China and Cuba, and from 1960 to 1962 the party started the process of arming the population in the south of the country. This was also the time when Vieira entered the PAIGC. He abandoned his vocational training and joined the party in 1960. Vieira quickly made an impression within the PAIGC leadership and was one of the first combatants to be sent for military training in China, at the Nanjing Army Command College. Upon his return he was appointed military commander and political commissar of the southeast region of the country, in what is currently known as Tombali, and started to infiltrate and arm the region. Connecting the military and the political in this manner was a conscious decision taken by the PAIGC leadership, and a connection Vieira was later to use to his advantage as he positioned himself within the post-independence state.

Vieira's rise through the ranks of the PAIGC and its armed forces, the FARP,[7] was remarkable. Despite his poor background and lack of education, he quickly gained the confidence of the party leadership and showed himself to be a convincing agitator as well as a distinguished soldier and commander (Weston 2009). His military unit set up their base in the forest surrounding Catió, the regional capital of the southeastern part of the country, and he led the first PAIGC attack on the Portuguese military on 23 January 1963, capturing the barracks in Tité. The attack was the first coordinated large-scale military assault on the Portuguese, and was to be the start of a decade of fighting in which the PAIGC made progressive advances. The liberation movement succeeded in liberating large parts of the country within the first few years, and by 1965 they were fighting the Portuguese on three fronts. From 13 to 17 February 1964, the first PAIGC congress was held in the liberated areas of the country, in Cassacá in the southern region of Guinea-Bissau, flaunting the movement's presence and consolidation in the country and, hence, the Portuguese lack of control over its territory. For Vieira personally, the triumph was no less remarkable. At the age of twenty-five he was made commander of the whole of the southern front, as well as a member of the Politburo, i.e. the Central Committee of the party, granting him a major political and military position in the PAIGC (Mendy and Lobban 2013: 419).

Fighting under the *nom de guerre* of "Nino" and "Kabi Nafantchamna",[8] Vieira grew increasingly famous as a resilient and tactically cunning guerrilla fighter. He was not only a strategist, calling the shots from a safe distance behind the front lines, but actively engaged in some of the most decisive battles of the independence war. Besides being in charge of transforming the liberated area in the south to align with the PAIGC political program, he managed to make the southern front the most feared area of engagement for the Portuguese troops. He gained mythical status as a commander within the PAIGC, as he headed his troops on the southern front during some of the most notorious battles in the war, most notably the battle of Guileje and the defense of Como island in 1964, where – outnumbered by four to one – he held off the Portuguese invasion of the island for seventy-one days, surviving strikes from Portuguese land troops, the navy and the air force. In fact, Vieira's military abilities and tactical knowledge were seen to be so impressive that he was granted full command of the FARP in 1971.

Although he excelled as a soldier, his political ambitions remained intact and in 1972 he was elected a member of the National People's Assembly, and served as its chairman from 1973. Vieira emerged, as such, from the war as both an influential military figure and politician. As it came to an end he was to be the one to announce the unilateral declaration of independence and declare the sovereign rights of the two territories of Guinea-Bissau and Cape Verde on 24 September 1973. The declaration started the countdown to the de facto decolonization of Guinea-Bissau, as well as to the carnation revolution in Portugal and the fall of the Salazar regime, on 25 April 1974. Yet it also started the post-war separation of military and political powers. The PAIGC leadership had accepted the need to become soldiers during the liberation struggle, but maintained that they wanted a clear division between politics and the military in the future. With the war coming to an end, the organization moved toward a less militant mode of functioning; however, as we shall see, Vieira never lost his grasp of the political dimensions of power, or his control of the army, which he was later to staff with people belonging to his military faction during the war. Though a warlord, he had substantial political influence and ambitions and set out to consolidate his power within both. As Guinea-Bissau gained its independence, Vieira was given the rank of general and the position of commander-in-chief of the FAG. He was, in other words, made head of the armed forces but was, furthermore, made *Commissar* (minister) of defense in the newly established national government led by President Luís Cabral and Prime Minister Francisco Mendés.[9]

From warlord to politician

The early independence years were full of optimism and progressive potential. After the end of the liberation war, the PAIGC split the movement into a military and a political branch and moved toward a post-conflict line of governance. As a result, the country not only received the backing of a number of socialist and communist states but was also embraced by the Nordic countries, especially Sweden, as they envisaged the emergence of a social democratic state in West Africa (see Mendy and Lobban 2013: 381). The country was in other words off to a promising start. Yet, though built on noble ideals, the Afro-socialist dream of the PAIGC never materialized. Instead of emerging from the independence struggle as a free and independent nation, Guinea-Bissau quickly became a repressive regime, which was almost completely dependent on development aid. As the country became poorer and poorer, it failed to live up to its promises of being a society of equals, "a people's state", able to provide for all its citizens and turned, instead, into an increasingly polarized society in which the PAIGC elite enjoyed the spoils of power whilst the general population were forced to live in abject poverty with limited civil liberties.

In similar vein, Vieira's initial role in post-independence Guinea-Bissau was not post-conflictual, progressive or democratically inclined. After the mayhem of the early liberation days he settled into office as chief of staff. However, it did not take long before his skills as a warlord were once again put to use with drastic security outcomes to follow. Where he had formerly fought against an external, colonial other, his military know-how was this time directed toward purging the party and population of dissidents and non-conformists. As head of the army, he allegedly ordered and planned, together with the head of the military police António Buscardini, the killing of a number of former Commandos Africanos, the local Guinea-Bissauan troops who had fought for the Portuguese against the PAIGC.[10] But the purges also cut into the PAIGC proper, as the same accusation of collaboration with the Portuguese was used by Vieira to legitimize the persecution of a number of party members and purge the party of opposition, most notably the former vice-president of the party, Rafael Barbosa, in 1976 (Chabal 1981: 81). The early years of independence were both busy and bloody times for Vieira.

In 1978 the death of the country's prime minister, Fransisco Mendès, once again changed the configurations of power and propelled Vieira further up the political hierarchy within the one-party state. Mendès died in a car accident, said at the time to be an assassination, and his (un)timely death allowed Vieira to take his position as prime minister and assume the leadership of the government. Furthermore, the death of Mendès enabled Vieira to move formally from soldier to politician. Yet Vieira was content neither with his new position of power nor with the leadership of his superior, President Luís Cabral, and on 14 November 1980 he led a coup, together with his long-time brother-in-arms Asumané Mané, in which he ousted President Cabral, disbanded the existing National People's Assembly and positioned himself as the leader of the Revolutionary Council, making him the autocratic ruler of the country.

The coup not only positioned Vieira in power but also contained a larger agenda of cleansing the local political environment of the influential Cape Verdean elite. Vieira did so by securitizing the Cape Verdean population group as a foreign influence working against the common good of the country's citizens. The Cape Verdean elite had constituted the bulk of the colonial administration before the war, and dominated the leadership of the PAIGC during and after it, yet their perceived homeland, the Cape Verdean Islands, lay 1,000 miles into the Atlantic, and their former affiliation with the Portuguese colonial power made it possible for Vieira to counter-identify them as both foreign and dangerous to the new nation's security and prosperity. Though many within the Cape Verdean community were born and bred in Guinea-Bissau, it was a creolized ethnic group that was constituted by the very arrival of the Portuguese, and Vieira used this to position them as non-indigenous. As a consequence, he set up a new leadership of the country, after the coup in 1980, largely composed of people of local Guinea-Bissauan descent.

The coup itself was triggered by a perceived Cape Verdean push into the higher ranks of the armed forces. In 1979, a quota system had been introduced regulating the possibility of promotion to the rank of commissioned officer within the armed forces. The system was seen to favor Cape Verdeans at the cost of the Guinea-Bissauan foot soldiers who actually fought the war on the front lines, causing dissatisfaction among troops from local ethnic groups. The coup was accordingly designated and legitimized as a "readjustment movement", and defined as a move toward getting Guinea-Bissau back on track, yet it seems to have gained its momentum and support by exploiting the historical tension between Guinea-Bissauans and Cape Verdeans.

The move can be seen as a tactical stroke of genius by Vieira. His great disadvantage in the game of politics in Guinea-Bissau was that he belonged to the Papel ethnic group, a minority constituting only 5% of the population, and so had little reliable support in a country where ethnic allegiances and networks play an important part in the configurations of power. By securitizing the Cape Verdean population group and counter-identifying them with the general population in Guinea-Bissau, Vieira managed to introduce a political fault line that excluded his rivals whilst including himself in the in-group of "true" Africans, thus moving him from a position as representative of a minority to that of a majority. He furthermore managed to divide the PAIGC, creating a schism between those who had made the real sacrifices on the battlefield and the privileged Cape Verdean elite who merely called the shots at a safe distance, from their headquarters in the neighboring country of Guinea Conakry, enabling him to purge the party to his advantage. Placing the "true" Guinea-Bissauans within the former and the "foreigners" within the latter, Vieira racialized and primordialized the liberation movement and granted his own military faction a forceful claim to power (see De Sá 2010: 24–28).

The new regime was presented as a champion of reform and justice. Yet Vieira's rule quickly proved itself worse than its predecessor on almost all accounts. In the years to follow, Vieira put his tactical prowess to use in removing any opposition to his reign. He governed Guinea-Bissau through a combination of paranoia and overexertion of power, taking what he wanted, distributing the spoils to his supporters as he saw fit, and punishing those who objected. In other words, having overthrown President Cabral, Vieira set to work creating a repressive and lawless society in which he was free to exploit the country, and to arrest, torture and execute perceived rivals with impunity (see Cardoso and Sjöberg 2011).

From dictator to democrat

Following the purge, Vieira appeared more powerful than ever. He was installed as head of state, commander in chief and general secretary of the country's sole political party, the PAIGC, in 1984. As the four-year-old Revolutionary Council adopted a constitutional government during the fourth Congress of the PAIGC in 1986 (US Department of State 1987), he was "re-elected" party leader, subsequently taking office in the newly created position of President of the Republic. However, though the reinstitution of the National People's Assembly may have given his rule an air of political legitimacy, it did not appease his fears of losing power, and the calm did not last long. Two years after reinstating the National People's Assembly, Vieira once again purged the political elite of an ethnic group that he saw as threatening his position. This time, however, his former allies within the Balanta ethnic group, the largest in the country, were the target of his purge.

Vieira feared a Balanta demand for a distribution of power that would reflect the ethnic group's size and importance within Guinea-Bissau. In order to quell the growing political awakening within the Balanta community Vieira ordered the eradication of the Balanta political and military elite in the interests of national security. In a combination of political killings, torture, disappearances, denial of fair public trials, and repression of free speech and the press he purged the PAIGC of its leading Balata figures. Along with sixty others, the recently appointed Prime Minister Correia was arrested on charges of plotting a coup against Vieira, and Correia was to lose his life together with ten of his closest allies, as they were convicted of conspiracy and executed (Mendy and Lobban 2013: 281). In hindsight, the elimination of the political representatives of the Balantas seems to have been short-sighted and ill-advised. It may have secured him an extra decade in power but, as we shall see, it also led to his fall. His purging of the Cape Verdean elite had been controversial, yet relatively safe as the group's power base was located over 1,000 kilometers into the Atlantic on the Cape Verdean Islands. The Balantas, however, were not only Guinea-Bissau's largest ethnic group but also dominant within the armed forces and thus a far more powerful enemy to acquire.[11]

Having purged the political scene, Vieira once again began intensifying the democratization process. The transition to multiparty democracy was launched with a PAIGC congress in January 1991 in which the proposal to remove the constitutional article granting PAIGC a monopoly of power was passed. In May of the same year the National Assembly approved a corresponding amendment to the constitution,[12] and half a year later a bill granting freedom of the press was passed. In December 1995 the fifth Congress of the PAIGC finally allowed multiparty elections, clearing away the last constitutional hurdle to the process (Mendy and Lobban 2013: 447).

In terms of electoral strategy, Vieira had taken the final steps toward transforming the PAIGC from a politico-military complex to a democratic party, and himself from a warlord to a democrat. He was now leading a government on the path to democratic reform, yet despite the road being cleared for the first democratic elections in the country's history, his abuse of power was on-going and included silencing the opposition and the media, as well as general distortion of the electoral procedures, including a range of confusing calls for elections in 1992, 1993 and early in 1994 (International Republican Institute 1994). Actual elections were not held until July 1994, when Vieira won 46.2% of the vote and became one of the two candidates to progress to the second round. Vieira won the second round with 52% of the votes and was subsequently installed as the country's first democratically elected president in early autumn 1994.

Spoils and the democratic façade

The election results were recognized as free and fair by international observers and the result was a massive triumph for Vieira. Not only had he managed to win but also to appease the international community by paving the way for a systemic change, setting up democratic institutions, and gaining formal acknowledgement of the balloting. It was, pro forma, a successful and remarkable political transformation, ultimately steering the country away from its former socialist agenda and into the world of capitalist democracies.

However, while Vieira may have moved toward a position of greater legitimacy from an international perspective, the actual depth of the political transformation was less impressive. First of all, the process of democratization in Guinea-Bissau did not include a concomitant move toward an equalization of power or the rule of law (Rudebeck 2001). Second, in the years following the 1994 election Guinea-Bissau did *not* develop into a society that was politically stable, where politics was defined by rational legal structures, human rights and security, but remained characterized by corruption, repression and a lack of transparency. Vieira's democratic regime persistently persecuted his opponents, obstructed the freedom of the press, and assassinated his main rivals. It remained, in other words, a forceful human rights violator where democracy amounted to little more than ritually instantiated dictatorship – autocracy measured in four-year units. His democratic government remained a political system in which the "conditions favouring 'citizenship' ... [were] still much more rare than conditions pressing people into 'subjection'" (Rudebeck 2001: 11).

The state of democracy in Guinea-Bissau came, in any case, to exemplify the untenability of the notion that democratization necessarily leads to growth and stability. The country may have been put on the "track to democracy" (Akopari and Azavedo 2007: 1), but the extreme levels of poverty that characterize everyday life for most of the Guinea-Bissauan population had not improved, undermining the fundamental principles of the political system. "Here we vote with our stomachs" an informant told me in Bissau, explaining why one corrupt and crooked politician after another is voted into power in the country. For a population as destitute as that of Guinea-Bissau, democracy is, as such, less a question of ideological reasoning than of people voting for the patron believed likely to pass most spoils their way. Similarly, while Vieira might have been a democrat in minimal institutional terms, his move toward democracy provides a prime example of how one may stage a transformation to democracy yet maintain autocratic control over both political institutions and the population. In an environment conducive to personalized politics, Vieira controlled both the judiciary and the military. His old comrade in arms and personal bodyguard Asumané Mané was chief of staff, guaranteeing military cooperation; the judges in the high court were appointed directly by him; and an effective secret service allowed the president to keep the population compliant through fear. Vieira's victory may have shown the world that he was a legitimate leader, but changes on the ground were limited to an adjustment from being ruled by a brutal dictator to being ruled by an equally brutal democrat.

The move toward democratic constitutionalism and multiparty democracy also demonstrated Vieira's ability to navigate the ebb and flow of political change. He was an opportunist who converted to democratic reform as a way of maintaining power by manipulating a political system that would enable him to continue to funnel international development aid into his own bank account and use state institutions for his personal gain. Guinea-Bissau was, at the time, one of Africa's poorest countries, yet Vieira had become one of continent's richest men. He had not only spent his time in power to direct development aid into his own pockets, but also used the military and state apparatus to engage in various kinds of illicit and illegal trade, from the selling of the country's fishing quotas, to the logging of its hardwood and the smuggling of arms from the Soviet bloc. In the Cold War era, when geo-political tensions and ideological fault lines overshadowed issues of good governance and accountability, Vieira put his knowledge of the region's shadow economies and formations, acquired during his time as a guerrilla commander in the liberation war, to good use and skillfully maneuvered between state and non-state formations of power.

However, as the fall of the Berlin Wall changed both flows of aid and the recognition of political legitimacy, Vieira needed to reinvent himself in order to keep donors content. Being democratically elected elevated Vieira's political standing, both regionally and internationally, thus allowing him continued access to the international subventions that he had come to treat as his personal endowment. As we shall see, it was precisely this illicit use of state resources and institutions that led to his downfall: ousted before the end of his first presidential term and killed before the end of his second.

The loss of command

In 1998 a series of events led to a year-long civil war and subsequent coup in the country. The coup, led by the former chief of staff and long-term ally of President Vieira, Asumané Mané, was initiated only a few months before the second multiparty elections in the country's history. The decisive factor for its instigation was related to the sales of arms from the FAG to the Movement of Democratic Forces of Casamance (Mouvement des Forces Democratique de Casamance, MDFC) rebels in Casamance,[13] southern Senegal, and the coup provides an interesting case study of the workings of Vieira's democracy and the warlord practices behind it.

Half a year before the start of the war, Asumané Mané had been suspended following accusations of arms sales to the rebel movement. During their fight for independence, the MDFC had close connections to Guinea-Bissau, as they used the northern, Diola/Felupe-dominated areas of the country as a safe haven for tired soldiers recuperating from the independence struggle. With Guinea-Bissau's entry into the West African Monetary Union and the gradual alignment of President Vieira's politics with the French sphere of influence in West Africa, which favored the Senegalese side of the Casamance conflict, there was increased focus on Guinea-Bissau's role in supporting the MDFC struggle.

In light of increased diplomatic pressure from Senegal and France, Vieira singled out Brigadier Mané to bear the blame for the arms sales, and a parliamentary investigation was launched on 27 February (Amnesty International 1999: 4). The report, which was due on Monday 8 June, was said to have been heavily influenced by the president, freeing him of blame while clearly incriminating Mr. Mané. It was never made public, however, as Mané gathered a group of allied troops around him and launched his coup d'état the day before the Parliamentary Commission was to announce its conclusions (Kovsted and Tarp 1999: 11; Forrest 2002: 255-259). It remains unclear who was actually in charge of the weapons sales, yet it seems safe to assume that both Mané and Vieira were aware of and profited from it, and that they had done so in tandem for many years. In any case, the split between them resulted in a division not just within their old military faction but also within the Guinea-Bissauan army as a whole. Vieira found himself challenged by the person who had otherwise remained most loyal to him, as well (he was subsequently to learn) as by the vast majority of the country's soldiers, who opted to join Asumané Mané's side of the conflict.

His closest ally had become his greatest enemy, and the population whose backing he had claimed since winning the election now flocked to the opposite side of the conflict. His purge of Balanta dissidents in the army in the 1980s had backfired, leaving the president without the support of the largest ethnic group in the country and the armed forces. And things were to go from bad to worse for the president, as Mané gained support from a large influx of veterans of the independence war. Vieira seemed to have underestimated the reaction of the common soldier and the general Guinea-Bissauan population to the emerging conflict. However, the few hundred men, mostly officers and the presidential guard, who did choose to stay on Vieira's side of the conflict were quickly supported by an artillery battalion from Guinea Conakry as well as 1,300 Senegalese commandoes. An influx of foreign troops saved him in the moment, yet its presence had the effect of further strengthening popular support for Asumané Mané's side of the conflict, now calling itself the "Junta Militar".[14]

What we see, when we observe the early stages of the war, is thus a conflict between a democratically elected president backed by a number of high-ranking officers, a few loyal local troops and a contingent of Senegalese and Conakrian military personnel, fighting against a Junta Militar backed by a large majority of local military personnel as well as an unknown number of MDFC troops,[15] with the support of the population in general. Despite his claimed political legitimacy Vieira was not able to gain local support and within the next fifty days the Junta Militar had seized control of the majority of the country, leaving Vieira in power over the Prabis peninsula, the cities of Bafata, Gabu, the Bijagos islands and a hemmed in area of Bissau,[16] with the frontlines drawn along the city's outer suburbs. A number of ceasefires, coordinated jointly by the Community of Portuguese Language Countries (Comunidade dos Países de Língua Portuguesa, CLCP) and the Economic Community of West African States (ECOWAS),[17] were attempted but by this stage it was clear that Vieira was fighting an uphill battle and merely buying himself time in order to make the best of the coming peace (Vigh 2006: chapter 3).

Vieira gradually lost control of the major strategic positions within Guinea-Bissau, to the point where his troops were pushed back to the capital and the Bijagos islands outside of it. On the morning of 7 May 1999 the Junta entered Bissau. Capturing the city, which was Vieira's last stronghold, they caught Vieira by surprise. The former warlord was a shadow of himself as he was apprehended by Junta troops while trying to hide in the French Cultural Centre in the middle of town. The pictures taken during the incident show an image of a man defeated and deflated. The Big Man was reduced to a frightened and fragile figure. At the time Vieira certainly had cause to fear for his life. Besides Asumané Mané, whom he had tried to blame for the arms trade to the Casamance rebels, the core figures of the military junta consisted of people he had persecuted and tortured during his purge of the Balanta elite in the mid-1980s, and his fate must have seemed grim as his triumphant capturers dragged him from the building. Yet instead of being killed by his captors, Vieira managed to negotiate his exile with the head of the Junta, Asumané Mané, and gain refuge in France and Belgium. Robbed of his military and political power, subjugated and expatriated, the episode seems to constitute a fitting end to the story of Vieira as a warlord democrat.

Democratic drug lord

However, Vieira was far from beaten. In fact, returning to power in 2005 after winning yet another presidential election, he was once again to prove his mastery of navigating both the underlying warlord networks and official democratic façade of Guinea-Bissauan politics.

Having lost the backing of his former party, the PAIGC, after his ousting, Vieira changed electoral strategy and announced his intention to run as an independent candidate in the presidential elections from his exile in Europe. I was in Bissau at the time, and his proclaimed return to the country was greeted with a mixture of disbelief and optimism. Taking Vieira's earlier brutal and corrupt rule into consideration, the optimism seemed strange. However, the excitement reflected not so much a longing for legitimacy as for order, however repressive it may have been. His return was seen as a possible road to stabilization of the country, which, since his ousting in 1999, had been caught in unprecedented turbulence which had made life ever more difficult for the small state's population. Vieira's ousting had left a number of influential politicians and military figures struggling for power, leading to four coups and military revolts in as many years. In comparison to the subsequent chaos, the many years with Vieira in power seemed almost pleasantly autocratic.

As regards the disbelief, the discussion was centered on whether Vieira would be allowed to return safely. The military had, by this point, become politically dominant and was headed by Tagme Na Waie, a Balanta general who Vieira had had tortured in the mid-1980s. The question was, who would protect Vieira if he were to come back, with most people thinking that Na Waie would strive to kill him as retaliation for his suffering. The election was scheduled for 10 June 2005. On 7 April Vieira landed by the national stadium in Bissau in order to register for the election. He was helicoptered in by the Guinea-Conakrian air force, emphasizing his backing by the neighboring country's president. As he entered Bissau he was greeted by a euphoric crowd of supporters, and instead of being targeted by Na Waie, he was protected by an army escort ordered by the general.

Approximately a month after registering for the election, Vieira was named as an officially recognized candidate for the coming election, as the Supreme Court published its list of contenders for the post. The acceptance of Vieira's candidacy caused a number of the other candidates to object to his official return to politics in the country, yet Vieira entered the elections as confident as ever. Unchallenged by the military that had previously exiled him and sanctioned by the courts, he proclaimed himself to be the only veteran of the war of independence who could unify the country and take it forward. Guinea-Bissau had been in complete disarray since the war in 1999 and it did not take more than an unsubstantiated promise of order and progress for Vieira to come second in the first round of elections, before going on to beat Malam Bacai Sanha in the second round on 24 July 2005. Once again the election was considered free and fair, and as the Electoral Commission confirmed the result on 10 August, Vieira was ready to take up his second period as the country's democratically elected president on 1 October 2005.

The election was an amazing turn of events, testament both to the political perseverance of Nino Vieira and the exceptional unpredictability of Guinea-Bissauan politics. From being a hated figure after the war, publicly spoken about as a thief and tyrant, he returned as the long-lost father of the nation; as "God's gift to Guinea-Bissau" (BBC News 2009), a providential figure able to generate stability and economic growth. In the eyes of the many who voted for him, his capacity to control and manage the various factions in the country's armed forces made him the only person capable of ruling the country. Vieira's return was an exceptional example of the workings of a warlord democrat. He managed simultaneously to use the political system to his advantage, calling for his right to be judged by the people and profiting from the legitimacy gained thereby, as well as to negotiate his return to Bissau by manipulating the dominant militant faction within the country through a proposal for mutual benefit and power. In other words, he did not return empty-handed, but with a business offer. As was to become clear later, he had struck a deal with the Balanta strongmen in the military, offering them a cut of the profits of an exceptionally lucrative and illegal trade.

Initially Vieira took office proclaiming his intention to mend the conflictual divides that had troubled the country, and salvage it from the economic abyss. Yet it did not take long before news started emerging of a very different agenda. The deal offered was one that put the remnants of the state to use in the country by offering its patronaged institutions to transnational criminal networks. Rumors in Bissau had been rife of Vieira making parts of his fortune by facilitating the smuggling of cocaine in the past. Undocumented as these rumors may have been, he re-entered Guinea-Bissauan politics by introducing an exceptionally profitable commodity into the almost bankrupt country. Rekindling a former smuggling connection, he had apparently convinced various key figures in the country's army to facilitate the trafficking of cocaine from Latin America into Europe by selling the services of the state apparatus to the cocaine cartels and passing on parts of the spoils to influential figures within the army, navy and police force. Vieira started his second mandate as the country's president by making Guinea-Bissau a key transit hub in the transatlantic trafficking of cocaine, using political offices and institutions to enrich and empower military positions and figurations. As he reassumed power, the cocaine trafficking in and through Bissau soared. In fact, the profit from the cocaine trade is currently said to dwarf the GNP (gross national product) of the country,[18] but rather than being distributed broadly and trickling down to the population at large, it is shared among a few key political and military figures, fed into the inner circles of patrimonial networks and overseas bank accounts (Vigh 2014).

President Vieira was literally back in business. Turning Guinea-Bissau into a trans-shipment hub by allowing the cartels to hide in the shadows of sovereign state was homologous to his own political practice of using official politics to further his illicit and illegal dealings. "The hyena [lobo] is back", people said of his return, and its ravening hunger was soon manifest. Controlling and distributing the spoils to his conspirators, he made a few people tremendously wealthy and started to consolidate his power by re-engaging many of his former political allies and partners in his new regime, working towards establishing a similar level of control to that he had possessed before his ousting.

However, cocaine is a volatile commodity and in terms of security outcomes his new move into the presidency was dire. First of all, it became – once again – clear that his role as a democrat was not a peaceful one. The intimidation and extrajudicial punishments that had characterized his earlier reign resurged. Second, after almost four years in office the political tensions started to increase between various figures benefiting from the illegal trade in the country. As fortunes were made, new political and military factions were forged bidding for higher and higher stakes in the profitable trade, and Vieira found himself in a situation where he was increasingly unable to control the configurations of power and profit that he had created. In theory, he was the country's president seeking to convince the outside world that he was doing his best to combat the cocaine trafficking that had now become prominent in Guinea-Bissau. In fact, he was trying to combat the political factions and networks, which increasingly competed for larger rewards of the trade at his expense.

The insecurity that follows in the wake of large-scale cocaine trafficking is well known from around the world. In Guinea-Bissau, the competition for power resulted in a number of assassinations, leading us back to the start of this chapter, with Vieira being attacked, shot and mutilated on 2 March 2009. The desecration of his corpse was an act of illumination, or "vivisection", as Appadurai (1998) has termed it – an attempt to decrease uncertainty by dismantling complex bodies and relationships into concrete parts. It was a demonstration, by his attackers, that the former hero of the war of independence had finally lost his powers and his uncanny potential for returning to power.

Conclusion

When in Bissau shortly before the presidential elections in 2009, I asked a group of interviewees what candidate they wanted to win. The question resulted in shrugged shoulders and despondent sighs. After a brief silence one of them, Djarnis, looked at me and said, "It doesn't matter. Politicians will do as they are wont to, eating money and telling lies". Trying to probe the issue further, I asked if they did not think that there was a good candidate running in the election? If there was not one who they thought "would work for the people, who will obey the law and be 'honest'"? Djarnis raised his head again and looked at me with an air of disbelief at the naiveté of the question, "But he would be killed, quickly!" At the time I did not fully understand the answer. Why? If people voted for an honest politician then surely he would be president? Was that not the name of the game? A bit later it dawned on me that it was not a question of me not understanding the rules of democracy, but rather me not understanding the elementary rules of contemporary politics in Bissau. What my interlocutor was trying to tell me was, of course, that if people voted for a politician who was *not* corrupt, criminally engaged and dictatorial, who did *not* condone the illicit use of state, and the illegal trade through it, then voting for him would be to waste one's vote, as he would be working against a dominant order that would simply get rid of him. In other words, if an honest politician stood to win, he would be taken out of the game by those who profit from the corruption and criminal activity that is rife under the democratic façade. Being democratically inclined in the "official" way will get you killed.

The awkward group interview speaks directly to the chapter and its policy relevance. It testifies to the banal fact that "democratization" and "statehood" may be different practices and have very different modalities of being than we might expect from a European perspective. This is, of course, an old truth in anthropology, yet if we look at political science, international organizations and relations it still seems that democracy is often approached as a political system naturally imbued with a potential for progress, freedom, peace and prosperity. Vieira ran as presidential candidate for the PAIGC in 1994 and as an independent candidate in 2005. He was elected into office in both campaigns. He put the country on track towards democratic constitutionalism and multiparty democracy. Yet while he may have been a democrat in in minimal institutional terms, his move toward democracy provides a prime example of how one may stage a transformation to democracy in order to maintain or even further autocratic control over both political institutions and the population. In fact, his move from warlord to democrat reads as a textbook example of the move from weak state to failed state to state capture – i.e. from functional failure to institutional failure to the wholesale use of state functions to serve non-public needs (Helpman et al. 2000).[19]

Democratization has gone hand in hand with a criminalization of the Guinea-Bissauan state. Both have been motivated by a desire to direct resources into political networks and consolidate or further patron-client relations. The many human rights violations which are ascribed to Vieira and his regime can in this perspective be seen to be motivated by much the same concerns, that is, as desperate attempts to secure the flow and access of resources into such socio-political networks. Tracing the political career of Nino Vieira and his various political representations has highlighted how the move from political tyrant to democratically elected president may imbue the latter with an alternative practical logic, bypassing presumed dimensions of democracy as rule of law, respect for human and civil rights, and a legitimate monopoly on violence. Vieira's qualities as a warlord, his ruthless control of the various military factions, and his ability to make the most out of a limited space of political and economic possibilities enabled him to win two democratic elections. As a politician he showcases the way democracy can be manipulated in order to serve essentially non-democratic purposes: he was the head of a democratic regime which governed without equalization of power or the rule of law, and worked through subjugation and domination rather than freedom and rights. What we see in Guinea-Bissau is a political system which may be attuned to democracy in the institutional sense, but where corruption, a lack of transparency, nepotism and embezzlement are part of democracy in the practical sense – not as a contrast but as a social logic that substantiates the entire political system.

If we look at actual process of democratization in Guinea-Bissau what we see is a process which may have included electoral strategies, official rights and regulations, and been practiced according to the rules, but which, rather than alleviating insecurity, resulted in human rights abuses and the criminalization of politics as security outcomes. Within the last twenty years, democratization has, in Bissau, led to an increasing criminalization of politics, which has gone hand in hand with human right abuses, coups d'état and chronic instability. Furthermore, the problem does not seem about to go away with the death of Vieira. As I write, the Guinea-Bissauan population has just voted a new president into power. Perhaps an estimable person, yet also a politician who is accused of embezzling €9 million of development aid, and who has vowed to "forgive" the criminal activity that has characterized the last ten years of institutionalized transnational organized crime in the country (Farge 2014). Despite the ongoing questioning of his honesty by national and international agencies, he won the second round of elections comfortably, backed by a military that exists outside the rule of law and in effect rules with impunity.

Notes

1 The Mouvement des forces démocratiques de Casamance, is a primarily Diola-based liberation movement in the Casamance region of southern Senegal. The Diola (in Guinea-Bissau known as Felupe) are the traditional inhabitants of parts of northern Guinea-Bissau and there has been movement of soldiers, goods and guns across the border.

2 Guinea-Bissau is rumoured to be used not just as a hub for the movement of cocaine from the Americas to Europe but equally as a transhipment point for Asian-produced drugs moving the other way. While the connection to Columbian and Venezuelan cartels is evident in Bissau, I have yet to have the latter confirmed, although there is evidence that points in the direction of close cooperation between agents on the various continents. See also:http://edition. cnn.com/2014/02/24/world/asia/philippines-mexico-sinaloa-cartel; http://www.scmp. com/news/hong-kong/article/1403433/ hong-kong-triads-supply-meth-ingredients-mexican-drug-cartels.

3 As their destinies, as Na Waie phrased it, were joined together (Vigh 2014).

4 A battalion of Balanta soldiers from the barracks in Manson.

5 The pictures of his battered body showed signs of multiple slashes to his head and torso.

6 As a reaction to the shooting of dockworkers demonstrating for higher wages in the harbours of Bissau, known as the Pinjiguiti massacre.

7 Forças Armadas Revolucionarias do Povo.

8 A name given to him by the Balanta, the ethnic group he was fighting and living with in the south of the country and whose young soldiers were later to kill him.

9 Cabral and Mendéz were, respectively, Presidente do Conselho de Estado and Comissário Principal of the National People's Assembly.

10 The evidence testifying to this is substantial (see for example Correio da Manhã 2010), yet no one has been held accountable, despite the fact that it was confirmed that the PAIGC was directly involved in the misdeed (Munslow 1981).

11 For further historical work on the political development in Bissau see also Lyon (1980), Forrest (1992, 2003: 222–232), Kovsted and Tarp (1999: 12) and Rudebeck (2001).

12 Primeira Revisao Constitucional, publicado no Suplemento ao B.D., no. 18, 9 May 1991.

13 Casamance, the southern part of Senegal bordering Gambia and Guinea-Bissau, has been the scene of a liberation war waged by the predominantly Diola (Felupe) based Mouvement des Forces Democratique de Casamance since 1982.

14 That is, a united military.

15 *Publico*, 24 September 1998.

16 The areas of prime strategic importance were, according to my high-ranking informants, primarily Bissau and the Bijagos islands, securing the government side access to both a port and an airstrip.

17 Report on the situation in Guinea-Bissau, prepared by the ECOWAS executive secretary, UN Security Council, 16 April 1999. ECOWAS is the Economic Community of West African States.

18 Testifying both to the poverty of the place as well as the lucrative possibilities of the informal economy. According to the UNODC (United Nations Office on Drugs and Crime), the value of the drug trade in Bissau is currently higher than the country's GNP. For an economy in which 80% of official revenue comes from development assistance, however, this probably does not say much. Yet the point is that the cocaine business and the subsequent flow of money it feeds into the country have become primary sources of income for groups like the police, military and navy, who have otherwise been paid irregularly, if at all, and feed off the country's population in order to gain an income.

19 The non-bureaucratic work of state is arguably more complex than the development theory of the demise of the post-colonial state may grasp (see de Sardan 1999; Blundo and de Sardan 2006).

Bibliography

Akokpari, J. and E. Azevedo. 2007. "Post-Conflict Elections in Africa. Liberia and Guinea-Bissau in Comparative Perspective." *African Journal of International Affairs* 10 (1-2): 73-92.

Amnesty International. 1999. *Guinea-Bissau: Human Rights in War and Peace*. Available from http://www.refworld.org/pdfid/45c06f252.pdf.

Appadurai, A. 1998. "Dead Certainty: Ethnic Violence in the Era of Globalization." *Development and Change* 29 (4): 905-925.

Bayart, J. F., S. Ellis and B. Hibou. 1999. *The Criminalization of the State in Africa*. Oxford: International African Institute.

BBC News. 2009. "Obituary: President Vieira of Guinea-Bissau." *BBC News*, 2 March. Available from http://news.bbc.co.uk/2/hi/africa/7918462.stm.

Blundo, G. and J.-P. O. de Sardan. 2006. *Everyday Corruption and the State*. London: Zed Books.

Cardoso, F. P. and A. Sjöberg. 2011. "Guinea-Bissau." In *The Security Sector and Gender in West Africa: A Survey of Police, Defense, Justice and Penal Services in ECOWAS States*, ed. M. Gaanderse and K. Valasek. Geneva: DCAF.

Chabal, P. 1981. "National Liberation in Portuguese Guinea, 1956-1974." *African Affairs* 80 (318): 75-99.

Correio da Manhã. 2010. "'Portugal desprezou soldados africanos'" [Portugal Despised its African Soldiers]. *Correio da Manhã*, 27 June. Available from http://www.cmjornal.xl.pt/domingo/detalhe/portugal-desprezou-soldados-africanos.html.[[5.24]

De Sá, F. G. C. 2010. *Os Sucessivos Golpes Militares No Processo da Democratização na Guiné-Bissau* [The Successive Military Coups in the Democratization Process in Guinea-Bissau]. Thesis: Universidade Federal do Rio Grande do Sul.

Farge, E. 2014. "Leading Candidate for Bissau's April Vote Faces Legal Objection." *Reuters*, 7 March. Available from http://www.reuters.com/places/africa/article/2014/03/07/us-bissau-election-idUSBREA2614H20140307.

Forrest, J. B. 1992. *Guinea-Bissau: Power, Conflict, and Renewal in a West African Nation*. Boulder, CO: Westview Press.

Forrest, J. 2002. "Guinea-Bissau." In: *A History of Postcolonial Lusophone Africa*, ed. P. Chabal. London: Hurst.

Forrest, J. 2003. *Lineages of State Fragility: Rural Civil Society in Guinea-Bissau*. Athens: Ohio University Press.

Helpman, J., G. Jones, and D. Kaufman. 2000. "Seize the State, Seize the Day." *World Bank Policy Research Working Paper* 2444.

International Republican Institute. 1994. *Guinea: Presidential Election Report 19 Dec 1993*. Available from http://www.iri.org/sites/default/files/Guinea's%201993%20Presidential%20Election.pdf.

Kovsted, J. and F. Tarp. 1999. *Guinea-Bissau. War, Reconstruction and Reform*. Working Papers 168. Helsinki: UNU World Institute for Development Economics Research.

Lyon, J. M. 1980. "Marxism and Ethno-nationalism in Guinea-Bissau, 1956-76." *Ethnic and Racial Studies* 3 (2): 156-168.

Mark, P. 1999. "The Evolution of 'Portuguese' Identity: Luso Africans on the Upper Guinean Coast from the Sixteenth to the Nineteenth Century." *Journal of African History* 40 (2): 173-191.

Mark, P. 2002. *Portuguese Style and Luso-African Identity*. Bloomington: Indiana University Press.

Mendy, P. K. and R. A. Lobban. 2013. *Historical Dictionary of the Republic of Guinea-Bissau*. Plymouth: Scarecrow Press.

Munslow, B. 1981. "The 1980 Coup in Guinea-Bissau." *Review of African Political Economy* 8 (21): 109-113.

Rudebeck, L. 2001. "On Democracy's Sustainability: Transition in Guinea-Bissau." *Sida Studies* No. 4. Swedish International Development Cooperation Agency.

US Department of State. 1987. *Country Report on Human Rights Practices for 1986*. February. Available from http://www.ecoi.net/local_link/239075/348306_en.html.

Vigh, H. E. 2006. *Navigating Terrains of War: Youth and Soldiering in Guinea-Bissau*. Oxford: Berghahn Books.

Vigh, H. E. 2008. "Crisis and Chronicity: Anthropological Perspectives on Continuous Conflict and Decline." *Ethnos* 73 (1): 5-24.

Vigh, H. E. 2009. "Conflictual Motion and Political Inertia: On Rebellions and Revolutions in Bissau and Beyond." *African Studies Review* 52 (2): 143-164.

Vigh, H. 2011. "Vigilance: On Negative Potentiality and Social Invisibility." *Social Analysis* 55 (4): 93-114.

Vigh, H. E. 2014. "La Marginalité Centrale: Sur les Réseaux, la Cocaïne et la Criminalité Transnationale en Guinée-Bissau" [Central Marginality: Networks, Cocaine and Transnational Crime in Guinea-Bissau]. *Socio* 3 (1): 289-313

Weston, M. 2009. *Joao Bernardo Vieira: A Turbulent Life in a Turbulent Country*. Global Dashboard. Available from: http://www.globaldashboard.org/2009/03/02/joao-bernardo-vieira-a-turbulent-life-in-a-turbulent-country/.

6 | Shape-shifters in the struggle for survival: post-war politics in Sierra Leone

Mimmi Söderberg Kovacs and Ibrahim Bangura

Introduction

The civil war in Sierra Leone was born out of a widespread failure of governance characterized by discriminatory practices and lack of respect for human rights and the rule of law. Almost a decade of violent conflict further contributed to an escalating cycle of repression and state collapse. Strengthening and reinforcing democratic institutions and practices was therefore a key priority in the peacebuilding process after the end of the war. In November 2012, the third post-war elections in Sierra Leone were held, and a large body of domestic and international election observers unanimously declared the process generally free of manipulation and malpractice. As such, the country has come a long way in breaking with its past. Yet, at the same time, the legacy of warfare is evident in post-war politics. A plethora of former military men – rebel combatants, militia and army soldiers – have navigated their way from the armed struggle into democratic politics. In a society where power and resources are still largely concentrated at the centre, most flagrantly in the office of the executive, the temptation to get involved in politics is high, and the potential benefits are many for those that succeed in carving out political space for themselves. Key personalities who rose to prominence during the civil war have therefore continued to pursue their struggle for political influence and significance as the context has shifted from war to peace and from military rule to democratic politics. In spite of this, very little is known about the effects of their participation on post-war politics. In particular, we lack a more detailed understanding of why some of these individuals have used their wartime legacy to instigate insecurity and violence while others have not. This is the research problem that motivates this study.

In this chapter, we take a closer look at three such prominent shape shifters, who all played key roles during the war, albeit in different organizations and during different time periods, but whose post-war political behavior displays a range of interesting variations that warrant further exploration. Samuel Hinga Norman, founder and leader of the Kamajors – a civil militia from the southeast which emerged as one of the key warring parties during the civil war in their resistance against both the rebel forces and turncoat army soldiers – assumed the position of deputy minister of defense during the wartime administration of the Sierra Leone People's Party (SLPP) and President Ahmad Tejan Kabbah. As such, he did not run for an elected position during the first post-war elections in 2002, but supported the flag-bearer of the party with the ambition of being reappointed. After the SLPP secured an overwhelming electoral victory, he was appointed minister of internal affairs under the second Kabbah administration. While in office, Norman had everything to gain from reinforcing the image of himself as a war hero and a stout supporter of the fragile peace process. However, after the Special Court for Sierra Leone (SCSL) indicted him for war crimes, Norman bitterly engaged in statements and behavior that served to securitize wartime identities and possibly even encourage incidents of organized violence by his former militia men. Because he was still in prison at the time of the run-up to the 2007 elections, he was personally prevented from running for office, but he publicly and vocally engaged in the campaign to mobilize votes for the SLPP breakaway party the People's Movement for Democratic Change (PMDC). There is little doubt that the reason for his behavior, including his radical switch, was primarily personal in nature and driven by his fall from the throne. Brigadier General Julius Maada Bio was for a brief period head of state during the war under the military junta known as the National Provisional Ruling Council (NPRC). After a decade in exile, he returned to the country after the war and joined the SLPP. In 2011, he succeeded in winning the internal party nomination for presidential candidate in the 2012 elections, largely due to his background as military strongman. Although very careful to publicly dissociate himself from any incidents of low-level organized violence committed by his supporters, Maada Bio's electoral career has undoubtedly benefited from his association with militarism and violence. While there is little if no concrete evidence that such violence has been directly ordered or organized by Maada Bio himself, it is highly improbable that it could have taken place without his open or tacit consent. Eldred Collins was spokesperson of the rebel group the Revolutionary United Front (RUF) throughout the civil war, and continued in this position after the group transformed into a political party, the Revolutionary United Front Party (RUFP), in the run-up to the first post-war elections in 2002. He subsequently tried to join other parties, but was eventually elected as the presidential flag-bearer for the revived RUFP in 2012 and personally ran for office for the first time. While still retaining a party name that evokes memories of the armed group and in spite of still appealing to political issues close to the hearts of many former combatants, Collins deliberately downplayed the origins of the party and made great efforts to distance himself personally from his wartime legacy during the campaign. Considering the lingering negative perceptions of the rebels in the mind of the electorate as well among other political parties, this was his only chance at a post-war political career.

This chapter is structured as follows. First, a short background section is provided, in which some of the main trajectories of the civil war are discussed. In addition, the key events of the post-war period are traced through the holding of three general elections in 2002, 2007 and 2012 respectively. Second, each of the selected warlord democrats is discussed in more detail as they navigate their way from wartime to peacetime politics. In the third and concluding section, we draw attention to the similarities and differences between the cases and suggest some findings in regard to their various outcomes. Some of the potential implications for policy priorities for local and international actors involved in post-war peacebuilding processes are also discussed.

The transition from war to peace in Sierra Leone

On 18 January 2002, the civil war in Sierra Leone was officially declared "don don" (over in the Krio language). A few months later, in May 2002, the first post-war elections were held. Since then, security has been stabilized throughout the country, and over a decade down the road the country is oftentimes referred to as a success story in terms of both its durable peace and its strengthening of democratic institutions. In light of its political history, this may be considered a remarkable break with the past. But it is equally true that the legacy of the past is constantly present in post-war politics, not least in the continuous existence and recycling of a number of key political figures with their political roots in the dynamics of the civil war. For an understanding of the dynamics of post-war politics in Sierra Leone, it is essential to understand the political context that shaped the emergence of the individuals in focus in this study.

In March 1991, the RUF together with a small group of regional mercenaries attacked villages in the eastern and southern parts of the country. It was soon announced over the radio that their proclaimed political goal was to overthrow the one-party regime of the All People's Congress (APC) and restore multiparty democracy to Sierra Leone (Richards 1998). Although the political maturity of this essentially military enterprise would eventually be questioned in the light of widespread atrocities against the civilian population, the group was initially able to play on widespread sentiments of resentment due to years of bad governance, political ostracization and disrespect for the rule of law. In particular, young people with few viable alternatives for survival and prospects for influence made up an easy pool of recruits (Bangura and Specht 2012: 55). The ensuing armed conflict caught the dilapidated state military off-guard. In April 1992, a group of lower ranking young soldiers from the front line protesting over the poor conditions of service stormed Freetown and established the NPRC. In spite of initial enthusiasm among large parts of the population it soon became evident that the politically inexperienced soldiers were ill-equipped for governance (Abraham 2004). Evidence soon emerged that soldiers were cooperating with the rebels in the illegal diamond trade in rebel-controlled territories and in the looting of the civilian population, giving birth to the expression "sobels": soldiers by day, and rebels by night (Abdullah and Muana 1998: 182). In response to the deteriorating security situation, various local defense militias began to appear, including the southeastern-based civilian militia, known as the Kamajors.

Facing mounting internal and international criticism, the unity of the NPRC began to crumble and an internal palace coup brought Brigadier-General Julius Maada Bio to power in January 1996. However, a road map for the transition to civilian rule had already been agreed and, in spite of attempts by Bio to postpone them, the scheduled elections were held in March the same year, and four years of military rule came to an end. President Kabbah and the SLPP secured an overwhelming electoral victory at the polls. One of the first tasks of the new government was to continue the peace talks that had already been initiated between the NPRC and the RUF and in November 1996 the Abidjan Peace Agreement was eventually signed. However, the RUF soon stalled on its commitment to the peace accord and refused to adhere to its terms. The last hope that the rebels would abide by the peace process died on 25 May 1997, when a new military coup took place in Freetown. Major Johnny Paul Koroma was announced as the leader of the new Armed Forces Revolutionary Council (AFRC), which was made up of an alliance between some junior officers and elements within the army and representatives of the RUF, including Collins. Kabbah and most of his administration – with the critical exception of Norman – went into exile, while Koroma dissolved the parliament, suspended the constitution and banned all political activities.

In the wake of further diplomatic failures, troops from the Economic Community of West African States Monitoring Group (ECOMOG), in cooperation with the civilian militias under the lead of Norman, chased the AFRC out of power in February 1998 and reinstated Kabbah. Several junta members and some of their supporters were charged with treason and arrested. Norman continued to serve as the deputy minister of defense, the position he held before the 1996 coups d'état. However, in January 1999 former soldiers in collaboration with the RUF attacked the capital again. International actors pressured Kabbah to seek another diplomatic alternative and in July 1999 the Lomé Peace Agreement was signed. The accord was a far-reaching version of a power-sharing agreement, which provided four cabinet posts for the RUF in the government and four deputy-ministerial positions for the duration of the term of office of the government.

The agreement also requested the United Nations Observer Mission in Sierra Leone (UNOMSIL) and ECOMOG to jointly comprise a peacekeeping force to oversee the implementation. These were later replaced by the United Nations Mission in Sierra Leone (UNAMSIL), acting under Chapter VII of the UN Charter. However, the implementation of the agreement was slow and marked by setbacks. In May 2000, the parties returned to open hostilities, leading to a British military invasion to help stabilize the situation in the country. The event also triggered a massive civil protest in Freetown outside Sankoh's residence, which turned violent. Sankoh fled but was subsequently arrested and incarcerated alongside a large number of other leading RUF personalities, including Collins. In subsequent months, an alliance of UN and British troops in collaboration with the civil militia and former AFRC soldiers led by Koroma successfully recaptured several strategic areas previously under rebel control, and in November 2000 a ceasefire agreement was signed in Abuja, Nigeria. Fighting resumed however, and, in May 2001, the parties met yet again in Abuja for a review of the agreement, followed by the re-initiation of the disarmament process.

The first post-war elections were held in May 2002. For the incumbent president and the SLPP it was a landslide victory. Both the RUFP and the People's Liberation Party (PLP) led by former APRC leader Koroma participated in the elections but none of them received more than a fraction of the votes (Kandeh 2003). In the spring of 2003, the SCSL, which had been established as a direct response to the events of May 2000 when the RUF returned to war, issued its first indictments. Altogether thirteen people from the key leadership circles of the warring parties since 1996 – including Norman – were indicted for war crimes, crimes against humanity and violation of international humanitarian law. A few months later, the court also indicted Charles Taylor, the President of Liberia.

In 2007, in the second post-war elections, the competition was fierce between the incumbent SLPP and the opposition APC. The APC, which had spent the early post-war years trying to remake the tarnished image of the party, went to the polls with a political promise to bring development to the country, a message that went down well with large parts of the population who had yet to share the spoils of peace. Another key contribution to the success of the APC was attributed to internal fragmentation in the SLPP. The formation of a breakaway party, PMDC, was to split the traditional SLPP voter base in its stronghold areas in the south and the east. Many well-known SLPP figures, including Norman, decided to publicly support the new party. The divorce was instrumental in the victory of the APC, which eventually emerged with the majority of the votes in a violent run-off (Kandeh 2008).

The period following the coming to power of the APC saw an intense leadership struggle in the SLPP, eventually resulting in the coming to power of Bio in 2011 as the new flag-bearer of the party. Somewhat surprisingly, the RUFP, which had been declared bankrupt and closed down its party offices prior to the 2007 elections, also re-emerged as a contender in the run-up to the third post-war general elections in 2012, with former RUF spokesman

Collins as the new party leader and presidential candidate. Much like previous elections, the 2012 election campaign had only little to do with competing ideas and policies, and more to do with a fierce struggle for power, access to resources and political survival. The race was again very close between the APC and the SLPP, with tension mounting in various parts of the country including Freetown. President Koroma eventually received 58.7% of the votes, with Bio coming in second with 37.4% (BBC News 2012). The SLPP contested the result on the grounds of fraud and malpractice, but on 14 June 2013 the Supreme Court eventually struck off the petition due to procedural technicalities (Awareness Times 2013). Both parties have subsequently faced an intense power struggle over who will represent them in the 2017 elections.

The ex-militaries and their road to electoral politics

The betrayed war hero: Samuel Hinga Norman Born in Mongeri in Bo District in southern Sierra Leone in 1940, Sam Hinga Norman joined the military at an early age and rose to the rank of captain. Already at this time he was known to be a supporter of the SLPP, and was imprisoned for his involvement in a coup against Siaka Stevens in 1967 (Hoffman 2011: 94). In 1972, Norman left the army and went into self-imposed exile, spending several years in Liberia (Gberie 2005: 85). Under the NPRC junta, he was appointed regent-chief of Jaiama-Bongor chiefdom, neighboring his home village (Hoffman 2011: 39). In response to the widespread insecurity that followed the breakout of the war, civil defense units mobilized across the country to protect their communities from both rebels and renegade soldiers, partly drawing on traditions and mythologies of local hunters, and sometimes in association with the chiefdom structures. Some of these units emerged as the Tamaboros, Gbetis and Kapras in the Northern Province, the Donsos in the east (Kono District) and the Kamajors in the southern and eastern regions. The Kamajors eventually became the most prominent among these community defense groups (Muana 1997). Some of its reputed organization during the war may have been owed to Norman's military background as he rose to become the head of the Kamajors.

After the return to civilian and democratic rule in March 1996, President Kabbah named Norman his deputy minister of defense. Norman's appointment was viewed with suspicion by the army – still largely dominated by northerners from the days of the APC regime – as they believed that the SLPP government was promoting the Kamajors over the established state army. This impression was further aggravated by Kabbah's plans to significantly downsize the army (Keen 2005: 197–202). Soon after Norman's appointment, parliament legalized the use of arms by the militias, thereby effectively legitimizing them as regular state troops. Norman was thus able to continue to recruit, train and arm the Kamajors across the south and the east during his time in office, and armed confrontations between the army and the militia upcountry was commonplace (Hoffman 2011: 42, 94–95; Gberie 2005: 86). Kabbah (2010: 58) admits in his memoir, "[m]y appointment of Chief Sam Hinga Norman ... seemed to have angered certain sections of the military hierarchy, who mischievously told their fellow soldiers that I intended to create a parallel force that would rival the Constitutional Army". Having spent less than a year in power, the government of Kabbah was overthrown on 25 May 2007 by the AFRC. One of their first moves was to outlaw the Kamajors, and go on an offensive against towns and villages believed to support the militia (Gberie 2004: 156).

As the only member of cabinet to stay in the country throughout the junta period, Norman became one of the leading organizers of the armed resistance against the AFRC. All existing civil militia units in the country were brought together under a single united command, to be known as the Civil Defense Force (CDF). Although Kabbah was formally named the supreme head of the CDF, Norman became the effective coordinator of the CDF and worked closely with the regional peacekeeping force, ECOMOG, and other forces loyal to Kabbah (Gberie 2005: 108–109). ECOMOG forces eventually captured Freetown in February 1998 and returned Kabbah to power. With his reinstatement, Kabbah maintained Norman as his deputy minister of defense. However, the relationship between Kabbah and Norman appeared to have become strained during the year in exile. Allegedly, Norman frequently complained that Kabbah did not provide enough support to the Kamajors, and oftentimes carelessly voiced his desire to one day assume power. Kabbah, for his part, is likely to have begun to see Norman as a potential threat, and after his return he took several steps to diminish his reliance on the military power of the CDF (Hoffman 2011: 47).

As a minister appointed by the sitting president, Norman did not run personally for office in the first post-war elections in 2002 but actively supported Kabbah's re-election. After Kabbah and the SLPP had secured an overwhelming victory, Norman was reappointed to cabinet, but this time as minister of internal affairs. Some argue that the reason was that Kabbah wanted to promote Norman to a full cabinet position as a reward for his support during the war. Others, however, argue that Kabbah's primary concern was to remove Norman from the Ministry of Defense to appease the anti-Norman factions in the military.[1] As long as Norman remained in government, he was known as a supporter of the largely SLPP-administered peace process. Widely considered a war hero and one of the key personalities responsible for defeating the rebels and returning the country to peace and democracy, Norman had everything to gain from further reinforcing this picture of him and his former CDF fighters as custodians of peace.

However, all this changed abruptly when the newly established SCSL issued its first indictments on 10 March 2003. Norman was named as one of eventually a total of twelve top commanders of the armed factions who would be arrested and tried for bearing "the greatest responsibility for war crimes, crimes against humanity and violation of international humanitarian law" committed since the 1996 peace accord.[2] The Kabbah administration – of which Norman was a member – had originally intended the court to exclusively target the RUF for atrocities during the war (United Nations 2000). It was only later decided that the investigation was going to include potential war crimes committed by all the warring parties.[3] Hence, when Norman and two other high-level CDF leaders were indicted, many Sierra Leonean expressed shock and disbelief. Three days after the announcement, Norman was arrested in his office and brought to a detention centre on the Bonthe Islands (Gberie 2005: 213).

Norman's arrest became one of the most serious security challenges to the peace process in the post-war period. Special security measures were taken with regard to Norman's detention, as rumors spread that Kamajors and former CDF members were planning a march on the capital. Although it was later revealed that these rumors were likely to have been exaggerated, many in his stronghold areas in the south and the east considered his arrest a betrayal and a craftily devised political ploy to remove Norman from the political scene (ICG 2003: 5–7). As stated by one supporter: "Norman was an agent of democracy and should have been protected rather than left under the claws of the Special Court. They wanted him out because he had the intention of leading the SLPP and was very popular and loved by us his people."[4]

Norman's own statements and behavior during his arrest only served to further fuel such sentiments. When asked specifically in an interview if he felt betrayed or let down by President Kabbah, Norman is alleged to have responded:

I feel more than being let down or betrayed [...] what I feel is that the impunity which is prevailing here today through the Special Court, with state complicity, if not checked, would plunge this country into another bloody conflict even when some of us are behind bars. (Quoted in ICG 2003: 7, n. 41)

On another occation, Norman had all his external communication and visits except for those with his lawyers restricted for fourteen days after the Special Court had intercepted a telephone conversation between Norman and an unidentified person. According to the official statement by the court: "The content of the intercepted conversation indicated his involvement in coordinating activities calculated to cause civil unrest in Sierra Leone ...[e]ffective immediately, Norman will no longer be able to make or receive telephone calls, except to his legal representatives." According to the Special Court's Chief Prosecutor David Crane, the telephone conversation "demonstrates that Hinga Norman may be prepared to call various factions to arms" (quoted in AllAfrica 2004).

Both these examples suggest that Norman deliberately attempted to securitize wartime identities during his time in prison, and possibly even encourage or instigate incidents of organized violence by his former CDF commanders, although evidence of the latter is scarce. Although Norman did not initially engage in such activities as a means to influence electoral politics, he later used similar rhetoric to mobilize electoral support for the SLPP breakaway party, the PMDC, in the run-up to the second post-war elections in 2007. Although Norman was behind bars at the time and thus prevented from personally participating in electoral politics, he was still an influential and popular political figure with considerable leverage in the public debate. His public endorsement of the PMDC thus contributed to boost support for the new party in traditional SLPP strongholds, especially in areas where the Kamajors were popular (World Press 2007). In what became a closely contested and violent election, the electoral success of the PMDC tipped the balance in favor of the APC when it publicly endorsed the latter during the second round of the presidential elections (Kandeh 2008).[5] However, Norman was never to experience the day of the elections. As the trial progressed his health deteriorated, and on 17 January 2007 he was flown to Senegal for surgery. On 22 February he was reported dead. His death provoked strong reactions and some of his supporters alleged that there might have been foul play involved. However, an investigation later established that Norman had died of natural causes (Special Court for Sierra Leone 2007: Paragraphs 2 and 3).

The reformed junta leader: Julius Maada Bio In January 1996, Brigadier General Julius Maada Bio overthrew his comrade Captain Valentine Strasser, the leader of the NPRC, following internal divisions within the military junta. The NPRC had been ruling the country since 1992, when they forced the one-party APC regime from power in a coup d'état. The culprits behind the coup were all lower-ranked frontline soldiers who had grown weary of the desolate conditions provided for them by the government. The junta was initially met with support among large parts of the population, who sympathized with the junta's declared ambition to end the war with the RUF and fight corruption. However, as the war dragged on, the inadequacies of the inexperienced junta leaders became increasingly apparent, and the support for the regime dwindled (Rashid 2004: 83–86). Instead of ending the war, rebels and soldiers colluded to share benefits derived from illegal mining and looting of the civilian population. Consequently, in 1995, the junta was forced by growing international and domestic pressure to agree to a timetable for election and a return to democratic rule (Abraham 2004).

In one of his first public statements, Maada Bio reassured the people of Sierra Leone that elections would be held as promised. However, his position quickly changed, and he spent his short time as Head of State trying to convince domestic public opinion that elections should be postponed until peace with the rebels had been established, a message he unsuccessfully put forth in the second so-called Bintumani conference – a broad-based consultative forum with societal and political organizations – held in mid-February 1996 (Kandeh 2004: 127–129). The attempt to remain in power failed, however, and the elections were held as scheduled at the end of February 1996 with a second round in the presidential elections in mid-March, which brought the SLPP and President Kabbah to office.[6]

Following his removal from power, Maada Bio retired from the army and was given a lucrative offer of a scholarship abroad. He first moved to France and later to the United States, where, among other things, he was to pursue his university studies.[7] It was not until after the end of the war and close to a decade in exile that Bio returned to Sierra Leone. In 2005, he signed up as an official member of the SLPP, and in the run-up to the second post-war elections scheduled for 2007 he made his first attempt to seek the party's ticket for the presidential election. However, most observers agree that the outcome of the nomination process was settled beforehand, and it was well known that President Kabbah favored Solomon Berewa – who had served as vice president since 2002 – as his successor (Kandeh 2008: 611). According to Maada Bio, he was well aware that the nomination process was in reality "a done deal", and his main purpose of running was not based on the hope of winning but rather to use the opportunity to "present himself as a civilian".[8] After his loss, Maada Bio publicly supported Berewa during the 2007 election campaign as his personal security detail (Standard Times 2007a, 2007c). As such, he was accused of mobilizing youth gangs who were responsible for several of the violent attacks conducted in the highly contested election campaign (Standard Times 2007b).

At the time of the third post-war elections in 2012, the political landscape had changed completely. The APC's first term in office was accompanied with a widespread public perception that Koroma's administration was able to deliver much-needed reforms and development, not least in terms of urban infrastructure and health care. Consequently, the party was gaining popularity far beyond its traditional northern support base. Internally, the SLPP faced a deep identity and leadership crisis. One of the factors contributing to the SLPP's loss at the 2007 polls was the split in the traditional SLPP vote caused by the formation of the PMDC by SLPP veteran Charles Margai. The competition between the SLPP and the PMDC in the 2007 elections was fierce and sometimes violent. Tensions peaked during the campaign period for the second round of the presidential elections, after the PMDC publicly endorsed Koroma, a move that eventually gained the party four ministerial positions in the new cabinet (ICG 2007, 2008).

Following the elections, many SLPP supporters and party representatives across the country voiced the need for substantial internal party changes in order to be able to challenge the APC in the 2012 elections. Among these voices, many advocated their desire for a more youthful and belligerent leadership, who would be able to counter the APC's perceived aggressiveness, a reputation acquired during the years of the one-party state.[9] Against this background, Maada Bio stated his intention to run in the internal SLPP race for presidential candidate in 2011. Altogether, there were nineteen contenders for the post and uncertainty about the outcome created intense speculation among SLPP supporters.[10] While outsiders to the party often dismissed Maada Bio as a credible alternative due to his political past, it was most likely precisely his military background that eventually earned him the party's ticket. Many in the party believed that only a former militarist like Bio would stand a chance of winning power back from the APC (The Patriotic Vanguard 2011a, 2011b). The term "Tormentor" was commonly used as a campaign slogan, referring to Bio's legacy as one of the men who overthrew the one-party regime of the APC in 1992. Another alleged reason for Bio's success was the perception of him as the person who brought back democracy to Sierra Leone after years of military rule, and, by extension, brought the SLPP back to power in 1996 (The Patriotic Vanguard 2011b).

Widespread and persistent reporting implicated Maada Bio's supporters as key culprits of violence before, during and after the 2012 elections. For example, on the day of the SLPP convention, it was reported that young Bio supporters outside the SLPP office in Freetown verbally insulted both Chairman John Benjamin and the National Women's Leader Isatu Kabbah (The Patriotic Vanguard 2011a). In one of the most serious events during the election campaign, rival party supporters clashed in Bo in September 2011 after Bio was hit on the head by a stone during a campaign event. During the resulting street riots, the local APC office was burnt to the ground along with two other buildings. The situation descended into widespread violence and the police responded with teargas and live bullets. One man was subsequently confirmed dead and over thirty people were injured (The Patriotic Vanguard 2011a). Another alarming confrontation took place on 12 October 2012 when convoys of Maada Bio and President Koroma clashed in central Freetown (Sierra Leone Media Express 2012).

Hence, Maada Bio's electoral career has been marked by incidents of organized violence from the outset. Yet it is difficult if not impossible to determine with any certainty the extent to which such violence carried out in his name has been directly ordered by him or not, or even how much he has known about and encouraged these activities. However, it seems highly unlikely that they could have taken place without his open or tacit support, and it is clear that such violence has served him well in his pursuit of power. In Bio's public appearances he has frequently and repeatedly urged his supporters to remain law-abiding citizens and refrain from violence. During his acceptance speech at the convention, he repeatedly warned his supporters that they have "no immunity" in this respect (Awareness Times 2011). Likewise, when asked about these violent incidents initiated by his supporters, Bio is quick to condemn any acts of violence carried out in his name, claiming that he frequently takes measures to explain to his supporters that he does not encourage such actions.[11] Whether true or not, it is evident that he has taken careful and deliberate measures to publicly distance himself both from his image as a military man and from all violent acts carried out in his name or in support of his party.

As anticipated by many, the sitting President Koroma of the APC secured a second term in power with almost 59% of the votes cast in the November 2012 general election, thereby avoiding a run-off against Maada Bio, who received 37.4% of the votes (Sierra Leone Telegraph 2012). On 24 November, the day after the announcement of the results, Maada Bio publicly declared that his party was not going to accept the results of a rigged election and that election outcome did not reflect the true will of the population (Söderberg Kovacs 2012). Although simultaneously calling on his supporters to remain calm and law-abiding while awaiting the official action of the SLPP, his message was most likely interpreted by at least some of his supporters as a go-ahead for continued protests and violent resistance (Söderberg Kovacs 2012). The next couple of weeks saw several outbreaks of election-related violence, particularly in the south and the east, but all were effectively contained by the state's security forces, and did not escalate into any serious clashes.

Eventually, Bio also officially conceded his electoral defeat and the tensions gradually subsided. The SLPP did however petition a complaint against the process and the election outcome to the Supreme Court, but on 14 June 2013 the court ruled against the SLPP on procedural grounds (The New People Newspaper 2013).

The shadow man: Eldred Collins

Collins was born in 1954 in eastern Freetown. He attended secondary school at the Albert Academy but later left Sierra Leone for Jamaica together with an uncle. He subsequently went to Liberia, where he met with Foday Sankoh, who told him about his plans and ideas. Collins allegedly agreed to join the planned military intervention in Sierra Leone, and suggested to Sankoh he "could be in charge of the political side of things".[12] Because he lacked a military background, and because, in his own words, he "did not want to fight or carry a gun", his role in the rebel hierarchy was to be primarily administrative in character, belonging to the small group of men whose roles and responsibilities were vaguely defined as "spokesmen" of the movement.[13] According to the Truth and Reconciliation Commission's (TRC) report, the individuals who held these administrative positions in the RUF from the outset tended to remain influential leadership figures in the RUF throughout the war (TRC 2004: 49, Vol. II, Ch. II). This is in contrast to many of the original military leaders, who are well known to have been killed by Sankoh, since he perceived as rivals to his own ambitions for power (Abdullah 1998). According to former RUF rank-and-file members, Collins was one of five men in the absolute power circle around Sankoh who remained loyal to him rather than the rebel movement. These were also the ones who allegedly kept power in their own hands after Sankoh was removed from active leadership (Richards and Vincent 2008: 92–93).[14] According to a source close to the RUF High Command:

> Collins was with the movement throughout the war and played a leading role advising Sankoh and Sam Bockarie. In fact he was part of the political machinery that guided that movement after Sankoh was arrested in Nigeria. Mosquito and others listened to him and he was seen as the political guide that intended to provide the RUF with a philosophy.[15]

When asked about his own role during the early war years, Collins becomes defensive about the failed political project of the RUF and explains:

> We spent a lot of time trying to talk to people about the purpose of the movement. We tried to explain the politics to the people. I tried to talk to Sankoh and explain that we needed to educate the soldiers too. I said: No one who does not understand the ideology should be part of the movement. But he did not want to listen. He said: "This is not the time for politics; this is the time for war". So I was not successful. And we had great problems with the Liberian NPFL fighters, who were committing lots of atrocities and looting etc. They were not interested in these things.[16]

In 1997, when the RUF was invited to join the AFRC junta in Freetown, Collins was one of three RUF members to be granted a seat in the ruling council. However, as Collins himself readily admits, "[i]t was not really politics though. We had all these uneducated RUF people who were roaming the streets, causing trouble".[17] When the RUF was granted extensive power-sharing responsibilities according to the terms of the Lomé agreement in 1999, Collins was appointed to one of the four ministerial positions. However, he never had the opportunity to take up his position, as the rebels returned to open warfare in May 2000. Instead, Collins was among the 400 RUF members that were arrested by the police after the attack on Freetown and held in detention at the Pademba Road prison (Keen 2005: 264; Richards and Vincent 2008: 82). He was imprisoned for sixteen months, but was never charged and was eventually released.

After the end of the war and the defeat of the RUF as a military movement, the remnants of the former rebel group attempted to transform into a political party. The RUFP was officially registered as a political party, party offices were opened in downtown Freetown, Bo and Makeni, and the Nigerian government provided some training and technical equipment for party officers (Mitton 2008: 202). Collins continued in his role as spokesperson for the movement, although now officially termed Public Relations Officer (Gberie 2005: 194). However, it was an uphill struggle, and the party lacked both the necessary funds and the party structure to realistically establish itself as a viable political contender (ICG 2001). One key disadvantage was the lack of a principal figure. Because Sankoh was still imprisoned, Alimamy Pallo Bangura – a university professor and one of Collins' fellow AFRC cabinet ministers – was eventually named the presidential candidate. Collins did not personally run for any post, but only supported the party and its flag-bearer. The elections were held in May 2002. The RUFP received only a small fraction of the national votes, with 1.73% in the presidential elections and 2.1% in the parliamentary elections, hence failing to acquire a single seat in the Sierra Leonean parliament (Kandeh 2003).

After the elections, some former RUF members, including Collins, remained in the party for a while, but faced with great difficulties in sustaining themselves financially and experiencing further fractionalization in the party's leadership, many eventually resigned. After four of its top members were indicted in 2003, the situation was aggravated even further (ICG 2003). In 2005, Collins officially announced his resignation from the party (AllAfrica 2005). Allegedly, he subsequently attempted to join both the APC and the SLPP, but nothing concrete resulted. In 2007, in the run-up to the second post-war elections, the RUFP was publicly declared bankrupt and officially ceased to exist as a party. According to reports at the time, the remnants of the party joined the APC (Kandeh 2008: 612; Mitton 2008: 202). However, this was subsequently denied both by the RUFP and the APC.[18] In 2009, the RUF-P suddenly re-emerged with the announcement that Collins had been elected acting interim leader of the party, replacing Issa Sesay who had been sentenced by the Special Court (The Patriotic Vanguard 2009). In August 2012, at the national party convention in Kenema, Collins was elected as the flag-bearer of the party for the upcoming presidential elections (Awareness Times 2012). The party expanded its infrastructure across the country and succeeded in nominating candidates for seats in the parliament and for local councillorships (Al Jazeera 2014).

During the election campaign, Collins focused his political message on the need for economic development, education and health care (Politico 2012). Although these are issues that a large number of former RUF combatants are generally believed to consider important, the same may be said for the population at large. Hence, there is little to suggest that Collins attempted to use his wartime legacy to mobilize voters or deliberately appeal to his former wartime constituency, other than in a more general sense taking advantage of widespread feelings of marginalization and exclusion from the peace dividends shared by the great majority. In fact, it appears as if Collins during his campaign deliberately distanced himself from his past with the realization that such a strategy was likely to have negative effects on his ability to mobilize votes:

> When I went campaigning, I never spoke of the war. I never mentioned it. I talked about development. I am even thinking about re-branding the party, changing its name. I want to remove the "R" in the RUFP. People associate the name with what the RUF did and the atrocities during the war. But the others in the party disagree.[19]

When asked if he had experienced any problems or opposition during his campaign due to resentment regarding the association with the RUF, Collins is quick to separate himself from the rest of the armed movement in general: "Not me personally. Never. People know me, and what I stand for. They came to see me. But others, former combatants, were attacked during the campaign as the party brought back old memories and antagonized people".[20] Hence, Collins' participation in post-war electoral politics does not appear to have had any negative security implications, at least not in any direct or substantial way.

In spite of relatively bleak prospects for the revived RUFP in the fiercely contested 2012 general elections, Collins was optimistic about the outcome. During an interview at the new party headquarters on the outskirts of eastern Freetown only a few days before the announcement of the election results in November 2012, Collins expressed his strong conviction that the party would fare well in the elections. However, it was also clear that, perhaps somewhat more realistically, he hoped for a close race between the APC and the SLPP, in which neither of them would acquire the necessary 50% needed to avoid a runoff.[21] A runoff would have opened up a possible bargaining situation, and hence also prospects of personal gains, power and influence. However, after the announcement of the result, it was clear that Collins had been unable to mobilize the voters, with only 0.6% of the votes cast in the presidential election and no seats gained for the RUFP in the parliamentary race. In addition, Koroma and the APC had won the race with significant margins, and Collins was thus forced to accept a continued role in the political periphery.

His electoral defeat does not seem to have particularly disappointed Collins, however, and by December 2013 he was in the process of seeking out new avenues for his political survival. At the time, he was primarily considering two options, either to radically "re-brand" the party by changing the name to distance it further from the association with the RUF, or to join another party. Apparently, at the time, he had already approached the APC to negotiate his possibilities for joining the party. Rumors about an upcoming reshuffle in the cabinet raised his hopes for another successful shape-shifting strategy. Or, as put by Collins in passing, when reflecting on the different choices people make, "you have to be creative and find opportunities. You cannot, like most of my people, just sit and beg".[22]

Conclusions

Shape-shifting is a frequently used and sometimes necessary strategy for political survival in Sierra Leone. The transition from war to peace saw a large number of individuals with backgrounds in the multitude of armed groups and militarized movements that existed during the civil war emerge as contenders in the post-war political arena. The three individuals under scrutiny in this chapter are in many ways prototype shape-shifters, who have navigated their way through the transition from war to peace and from military rule to democracy. But the security implications of their participation in post-war politics have varied considerably.

After the end of the war, President Kabbah appointed Norman as his minister of internal affairs. However, in 2003 the SCSL indicted him for war crimes and Norman was arrested and put in detention. This decision did not only abruptly end Norman's post-war political career, it also came to radically change his attitude and behavior towards both the regime he had loyally worked for and, by extension, the SLPP-administered peace process. Soon after his arrest, Norman began to publicly vent his feelings of bitterness and resentment regarding his own predicament. Some of his statements and activities suggest that at times Norman attempted to securitize wartime identities and perhaps even instigate violence by his former combatants, although the latter is difficult to prove. Across the country, but particularly in strongholds of the Kamajors in the south and the east, people were infuriated over the decision to indict Norman and his fellow CDF commanders, and against this background his statements had potentially dangerous and far-reaching security implications. The reasons for Norman's behavior must be considered primarily personal rather than political in character, at least in the early years. However, after Norman came out as a vocal supporter of the PMDC in the run-up to the 2007 elections, he used his personal experience to mobilize electoral support for the SLPP breakaway party.

Maada Bio has deliberately and relatively successfully used his military past as a tool to mobilize support in post-war politics, both internally in the struggle against his political contenders in the SLPP, and externally towards the electorate. In the 2012 elections, he ran as the presidential candidate for the SLPP in an electoral campaign that was marred by violence and insecurity. Although he has been careful to publicly distance himself from his group of violent youth supporters who have carried out several well-documented incidents of organized violence, it is clear that such violence has provided a useful tool for his political ambitions. The reasons for his behavior must thus be sought in perceived electoral benefits stemming from this display of militarism and force. It remains an open question to what extent he has deliberately ordered or actively encouraged such incidents, but it is highly unlikely that these events have taken place without his knowledge and support.

Collins is perhaps the most elusive character of them all. He has mostly operated outside the public view and has navigated his way through peacetime politics searching for political relevance. It was not until the 2012 elections that Collins ran for public office for the first time, as the presidential candidate for the revived RUFP. During the campaign, he deliberately attempted to distance himself and the party from the violent legacy of the past, and instead tried to carve out political space in the middle, emphasizing national unity, and hoping to gather enough support to use as a bargaining chip with either of the two major political parties that have dominated post-war politics. Although his political message appealed to the grievances shared by a large number of former RUF combatants in the post-war period, such political sentiments are also widely held by many others across the country. The reason for Collins' behavior must be considered pragmatic and based on a realistic understanding of which strategy would gain him most potential votes. A more belligerent strategy was thus never an option for a man and a party already so strongly associated with negative perceptions. However, Collins' decision to refrain from any activity that could compromise security has not contributed to consolidate the peace process in any significant manner beyond its possible symbolic relevance, primarily because of the marginal influence of the RUFP in electoral politics.

This brings us to another important finding. Beyond individual-level explanatory factors, there are also important contextual factors that can serve to explain why some warlord democrats, such as Maada Bio, have engaged in electoral activities with negative security implications, while others, such as Collins, have not. In post-war Sierra Leone, there are few wartime divisions and issues that remain politically salient and relevant to use as tools for mobilizing voters. Post-war politics, at least after the 2002 elections, has primarily been characterized by a return to the political dynamic that used to characterize the country prior to the outbreak of the war and dating back to the early days of independence. This dynamic is strongly driven by an overlapping pattern of ethnic and regional competition, with the most prominent dividing line running between the northern region, the Temne and Limba ethnic groups and the APC on the one hand, and the southern and eastern regions, the Mende ethnic group and the SLPP on the other hand. Competition between the APC and the SLPP has been fierce in the post-war period, with high stakes, close races and widespread impunity for violence. Warlord democrats involved in this political competition are therefore much more likely to have political leeway and resources at their disposal to resort to belligerent strategies, while the room for maneuver for other actors has been strongly curtailed. Maada

Bio's entry into post-war electoral politics was strongly shaped by this logic, and his background as a youthful military strongman was considered a useful asset by people within the SLPP and among its supporters who were eager to find a counterweight to the perceived aggressiveness and forceful nature of the APC. Maada Bio's strongest political asset was thus his links to the past and his display of forceful determination, a narrative that he used to carve out a political career for himself. Without this strong and sometimes violent competition between the parties, this is unlikely to have been a useful political card to play.

In line with this finding, it is also likely that the political space for any large-scale negative security moves, such as organizing extensive and widespread violence, has been curtailed by the overall strong support for the peace process. Hence, although Norman was able to securitize wartime identities and Bio has been implicated in the orchestration of low-intensity electoral violence for electoral benefits, any warlord democrat who wants to navigate the post-war Sierra Leonean landscape also needs to employ self-imposed constraints stemming from an understanding of what behavior would be deemed "acceptable enough" by both the domestic audience and concerned international donors and third party actors with a keen interest in protecting the hard-won peace. This does not imply that contextual factors or the overall political and electoral context in which these warlord democrats operate is more important than the individual agency of the warlords themselves. Only that they, much like all other political actors who want to gain power through the ballot box, make choices based on an overall consideration of what strategies and tactics are the most likely to pay off at each point in time, and in relation to a particular audience. However, their own historical legacies, memories, skills, resources and networks also impose important constraints on what options are available and desirable to them.

However, and additionally, there is little from the post-war Sierra Leonean experience suggesting that it makes a great difference exactly how a warlord democrat engages in electoral politics – whether this is through the trans-formation of a formerly armed group to a political party (such as Collins) or through participation in already existing parties (such as Norman and Maada Bio) – for determining their behavior. What appears to matter more is the overall political dynamic that shapes post-war electoral politics and whether such politics encourage or discourage the use of militant and violent slogans and behavior as an electoral strategy, for individuals as well as parties. As long as the underlying dynamics of politics continues to be driven by a winner-takes-all mentality and widespread impunity for violence as an electoral strategy, there is always the risk that former warlord democrats will make use of their past to get the upper hand in competitive electoral politics. Much remains to be done in terms of the depoliticization of society and deconcentration of political and economic power at the centre before we can expect this to change.

The findings from Sierra Leone also suggest the relevance of building institutions that are able to at least manage such behavior. In the case of Sierra Leone, the strong engagement of both domestic and international actors has contributed to the emergence of an institutional electoral framework, notably a relatively efficient and independent Electoral Commission, that has succeeded in establishing a range of de facto checks and balances on the statements and activities of the political actors. Such rules of the game serve to establish important limits on the extent to which any warlord democrat is able to engage in activities with negative security implications.

Notes

1 Author interview with a former cabinet minister in the Kabbah administration, Freetown, 9 February 2014.

2 See http://www.rscsl.org/Documents/ Decisions/CDF/785/SCSL-04-14-T-745.pdf (accessed 17 February 2014).

3 Author interview with a former cabinet minister in the Kabbah administration, Freetown, 9 February 2014.

4 Author interview with SLPP supporter, Freetown, 1 February 2014.

5 Many in the same group would also be among those who later threw their support behind Julius Maada Bio in the lead-up to the third post-war elections in 2012, as they saw Bio as a new Norman, a strong leader with a military background who genuinely has their interest at heart. Author interview with a university professor of political science at the University of Sierra Leone, Freetown, 2 February 2014.

6 The Constitution of Sierra Leone dictated that no one under the age of forty could run as a candidate in the elections, which prevented anyone from the youthful NPRC considering this option.

7 Author interview with Bio, Freetown, 13 December 2013.

8 Ibid.

9 Author interviews in the southern and eastern regions of Sierra Leone in January 2011.

10 Ibid.

11 Author interview with Bio, Freetown, 13 December 2013.

12 Author interview with Collins, Freetown, 11 December 2013.

13 Ibid.

14 It is worth noting that three of the key individuals in the leadership circle – Sam Bockarie (Mosquito), Issa Sesay and Augustine Gbao – were later indicted by the Special Court along with Sankoh himself, while the fourth – Dennis Mingo (Superman) – was killed before the end of the war.

15 Author interview conducted with former RUF member, 16 April 2014.

16 Author interview with Collins, Freetown, 11 December 2013.

17 Ibid.

18 Author interview with Collins, Freetown, 20 November 2012; Author interview with former senior member of the APC, Freetown, 12 December 2013.

19 Author interview with Collins, Freetown, 20 November 2012; Interviews with a large number of party members and supporters at the RUFP headquarters on 20 November confirm this picture. Many became very angry when asked if they had considered changing the party name.

20 Author interview with Collins, Freetown, 20 November 2012.

21 Ibid.

22 Ibid.

Bibliography

Abdullah, I. 1998. "Bush Path to Destruction: The Origin and Character of the Revolutionary United Front/Sierra Leone." *Journal of Modern African Studies* 36 (2): 203–235.

Abdullah, I. and P. Muana. 1998. "The Revolutionary United Front of Sierra Leone. A Revolt of the Lumpen Proletariat." In *African Guerrillas*, ed. C. Clapham. Oxford: James Currey.

Abraham, A. 2004. "State Complicity as a Factor in Perpetuating the Sierra Leone Civil War." In *Between Democracy and Terror. The Sierra Leone Civil War*, ed. I. Abdullah. Dakar: CODESRIA.

Al Jazeera. 2014. "Ghosts of Civil War Haunt Sierra Leone Polls." *Al Jazeera*, 25 March. Available from http://m.aljazeera.com/story/20121116104035514355.

AllAfrica 2004. "Sierra Leone: Special Court Accuses Indicted Militia of Inciting Civil Unrest", *AllAfrica*, 22 January. Available from http://allafrica.com/stories/200401220106.html.

AllAfrica. 2005. "Sierra Leone: Eldred Collins Resigns from the RUFP." *AllAfrica*, 3 May. Available from http://allafrica.com/stories/200505130018.html.

Awareness Times. 2011. "Live Updates of SLPP's July Convention Activities." *Awareness Times*, 2 August. Available from http://news.sl/drwebsite/exec/view.cgi?archive=7&num=18397&printer=1.

Awareness Times. 2012. "In Sierra Leone, Revolutionary United Front Party (RUFP) Elects Eldred Collins as Presidential Flag Bearer." *Awareness Times*, 4 September. Available from http://news.sl/drwebsite/exec/view.cgi?archive=7&num=18397&printer=1.

Awareness Times. 2013. "Supreme Court throws out SLPP's Illegal Petition." Awareness Times, 17 June [cited 27 April 2014]. Available from http://news.sl/drwebsite/exec/view.cgi?archive=9&num=22993&printer=1.

Bangura, I. and I. Specht. 2012. *Work Not War: Youth Transformation in Liberia and Sierra Leone*. Conciliation Resources Accord Issue 23, UK.

BBC News. 2012. "Sierra Leone: Ernest Bai Koroma Wins Presidential Poll." BBC News, 23 November. Available from http://www.bbc.co.uk/news/world-africa-20472962.

Gberie, L. 2004. "The May 25 Coup d'état in Sierra Leone: A Lumpen Revolt?" In *Between Democracy and Terror. The Sierra Leone Civil War*, ed. I. Abdullah. Dakar: CODESRIA.

Gberie, L. 2005. *A Dirty War in West Africa. The RUF and the Destruction of Sierra Leone*. London: Hurst & Company.

Hoffman, D. 2011. *The War Machines. Young Men and Violence in Sierra Leone and Liberia*. Durham and London: Duke University Press. .

ICG (International Crisis Group). 2001. *Sierra Leone: Ripe for Elections*. Africa Briefing No. 6. Freetown/Brussels.

ICG (International Crisis Group). 2003. *The Special Court for Sierra Leone: Promises and Pitfalls of a "New Model"*. Africa Briefing No. 16. Freetown/Brussels.

ICG (International Crisis Group). 2007. *Sierra Leone: The Election Opportunity*. Africa Report No. 129. Freetown/Brussels.

ICG (International Crisis Group). 2008. *Sierra Leone: A New Era of Reform?* Africa Report No. 143. Freetown/Brussels.

Kabbah, A. T. 2010. *Coming from the Brink in Sierra Leone*. Accra: EPP Books.

Kandeh, J. D. 2003. "Sierra Leone's Post-conflict Elections of 2002." *Journal of Modern African Studies* 41 (2): 189–216.

Kandeh, J. D. 2004. "In Search of Legitimacy: The 1996 Elections." In *Between Democracy and Terror. The Sierra Leone Civil War*, ed. I. Abdullah. Dakar: CODESRIA.

Kandeh, J. D. 2008. "Rouge Incumbents, Donor Assistance and Sierra Leone's Second Post-conflict Elections of 2007." *Journal of Modern African Studies* 46 (4): 603–635.

Keen, D. 2005. *Conflict and Collusion in Sierra Leone*. Oxford: James Currey.

Mitton, K. 2008. Engaging Disengagement: The Political Reintegration of Sierra Leone's Revolutionary United Front. *Conflict, Security and Development* 8 (2): 193–222.

Muana, P. K. 1997. "The Kamajoi Militia: Civil War, Internal Displacement and the Politics of Counter-Insurgency." *Africa Development* 22 (3/4): 77–100.

Politico. 2012. "Interview: RUFP Presidential Candidate Speaks Out." *Politico.* Available from http://politicosl.com/node/646.

Rashid, I. 2004. "Student Radicals, Lumpen Youth, and the Origins of Revolutionary Groups in Sierra Leone, 1977–1996." In *Between Democracy and Terror. The Sierra Leone Civil War*, ed. I. Abdullah. Dakar: CODESRIA.

Richards, P. 1998. *Fighting for the Rain Forest. War, Youth and Resources in Sierra Leone*. 2nd ed. London: James Currey.

Richards, P. and J. Vincent. 2008. "Sierra Leone: The Marginalization of the RUF." In *From Soldiers to Politicians. Transforming Rebel Movements after War*, ed. J. de Zeeuw. Boulder, CO: Lynne Rienner.

Sierra Leone Media Express. 2012. "Lawless and Defiant… Maada Bio Blocks Presidential Convey in Sierra Leone." *Sierra Leone Media Express*, 9 October. Available from http://www.sierraexpressmedia.com/?author=6&paged=147.

Sierra Leone Telegraph. 2012. "Sierra Leone's opposition SLPP reacts to the declared election results." Available from http://www.thesierraleonetelegraph.com/?p=3012.

Special Court for Sierra Leone. 2007: *Special Court Orders Inquiry into Death of Hinga Norman*. 23 February.

Standard Times. 2007a. "A Dangerous Political Romance… The Self-Style National Provisional Ruling Council Junta Generals of SLPP." *Standard Times*, 19 July. Available from http://www.standardtimespress.org/cgi-bin/artman/publish/article_1655.shtml.

Standard Times. 2007b. "Attack on Charles Margai… PMDC Publicity Secretary Accused Maada Bio and Tom Nyuma." *Standard Times*, 19 July. Available from http://www.standardtimespress.org/cgi-bin/artman/publish/article_1660.shtml.

Standard Times. 2007c. "Brigadier General Maada Bio Turns Security Guard for Vice President Berewa." *Standard Times*, 19 July. Available from http://www.standardtimespress.org/cgi-bin/artman/publish/article_1656.shtml.

Söderberg Kovacs, Mimmi. 2012. "'Ampa Ampoh'!: Sierra Leone after the Announcement of the 2012 Election Results." Blog guest post on 11 November. Available from https://matsutas.wordpress.com/2012/11/30/ampa-ampoh-sierra-leone-after-the-announcement-of-the-2012-election-results-guest-post-by-mimmi-soderberg-kovacs/.

The New People Newspaper. 2013. "Supreme Court Disappoints SLPP." *The New People Newspaper*, 15 June. Available from http://standardtimespress.org/?p=2200.

The Patriotic Vanguard. 2009. "Collins Assumes RUF Leadership." *The Patriotic Vanguard* 21 July. Available from http://www.thepatrioticvanguard.com/spip.php?article4359.

The Patriotic Vanguard. 2011a. "Reflections on the SLPP Convention of 2011." *The Patriotic Vanguard*, 5 August. Available from http://www.thepatrioticvanguard.com/spip.php?article6095.

The Patriotic Vanguard. 2011b. "Further Comments on the SLPP Convention of 2011." *The Patriotic Vanguard*, 18 August. Available from http://thepatrioticvanguard.com/spip.php?article6124.

TRC (Truth and Reconciliation Commission of Sierra Leone). 2004. *Truth and Reconciliation Commission's Report*. Vol. II. Freetown, Sierra Leone.

United Nations. 2000. *Letter dated 9 August 2000 from the Permanent*

Representative of Sierra Leone to the United Nations addressed to the President of the Security Council, S/2000/786, 10 August. Available from http://www.rscsl.org/Documents/Establishment/S-2000-786.pdf.

World Press. 2007. "Voices from Confinement: Former Warriors Declare Their Support for the P.M.D.C. in Sierra Leone." *World Press*, 5 March. Available from http://www.worldpress.org/Africa/2702.cfm.

7 | Riek Machar: warlord-doctor in South Sudan[1]

Johan Brosché and Kristine Höglund

Introduction

In mid-December 2013, fighting broke out in Juba, the capital of South Sudan, quickly spreading across the country. Within only a few months, more than 10,000 people had been killed and over a million were displaced. These events constitute the culmination of a long-lasting crisis of governance and power struggle between President Salva Kiir and the former Vice-President Riek Machar, both of whom earlier held prominent positions in the Sudan People's Liberation Movement/Army (SPLM/A) rebellion against the regime in Khartoum. In particular, the crisis represented an escalation of the competition between Kiir and Machar to become the SPLM/A candidate for the next presidential elections that were planned for 2015. The conflict has taken on an ethnic dimension, since Kiir is from South Sudan's largest ethnic group, Dinka, and Machar is from the second largest, the Nuer (ICG 2014; Amnesty International 2014).

This chapter analyses the influence of ex-militants on politics and violence in South Sudan. More specifically, we will focus on Riek Machar, an ex-military who became involved in politics after the end of the north–south war and who has been involved in both political and violent practices since then. As vice-president he was involved in the process of transforming SPLM/A from a rebel group into the ruling political party of South Sudan. However, Machar resumed the position as rebel leader in 2013, after the falling out with President Kiir, and he headed the newly formed rebel group SPLM/A – In Opposition (SPLM/A-IO), with Nuer communities as its prime support base. After a peace agreement was signed in August 2015, ending the worst of the fighting, Machar returned to Juba in April 2016 and again took up the position of vice-president. In July, heavy fighting re-erupted in Juba and Machar fled the country. The government seized the opportunity to replace Machar and on 26 July 2016, SPLM/A-IO's former chief negotiator Taban Deng was sworn in as vice-president (ICG 2016). Thus, Riek Machar has made several transitions: from rebel to vice-president and back.

This chapter has four core components. First, we highlight how warlord democrats, as a specific type of political leader in post-war contexts, are instrumental in instigating violence. To this end, we develop a theoretical framework to understand the links between individual leaders and different kinds of security outcomes, in particular organized violence. We suggest that two dimensions are important in understanding how the actions taken by warlords are linked to violence: first, they provide leadership in the framing – including the securitization of identities – of contentious actions and, second, they are instrumental in the implementation of violence. Second, we apply the theoretical framework to the case of Sudan in general, and Machar in particular. We show that Machar has made use of several electoral strategies. In the aftermath of the peace agreement in 2005, he was involved in the process of transforming the SPLM from a rebel movement to become a political party. During this time, however, he also wanted to strengthen his power by circumventing President Kiir's influence. In March 2013, Machar declared the intention of challenging Kiir as leader of SPLM, which later led to the formation of SPLM/A-IO. We argue that in South Sudan, the involvement of ex-militants as political leaders has contributed to securitize wartime identities, organized violence and foster human rights abuses. Third, and most importantly, we conduct an in-depth study of the processes that lead to organized violence, one of the security outcomes of Machar's engaging in electoral politics. We first identify conditions in South Sudan that explain why Machar has chosen to engage in violent tactics. We suggest that weak political institutions and a strong militarization of society create a situation where military democrats are prone to engage in violent tactics. In addition, the prize attached to holding state power and controlling government resources is immense. It is a prime means for individual politicians to achieve personal wealth, and also to secure benefits for their key constituencies, including their ethnic group. Another important factor to understand the dynamics in South Sudan is the increasingly authoritarian manner by which Salva Kiir has ruled SPLM/A, and thereby South Sudan, as it is, in practice, a one-party state, which has served to increase tensions between Kiir and Machar. In the main part of the analysis, we show that Machar has been able to draw on his experience and status from the war to use all means available in his ambition to become the top leader of SPLM/A. Finally, we identify two additional relevant security outcomes – the securitizing of wartime identities and rising human rights abuses. We find that Machar has played an important role in framing the political landscape in South Sudan in a way that has securitized wartime identities and increased the risk of organized violence. Moreover, he has launched insurgencies and encouraged human rights abuses targeting particular ethnic communities as part of his tactics to implement his political ambitions.

Warlord democrats, political leadership and violence

Moments of social change, such as war-to-democracy transitions, create uncertainties and challenges for political leaders. Structural changes may threaten the power position of elites and encourage violent mobilization for political leaders to gain advantage in an election and retain power. In post-war societies, political space often opens up which may be used by opportunistic leaders for militant mobilization. Elites can take advantage of their control over government, the economy and mass media to manipulate public debates. In such instances, nationalism can serve as an instrument for powerful groups that aim to retain power (Snyder 2000: 32). The opening up to electoral competition is particularly risky in a post-civil war context where grievances and identities created during the war can be utilized in the political game after the war has ended. In this context, former commanders who join the political competition – "warlord democrats" – have a unique position since they can use their networks from the war to bolster their power. But what, more specifically, is the role of warlord democrats as political leaders in the mobilization for violence at election times in a post-war context?

The function of leaders in instigating violence In the mobilization for violence, political leaders play an instrumental role. Violence during transitional periods can take different forms. Political violence may be part of a larger violent political struggle and a mobilization process to overturn or reform the political system. In some instances, the violence makers have a more limited aim: they are opposed to the peace process and use violence to sabotage it (Stedman 1997). In other instances, a political movement may be using a dual strategy of violence and participation in the electoral process. But even when this is the case, there are differences in terms of situations where mobilization primarily happens around an election to influence its outcome, or if mobilization is part of a parallel political struggle waged by an insurgent or rebel group to seize power (Weinberg et al. 2009).

Generally speaking, leaders serve a directive function to the collective or a political community. This function contains three different phases: (1) diagnostic, which includes formulation of the problem, or situation, facing the collective, (2) prescriptive, which entails the formulation of the responses and actions necessary, and (3) mobilization, which involves garnering support for political action or implementation (Tucker 1981: 15–19). Building on this conceptualization of the directive function of leaders, we suggest two main links between the involvement of warlord democrats in politics and mobilization for violence. Firstly, warlord democrats are important because they have a *framing* function. They diagnose the problem and prescribe action – in essence, they formulate discourse upon which mobilization for violence take place. Secondly, warlord democrats are important because they have an *implementing* function – they have power over support for an organization, and thus have control over resources for action. Mobilization is, thus, broadly understood as the process in which individuals are motivated and recruited to take action for a common goal (Gurr 2000: 74). The two main functions are closely related to two terms in the literature on social movements and collective action – collective and selective incentives (Olson 1965).

FRAMING FUNCTION A first function is to frame the discourse upon which to mobilize for violence. While the driving forces behind a warlord democrat can be linked to a set of motives – ranging from legitimate social goals to selfish ambition – political leaders and organizations need to be perceived "to serve and stand for *something* apart from themselves" (Kane 2001: 10). A key function of political leadership is the "capacity to persuade – and perhaps inspire – others" (Whitehead 2002: 43). The rhetoric of warlord democrats as forming a common identity and goals thus becomes important. The rationale upon which people are mobilized is often formulated in "symbolic frames" which provide the link between the leaders and the mass level, constituency or group (Pappas 2008: 1122-1223). Frames often take simple binary oppositions, formulated in "us" vs "them" terms (rich vs poor, core vs periphery etc.). In many instances, it is references to ethnic group identity or political party affiliation which provide symbolic frames. In this sense, leaders can "shape the political 'market' of ideas and loyalties" (Lyons 2005: 43). To use the terminology of collective action, leaders provide collective incentives through appeals to ideology, identity or solidarity which will benefit the entire group "indiscriminately" (Olson 1965: 51).

Certain types of "frames" are especially important in shaping a climate conducive for political violence. For instance, appeals to exclusive or extremist group identities or ideologies commonly form the basis for violent mobilization. In essence, frames that serve to securitize wartime identities are crucial in a post-war context (see Introduction to this volume), but new conflict identities may also be created as part of a mobilization process. While the securitization of identities does not by definition result in violent outcomes, it forms a stepping stone – sometimes even a necessary one – for political leaders who mobilize for violence.

The tendency to mobilize around exclusionist identities often grows when insecurity is widespread.[2] Research on radical mass movements indicates that a frame involving a strong injustice component is more likely to motivate people for radical action (Pappas 2008: 1122-1123). For instance, political violence has sometimes been legitimized as an acceptable mode of campaigning with a rhetoric linked to a rights discourse. In countries that have already experienced protracted conflict, political mobilization is likely to be along conflict lines (Paris 2004). Differences rather than similarities are emphasized to win votes. To signal commitment to a cause, warlord democrats may use strategies of outbidding in power struggles with competing groups. Such outbidding usually takes the form of non-conciliatory and extremist discourse in which competitor groups are portrayed as uncommitted. Outbidding can under certain conditions also be manifested in violence against rival groups.

The creation of enemy images is particularly important in mobilization for violence. By framing certain groups as enemies, warlord democrats respond to questions of why a certain group is a legitimate target of political violence. Dehumanization and deindividualization are powerful instruments in reducing empathy for entire groups which will no longer be awarded protection from the norms against aggression which usually exist within social communities (Pruitt and Kim 2004: 111). Militant rhetoric plays a role in the creation of enemy images. Electoral politics are particularly susceptible to violence-inducing rhetoric, since the rhetoric around elections is filled with military connotations and metaphors. "The parties wage 'campaigns', employing 'strategies and tactics'. Party faithful are called 'cadre', and areas with many supporters are known as 'strongholds' or 'citadels'" (Rapoport and Weinberg 2001: 31). Such militant rhetoric may fuel a sense of insecurity, which in turn can instigate violence. In a post-war society, such rhetoric may be even more perilous than in societies spared from violent conflicts.

IMPLEMENTING FUNCTION In order to carry out the actual violence – to *implement* the decision – the mobilization process is taken one step further. A first aspect in the implementation of violence is to provide incentives for those involved in carrying out the violence. It is a matter of creating a conflict constituency, which perceives benefits from violence (Menkhaus 1998). The incentives must be selective, operating directly on the individual involved in the activities, meaning that those involved gain something specific which others do not (Olson 1965: 51). Such incentives are often channeled in the form of patronage and are used by leaders in mobilization processes to gain the support of key constituencies and to recruit individuals to carry out the violence. Incentives may be positive and negative, short-term and long-term. Short-term incentives can include cash payments, provision of food, alcohol or drugs, or security in terms of protection. Longer-term incentives may include expectations of getting jobs for family members, gaining powerful positions or state contracts. In the Sierra Leonean general election in 2007, ex-combatants remobilized based on expectations of benefits they would receive. While short-term benefits such as security, basic foodstuffs and money were important, it was mainly future prospects that appear to have been the most significant driving force (Christensen and Utas 2008).

The resources warlord democrats have available in political contestation are also dependent on whether they are the incumbent or part of the challenger side. Incumbents have state resources available which can be misused for violent suppression of political opponents. State power often means disproportionate access to material resources, control over state contracts and jobs, and welfare benefits which can be used for political patronage. State resources – vehicles, arms etc. – can also be employed to carry out violence. Warlord democrats holding state power can use their personal security, provided by the state security forces, to intimidate voters and candidates. To what extent state resources are misused ultimately depends on legal constraints and how well they are respected and enforced. Clearly, warlord democrats are not entirely independent in taking action. A dependency often develops: the leaders need followers, often ex-combatants and army deserters, for their protection and to carry out violence. At the same time, the recruits are dependent on the leaders for assets such as protection, arms, money, food and circumventing legal measures.

A second aspect of implementation relates to the social networks and relationships between leadership at different levels in society or in an organization (Brosché 2014; Kalyvas 2006). In order to mobilize followers, warlord democrats usually need to tap into existing social networks for recruitment. Such networks can be of different kinds – religious, ethnic or economic. Leadership at the mid level of society often serves as an intermediary and is needed to establish the link between the top leadership and those who carry out the violence (Themnér 2011). Previous research has pointed to the importance of understanding a leader's "span of control". In essence, leaders can only have control over a limited number of individuals at the same time, due to limited cognitive and monitoring capacity. This explains leaders' dependence on existing networks at different levels in society (Graicunas 1937; Themnér 2011).

To recapitulate, warlord democrats have two distinct functions in the mobilization of political violence in transitioning societies. They can be viewed as "political entrepreneurs", with control over both collective and selective incentives (Lyons 2005), as summarized in Table 7.1:

Methods for framing (motivation)	Methods for implementing (recruitment and organization)
• symbolic frames • outbidding • enemy images, including militant rhetoric	• short-term and long-term incentives • social networks, including leadership at different levels

Table 7.1 Warlord democrats and their core functions in the mobilization for violence

South Sudan: the world's newest nation

On 9 January 2005, Sudan's longstanding north–south war ended through the signing of the Comprehensive Peace Agreement (CPA) by the Government of Sudan and the rebel movement SPLM/A. The agreement ended Africa's longest conflict, which had killed more than 2 million people. The conflict had its origin in the centralization of economic, political and cultural power in Khartoum, in the north of Sudan, where the peripheries – the south of Sudan in particular – remained severely marginalized. The north–south divide was further entrenched by the north being more Muslim and Arabic, whereas the south is predominantly Christian and African.

The CPA fundamentally changed South Sudan as a political entity by granting the region extensive autonomy and by establishing the Government of South Sudan (GoSS) as the prime ruling authority of the area. When GoSS was established it was led by President of South Sudan John Garang, with Salva Kiir as vice-president. Six months after the signing of the CPA, however, Garang died in a helicopter crash and Kiir took up the position as President of South Sudan with Riek Machar as the new vice-president. The CPA also called for general elections, which were held in April 2010.[3] The elections resulted in an overwhelming victory for SPLM. Kiir won the presidential election with 93% of the vote, leaving 7% to his sole rival, Lam Akol of the SPLM – Democratic Change (SPLM-DC). In addition, Machar, who ran as a candidate for the vice-presidency on Kiir's ticket, remained as vice-president after the elections (LeRiche and Arnold 2012; Brosché 2009).

The CPA also resulted in power-sharing institutions, such as the Government of National Unity with representation from the north and south, wealth-sharing arrangements for the oil, and the formation of new armed forces. In addition, the agreement stipulated a referendum for the independence of South Sudan. On 9 January 2011, 99% voted in favor of independence and the country was born on 9 July 2011 (LeRiche and Arnold 2012). South Sudan is one of the world's poorest states and the national economy is dominated by oil, which prior to the 2013 crisis accounted for 98% of the government's revenues (Johnson 2006; ICG 2014).

Since the SPLM/A was founded in 1983, the movement has suffered from severe intra-party power struggles. To deal with such fractionalization tendencies, the SPLM/A has attempted to suppress internal divisions by force rather than by reaching consensus. Moreover, the organization is very top-down and John Garang ruled the movement in an autocratic manner (LeRiche and Arnold 2012). When Salva Kiir succeeded Garang as the leader of SPLM/A, this partly changed and he often consulted at least some of the other elites within the movement (ICG 2011). This approach was used in an attempt to heal South Sudan, which was heavily divided when the CPA was signed in 2005. Furthermore, during his first years in office as president, Kiir tried to consolidate his power by co-opting political players that constituted a threat to the government. For some years, the strategy was fairly successful and South Sudan did not – in contrast to what many had anticipated – descend into full-fledged civil war. However, this approach also caused severe problems and SPLM/A became an organization consisting of many different actors, many of which had fought each other during parts of the north–south war. A particularly important development was the inclusion of former militias in the army structures, which resulted in a deeply divided army. By the end of 2010, Kiir's strategy partly changed and he began to rely more on a few close advisers, while increasingly threatening opponents and punishing dissent (LeRiche and Arnold 2012). With activities to undermine him politically continuing, including rebellion, Kiir had become less confident that co-optation could safeguard his power (email correspondence Matthew LeRiche, 26 August 2014).

Electoral politics and patterns of violence in South Sudan

This section outlines electoral politics and patterns of violence in South Sudan since the signing of the CPA. Predictions at the time assumed that South Sudan would rapidly disintegrate into a full-fledged civil war. However, a five-year period after the signing of the CPA was relatively peaceful. Some violent communal conflicts took place, but there was no insurgency challenging the Government of South Sudan (UCDP 2014).

Violence in the 2010 election In spite of some harassment and intimidation ahead of the 2010 election, it was generally peaceful (Carter Center 2010). However, in its aftermath several violent conflicts were initiated with clear links to electoral politics. Two rebellions were launched soon after the elections by candidates who lost (UCDP 2014). A first insurgency was started by George Athor, a former commander in the SPLA from the Padeng Dinka community, who ran as an independent candidate for governor of Jonglei state. Following his defeat at the polls, Athor accused the SPLM of manipulating the voting and declared the results invalid. He then called for the government of South Sudan to be dissolved. Athor founded a rebel group called the South Sudan Democratic Movement/Army (SSDM/A) and initiated fighting against the regime in Juba. In late 2011, George Athor was killed in battle but other elements of the SSDM/A continued the rebellion. Another insurgency in Jonglei was launched by David Yauyau in May 2010. This uprising started after Yauyau lost the election for a parliamentary seat. Yauyau is from the Murle community, and an essential cause of this rebellion was intense discontent among the community with regard to how they were treated by the regime in Juba. Yauyau joined the government in 2011, but left in April 2012 (Small Arms Survey 2013). A ceasefire agreement was signed with the government in late January 2014 (Sudan Tribune 2014). In 2015, a faction from the SSDM/A defected and joined the SPLMA-IO (Sudan Tribune 2015), but David Yauyau remained with the government.

In 2011, a new rebellion was launched in South Sudan when the South Sudan Liberation Movement/Army (SSLM/A) took up weapons against the regime in Juba. The group was led by Peter Gadet, a commander from the Bul Nuer community (Small Arms Survey 2013). Compared to the two rebellions described above, this one was less linked to electoral dynamics and was initiated several months after the elections. Nevertheless, when launching the rebellion, the SSLM/A stated that "[t]he noises of victory by the SPLM in the last elections in the South are preposterous and ludicrous" (Sudan Tribune 2011). The group also called for a caretaker government to rule South Sudan until new elections were held. However, the real motivation for the rebellion can be found in a search for economic and political advantages, and divisions created during the north–south war. Gadet shifted sides several times during the war: at times he fought for SPLM and at other times for the Sudanese government. Gadet signed a peace agreement with the regime in Juba in August 2011, but other sections of SSLM/A have continued to fight against the South Sudanese government (Small Arms Survey 2013). As part of the SPLM/A-IO rebellion, however, Gadet defected again and became the military commander of that movement (Young 2015).

The 2013 crisis The severest challenge to South Sudan since the signing of the 2005 peace accord is a result of the crises which erupted in mid-December 2013, when fighting between different factions of the presidential guard broke out in Juba. Within just a few months, more than 10,000 people were killed and over a million people displaced, with approximately 950,000 people internally displaced in South Sudan and close to 300,000 having fled to neighboring countries (Amnesty International 2014). It is exceedingly difficult to make an assessment of the total number of fatalities in the war, but in March 2016 an unnamed UN source estimated that 50,000 had been killed (Al-Jazeera 2016).

The conflict has its origin in the struggle for power within the SPLM, which in turn had implications for the elections that were planned for 2015.[4] In mid-March 2013, then Vice-President Riek Machar declared his intention to challenge President Salva Kiir over the leadership of the SPLM at its third extraordinary national convention scheduled for May 2013. However, the convention was repeatedly delayed, as were other important meetings of the SPLM, for instance, the National Liberation Council (NLC) and the SPLM Political Bureau. One reason was that Machar appeared to have stronger support than Kiir at such meetings (ICG 2014). To safeguard his power, Salva Kiir sacked the entire government – including Riek Machar – in July 2013. When the government was reinstalled, politicians perceived as posing a threat to Kiir were replaced with those assumed to be more loyal to the president. The criticism of President Kiir continued, however, and on 6 December 2013 a political coalition led by Machar, SPLM/A-IO, was formed. In an attempt to curtail the crisis, a meeting of the NLC was held on 14 December. During the tense meeting Kiir succeeded in removing some of his critics and as a result sacked officials boycotted the next day's session. On the evening of 15 December, fighting erupted after the president decided to disarm presidential guards from the Nuer community, and to arrest leaders of the SPLM/A-IO accused of a coup attempt (ICG 2014). While disputed, most independent analysts consider the alleged coup to be unlikely. Intense fighting broke out and within a few days most of the leading critics were arrested, but Riek Machar managed to escape from Juba (ICG 2014).

The fighting has been intense and control over strategic towns such as Bentiu, Bor and Malakal has shifted several times. An integral part of the fighting has been numerous massacres, where people have been targeted because of their ethnic belonging, primarily pitting Dinka against Nuer. Still, it should be noted that there are Dinka elements that are fighting on the side of the rebels and that some Nuer groups are fighting with the government (LeRiche 2014).

At an early phase of the fighting, SPLM/A-IO advanced towards Juba and it is widely believed that without support from Uganda, the South Sudanese government would not have been able to keep control of the capital.[5] The regime has also been supported by Sudanese rebel groups, notably JEM (Justice and Equality Movement), an opposition movement based in Darfur. Moreover, there are allegations that Machar is supported by Eritrea, but no proof has been presented (ICG 2014, 2015; Amnesty International 2014). The role played by Sudan is particularly complicated. Officially it has supported the regime in Juba, and Khartoum has been active as a mediator in the Intergovernmental Authority on Development (IGAD)-led negotiations. At the same time, it allows SPLM/A-IO to use rear bases in Sudan, and has given funds and weapons to Machar's forces. Sudan is balancing between several crucial interests. Economically it is important for Khartoum to uphold a working relationship with Juba. Currently all oil produced in South Sudan is transferred through a pipeline in Sudan and the fee Juba pays for usage is economically important for Khartoum. Therefore, the Sudanese government has provided arms and money to Machar to prevent him from attacking the oilfields and the pipeline (de Waal 2015). In addition, since Sudanese rebels – and Sudan's arch-enemy Uganda – are fighting alongside the South Sudanese government, the Sudan–South Sudan relation risks deteriorating (ICG 2015).

The international community has pushed for a negotiated solution to the crisis and the IGAD has led negotiations in Addis Ababa. Under increasing pressure from the international community, the two parties signed a peace agreement in August 2015. However, the implementation of the agreement was slow and Machar did not return to Juba until April 2016. Tensions between Machar and Kiir remained high and in July the two parties once again fought each other fiercely in Juba. Around 300 people died. Machar first fled into the bush and later left the country. Yet the clashes ceased after a few days and did not lead to a return to a full-fledged civil war. In a tactical move to reduce the power of Riek Machar, the South Sudanese government swore in Taban Deng, the former chief negotiator of SPLM/A-IO, as vice-president. To decrease the risk of further escalation of the conflict the UN Security Council authorized a regional protection force of 4,000 men to complement the 13,000 UN troops and police currently in South Sudan (ICG 2016).

To sum up, instead of fostering a democratic culture, the introduction of elections in South Sudan has contributed to several destructive conflicts. Pivotal to the destructive path South Sudan has taken lately is the actions taken by warlord democrats such as Salva Kiir and Riek Machar. Next, we focus on Machar, his involvement in violence and electoral politics, and the consequences of his actions.

Riek Machar: warlord doctor with ambitions

Riek Machar is from Leer in Unity State and is the son of a chief in the area. Machar trained as an engineer at the University of Khartoum and later went to the University of Bradford, where he graduated with a PhD in engineering in 1984. The same year, he joined the SPLM/A in its struggle against the regime in Khartoum. He fought with the movement until 1991 when – together with Lam Akol and other commanders in SPLM/A – he launched a coup against John Garang. The attempt to oust Garang resulted in a split in SPLM/A. Machar and Akol formed a new group called SPLM/A-Nasir faction. In this process, both Garang and Machar played the ethnic card, and mobilized their respective ethnic group against the other. A main result of the split, therefore, was large-scale Dinka–Nuer violence (Jok and Hutchinson 1999).

After the split, Machar's group was supported by the Sudanese government due to having a common enemy in Garang. However, in 2002, the relationship between Machar and Garang was mended and Machar rejoined SPLM/A as a senior commander. Because of his prior involvement with the Khartoum regime, many southerners continued to view him as a traitor. Machar remained within the SPLM/A structures between 2002 and 2013, but throughout this time he was looking for an opportunity to become the leader of SPLM/A. Machar's determination is captured by the South Sudanese expert Jok Madut Jok: "he [Machar] is very ambitious to take the top office in the land, and nothing else matters" (Reuters 2013). Furthermore, Douglas Johnson, another expert on South Sudan who is personally acquainted with Machar, believes that Machar is genuine in his belief that he can do a better job than Kiir (Reuters 2013). Thus, although the prime motivation for Machar to gain power is personal, there are also indications that he believes South Sudan stands to benefit if he assumes power.

Machar's struggle to take power in South Sudan must also be understood against several structural features, which provide a fertile breeding ground for political violence. Most importantly, the highly centralized and hierarchical structure of political power means that the prize attached to holding state power and controlling government resources is significant. It is a prime means not only for personal wealth for individual politicians, but also for their key constituencies, including their ethnic group. Weak and exclusionary political institutions, as well as a high level of militarization, further increase grievances. The authoritarian approach by which Salva Kiir has ruled SPLM/A has also augmented tensions in South Sudan generally, and between Kiir and Machar specifically (De Waal 2014; LeRiche and Arnold 2012).

As part of Machar's ambition to take over Salva Kiir's position, he attempted to circumvent Kiir's influence by, for instance, blocking important decisions (LeRiche and Arnold 2012). Despite this ambition and Machar's violent history his involvement was limited in the violence connected to the 2010 elections. Instead of openly challenging Kiir during the interim period stipulated in the CPA (2005–2011), Machar accepted the position of vice-president. However, in order to succeed in his political ambition to become the leader of South Sudan he forged secret deals with different influential military personalities (Jok 2014). With South Sudan's independence achieved and with increased criticism towards how Kiir governed the country, it is reasonable to believe that Machar perceived that he had a good opportunity to challenge the incumbent leader.

What actions has Machar taken to empower himself and why has his approach had violent consequences for South Sudan? The next sections seek answers to these questions by focusing on the methods for framing and implementation that Machar has used.

Framing motivation

Riek Machar faces a difficult predicament in his efforts to motivate people and politicians to side with him. The forces fighting for Machar are primarily Nuer and in order to secure support and recruits from his community he needs to be perceived as the Nuer leader who best represents their interests. At the same time, he needs broad multi-ethnic support in order to be portrayed as a better alternative than Salva Kiir – in particular since he accuses Kiir of being ethnically biased in favor of the Bahr-el-Ghazal Dinka community to which he belongs. This predicament has important implications for the way in which Machar has framed the cause.

Portraying conflicts in ethnic terms to mobilize political support has a long tradition in South Sudan and constitutes the most obvious symbolic frame that leaders resort to. To downplay their responsibility, ambitious political leaders regularly try to cover the role of their individual interests and stakes in the conflict (Interview with Leben Moro, 21 March 2011, Juba, South Sudan). It is generally believed that people are not willing to support a politician motivated by an agenda to strengthen their personal influence and that such motivations would harm the politician's reputation. Framing the conflict as if tribal wealth is threatened is therefore a way to persuade communities to participate in conflicts (Hutchinson 2001).

An important framing tactic used by Machar, which ties into ethnic conflict as a symbolic frame, has been to portray the government as being a Dinka hegemony. In 2013, Machar's critique of Kiir became increasingly open. He accused Salva Kiir of promoting a "Dinkocracy" in South Sudan, meant to imply that important positions in the government and military are held by individuals who are ethnically biased in favor of Kiir's Dinka community (Reuters 2013). Although the criticism is partly correct, as the regime in Juba tends to favor Dinka over non-Dinka (Brosché 2014), such statements contribute to securitize ethnic identities and to the violence taking on an increasingly ethnic nature. Furthermore, such rhetoric disguises the fact that the Dinka are not a homogenous group, but are highly diverse. In fact, the group consists of twenty-five different tribal factions. Although all tribes in South Sudan are diverse to some extent, the heterogeneity of the Dinka is extraordinary because it is the largest group and one that is present in most areas across South Sudan. This diversity implies that there is fertile ground for intra-Dinka conflict. The history of the Dinka reveals several such examples, and many of the main opponents to highly positioned Dinka leaders have come from inside this community (Johnson 2006). Despite this caveat, those within the government cannot take decisions that are viewed as being too unfavorable to the communities from which they originate. With the Dinka holding many powerful positions, this means that they are often treated more favorably than other communities. In addition, and essential for the dynamics in South Sudan, perceptions about Dinka dominance prevail among the non-Dinka communities in South Sudan. Although the government does not treat all communities equally, the perception of a Dinka hegemony does not fully match reality (email correspondence with Matthew LeRiche, 12 October 2013). Machar has capitalized extensively on this perception to enhance his support.

Machar has a long history of motivating Nuer communities to fight for his personal cause, while framing the conflict in such ways that his own ambitions remain concealed. In particular, appeals to the Nuer community have been tied to ethnic outbidding as a tactic around which Machar has garnered support. Support for his cause has been framed based on his association with widespread grievances among the Nuer communities. Early on in the crisis in 2013, the government targeted Nuer in Juba extensively, resulting in hundreds of deaths. This contributed to an ethnification of the conflict and caused widespread resentment against the government among Nuer communities. The prime reason why Nuer were targeted was not ethnicity per se, but rather that they were perceived as supporters of Machar. Thus, they were targeted in order to counter the threat they posed to President Kiir (LeRiche 2014).

The killings have contributed to increasing support for Machar. The bitterness caused by the killings is actively used by commanders in the SPLM/A-IO who, in order to keep the communities mobilized, exploit these grievances and capitalize on ethnic resentments by directing it towards the government. This mobilization approach has been successful and Machar has widespread support from the Nuer community which largely views him as representing Nuer interests. However, this support is mainly a result of Machar's success in associating himself with Nuer grievances (revenge and an end to Kiir's rule) and not a strong commitment among the fighters to the political ambitions of Machar (Small Arms Survey 2014). Yet the two strands of incentives go hand in hand, which helps to motivate people to fight for Machar.

In order to mobilize for the struggle, Machar skillfully uses different aspects of Nuer traditions to create enemy images that suit his interests. In the Nuer communities, there are strong traditions about the social and spiritual consequences for individuals involved in killings. In the late 1980s and early 1990s, Machar initiated an ideological campaign to mobilize individuals to join in the war against the government, by trying to convince civilians and rank-and-file that there were actually two kinds of wars. Killings committed in a "government war" were free of traditional consequences because of their secular and impersonal nature. Instead, spiritual consequences for killings only applied to "homeland wars". Later, after the SPLM/A split in 1991, Machar used the same distinction about enemy images to motivate communities to fight against Garang.[6] This policy was also intended to remove any mediating structures – including factors such as kinship, community and spirituality – between Machar and the loyalty of his troops (Hutchinson 2001). Although Machar has attempted to remove spiritual factors that risk undermining his influence, he has used other spiritual attributes to bolster his stature as a prominent Nuer leader. For instance, Machar has managed to get his hands on a ceremonial stick, once belonging to the famous Nuer prophet Ngundeng Bong, called the "dang" stick, which he uses politically, but also for his own superstitious purposes (Reuters 2013). Thus, Machar uses various framing tactics and plays on different enemy images to present the conflict in terms that suit his interests. In this process, Machar sometimes downplays the moral aspect of participating in fighting, while simultaneously increasing his authority by using traditional attributes.

In addition to securing support from Nuer communities, Machar has sought to widen his support base as a way to increase his political opportunities. In essence, this is an attempt to create a counter frame or a complement to the ethnic conflict frame and involves efforts by Machar to portray himself as the leader of a multi-ethnic coalition. In order to reduce the perception of being solely a Nuer movement, the SPLM/A-IO has tried to recruit from other disaffected groups, such as the Equatorian, Murle and Shilluk communities. The purpose has been to galvanize multiethnic resistance towards the government by convincing other communities to openly resist President Kiir (Small Arms Survey 2014).

Another example of Machar's attempt to frame himself as a national – rather than solely Nuer – leader was when in 2011 he apologized for the Bor Massacre. In 1992, at least 2,000 Dinka civilians were killed in Bor (capital of Jonglei and John Garang's hometown), which made it one of the severest examples of the Dinka–Nuer violence that followed after the 1991 split of SPLM/A (ICG 2009). This attack was ordered by Machar, but for two decades he denied responsibility. In 2011, however, he admitted responsibility and asked the Dinka Bor community to accept his apology (Sudan Tribune 2011). Most analysts view this expression of regret as an attempt to increase his political support. Salva Kiir is a Dinka from the Bahr el-Ghazal Dinka community, which is involved in a competition over power with the Bor Dinka. To empower himself, Riek Machar has tried to improve his relation with the influential Bor Dinka community and the apology should be viewed against this background (ICG 2014; Sudan Tribune 2011).

The formation of SPLM/A-IO was an important achievement by Machar, presenting himself as a political leader not only for the Nuer community. In December 2013, Machar led a group of politicians who had been dismissed from the government to publicly challenge Kiir and accuse him of "dictatorial tendencies" (Sudan Tribune 2013). The group was multiethnic in its composition and also included politicians from the Dinka community. Importantly, Machar had managed to convince several senior politicians associated with John Garang (including his widow, Rebecca Garang) to join the SPLM/A-IO. The coalition also included prominent political figures from several other communities, such as Ngok Dinka (who were disappointed in how Kiir had handled Abyei, an area disputed between Sudan and South Sudan), Bari (representing the Equatorians) and Bahr el-Ghazal Dinka (President Kiir's home area) as well as influential militaries. To unite such a diverse group was a major achievement by Machar, especially since many of these politicians had fought against Machar during periods of the north–south war. This broad coalition presented a coherent political agenda that focused on the democratization of SPLM and constituted the severest threat to Salva Kiir since he became the leader of SPLM/A (Small Arms Survey 2014).

However, the diversity of the group also constituted a problem. The prime unifying factor was their ambition to oust Kiir (all main actors in SPLM/A-IO had previously been distanced from the center of power by Kiir), rather than other common interests. This had significant implications for the dynamics that followed after the alleged coup. Importantly, many of the politicians involved in the coalition have distanced themselves from Machar. For instance, when the negotiations in Addis Ababa, that had started in January 2014, temporarily broke down in March 2015, a group of Kiir's opponents formed an independent group called "former detainees",[7] which began to participate as a separate bloc. While the group remains committed to its opposition to the incumbent government, it does not recognize Riek Machar as its leader. This has created bitterness among the SPLM/A-IO leadership. However, SPLM/A-IO is careful not to encourage criticism and thereby risk distancing itself too much from non-Nuer opposition figures. A main reason for the failure to build an opposition platform that transcends ethnicity was the government's attack on Nuer in Juba. This event led to a severe ethnification of the conflict and coalitions that cut across ethnic affiliations became harder to uphold. For the armed Nuer, the war was a fight for survival against a government that used ethnic cleansing against them. The former detainees, however, focused on political reform, in particular the removal of President Kiir. As a result, the multiethnic coalition that Machar had fought hard for dissolved. This represents a severe political setback for Machar. Not only does it decrease his political support, it has also exposed him to the accusation that he is dividing South Sudan along ethnic lines (Small Arms Survey 2014).[8]

To sum up, Riek Machar's framing approach has been twofold. First, he has portrayed himself as the prime Nuer leader and contributed to the ethnification of political competition in South Sudan. Second, he has attempted to also be perceived as a national leader. Whereas the first approach has been fairly successful – primarily because of extensive Nuer grievances against the regime in Juba – the second has largely failed and most South Sudanese do not see him as a national leader (Reuters 2013).

Implementation: incentives for recruitment and organization of SPLM-IO

The violence that erupted in mid-December 2013 quickly spread to large areas of South Sudan and had an intensity that shocked observers and South Sudanese alike. How was it possible for the violence to become so widespread in such a short time? This section addresses this question by highlighting both immediate and more enduring incentives, and the social networks facilitating violence, including the interactions between leaders at different levels. While these dimensions relate to the specific implementing approach used by Machar to mobilize and recruit for violence, the broader political landscape in South Sudan also encourages violence.

A significant and enduring incentive to mobilize for violence relates to the benefits of being associated with the political leadership of South Sudan. The stakes in South Sudan's political struggle are high. The state controls significant oil resources and other important economic assets, including land. Moreover, state and party arrangements are very hierarchical and currently dominated by SPLM/A (ICG 2014). Combined with institutionalized corruption, there are ample opportunities for those in power to enrich themselves (de Waal 2014).

But political power is not only important for those at the top. Leaders in South Sudan are obliged to provide resources to their community, tribe or family. This means that extended family or members from the leader's community are offered positions in the administration across a range of levels, from ministerial posts and advisers, to drivers (LeRiche 2014). These kinds of incentives become very important in a context where there are limited opportunities to garner wealth without access to government structures and the circles of power (ICG 2009). For commanders, rank-and-file and communities, it becomes important that "their" patron is a top leader. The belief that a shift at the top level would entail drastic changes in how the state is organized is a key explanation of why so many people are willing to fight for Machar.

More specifically, the incentive structure of South Sudan favors violence over non-violent means in several ways. First, to be part of a rebellion includes several short-term benefits, such as opportunities to mete out revenge and to loot resources. In particular, the prospect of raiding cattle is an important enticement for many people to join an insurgency. Cattle are of economic and cultural importance for many communities in South Sudan (Hutchinson 1996; Willems and Rouw 2011). Land is another political asset that is used as an incentive to get people to fight for an armed insurgency. Land is of importance for both agriculturalists and pastoralists, and politicians in power have far-reaching control over landownership.[9] The current government tends to favor the Dinka community in land disputes, which causes frustration among non-Dinka communities. A prevailing anticipation among many South Sudanese is that the land policy will change if the incumbent regime is toppled, which again increases the motivation to join opposition movements.

Second, the political structures of South Sudan since the signing of the CPA in 2005 have made the threat of violence a powerful tool to gain concessions and influence (LeRiche 2014). In fact, the contemporary political scene in South Sudan is largely dominated by militaries. It is very difficult for an individual who is not a veteran of the war to gain an influential position. South Sudan gained its autonomy, followed by independence, through the 2005 peace agreement. The accord gave almost all power to military actors while other political movements were excluded (Mamdani 2014). In post-agreement South Sudan, this situation endures. Government positions are predominately occupied by militaries and influential generals are sometimes more powerful than ministers and can dictate how ministers allocate the resources they have at their disposal (de Waal 2014). This means that the opportunities to become influential through ordinary political means decreases, which, in turn, increases motivation to join an armed movement. In particular, elites are given prominent positions depending on how great a threat they constitute (Interview with

SPLA veteran, 14 October 2011, Juba, South Sudan). During his first years in office, Salva Kiir's approach was to deter groups that were threatening his power by incorporating them in governmental structures. Instead of fighting off rivals, they could fight for a while and later become part of the state. As part of this "big tent" policy, the rank-and-file of these groups were included in the armed forces, whereas the leaders gained high positions in the army and were sometimes included in the government (ICG 2014). Paradoxically, the policy of incorporating insurgents in the army has also made joining an armed rebellion a route into the state forces for ordinary citizens. Most of the population lives on less than US$1 a day. By contrast, the lowest-ranking soldiers in the army are paid approximately US$140 a month (Mamdani 2014). This makes it very attractive to become part of the army. Thus, incentives for rebellion were created among both elites and regular soldiers.

Third, this policy reduced the opportunity costs of joining armed rebellion since the strategy included a widespread use of amnesties. South Sudan has a long history of atrocities going unpunished, reducing the expected costs associated with using violence as part of political competition (Rift Valley Institute 2014).

The long history of war in South Sudan has also influenced the incentive structure by creating a society where military achievements are central to obtaining prestige. Such attitudes created by the long war also make it easier for military "strong men", like Machar, to maintain their standing within society. In this system, political and military leaders often offer weapons to secure a powerful position in their community (Interview with James Ninrew, 12 October 2011, Juba, South Sudan). In this milieu, it also becomes important to take revenge for injury done to an individual or to a community. Thus, retaliation is crucial and many conflicts are retributions for earlier conflicts (Harragin 2011), which serve to further contribute to violent outcomes.

Another factor that is essential to explain the implementation of violence in South Sudan relates to social networks in general and the organization of Machar's SPLM/A-IO in particular. The "big-tent" policy served to create a basis for the organizational structures of different armed factions, including the SPLM/A-IO. At the start of the 2013 crisis, the South Sudanese army was severely divided and constituted a coalition of various militias rather than a unified national army (Mamdani 2014). Importantly, most fighters in these militias were Nuer, which created an army where a majority came from this community (ICG 2014). When events unfolded in late 2013, Machar did not need to build up his rebel group. Instead, the national army split in two halves and the SPLM/A-IO was well armed at its birth. Furthermore, many of the former militias had fought with Machar during the war and he could capitalize on these networks. For example, Peter Gadet, the current military commander of SPLM/A-IO, fought alongside Machar during periods of the north-south war (Johnson 2006). More generally, prevalent networks in South Sudan are largely a legacy of linkages created during the north-south war. At the top level, these wartime networks created bonds between commanders at different levels used to launch rebellion. Likewise, prevailing linkages between soldiers and their commanders are strong in South Sudan and influence incentive structures. During the north-south war, commanders carried out extensive predation in the areas they controlled. Many commanders paid dowry for their soldiers, which enabled them to get married. This created a social contract with wide-reaching obligations that kept the lower strata of these networks dependent on these leaders. Dependency did not end with the termination of the north-south war. Instead, the intimate ties developed during the war ensured that commanders could preserve their powerful positions in a post-war setting (Pinaud 2014). These networks thus include a dual dependency between powerful commanders and regular soldiers, where the leaders need their soldiers in order to remain powerful and the rank-and-file need their commanders as their influential positions allow them to distribute assets. For warlords who want to employ violence, these established military networks are beneficial since they can make use of the existing structures, instead of building up new networks.

Conclusions

This chapter has studied how the political actions taken by Riek Machar – a militant turned politician, and then back again – in relation to the electoral process have created a humanitarian disaster in South Sudan. Machar has been involved in several election-related strategies. After the death of Garang he reluctantly accepted the role of vice-president and was involved in transforming the SPLM from a rebel group to a political party. In March 2013, he declared that he would challenge Kiir as the leader of SPLM, which later led to the formation of the SPLM-IO. As leader of the SPLM-IO, Machar has organized collective violence, resecuritized wartime identities and committed human rights abuses in South Sudan. The SPLM/A-IO has carried out numerous attacks against civilians (primarily targeting the Dinka community). The violence has served to further securitize wartime identities. This does not mean, however, that the incumbent President Salva Kiir is without guilt for the deplorable situation in the country. The president is responsible for the targeting of Nuer civilians in Juba. Kiir's increasingly authoritarian rule, and a number of factors conducive to violence, including weak institutions, a high centralization of political power and pervasive militarization of society, are critical for understanding the war dynamics in South Sudan. These factors have played into the frames around which Machar has been able to mobilize support for his cause. While mobilizing support by reference to the protection of the Nuer community, he has also attempted to build broad-based support in response to Kiir's authoritarian and allegedly Dinka-dominated rule. Moreover, the rapidity with which events unfolded and escalated into large-scale violence must be understood in relation to the resources leaders have available to implement violence. While Machar has used violence primarily to empower himself, he has been able to mobilize elites and followers to use violence due to close ties and social networks created between commanders and soldiers during the north-south war. Moreover, potential costs for violence are very low, since impunity is widespread and militant behavior rewarded both economically and politically.

This chapter identifies several insights useful for policy makers. A first such insight relates to amnesties. In South Sudan, the short-term effects of widespread amnesties to rebel leaders (and their fighters) were positive as they helped to spare South Sudan from a civil war right after the CPA was signed. However, the long-term effects of this policy have been devastating and created a milieu where the incentives to join a rebellion are significant and the disincentives almost non-existent. Thus, our analysis suggests that if amnesties are used, they need to be time-restricted to prevent a complete undermining of the political landscape, as has been the case in South Sudan. A second policy implication relates to peace-building and democratization in a de facto one-party state, such as South Sudan. The SPLM dictates politics in the country and its leader is destined to become the head of state. In this context, the outcome of the electoral process is determined long before the actual elections take place and is contingent on intra-party competition and the internal processes of the dominant party. In addition, in a place torn by violent conflicts, political contests are often between warlord democrats with the means and resources readily available to mobilize for violence.

Notes

1 This chapter partly builds on text and ideas published in Brosché and Höglund (2016). Reprinted with permission from Cambridge University Press.

2 On choice and development of identity around which to mobilize in secessionist conflicts, see Saideman et al. (2005).

3 The CPA stipulated that elections were to be held in July 2009, but they were delayed. A prime reason was problems with the census – a prerequisite for the elections. In addition, Garang's death impeded the implementation of the accord (Brosché 2009).

4 In May 2014, President Kiir announced that the elections would be postponed until 2017 or 2018 because of the crisis that began in late 2013 (BBC 2014).

5 Salva Kiir and Uganda's President Yoweri Museveni are close allies. When Kiir was under threat, Uganda sent troops to support him.

6 Another frame that Machar used to motivate people to fight for him during his conflict with Garang was the issue of independence. While Garang was fighting for a "New Sudan", where the whole of Sudan would be transformed, Machar declared that he wanted an independent South Sudan. As part of this strategy – and to rally support among his troops – Machar renamed his movement:

from SPLM/A-Nasir to the South Sudan Independence Movement/Army (SSIM/A) (Hutchinson 2001; Johnson 2006). As independence was the ultimate goal for most southerners, this was a factor that increased support for Machar.

7 They are referred to as "former detainees" as they were detained by President Kiir after he accused them of being part of the alleged coup. Later, they were released and formed this opposition group.

8 In addition to these tensions, there are also strains between different Nuer factions in the SPLM/A-IO, illustrated by the nomination of Taban Deng as vice-president. Deng is, like Machar, of Nuer origin.

9 All subterranean natural resources are in fact government-owned, which also raises the stakes in central politics (Mertenskoetter and Luak 2012).

Bibliography

Al-Jazeera. 2016. "UN: Tens of Thousands Killed in South Sudan War." *Al-Jazeera*, 3 March.

Amnesty International. 2014. *Nowhere Safe: Civilians under Attack in South Sudan*. London: Amnesty International.

BBC. 2014. "South Sudan's Elections Postponed, Says President Kiir." BBC, 12 May.

Brosché, J. 2009. *Sharing Power – Enabling Peace? Evaluating Sudan's Comprehensive Peace Agreement*. New York and Uppsala: Uppsala University and the Mediation Support Unit, Department of Political Affairs, United Nations.

Brosché, J. 2014. *Masters of War: The Role of Elites in Sudan's Communal Conflicts*. Uppsala: Uppsala University Press.

Brosché, J. and K. Höglund. 2016. "Crisis of Governance in South Sudan: Electoral Politics in the World's Newest Nation." *Journal of Modern African Studies* 54 (1): 1-24.

Carter Center. 2010. *Observing Sudan's 2010 National Elections April 11–18*, Final Report.

Christensen, M. M. and M. Utas. 2008. "Mercenaries of Democracy: The 'Politricks' of Remobilized Combatants in the 2007 General Election, 2007." *African Affairs* 107 (429): 515-539.

De Waal, A. 2014. "When Kleptocracy Becomes Insolvent: Brute Causes of the Civil War in South Sudan." *African Affairs* 113 (452): 347-369.

De Waal, A. 2015. *The Real Politics of the Horn of Africa*. Cambridge: Polity Press.

Graicunas, V. A. 1937. "Relationship in Organization." In *Papers on the Science of Administration*, ed. L. Gulick and L. Urwick. New York: Colombia University Press.

Gurr, T. R. 2000. *People Versus States: Minorities at Risk in the New Century*. Washington, DC: United States Institute of Peace Press.

Harragin, S. 2011. *South Sudan: Waiting for Peace to Come: Study from Bor, Twic East and Duk Counties in Jonglei*. Copenhagen: Local to Global Protection. Available at http://www.local2global.info/wp-content/uploads/L2GP_Jonglei_S_Sudan_TR_FINAL.pdf.

Hutchinson, S. E. 1996. *Nuer Dilemmas Coping with Money, War, and the State*. Berkeley, CA: University of California Press.

Hutchinson, S. E. 2001. "A Curse from God? Religious and Political Dimensions of the Post-1991 Rise of Ethnic Violence in South Sudan." *Journal of Modern African Studies* 39 (2): 307-331.

ICG (International Crisis Group). 2009. *Jonglei's Tribal Conflicts: Countering Insecurity in South Sudan*. Brussels: International Crisis Group

ICG (International Crisis Group). 2011. *Politics and Transition in the New South Sudan*. Brussels: International Crisis Group.

ICG (International Crisis Group). 2014. *South Sudan: A Civil War by Any Other Name*. Brussels: International Crisis Group.

ICG (International Crisis Group). 2015. *Sudan and South Sudan's Merging*

Conflicts. Brussels: International Crisis
Group.

ICG (International Crisis Group). 2016.
South Sudan's Risky Political Impasse.
Brussels: International Crisis Group.

Johnson, D. H. 2006. *The Root Causes of
Sudan's Civil War.* Bloomington, IN:
Indiana University Press.

Jok, J. M. 2014. *South Sudan and the
Prospects for Peace Amidst Violent
Political Wrangling.* Juba: Sudd
Institute.

Jok, J. M. and S. E. Hutchinson. 1999.
"Sudan's Prolonged Second Civil
War and the Militarization of Nuer
and Dinka Ethnic Identities." *African
Studies Review* 42 (2): 125-145.

Kalyvas, S. 2006. *The Logic of Violence
in Civil War.* Cambridge: Cambridge
University Press.

Kane, J. 2001. *The Politics of Moral Capital.*
Cambridge: Cambridge University
Press.

LeRiche, M. 2014. "South Sudan: Not Just
another War and another Peace in
Africa." *African Arguments,* 28 January.

LeRiche, M. and M. Arnold. 2012. *South
Sudan from Revolution to Independence.*
London: Hurst.

Lyons, T. 2005. *Demilitarizing Politics:
Elections on the Uncertain Road to
Peace.* Boulder, CO: Lynne Rienner
Publisher.

Mamdani, M. 2014. "South Sudan and its
Unending Bloody Conflict: No Power-
sharing without Political Reform." *The
East African,* 15 February.

Menkhaus, K. 1998. "Somalia: Political
Order in a Stateless Society." *Current
History* 619: 220-224.

Mertenskoetter, P. and D. S. Luak. 2012.
"Overview of the Legal System and
Legal Research in the Republic of South
Sudan." *GlobaLex,* Hauser Global Law
School Program, New York University.

Olson, M. 1965. *The Logic of Collective
Action: Public Goods and the Theory
of Goods.* Cambridge, MA: Harvard
University Press.

Pappas, T. S. 2008. "Political Leadership
and the Emergence of Radical

Mass Movements in Democracy."
Comparative Political Studies 41:
1117-1140.

Paris, R. 2004. *At War's End: Building
Peace after Civil Conflict.* Cambridge:
Cambridge University Press.

Pinaud, C. 2014. "South Sudan: Civil War,
Predation and the Making of a Military
Aristocracy." *African Affairs* 451 (113):
192-211.

Pruitt, D. G. and S. H. Kim. 2004. *Social
Conflict: Escalation, Stalemate, and
Settlement,* 3rd ed. New York: McGraw
Hill.

Rapoport, D. C. and L. Weinberg. 2001.
"Elections and Violence." In *The
Democratic Experience and Political
Violence,* ed. D. C. Rapoport and
L. Weinberg. London: Frank Cass
Publishers.

Rift Valley Institute. 2014. *South Sudan:
Is Peace Possible?* Nairobi: Rift Valley
Institute.

Reuters. 2013. "Riek Machar: South Sudan's
Divisive Pretender for Power." *Reuters,*
20 December.

Saideman, S. M., B. K. Dougherty and
E. K. Jenne. 2005. "Dilemmas of
Divorce: How Secessionist Identities
Cut Both Ways." *Security Studies* 14
(4): 607-636.

Small Arms Survey. 2013. *SSLM/A.*
Geneva: Small Arms Survey.

Small Arms Survey. 2014. *The SPLM-
in-Opposition.* Geneva: Small Arms
Survey.

Snyder, J. 2000. *From Voting to Violence.*
New York and London: W. W. Norton
& Company.

Stedman, S. J. 1997. "Spoiler Problems in
Peace Processes." *International Security*
22 (2): 5-53.

Sudan Tribune. 2011. "The Mayom
Declaration" *Sudan Tribune,* 11 April.

Sudan Tribune. 2013. "Senior SPLM
Colleagues Give Kiir Ultimatum
over Party Crisis." *Sudan Tribune,* 6
December.

Sudan Tribune. 2014. "South Sudanese
Government, Yau Yau Rebels Sign
Ceasefire." *Sudan Tribune,* 31 January.

Sudan Tribune. 2015. "Murle Faction Announces Defection to S. Sudan rebels." *Sudan Tribune*, 14 February.

Themnér, A. 2011. *Violence in Post-Conflict Societies: Remarginalization, Remobilizers and Relationships*. London and New York: Routledge.

Tucker, R. C. 1981. *Politics as Leadership*. Columbia: University of Missouri Press.

UCDP (Uppsala Conflict Data Program). 2014. *UCDP Database*. Uppsala: Department of Peace and Conflict Research, Uppsala University.

Young, J. 2015. *A Fractious Rebellion: Inside the SPLM-IO*. Geneva: Small Arms Survey.

Weinberg, L., A. Pedahzur and A. Perlinger. 2009. *Political Parties and Terrorist Groups*, 2nd ed. London: Routledge.

Whitehead, L. 2002. *Democratization: Theory and Practice*. Oxford: Oxford University Press.

Willems, R. and H. Rouw. 2011. *Security Promotion Seen from Below: Experiences from South Sudan*. Utrecht: IKV Pax Christi.

Conclusion | Ambiguous peacelords: the diminishing returns of post-war democracy

Anders Themnér

> When international agents encounter war criminals, drug dealers, and human rights violators, they can choose whether to make them partners or enemies. While particular circumstances might justify one course of action or another, these choices have an impact on the goal of building a sovereign state. (Ghani and Lockhart 2008: 177)

In post-civil war societies electoral politics often becomes a competition between different warlord democrats. The political maneuverings of such Big Men often provoke strong reactions from local and international actors alike; not only may the former have orchestrated wartime atrocities, but oftentimes they continue to possess the capacity needed to instigate new forms of violence. So far there is a lack of studies investigating the security impacts of including WDs in post-war electoral politics. In fact, previous research has instead stressed the importance of building strong and democratic institutions and political parties. Manning (2004: 55), for instance, holds that "[t]he quality and durability of democratic political settlement ... depends largely on the establishment of viable political parties willing and able to compete in the electoral arena". But what happens when there are no strong democratic political parties or institutions to fall back on, and it will arguably take years before the necessary organizational structures are set in place? Under such circumstances the best chance to support peace and democracy may be to transform "warlords" into "peacelords". In this volume we have investigated whether this is possible. More specifically we have done this by addressing the following questions: (1) does the electoral participation of WDs tend to have a positive or negative effect on post-civil war security; and (2) if there are negative implications, how do they manifest themselves? In our efforts to answer these questions, we have compared the personal trajectories of a number of African WDs – Antipas Mbusa Nyamwisi (DRC); João Bernardo Vieira (Guinea-Bissau); Sekou Conneh and Prince Johnson (Liberia); Afonso Dhlakama (Mozambique); Paul Kagame (Rwanda); Julius Maada Bio, Eldred Collins and Samuel Hinga Norman (Sierra Leone); and Riek Machar (South Sudan). Even if the main aim has been to establish whether WDs who run for office tend to promote or undermine security, the chapter authors have also sought to inductively identify why they have done so. In the following, the book's main findings and contributions are summarized, while a number of practical and policy-oriented implications derived from these findings are discussed.

Electoral maneuverings and political outcomes

The WDs investigated in this volume employed a myriad of electoral strategies during their post-war careers. Their choice of strategy – and to some extent their electoral success – largely hinged on the amount of power they had amassed by the end of the civil wars. At one extreme one finds Paul Kagame (Rwanda), João Bernardo Vieira (Guinea-Bissau) and Riek Machar (South Sudan), who came to embody, or at least have a major impact on, their countries. Even if Kagame was initially only vice-president, he de facto controlled the reins of government after the end of the war. In this capacity he oversaw the transformation of Rwandan Patriotic Front (RPF) into a political party. In 2000 he formalized his power by becoming Rwanda's president, a position that he defended in two consecutive elections (2003 and 2010) as the standard-bearer of RPF. As a celebrated freedom-fighter Vieira was able to position himself as general secretary of African Party for the Independence of Guinea and Cape Verde (PAIGC) – Guinea-Bissau's sole party – and president in 1984. In the country's first free elections, he confirmed his position as head of state and subsequently reaffirmed PAIGC's hold on power. Interestingly, despite being sidelined by PAIGC after his fall from power in 1999, Vieira was able to make a spectacular political comeback and win the 2005 presidential elections. The fact that he did this as an independent candidate is witness to the resources, networks and prestige that he possessed. Even if Machar was never head of state, he was arguably the second most powerful individual in South Sudan. In 2005 Machar became vice-president after the death of Sudan People's Liberation Movement (SPLM) leader John Garang. In this capacity Machar played a pivotal role in helping to cement SPLM's dominance over South Sudan's political and economic life. With the 2010 elections, Machar reconfirmed his position as vice-president, after supporting SPLM leader Salva Kiir's presidential bid. In 2013 Machar openly challenged Kiir for the leadership of SPLM and by extension who would rule South Sudan.

At the other extreme one finds the likes of Eldred Collins (Sierra Leone) and Sekou Conneh (Liberia). By the beginning of the Liberian and Sierra Leonean peace processes, both had become somewhat marginal figures; while Collins' Revolutionary United Front (RUF) had been militarily defeated and its top leaders arrested by the Special Court, Conneh had lost control over parts of Liberians United for Reconciliation and Democracy (LURD) after a power struggle with his former wife. However, both Collins and Conneh tried to make the most out of their difficult positions. Collins initially acted as spokesperson of Revolutionary United Front Party (RUFP) – the political heir of RUF – but left the party after it was decisively defeated in the 2002 national elections. Having failed in his efforts to gain a position of influence in other parties, he reemerged in 2009, relaunched RUFP (it had ceased to exist in 2007 after going bankrupt) and ran as the RUFP's presidential standard-bearer in the 2012 elections. Meanwhile, Conneh created a completely new party – Progressive Democratic Party (PRODEM) – to support his bid to become president in 2005. PRODEM was, however, little more than a front for Conneh's personal ambitions. The electoral results also mirrored Collins' and Conneh's political difficulties; both only retained 0.6% of the votes.

In between these two extremes one finds Afonso Dhlakama (Mozambique), Antipas Mbusa (DRC), Prince Johnson (Liberia) and Julius Maada Bio and Samuel Hinga Norman (Sierra Leone). Dhlakama and Bio headed relatively well-established and popular opposition parties. The only difference was that Dhlakama had transformed his rebel movement RENAMO into a political party, while by 2011 Bio had maneuvered himself to the top of the Sierra Leone People's Party (SLPP), a party that had existed long before the outbreak of the civil war. Both WDs dominated their respective parties and RENAMO and SLPP had a substantial presence in the legislatures of Mozambique and Sierra Leone thanks to strong electoral showings. Meanwhile, as a renowned war hero – credited by many for having saved Sierra Leone from abusive rebels and rogue soldiers – Norman was instrumental in shoring up support for the SLPP regime (1996–2003), especially during the 2002 elections. For these endeavors he was handsomely rewarded, first with the position of deputy minister of defense and later as minister of internal affairs. Even after he was arrested by the Special Court in 2003, Norman continued his political maneuverings; bitter because of SLPP's failure to prevent his incarceration, he switched sides and encouraged his supporters to vote for the People's Movement for Democratic Change (PMDC) opposition during the 2007 elections. In addition, as leader of Congolese Rally for Democracy/Kisangani-Liberation Movement (RCD/K-ML), Mbusa spearheaded the transformation of his armed group into a political party after the 2002 peace accord; an organization that largely followed his political will. Even if he failed to win the presidency in both the 2006 and 2011 elections, he was able to ensure that RCD/K-ML gained a fair number of seats in the national assembly. Initially Mbusa used his political influence to support President Joseph Kabila's regime, but after being marginalized by Kabila within the government, he switched to backing the opposition. Finally, Prince Johnson – a controversial figure who, as head of Independent National Patriotic Front of Liberia (INPFL), had executed President Samuel Doe in 1990 – perhaps comes closest to embodying the notion of an electoral navigator. After having spent much of the war in exile, Johnson returned to Liberia in 2004 in order to take part in the 2005 elections.

Lacking support from a political party, he contested one of the senate seats allotted to his native Nimba County as an independent. Seen as having liberated members of the Gio and Mano ethnic communities from Doe's oppressive rule, Johnson succeeded in his efforts to become a senator. To increase his chances of winning the 2011 presidential elections, he formed the National Union for Democratic Progress (NUDP) and shocked many observers by coming third in the presidential race. Having fallen out with his NUDP colleagues, he was once again obliged to run as an independent to defend his senatorial position in 2014, which he successfully did.

Interestingly it appears that actually succeeding at the polls was not necessarily the main objective of all WDs. For some, taking part in elections rather seems to have constituted an opportunity to showcase themselves and the networks of clients that they possessed. Such actions were particularly important in the event of presidential elections requiring a second round, where benefits could be gained by offering support to one of the remaining candidates. Collins (Sierra Leone), Conneh and Johnson (Liberia) all hoped to position themselves as such king- or queenmakers. Of these it was, however, only Johnson that succeeded. Coming third in the 2011 presidential elections, with 11.6% of the votes, gave him much room for bargaining. Finally, he decided to back Johnson-Sirleaf. In return for his support, it is rumored that Johnson was given a substantial amount of money. Not even Dhlakama – whose Mozambican National Resistance (RENAMO) was in a much stronger position than Collin's RUFP, Conneh's PRODEM and Johnson's NUDP – saw elections as the most efficient route to gain political prominence. Instead he preferred to personally negotiate deals with subsequent Mozambican presidents, efficiently side-lining parliament as the main venue for political dialogue and decision-making. The main purpose of such agreements was to gain economic benefits to ensure the survival of his Big Man networks. When state leaders are uninterested in cutting such deals with WDs, it may be necessary for the latter to signal political resolve by mobilizing supporters in the street or rearming them in the countryside. In fact, displaying "wealth in people" (Bledsoe 1990) and a capacity to disrupt governance may then be the only way to gain the president's ear. This was true in the case of Dhlakama; after Guebuza became president in 2004, he refused to engage in new deals with Dhlakama and it was only after the latter challenged the government with arms that Guebuza changed his mind. When considering the centralization of political, economic and military power in the hands of the president in many African countries, it is perhaps not surprising that WDs prefer to focus their energy on cutting a deal with their heads of state (Bratton and van de Walle 1997).

In order to mobilize support for their political agendas, many WDs actively played on their wartime credentials. Conneh (Liberia), Machar (South Sudan),

Norman (Sierra Leone) and Johnson (Liberia) all alluded to their role in having defended their ethnic communities to rally voters or, as in the case of Machar, gather support in his struggle with President Kiir. Meanwhile, Bio (Sierra Leone) succeeded in becoming the SLPP's presidential flag-bearer by referring to his youth and militancy: only he could help the SLPP stand up against the perceived aggressions of the All People's Congress (APC) government. One reason why Vieira was re-elected to office in 2005 was that he was seen as the only person with the military authority and connections to reign in unruly elements within the armed forces. In fact, of the WDs analyzed in this book it was only Collins (Sierra Leone) who chose not to exploit his military background for political purposes. This was probably a function of his marginal status in Sierra Leone's post-war political scene; having more or less lost the war, being seriously tainted by RUF's wartime abuses, and lacking a clear ethnic base from which to mobilize supporters (RUF had never been linked to a specific ethnic community), Collins presumably had little to gain by reminding the electorate of his wartime past. Hence, it appears unrealistic to expect that WDs will be forward-looking politicians who will let the past alone; it is simply too tempting to employ wartime credentials to gain an edge over the competition. The efficiency of such electoral strategies partly contradicts some common assumptions found in previous literature, which have assumed that it is necessary for wartime actors to broaden their support base, utilize a more inclusive rhetoric and focus on a new peacetime agenda to truly succeed at the polls (Manning 2004: 59).

For the most part, the maneuverings of the WDs had a substantial impact on political dynamics in their respective countries. As heads of states – who controlled considerable formal and informal power – Kagame (Rwanda) and Vieira (Guinea-Bissau) possessed the greatest amount of agency and decided most aspects of government policy. For instance, Kagame initiated an ambitious program to achieve economic growth, reduce poverty and provide social services. In addition, he sponsored military operations in DRC. As previously touched upon, Vieira oversaw the introduction of multiparty elections in 1994 and was in 2005 re-elected as president without the backing of a political party. Meanwhile, through his decision to challenge President Kiir as the leader of SPLM, Machar plunged South Sudan into its most severe crisis since the end of the north-south war in 2005. As heads of Mozambique and Sierra Leone's main opposition parties – RENAMO and SLPP – Dhlakama and Bio were the only viable alternatives to the Mozambique Liberation Front (FRELIMO) and APC governments. In fact, while Bio came in second place during the 2012 presidential elections (with 37.4% as compared to 1.3% of the votes gained by third-placed Charles Francis Margai), Dhlakama came close to winning the 1999 presidential elections and would, according to some observers, have won had the government not engaged in electoral fraud. Even though Mbusa's (DRC) electoral track record cannot be compared to that of Dhlakama and Bio, he did play an instrumental role in shoring up support for President Kabila in parts of eastern DRC. In fact, by breaking rank with other ex-rebel leaders, he weakened the opposition against Kabila. In addition, Norman (Sierra Leone) played an instrumental role in the electoral defeat of SLPP in 2007. Norman's open support for PMDC – which had made a political alliance with APC – is believed to have split the Mende vote and paved the way for APC's first electoral victory since being ousted from power in 1992. Finally, as previously touched upon, Johnson became queenmaker during the second round of the 2011 presidential elections in Liberia, when he decided to throw in his lot with the incumbent Johnson-Sirleaf. Of the studied WDs it was only Collins (Sierra Leone) and Conneh (Liberia) who failed to have a major impact on political dynamics, even if the latter caused much media alarm when he declared his intention to run for president.

Once a military, always a military?

Given that the electoral participation of WDs tends to have a substantial impact on political outcomes, how does it affect post-war security? At first glance the prospect of WDs becoming "peacelords" appears discouraging. Of the ten WDs included in this volume, it was only Collins (Sierra Leone) who never took any action – such as supporting organized violence, securitizing wartime identities, criminalizing politics or fostering human rights abuses – which threatened to undermine the new peace order. In fact, Collins even refrained from inciting fears or trying to cement wartime cleavages. Instead, his speech acts were characterized by messages of national unity. Hence, somewhat ironically, Collins – whose movement had been one of Africa's most abusive armed groups – comes closest to embodying the ideal peacelord.

When comparing the forms of insecurity that the WDs sponsored, it is interesting to note that organized violence – arguably the most detrimental form of aggression – was a relatively rare phenomenon. In fact, there were only two clear cases of such types of violence – Dhlakama's rebellion against the Mozambican government and Machar's armed struggle against South Sudanese President Kiir. The magnitude of the violence was, however, severe. The civil war in South Sudan had killed over 10,000 people by 2015 and displaced another million, and even if the 2013-2014 hostilities in Mozambique only resulted in approximately 200 deaths they created fears that the country was about to slide back to the dark days of the 1980s. The observation that WDs are reluctant to resort to violence is in line with arguments – developed by de Waal (2009: 104) – concerning the behavior of African elites. According to him, "because most members of the elite are content with their personal stakes in the status quo, they rarely use violence among themselves". Hence, as long as WDs are not relegated to the margins of society – whereby they lose their elite status – it may be that they are not willing to take the risks associated with challenging the post-war order with arms.

There were also a number of unclear cases, where it is difficult to establish exactly what role the WDs had in instigating the violence. This was, for instance, the case for Bio (Sierra Leone) and Mbusa (DRC). What is interesting with these two WDs is that it appears as if they played on the ambiguity of their involvement. For instance, Mbusa purposely fanned rumors – that were difficult to verify – about his influence over a number of armed groups, ranging from Allied Democratic Forces (ADF) and segments of the Congolese armed forces, to M23. In this sense, he strategically deployed "conflict narratives as a mobilizing resource" to gain political advantages (see section "Misguided Militarized Posturing: Flirting with the M23?", Chapter 1). When it came to Bio, his supporters were involved in a number of violent incidents before, during and after the 2012 elections. Officially he denounced these acts and called on his followers to remain calm. However, having portrayed himself as a militant and defender of SLPP, his innocence is highly questionable. In this context it is also interesting to mention Norman, who was reported to have urged his supporters to take up arms in a phone call from detention. There are indications that Norman knew that his prison calls were tapped. It is therefore probable that the statement was more intended as a warning to the government or international community, rather than a sincere effort to ignite violence.

A somewhat more usual strategy was to attempt to securitize wartime identities. This was particularly common amongst WDs from the opposition. For instance, in 2011 Dhlakama (Mozambique) promised to oust FRELIMO from power if he did not gain concessions during talks with the government. Four years later, Dhlakama made similar remarks when he threatened to resort to arms if the regime did not adhere to his demands. Less direct threats were made by Conneh and Johnson (Liberia). During the 2005 presidential campaigns, Conneh proclaimed that only he could control the violent agency of ex-combatants, indicating that there would be no peace without him controlling the reins of power. Veiled threats were a particular trademark of Johnson, who employed such tactics throughout his electoral career. This was especially true after the creation of the Truth and Reconciliation Commission (TRC). Without directly implicating himself, Johnson warned that if the TRC did not cease harassing him, and other ex-military leaders, there was an imminent risk that new violence would erupt.

Another category of WDs that made efforts to securitize wartime identities were ex-militaries who had fallen out with their bosses. After Machar (South Sudan) was ousted as vice-president in 2013 he launched a smear campaign against President Kiir, accusing the latter of promoting a "Dinkocracy". The purpose of these verbal attacks was to polarize relations between Dinkas and other ethnic groups and rally the latter behind his political agenda. From having been an outspoken supporter of the peace process, Norman (Sierra Leone) made a number of disturbing statements after his arrest. For instance, he declared that the actions of the Special Court – in complicity with the government – amounted to nothing less than impunity, which risked plunging the country into new fighting. Although Norman never mentioned his own name, the message was clear: there would be no peace without his release.

There were also incidents of WDs fostering different types of human rights abuses. Such cruelties were carried out by WDs who were heads of state or embroiled in warfare. As president, Kagame (Rwanda) imprisoned political opponents, arrested independent journalists and ordered extrajudicial killings. Such actions were particularly prevalent during times of elections. Both of Vieira's (Guinea Bissau) presidential terms were characterized by human rights abuses. After his 1994 electoral victory repressions, persecution of opponents, obstruction of the press and killings of rivals were commonplace, while intimidation and extrajudicial punishments were carried out between 2005 and 2009. Finally, Machar (South Sudan) was also responsible for serious human rights encroachments. These were, however, not carried out until after the outbreak of a new civil war in late 2013 and should be seen in the light of these developments.

The least common form of aggression was the criminalization of politics. In fact, it was only Vieira who actively mixed crime and politics. During his second term as president, Vieira allowed Guinea-Bissau to become a transit country for international drug cartels. In return for handsome paybacks Vieira employed parts of the state apparatus to facilitate the movement of cocaine from Latin America to Europe. When setting up his criminal enterprise, Vieira made use of old arms-smuggling networks which he had previously developed.

Ambiguous peacelords

However, on closer scrutiny the results are not quite as discouraging as they first appear. When tracing the personal trajectories of the WDs, it is possible to make two important qualifications regarding the detrimental behavior of WDs. These provide some hope concerning the prospect of employing WDs as 'peacelords'.

Short-term benevolence, long-term belligerency The first qualification is based on the observation that several of the studied WDs began their electoral careers as benign leaders, only later switching to more belligerent activities. During much of the 1990s, Dhlakama (Mozambique) played a rather positive role in strengthening the peace process; as the leader of the largest opposition party in Africa, he was instrumental in ensuring political pluralism and checking authoritarian tendencies within the FRELIMO government. Meanwhile, Mbusa

229

(DRC) successfully transformed his armed group into a political party, participated in the 2006 elections and was seen by some as a pioneer of national reunification; it was only later that he began flirting with different armed groups. Similarly, Machar (South Sudan) refrained from undermining the post-war order until after being ousted as vice-president in 2013. During 2001–2003, Norman was a key proponent of peace in Sierra Leone and it was only after his arrest that he took a more aggressive stance. Finally, Vieira initially played a positive role in shepherding Guinea-Bissau to its first multiparty elections in 1994, which were deemed free and fair. It was only after entering office as an elected president that he began to foster human rights abuses.

It is, however, vital to stress that during these periods of non-belligerency it is questionable whether the WDs – with the possible exception of Dhlakama and Norman – can truly be seen as "transformational" peacelords who actively sought to solidify peace and "reconstruct their nationalist discourses" to emphasize peace and reconciliation (Kaufman 2006: 215). For instance, it was from a position of power that Vieira allowed the democratization of Guinea-Bissau's political life to proceed. He could therefore afford to be generous and not to pervert the 1994 elections. However, once in office he began clamping down on opponents. Meanwhile, even if Machar (South Sudan) and Mbusa (DRC) refrained from engaging in aggressive acts during periods of their time in office, there is no evidence that they took any concrete steps during this time aimed at building a more durable peace. Hence, if we are to classify this category of WDs as peacelords,[1] it is not because they took constructive steps to build positive and durable peace, but simply because they did not misbehave.

What implications do these findings have for the argument that democratic participation has the potential to socialize belligerent actors into benign democrats? The fact that four WDs – Bio (Sierra Leone), Conneh (Liberia), Kagame (Rwanda) and Johnson (Liberia)[2] – acted in a hostile manner throughout their political careers, while five – Dhlakama (Mozambique), Machar (South Sudan), Mbusa (DRC), Norman (Sierra Leone) and Viera (Vieira) – became more belligerent over time, casts doubt on this argument. How can this lack of socialization be explained? There are probably three possible answers to this question. First, perhaps "democratic institutions do not always produce peaceful democrats" (Jarstad and Sisk 2008: 23), because some actors are simply unable to acquire new norms and behaviors. It may be that most WDs will, at some point or the other, engage in aggression due to their military experiences; to recall previous research has documented a strong correlation between military service and low levels of agreeableness (see section "Warlord Democrats as Instigators of Insecurity", Introduction). Second, perhaps WDs are good at initiating democratic transitions, but bad at sustaining and entrenching them. As democratization and peacebuilding progress there is always a risk that WDs' power-bases – (in)formal military networks, wartime constituencies and economic resources – will begin to deplete. Maybe it is waning economic and human resources that push WDs to eventually undermine peace processes. Finally, perhaps there is a process of socialization, but in a different manner than expected. Instead of being socialized into functioning democratic systems, WDs learn how to navigate in political systems that are semi-authoritarian by nature and where threats, violence and abuse are accepted modes of behavior (for a more detailed discussion concerning which of these three arguments have most explanatory value, see section "Electoral Politics and the Schooling of Autocrats" below).

Two-faced blufflords The second qualification concerns the two-faced nature of belligerent WDs. In fact, when several of the latter engaged in aggression, they simultaneously took conciliatory steps. For instance, while Kagame (Rwanda) was fostering human rights abuses, he was also engaging in a systematic effort to address socioeconomic deficiencies in the country and desecuritize wartime identities. This dual nature of abuse and peacemaking was in line with his personality, which switched between being "austere and charming, imperious and friendly, fastidious and brutal" (see Chapter 2). These qualities gave Kagame an aura of being a Dr. Jekyll and Mr. Hyde character. Meanwhile, Conneh and Johnson (Liberia) made a habit of mixing veiled threats with messages of peace and reconciliation. Such dual discourses may be understood as an example of what Chowdhury and Krebs (2009: 379) have described as "rhetorical ambivalence", whereby actors who are part of different networks employ different discourses depending on the audience they speak to. According to this logic, Conneh and Johnson may have been engaging with different audiences when they sought to securitize wartime identities (for instance their constituencies) and made conciliatory remarks (the international community). By employing rhetorical ambivalence, they probably increased their chances of ensuring political relevance in the eyes of numerous actors. In the case of Mbusa (DRC), Bio and Norman (Sierra Leone), they utilized the ambiguity of their involvement in suspected or ongoing violence to their advantage. They thereby gained the benefit of being associated with the violence, without taking the security risks of claiming responsibility for it. Such a strategy is not uncommon amongst military leaders. This is because the perception of personal influence often matters "as much, if not more, than the actual reality" (Gormley-Heenan 2006: 21).

These two-faced WDs can be described as engaging in chameleonic leadership, a fluctuating form of leadership that alters according to the opinions of others and the context in which it exists (Gormley-Heenan 2006: 4). This finding speaks to the need to dismantle dichotomous labels commonly used to depict war- and peacetime leaders as either being hawks or doves, zealots or dealers (Gormley-Heenan 2006: 10). In this sense WDs are neither "good" nor "bad"; over time they switch between strategies and sometimes simultaneously engage in belligerent and benign acts. WDs are, in other words, "shape-shifters" (see Chapter 6) and "pompier-pyromanes" (see Chapter 1); they are both "warlords" and "democrats". However, such chameleonic tendencies should not necessarily be seen as an obstacle to peace, at least not when it concerns the likes of Bio (Sierra Leone), Conneh (Liberia), Johnson (Liberia), Mbusa (DRC) and Norman (Sierra Leone). On the contrary, in many instances chameleonic behavior is more about increasing one's bargaining range vis-à-vis political opponents than seeking military escalation. For instance, by employing a dual rhetoric of peace and violence, WDs can allude to their capacity to disrupt the new peace order, while at the same time promising to prevent such events from unfolding if they are elected into office or allowed to remain in power. Under such circumstances, WDs portray themselves as both villains and saviors. When faced with such WDs, it is crucial for peacemakers not to mechanically isolate them from forums of dialogue. If they do, there is always a risk that WDs will become the total spoilers they are often assumed to be (Stedman 1997).

Explaining the belligerency of warlord democrats

What then explains the WDs' decisions to either embrace peace or engage in more destructive behaviors – support organized violence, securitize wartime identities, criminalize politics or foster human rights abuses? Based on the inductive investigations conducted by the chapter authors, this section is dedicated to addressing this question and analyzing why some WDs switched from benevolent to more confrontational interactions during their electoral maneuverings. In this process one finding – which has received scant attention in the literature on peacebuilding and post-war democratization – deserves to be given special attention: the central role that brokerage plays in determining WDs' belligerency or benevolence.

Securitizing wartime identities Evidence suggests that it was predominantly electoral constraints – due to the authoritarian tendencies of governments, deterioration of patronage networks and limited electorates, or a combination of the three – that pushed WDs to securitize wartime identities. Dhlakama's (Mozambique) threat to remove FRELIMO from power in 2011 came after successive efforts by the regime to marginalize his and RENAMO's political influence. These efforts largely centered on restricting the freedom and fairness of elections and abusing RENAMO supporters, especially during times of elections. In addition, President Guebuza was less inclined than his predecessors to give economic concessions to Dhlakama through bilateral talks. What made things worse was RENAMO's decreasing presence in parliament and its lack of local government representation. A direct consequence of this was that RENAMO revenues were drying up. This constituted a serious threat to Dhlakama's political survival; with less patronage to distribute he was losing influence over key RENAMO supporters. Dhlakama's sense of being besieged was probably augmented by his insecure personality. By threatening violence, Dhlakama hoped to coerce the government into making economic and political concessions and subsequently solidify his networks of dependents. Similar dynamics can be identified in the case of Machar. After South Sudan's independence in 2011, President Kiir became more and more autocratic. These tendencies escalated after Machar declared his intention to challenge Kiir as SPLM leader in 2013 and Kiir dissolved the cabinet and removed Machar as vice-president. This fall from grace constituted a serious obstacle for Machar; without the backing of the SPLM Machar would not have access to the state patronage – which was substantial because of oil revenues – needed to win the elections. Even worse, after his dismissal as vice-president, Machar's ability to uphold his existing networks of clients was seriously challenged. Machar's decision to accuse Kiir of "Dinkocracy" should be seen in this light; by polarizing inter-ethnic relations Machar could ensure continued political relevance.

For Conneh and Johnson (Liberia), it was above all the small size of their electorates that pushed them to securitize wartime identities. Having lost influence over large segments of LURD, and coming from one of Liberia's smaller ethnic groups (Mandingos), Conneh had incentives to remind a broader segment of the population why they needed a strong military man to lead the country. For this reason, Conneh made a conscious effort to securitize the ex-combatant issue and declare that only he had the influence and knowledge to prevent ex-fighters from ravaging the country. Meanwhile, having spent twelve years in exile, Johnson had lost most of his followers when he returned to Liberia in 2004. By reminding the Gio and Mano electorate in Nimba that they were still not safe, and promising to protect them in case of renewed aggression from their Krahn neighbors, Johnson once again made his military credentials relevant. During subsequent elections, Johnson employed similar tactics, constantly describing the peace process as fragile and emphasizing how insecure Liberia was. Johnson's solution to these challenges were simple – only a military man, and devout Christian, could keep Liberians safe.

Hence, for some WDs efforts to securitize wartime identities can be seen as a rational reaction to the democratic deficiencies that characterize governance in many post-civil war societies. With few prospect of conquering the presidential office – due to electoral fraud or other malpractices – oppositional WDs can seek to securitize wartime identities in the hope of creating a kind of "hurting stalemate" (Manning 2004: 68); by keeping wartime fears, issues and divisions alive, they can hinder efforts by the government to marginalize them. Meanwhile, for WDs who head waning patronage networks and only have access to small electorates, securitizing wartime identities can help to pull back fledging clients and hesitant voters. In this sense "rhetorical deployments can have structural effects" and "change the game's structure" (Chowdhury and Krebs 2009: 382-383).

Even if electoral constraints were the most common cause for why the studied WDs securitized wartime identities, it was not the only one. In fact, the prospect of being convicted for war crimes was, at times, a contributing factor. Even if Johnson (Liberia) had already employed aggressive rhetoric during the 2005 elections, it escalated to a new level after the TRC began its work. Fearing that the TRC was a prologue to a war crimes tribunal, Johnson repeatedly warned that any effort to indict him, or other wartime leaders, would plunge Liberia into a new era of disorder. Meanwhile, Norman's (Sierra Leone) aggressive rhetoric was a direct reaction to his incarceration by the Special Court. By arguing that the actions of the Special Court threatened to unravel the country's peace process, Norman presumably hoped to pressure the authorities and international community into releasing him.

Supporting organized violence One revealing observation is that the two WDs that openly employed organized violence – Dhlakama (Mozambique) and Machar (South Sudan) – did so only after having first securitized wartime identities (predominantly due to electoral constraints). Electoral constraints can therefore be seen as a set of background factors which can initiate a process that eventually escalates into violence. Put differently, electoral constraints may be necessary, but not sufficient for WD-sponsored violence to take place. But why was it only Dhlakama and Machar that went from aggressive rhetoric to armed action? Conneh and Johnson (Liberia) also securitized wartime identities, but never chose to escalate things further.

This puzzle can largely be explained by referring to the capacity for and cost of misbehaving. Once President Kiir accused Machar of planning a coup against him and Mozambique's riot police started arresting RENAMO supporters, both Machar and Dhlakama had the capacity to rapidly mobilize for armed conflict. The former could, for instance, count on loyal supporters within the armed forces who quickly defected to fight on his behalf. Recruitment was also facilitated by the fact that South Sudanese society was highly militarized; not only was armed retribution for perceived injustices deemed acceptable behavior, social advancement was largely linked to wartime credentials. In addition, informal ties flourished between ex-combatants and commanders who had previously fought for Machar. This also made remobilization easier. Meanwhile, Dhlakama could quickly engage in violence thanks to his Presidential Guard; an armed unit – serving as Dhlakama's personal bodyguard – that had never been demobilized and was tolerated by the Mozambican authorities. The relative weakness of the Mozambican and South Sudanese armed forces, and the lack of peacekeeping troops, meant that the risk associated with re-engaging in violence was relatively low. Dhlakama and Machar's capacity to inflict harm was in sharp contrast to that of their Liberian counterparts. Not only had Conneh and Johnson's control over their ex-command structures seriously deteriorated by the first post-war elections in 2005, the 15,000-strong peacekeeping force made any efforts to engage in violence extremely hazardous.

What explains Bio, Norman and Mbusa's more ambiguous roles in supporting or calling for armed violence? Here it is not possible to pinpoint one dominant aspect; rather there were a myriad of factors at play. Just like Dhlakama (Mozambique) and Machar (South Sudan), Mbusa's (DRC) belligerency was a response to electoral constraints imposed on him. After falling out with Kabila in 2008, Mbusa struggled to uphold his patronage networks, a development which threatened his position as an influential WD. By associating himself with different oppositional armed groups, Mbusa hoped to once again make himself indispensable to Kabila; if the latter wanted to reach out to the armed opposition he would have to go via Mbusa. Meanwhile, Bio's covert fanning of electoral violence was a function of the structures that had propelled him into the leadership of the SLPP in the first place. Having convinced the SLPP grassroots to elect him as their presidential standard-bearer because of his youth, militancy and promise to stand up against the aggression of the ruling APC, he could not afford to back down once electoral tensions increased. Finally, Norman's decision to call his supporters to arms – in a phone call in 2003 – should probably be seen as a new attempt to coerce the international community and SLPP government into releasing him. To recall, Norman had made a similar attempt a few months earlier, when he claimed that the actions of the Special Court risked sparking new violence in the country.

However, one thing that Bio, Norman and Mbusa had in common was their lack of capacity to misbehave. In addition, Bio and Norman also had to take into consideration the high costs of engaging in such activities. The influence of these factors probably explains why their actions never escalated into more open and public support for violence. Even if all three, to some extent, had access to networks of ex-combatants, they did not control the loyalty of any armed units like Dhlakama and Machar. This made mobilization more difficult and time-consuming. In addition, Norman's possibility of organizing any armed activities was seriously curtailed by the fact that he was incarcerated and under close surveillance. In addition, Bio and Norman also had to take into consideration the wider military-political context in which they were operating. Not only was public support for the peace process high, there was also a strong commitment from the international community not to let Sierra Leone slide back into civil war. This arguably forced Bio and Norman to constrain themselves and, to some extent, their followers. This observation confirms some previous findings concerning how wartime actors behave during peace processes. According to Höglund (2008: 97), "[f]ormal criteria for inclusion in peace processes – often through ceasefire – may result in new forms of violence, since it is in the interest of the parties not to be associated with violations of the principles agreed to". For WDs this could entail refraining from openly supporting organized violence, and instead fuel narratives of conflict involvement and securitize wartime identities.

Fostering human rights abuses and criminalizing politics To recall, fostering human rights abuses and criminalizing politics were rather uncommon outcomes. In fact, only Vieira (Guinea-Bissau) engaged in the latter, while Vieira, Kagame (Rwanda) and Machar (South Sudan) did the former. Why was it so rare for WDs to foster such forms of belligerency and what explains Kagame, Machar and Vieira's decision to do so? On a general level there appears to be correlation between possessing the reins of government and the promotion of abuses and crime. Coordinating large-scale criminal activities, such as cocaine smuggling, necessitates a certain amount of state involvement, such as officials turning a blind eye and powerful politicians giving covert support. It would therefore have been difficult for oppositional WDs – such as Dhlakama (Mozambique), Conneh and Johnson (Liberia), Bio and Collins (Sierra Leon) – to set up similar enterprises. Meanwhile, it can be argued that it is foremost WDs who are part of the government that have the interest in and means to encourage human rights infringements. Such actions constitute a subtle way to control the opposition and few WDs coming from the latter possess the organizational capacity – due to disarmament, demobilization and reintegration (DDR) processes – to engage in systematic human rights abuses. The only exception was Machar (South Sudan). The abuses that took place under his leadership were, however, committed in the context of a horrendous civil war, where he had an armed rebel movement at his disposal. In this sense, Machar had, by late 2013, also attained the means to foster human rights abuses.

What, more specifically, prompted Kagame and Vieira to commit these acts of belligerency? Evidence suggests that electoral constraints was the most decisive factor. Due to Rwanda's ethnic composition – where Kagame's Tutsi community was in a clear minority – Kagame had little hope of staying in power without cracking down on the opposition or circumventing democratic principles. Thanks to RPF's resounding military victory and monopoly on violence, Kagame had the means to suppress oppositional elements. The ease with which Kagame fell back on this aggressive strategy can probably also be explained by the WD's authoritarian leadership style. When Vieira planned his electoral comeback in 2005, a major challenge was to mobilize the patronage needed to convince key actors to support his presidential bid. With few domestic resources to speak of, Vieira came up with the plan to establish Guinea-Bissau as a conduit for international drug smuggling. The promised rents generated from these activities sufficed to create a broad-based alliance in his support. The human rights abuses that Vieira engaged in once in power were a reaction to the need to fend off competitors seeking to capture part of the drugs trade and to retain his position as head of state.

Embracing peace The analysis above gives an indication of when we can expect that WDs are likely to act benevolently. This should primarily be the case under three circumstances: (1) when there are few electoral constraints (especially in the form of democratic infringements, limited electorates and weakening of patronage networks); (2) when WDs lack the capacity to misbehave; and (3) when the cost of belligerency is high. As we have seen, this was partly true for Dhlakama (Mozambique), Machar (South Sudan) and Mbusa (DRC). When the electoral constraints were low, the three WDs had little interest in aggression. Once constraints increased, they changed strategies; Mbusa – at least narratively – aligned himself with a number of armed groups, while Dhlakama and Machar first securitized wartime identities and later switched to supporting organized violence. The latter move was possible due the military units that they commanded, and the relative military weakness of their opponents.

Can the same set of factors also explain Collins' (Sierra Leone) choice not to engage in any form of aggression? To some extent it can. In the Sierra Leonean context there were limits to how belligerent a WD could be. As we have seen, there was a strong international commitment to uphold the peace. However, based on the experiences of Conneh and Johnson (Liberia), this should only have restrained Collins' willingness to engage in organized violence, not securitize wartime identities. In fact, just like Collins, Conneh and Johnson were constrained by determined peacemakers; with strong UN peacekeeping troops stationed in Liberia armed action was simply not a feasible alternative. In addition, all three WDs suffered from electoral constraints that hindered their political maneuverings. Despite this, it was only Conneh and Johnson that securitized wartime identities. How can these diverging outcomes best be understood? One interpretation is that there may be an inverted U-shaped correlation between electoral constraints – in the form of waning popular support and faltering patronage networks – and post-war belligerency. Initially such shortcomings may push WDs to act aggressively in order to gain concessions and pull back wavering followers. However, at some point support becomes so negligible and networks so minimal that threatening behavior either becomes non-credible or so infuriates public opinion that it becomes counterproductive. Perhaps this is what happened with Collins: by the time he ran for president, eleven years after the end of the war, he was such a marginal figure in Sierra Leone's networked society that any forms of verbal threats would have seemed hollow, to say the least. Even if Conneh and Johnson also experienced electoral constraints – many of the former's ex-fighters had aligned themselves with his ex-wife and the latter's network of followers had shrunk after having lived in exile for a long time – they were in a better position than Collins. Both could fashion themselves as liberators – Conneh for having evicted Taylor from power and Johnson for having executed Doe – and Johnson had a large ethnic electorate to fall back on (Gio and Manos). This was not an option for Collins; not only was it difficult for Collins to remind the electorate of any positive wartime accomplishments – on the contrary, RUF was widely despised for its large-scale abuses – Collins had no clear ethnic constituency that he represented.

Hence, it may be that WDs are most likely to stop playing on their wartime credentials, and begin to develop political visions that focus on the future, when they are severely tainted by wartime abuses and their patronage networks are all but gone.

Electoral politics and the schooling of autocrats To recall, a central finding of this volume is that electoral participation does not necessarily socialize WDs into becoming more benign democrats (see section entitled "Short-Term Benevolence, Long-Term Belligerency"). In fact, there are no examples of WDs becoming more conciliatory over time. On the contrary, those that were belligerent either employed such strategies throughout the time periods studied – such as Bio (Sierra Leone), Conneh (Liberia), Kagame (Rwanda) and Johnson (Liberia)[3] – or those who were initially benevolent became more aggressive over time – for instance Dhlakama (Mozambique), Mbusa (DRC), Machar (South Sudan), Norman (Sierra Leone) and Vieira (Guinea-Bissau). How can we understand these counterintuitive dynamics? There is limited evidence suggesting that it was the WDs' personality traits that compelled them to act more aggressively over time. It was only in the case of Dhlakama and Kagame that the chapter authors identified a connection between personal characteristics and belligerency. It is, however, questionable to what degree it was Dhlakama's insecure personality that explains why he securitized wartime identities and later launched a rebellion against the Mozambican authorities. Presumably this trait was also present during much of the 1990s, when Dhlakama was acting in a more conciliatory manner. It is true that the more permanent belligerency of Kagame probably can, at least partially, be explained by referring to his authoritarian personality. However, this factor cannot be isolated from the electoral constraints imposed on him by the small size of his Tutsi electorate. The dangers of reducing aggressive behavior to questions of personality have been eloquently expressed by Greenhill and Major (2006/2007: 36–37):

> Although leadership style and what might be thought of as "preference stickiness" can serve as lenses through which power is filtered, if custodians

of the peace shift the prevailing opportunity structures in their favor, in most cases parties to the process will alter their policies accordingly. ... Thus the key variable is not spoiler type. Instead, the distribution of relative power and the availability of sufficient carrots and sticks are the primary variables that determine whether a spoiler will undermine a peace process.

A more compelling argument for why the WDs did not become more benevolent over time is that the structures assigned to socialize them were semi-authoritarian, rather than democratic. In this sense, WDs learn that elections are not free and fair, and that democratization is molded in a manner that tends to reinforce the power of the incumbent. In this context power is acquired through threats, violence and abuse. What is more, while WDs are being socialized into a semi-authoritarian political system, it is not uncommon that their power base begins to fade away. As regimes regain strength, they have incentives to restrain the power and autonomy of WDs. This is what happened to both Dhlakama (Mozambique) and Mbusa (DRC) and, as we have seen, this process contributed to making both WDs more belligerent. From this perspective it can be argued that it is these two parallel pressures – authoritarian socialization and waning strength – that explain why some WDs become more aggressive over time.

The most important implication of these findings is that WDs should not be seen as reckless individuals that carelessly plunge their countries into the abyss. On the contrary, they appear to be highly rational actors who only engage in bullying behavior under very particular circumstances. In fact, many seem reluctant to challenge the new peaceful order, and before they escalate to violence they often begin by securitizing wartime identities. Acts of the latter can thus be seen as a type of early warning indicator of troubles to come.

The importance of brokerage To recall, the waning of WDs' patronage networks was a decisive factor in convincing ex-military turned politicians to engage in aggression. But how should we, more specifically, understand this behavior and what are the dynamics involved? Besides the WDs that were heads of state – Kagame (Rwanda) and Vieira (Guinea-Bissau) – few of the analyzed WDs possessed substantial resources of their own. In fact, what many of the WDs strived for was to attach themselves to the state in order to gain the patronage needed to safeguard their networks of clients. The goal was, in other words, to attain a position of brokerage, whereby they could funnel economic resources from the state to local communities. Systems of brokerage are not only about distributing patronage, however. Having actors who provide bridging functions is crucial in post-war societies permeated by distrust and fear, where old wartime networks are dissolved or reconfigured and new structures take shape. In such contexts WDs can use their wartime connections to bring disparate elites together and integrate their clients into the new post-war order being built. Several of the WDs analyzed in this volume played such a key role forging and changing political and military alliances (see Chapter 1, section "Two Wars and Two Intransitive Transitions").

Interestingly some of the WDs analyzed in this volume appear to have been willing to overlook democratic deficiencies, as long as their status as brokers was not threatened. For instance, it was when Dhlakama (Mozambique), Machar (South Sudan) and Mbusa (DRC) began to lose their broker positions – the Mozambican government ceased to make bilateral deals with Dhlakama, Machar was ousted from his position as vice-president and Mbusa was marginalized by President Kabila – that they securitized wartime identities or engaged in, or at least ambiguously supported, organized violence. It can be argued that by engaging in such forms of aggression, they hoped to force the regime to reconfirm their brokerage positions and, by extension, salvage their networks of clients. This strategy was particularly successful in the case of Dhlakama; not only did the latter compel President Guebuza to cut a new deal with him, RENAMO also increased its share of the vote in the first elections after the 2013–2014 fighting.

The literature on peacebuilding and post-civil war democratization has so far given scant attention to how such broker figures can have a profound impact on political, economic and military dynamics in war-ridden societies (see e.g. Gould 1998; Burt 2005). This is unfortunate; a number of studies have, for instance, shown the lengths that elites will go to in order to retain their broker positions. In fact, the prospect of losing their role as middleman has prompted individuals as disparate as ex-commanders in Liberia and local politicians in eighteenth century United States to take to arms (Gould 1998; Themnér 2015). Brokerage as a political phenomenon should therefore probably be seen as an example of what de Waal (2009) has termed the "African political marketplace", where governing elites engage in cyclical negotiations with oppositional elites for the cost of political reintegration. During such negotiations, oppositional WDs have incentives to signal their resolve and strength by threatening to employ violence (i.e. securitize wartime identities) or by doing so.

Dealing with warlord democrats

Based on the findings presented in this volume, what are some of the policy options available for local and international peacemakers confronted with WDs? Perhaps the most vital lesson is that ex-military turned politicians are not reckless, irrational actors bent on undermining peace. There is, in fact, little evidence suggesting that particular personality traits predetermine WDs to act belligerently. On the contrary, most WDs only engage in aggression under very particular circumstances. Hence, if the "optimal" conditions prevail – low electoral constraints (e.g. free and fair elections; WDs have a

240

large constituency and possess stable patronage networks), WDs have limited capacity to misbehave (e.g. their armed units have been formally demobilized) and there are high costs attached to misbehaving (e.g. strong security forces and international commitment to support the peace process) – then WDs are more likely to behave as peacelords.

Considering that semi-democratic contexts socialize WDs into belligerency, a central objective for peacemakers should be to truly and sincerely invest in the democratization of post-civil war societies. Put differently, it is time to re-evaluate contemporary strategies to condone democratic deficiencies in the name of stability. By dismantling the authoritarian structures, norms and behaviors that restrict most oppositional actors in contemporary Sub-Saharan Africa, WDs should be less inclined to undermine contemporary peace processes. What is more, if political systems become more democratic, it is not impossible that WDs are actually socialized into becoming "democrats'" rather than "autocrats".

A central theme in this volume has been to trace and highlight the political agency of WDs operating in a context of weak state institutions and political parties. Even if most of the book's WDs – with the possible exception of Collins (Sierra Leone) and Conneh (Liberia) – possessed the power and resources to shape political outcomes in their respective countries, there were differences in how constrained they were by contextual factors that peacemakers – given sufficient resources, political will and openings – can affect. Based on the chapter authors' findings it is possible to identify three such factors. First, efforts to develop efficient and independent electoral commissions can be fruitful. In Sierra Leone, for instance, the country's electoral commission established a number of checks and balances on the statements and activities of political actors like Bio. Second, greater attention needs to be given to monitoring intra-party politics and finding ways to strengthen intra-party democracy. The devastating effect that intra-party feuds, involving WDs, can have becomes evident when tracing the post-war navigations of both Bio and Machar (South Sudan). Finally, emphasis should be given to identifying strategies that curtail the military capacity of WDs. This can, for instance, be done by investing in DDR and security sector reform (SSR), whereby ties binding WDs to their commanders and fighters, and units within the armed forces, are at least weakened. Experiences have shown that there will always be some interactions between WDs and their wartime followers (Themnér 2012), but there is a qualitative difference if the latter are organized in formal armed units rather than connected by informal bonds. In this sense, it was probably no coincidence that it was Dhlakama (Mozambique) and Machar who engaged in open, organized violence, rather than Johnson (Liberia) or Mbusa (DRC). In this process, it is also vital to support the (re)construction of efficient and professional security forces, with democratic oversight. This should not only increase the cost of misbehaving, but also minimize the risk that WDs and their followers are victimized by security forces.

Addressing WDs' electoral deficiencies is more problematic. In the long term it may be desirable that WDs' constituencies diminish and the latter's patronage networks dissolve. Just as for Collins (Sierra Leone), such a process may marginalize WDs to a point where they no longer pose a threat to the new post-war order. The problem is, however, whether peacemakers and local communities are willing to pay the short-term consequences of such a policy. As we have seen, WDs often become more aggressive when their post-war power begins to wane. If relevant stakeholders perceive such developments as daunting, then it is vital to grant WDs the political and economic space needed to retain their Big Man status and efficiently compete in electoral politics. If this cannot be done through more traditional democratic means – for instance, salaries and generous per diems for elected officials and economic support for political parties represented in the legislature – it may be necessary to develop alternatives.

One such alternative is to employ WDs as brokers of peace. In return for keeping their constituencies calm, WDs can be given high-profile positions that provide them with access to economic resources, security and political influence. Such commitments can be more or less formalized. At one extreme, WDs are given unofficial positions, whereby they de facto function as government agents. In return for upholding security and mobilizing their followers on behalf of the regime, WDs can be given considerable autonomy in organizing economic and political affairs in their traditional fiefdoms. Such arrangements may also entail provision of state patronage in order to shore up support from key clients. Of the WDs analyzed in this volume, Mbusa (DRC), and his relationship with President Kabila, comes closest to personifying this type of broker. Kabila's dealings with Mbusa are, however, not unique in an African context. On the contrary, informal power-sharing agreements have a long tradition on the continent and some scholars argue that such arrangements are more efficient at upholding peace than the institutionalized versions (the latter are often supported by the international community) (Spears 2013). The benefit of informal broker arrangements is that peacemakers and national governments do not openly have to associate themselves with controversial WDs. In addition, by not institutionalizing such provisions it also becomes easier to amend or remove them when they have outlived their usefulness. However, due to the non-transparent manner in which such deals are struck and implemented, it is difficult for citizens to hold regimes, and their broker allies, accountable for any negative repercussions that may follow. In addition, the flows of patronage associated with similar systems of governance risk increasing levels of corruption at a time when most local and international peacemakers are presumably working to decrease such vices.

At the other end of the spectrum, one finds formalized arrangements where WDs are awarded official state positions. The latter may range from receiving seats in the cabinet or becoming presidential advisers, to being appointed as mayors, representatives of various state committees or national companies. The benefit of such arrangements is that it increases the prospect of holding WDs and their employers accountable for any transgressions. This is exactly what happened in Liberia after the end of the civil war. The National Transitional Government of Liberia (NTGL) (2003-2006) has often been condemned for its inefficiency and corrupt practices. However, as we have seen (Chapter 3) an alternative interpretation of this institution is that its shortcomings actually paved the way for long-term stability and democracy. Those WDs that took part in the NTGL – and engaged in what can only be described as large-scale corruption – were so tainted by their actions that they lost all public credibility. When some later attempted to run for office, they were decisively defeated.[4] Today the likes of Thomas Nimely, ex-leader of Movement for Democracy in Liberia (MODEL), are marginal figures in Liberia and pose no direct threat to peace and stability. Of course, by officially cooperating with WDs, peacemakers risk undermining other social goods, such as post-war reconciliation and justice. What is more, it may be difficult for Western governments to explain to their voters and taxpayers why they are embracing, rather than punishing WDs.

In the end, there are no optimal solutions concerning how to deal with the problem of WDs' electoral constraints. Which strategy to employ depends on the particular context in which the WDs are operating. For instance, what are the power relations between the WDs, other political actors and peacemakers; do international peacemakers have strong, national interests in the WDs' country; are there any public costs for the international peacemakers in cooperating with the WDs; and what is the relationship between the WDs and their local communities? Whatever path local and international peacemakers take, there are repercussions and dilemmas to tackle. It is therefore crucial for the peacemakers to be aware of these and develop contingency plans for how to address the negative consequences of either befriending or shunning WDs.

What can be done when peacemakers are confronted with WDs that have captured the reins of government? The discussion above has largely centered on how to minimize the damage caused by oppositional WDs or WDs allied to the state. However, dealing with Kagame (Rwanda) and Vieira (Guinea-Bissau), is very different from dealing with the likes of Dhlakama (Mozambique), Mbusa (DRC) and Collins (Sierra Leone). Unfortunately, this volume did not include any heads of state who refrained from acts of aggression – to recall, both Kagame and Vieira fostered human rights abuses, while the latter also criminalized politics – making it difficult to draw any conclusions based on a comparison between cases with contrasting outcomes. However, what can be said is that in the case of both Kagame and Vieira, the international community employed a strategy based on appeasement. Donors were, for instance, satisfied with the minimalistic version of democracy that Vieira crafted before and after his 1994 electoral victory. Meanwhile, despite considerable human rights abuses and a questionable democratic record it took years before Western powers began to criticize Kagame. Considering most WDs' preference for adapting to, rather than resisting, external shifts in power, it is plausible that Kagame and Vieira would have been more benevolent had foreign powers put more pressure on them. This is, however, speculation and a more definite answer can only be attained through further research.

Notes

1 The term peacelord would then only be applicable to the time periods when they acted benevolently.

2 Here it is important to remind the reader that the time periods analyzed for Bio and Conneh are rather limited.

3 Here it is important to remind the reader that the time periods analyzed for Bio and Conneh are rather limited.

4 Members of NTGL were only prohibited from taking part in the first post-civil war election in 2005.

Bibliography

Bledsoe, C. 1990. "No Success Without Struggle: Social Mobility and Hardship for Foster Children in Sierra Leone." *Man* 25: 70-88.

Bratton, M. and N. van de Walle. 1997. *Democratic Experiments in Africa-Regime Transitions in Comparative Perspective.* Cambridge: Cambridge University Press.

Burt, R. S. 2005. *Brokerage and Closure: An Introduction to Social Capital.* Oxford: Oxford University Press.

Chowdhury, A. and R. R. Krebs 2009. "Making and Mobilizing Moderates: Rhetorical Strategy, Political Networks, and Counterterrorism." *Security Studies* 18 (3): 371-399.

De Waal, A. 2009. "Mission Without and End? Peacekeeping in the African Political Marketplace." *International Affairs* 85 (1): 99-113.

Ghani, A. and C. Lockhart. 2008. *Fixing Failed States: A Framework for Rebuilding a Fractured World.* Oxford: Oxford University Press.

Gormley-Heenan, C. 2006. "Chameleonic Leadership: Towards a New Understanding of the Northern Ireland Peace Process." *Leadership* 2 (1): 53-75.

Gould, R. V. 1998. "Political Networks and the Local/National Boundary in the Whiskey Rebellion." In *Challenging Authority: The Historical Study of Contentious Politics,* ed. M. P. Hanagan, L. P. Moch and W. te Brake. Minneapolis: University of Minnesota Press.

Greenhill, K. M. and S. Major. 2006/2007. "The Perils of Profiling: Civil War Spoilers and the Collapse of Intrastate Peace Accords." *International Security* 31 (3): 7-40.

Höglund, K. 2008. "Violence in War-to-Democracy Transitions." In *From War to Democracy: Dilemmas of Peacebuilding,* ed. A. K. Jarstad and T. D. Sisk. Cambridge: Cambridge University Press.

Jarstad, A. K. and T. D. Sisk, eds. 2008. *From War to Democracy: Dilemmas to Peacebuilding.* Cambridge: Cambridge University Press.

Kaufman, S. J. 2006. "Escaping the Symbolic Political Traps: Reconciliation Initiatives and Conflict Resolution in Ethnic Wars." *Journal of Peace Research* 43 (2): 201-218.

Manning, C. 2004. "Armed Opposition Groups into Political Parties: Comparing Bosnia, Kosovo, and Mozambique." *Studies in Comparative International Development* 39 (1): 54-76.

Spears, I. A. 2013. "Africa's Informal Power-Sharing and the Prospects for Peace." *Civil Wars* 15 (1): 37-53.

Stedman, S. J. 1997. "Spoiler Problems in Peace Processes." *International Security* 22 (2): 5-53.

Themnér, A. 2012. "Former Mid-Level Commanders in Big Man Networks." In *African Conflicts and Informal Power: Big Men and Networks*, ed. M. Utas. London: Zed Books.

Themnér, A. 2015. "Former Military Networks and the Micro-Politics of Violence and Statebuilding in Liberia." *Journal of Comparative Politics* 47 (3): 334-353.

About the contributors

Ibrahim Bangura works as a consultant in Freetown and lectures at the Department of Peace and Conflict Studies, University of Sierra Leone.

Johan Brosché is an assistant professor in the Department of Peace and Conflict Research, Uppsala University.

Kristine Höglund is professor in the Department of Peace and Conflict Research, Uppsala University.

Mimmi Söderberg Kovacs is head of research at the Folke Bernadotte Academy, a Swedish government agency working in the field of peace and security, and an associate researcher with the Department of Peace and Conflict Research at Uppsala University and the Nordic Africa Institute.

Carrie Manning is professor and chair of the Department of Political Science at Georgia State University in Atlanta, Georgia.

Judith Verweijen is a postdoctoral research fellow at the Conflict Research Group at Ghent University.

Henrik Vigh is professor in the Department of Anthropology, University of Copenhagen.

Alex Vines is director of area studies and international law and head of the Africa Programme at Chatham House, London. He is also a senior lecturer at Coventry University.

Lars Waldorf is senior lecturer in the Centre for Applied Human Rights, University of York.

Index

Abuja Agreement (2000), 99
Adebajo, Adekeye, 100
Adriano, Faustino, 127
Afghanistan, 16
African Party for the Independence of
    Guinea and Cape Verde (PAIGC), 157,
    160, 161, 162, 163, 164, 165, 223
Ajello, Aldo, 126
Akol, Lam, 205, 209
All-Liberia Coalition Party (ALCOP),
    100, 109
All People's Congress (APC) (Sierra
    Leone), 14, 179, 181, 182, 185, 186, 187,
    190, 193, 194, 227
Alliance for the Presidential Majority
    (AMP) (Congo), 53, 54, 56
Alliance for the Renewal of the Congo
    (ARC), 53
Alliance of Democratic Forces for the
    Liberation of Congo-Zaire (AFDL),
    44, 48
Allied Democratic Forces (ADF)
    (Uganda), 51, 54, 55, 59, 61, 228
Anders, Gerhard, 13
Appadurai, Arjun, 172
Armed Forces for the Defense of
    Mozambique (FADM), 126, 127, 129,
    138, 139, 140, 150
Armed Forces of Liberia (AFL), 98
Armed Forces of the Democratic Republic
    of the Congo (FARDC), 52, 54, 55, 58,
    59
Armed Forces Revolutionary Council
    (AFRC) (Sierra Leone), 180, 183, 189
Arms for Tools program (Mozambique),
    128
Arusha Accords (1992), 71, 75, 76, 79, 80,
    81
Athor, George, 206

Balanta community (Guinea-Bissau), 164,
    165, 168, 169, 171

Bangilima militia, 48
Bangura, Alimamy Pallo, 190
Banyarwanda community, 48, 49; see
    also Hutu community and Tutsi
    community
Barbosa, Rafael, 162
Belgium, 69, 70
Bemba, Jean-Pierre, 2, 51
Benjamin, John, 187
Berewa, Solomon, 186
Big Men, 2, 3, 11, 12, 15, 19
Bio, Julius Maada, 2, 232, 236, 241;
    belligerency of, 230, 238; electoral
    performance of (in 2007, 186; in 2011,
    187); links to organized violence, 178,
    187, 188, 192, 194, 228, 231, 235; military
    career of, 180, 185; political career of,
    178, 181, 186, 193–4, 224, 226
Bissopo, Manuel, 137, 138, 143, 148
Bizimungu, Pasteur, 73, 77, 83
Boakai, Joseph, 115
Bøås, Morten, 98, 121, 122
Boley, George, 99, 100, 101, 105
Bomba, Adriano, 123
Booth, David, 80
Bor Massacre (1992) (Sudan), 213
Bosnia-Herzegovina, 22
Botha, Pieter, 125
brokerage, 42, 51
Brown, Michael, 4, 21
Brumskine, Charles, 115
Bryant, Gyude, 102, 111
burecation strategy, 57
Buscardini, António, 162

Cabral, Amilcar, 160
Cabral, Luís, 162, 163
Cahen, Michel, 136
Cambodia, 6
Cape Verde, 161
Cape Verdean community (Guinea-
    Bissau), 163, 164, 165

Catholic Church, 50, 51
Central African Republic (CAR), 74
Chabal, Patrick, 15
China, 160
Chissano, Joaquim, 121, 125, 131, 134, 136, 145
Chowdhury, Arjun, 231
Christina, Orlando, 123
Civil Defense Force (CDF) (Sierra Leone), 183, 184
Clapham, Christopher, 121, 122
Clark, Phil, 77, 78
clientelism, 10
Coalition for the Transformation of Liberia (COTOL), 104
Cobra warlords (Congo), 20
Collins, Eldred, 178, 180, 181, 182, 188–191 passim, 193, 223–7 passim, 236, 237, 238, 241, 242, 243; electoral performance (2012), 191, 193
Community of Portuguese Language Countries (CLCP), 169
Comprehensive Peace Agreement (CPA) (Liberia), 102, 106
Comprehensive Peace Agreement (CPA) (South Sudan), 204, 205, 215
Congo, Democratic Republic of (DRC), 42, 43, 46, 47, 74; 2002 peace accord in, 41; 2014–15 massacres, 59, 62; elections in (in 2002, 21; in 2006, 46, 53; in 2011, 46); electoral politics in, 46; ethnic identities in, 46; First Congo War, 44, 72; Global and All-Inclusive Accord, 60; militarization of, 46, 48, 61, 62; military integration in, 45, 46; patronage networks in, 57; political fragmentation in, 46, 47; Second Congo War, 42, 44, 45, 51, 72; transition to democracy in, 43
Congo, Republic of, 20
Congolese Popular Army (APC), 49
Congolese Rally for Democracy (RCD), 44–9 passim
Congolese Rally for Democracy/Kisangani–Liberation Movement (RCD/K-ML), 42, 44, 46, 47, 49–60 passim, 62, 224
Congolese Rally for Democracy–Liberation Movement (RCD-ML), 47
Congolese Rally for Democracy–National (RCD-N), 44, 51

Congress for Democratic Change (CDC) (Liberia), 104, 114
Conneh, Aisha, 104, 105, 106, 108, 109
Conneh, Sekou, 95, 101, 105, 223, 227, 232, 234, 236, 241; approach to reconciliation, 107; belligerency of, 230, 238; electoral performance of, 96, 104, 115, 224, 225; electoral strategy of, 14, 96, 97, 109, 115; electoral constraints on, 237; links to organized violence, 235; political career of, 106, 107; use of ethnic identities, 96, 108, 109; use of securitized identities by, 228, 231, 233
Conté, Lansana, 101, 105, 106
Correia, Carlos, 165
Cotonou Accord, 98, 99
Coventry, Dudley, 123
Crane, David, 184
Crystal Ventures Ltd. (Rwanda), 73
Cuba, 160
Cyiza, Augustin, 83

Dallaire, Roméo, 72
Daloz, Jean-Pascal, 15, 19
Darfur (Sudan), 74
De Waal, Alex, 227, 240
De Zeeuw, Jeroen, 69, 87
demobilization, 17
democracy, 6, 8
Democratic Green Party (Rwanda), 83
Democratic Movement of Mozambique (MDM), 141, 143, 144, 151
Democratic Republic of the Congo (DRC) see Congo, Democratic Republic of (DRC)
Democratic Republican Movement (MDR) (Rwanda), 80, 81, 83
democratization, 3, 6, 8, 15, 173, 230, 240
Deng, Taban, 199, 209
Devine, Richard, 104
Dhlakama, Afonso, 2, 121, 133–42 passim, 146, 149, 224, 225, 229, 236, 239, 243; and regional autonomy, 144, 145, 148; as broker, 240; electoral performance of (in 1999, 226; in 2014, 122, 142); leadership style of, 122, 136, 150, 151, 230; military career of, 123, 125, 126; personality traits of, 143, 233, 238; use of organized violence by, 152, 138, 227, 228, 234, 235, 241; use of securitized identities by, 232, 237

Dinka community (South Sudan), 199, 206, 209, 210, 211, 213, 215, 228
Diola community (Guinea-Bissau), 167
disarmament, 17
Disarmament, demobilization and reintegration (DDR), 76, 107, 129, 236 241
Doe, Cheyee, 106, 111
Doe, Samuel, 97, 98, 109
Dolo, Adolphus, 95, 104
Domingos, Raúl, 136, 137, 143, 145, 151
Donso militia (Sierra Leone), 182
Dos Santos, José Eduardo, 88
Dunn, Kevin, 121, 122

East Timor *see* Timor-Leste
Economic Community of West African States (ECOWAS), 98, 169
ECOWAS military monitoring group (ECOMOG), 98, 110, 180, 183
El Salvador, 6, 13, 23
elections, 6, 7, 225
electoral politics, 5, 9, 24, 194, 203, 222
elites, 2, 3, 7, 10, 227
Emerson, Stephen, 124
Equatorian community (South Sudan), 212
Eritrea, 75, 208
Ethiopia, 75

Farabundo Martí Front for National Liberation (FMLN) (El Salvador), 14
Farley, Kia, 104
Federalist Christian Democracy party (DCF) (Congo), 48
Federalist Christian Democracy party – Nyamwisi faction (DCF/Nyamwisi) (Congo), 48, 53, 56
Felupe community (Guinea-Bissau), 167
Forces du Renouveau (Congo), 53
Forum of Political Parties (Rwanda), 80, 81, 82
France, 168

Gadet, Peter, 207, 216
Gahima, Gerald, 77, 84
Gandhi, Jennifer, 82
Garang, John, 205, 209
Gbagbo, Laurent, 101, 103
géopolitique, 43, 48
Germany, 69, 74

Gettleman, Jeffrey, 74
Gio community (Liberia), 98, 111, 112, 114
Gizenga, Antoine, 54
Golooba-Mutebi, Frederick, 80
Greenhill, Kelly, 238
Guebuza, Armando, 137, 138, 140, 143, 151, 152, 225, 232
Guinea-Bissau, 156–62 *passim*, 167, 169, 170, 173; 1998 coup d'état in, 167, 168; cocaine trade in, 156, 157, 171, 172; constitution of, 165; criminalization of politics in, 157, 173, 174; democratization of, 166, 174; elections (in 1994, 165; in 2005, 170); human rights violations in, 157, 166, 173; Junta Militar, 168, 169
Guinea-Bissauan Armed Forces (FAG), 158, 162
Guinea-Conakry, 101, 168, 170

Habineza, Frank, 83
Habyarimana, Juvénal, 70, 78; killing of, 71
Hatløy, Anne, 98
Hitimana, Leonard, 83
Höglund, Kristine, 235
Horizon Group (Rwanda), 73
human rights abuses, 23, 26
Hutu community, 48, 69–72 *passim*, 76, 81; 1959 "social revolution", 70

identities: ethnic, 21; securitization of, 21, 22, 26, 202
Independent National Patriotic Front of Liberia (INPFL), 96, 98, 110, 224
Indonesia, 16
Ingabire, Charles, 84
Ingabire, Victoire, 86
institutions, 7, 8, 9, 15, 26
Intergovernmental Authority on Development (IGAD), 208
Interim Government of National Unity (IGNU) (Liberia), 98
International Criminal Court (ICC), 102
International Observer Military Team for the Cessation of Military Hostilities (EMOCHM) (Mozambique), 129
Ivory Coast, 101, 103

Jackson, Robert, 15
Jallabah, Malliam, 104

Janneh, Kabineh, 106
Jarstad, Anna, 88
Jervis, Robert, 27
Johnson, Douglas, 209
Johnson, Prince, 95, 104, 116, 224, 232, 236, 241; and Truth and Reconciliation Commission, 97, 112, 113, 115, 228, 234; belligerency of, 230, 238; electoral performance of, 96, 115 (in 2005, 112, 225; in 2011, 105, 114, 225; in 2013, 115); electoral strategy, 14, 15, 112, 113, 226; links to organized violence, 235; military career, 98, 109, 110; religious work of, 111; use of ethnic identities by, 96; use of securitized identities by, 96, 231, 233, 237
Johnson, Roosevelt, 99, 101
Johnson-Sirleaf, Ellen, 15, 100, 101, 104, 114
Jok, Jok Madut, 209
Justice and Equality Movement (JEM) (Sudan), 208

Kabbah, Ahmad Tejan, 178, 180, 182, 183, 184, 186, 192
Kabbah, Isatu, 187
Kabila, Joseph, 45, 47, 53, 54, 56, 57, 224, 227, 242
Kabila, Laurent, 44, 72
Kagame, Paul, 68, 69, 239, 244; and human rights abuses, 231, 236; as president, 73; beating of staff, 74; belligerency of, 230, 238; developmental agenda of, 73, 87; electoral participation of, 85, 87, 88; leadership style of, 77, 79; links to human rights abuses, 84, 87, 229, 243; military career of, 70, 71, 72, 75; personality traits of, 238; political career of, 73, 76, 78, 83, 223, 226; role in peace process, 84, 85, 87, 74; use of ethnic identities by, 85, 86
Kaine, Roland, 104
Kakule Sikuli, Lafontaine, 55
Kamajor militia (Sierra Leone), 177, 180, 182–5 passim, 192
Kamara, Idrissa, 13
Kamara, Losone, 106
Kamitatu, Olivier, 53
Kanyarengwe, Alexis, 72
Karake, Emmanuel Karenzi, 77

Karegeya, Patrick, 68, 77, 84
Karugarama, Tharcisse, 77, 78
Kasindien militia (Congo), 48
Kayibanda, Grégoire, 70
Kazini, James, 49
Kiir, Salva, 199, 200, 205–11 passim, 213, 214, 216, 217, 223, 233
Kombi, Hilaire, 58, 59
Koroma, Ernest Bai, 182, 186, 188,
Koroma, Johnny Paul, 181; and 1997 coup d'état, 180
Kosovo, 16
Kosovo Liberation Army (KLA), 22
Krahn community (Liberia), 97–9 passim, 101, 111, 114
Krebs, Ronald, 231
Kromah, Alhaji, 98–101 passim, 104, 109

Liberal and Patriotic Center (CLP) (Congo), 55, 56
Liberal Party (Rwanda), 79, 81
Liberia, 22, 97; civil wars in, 95, 97, 99, 100, 101; elections in (in 1985, 97; in 1997, 95, 99, 116; in 2005, 14, 97, 103, 109, 112, 116; in 2011, 14, 105, 113, 114; in 2014, 15, 105; in 2017, 15); warlord democrats in, 95, 96, 115
Liberia Action Party (LAP), 102, 111
Liberia People's Party (LPP), 100
Liberia Unification Party (LUP), 100
Liberian Peace Council (LPC), 99
Liberians United for Reconciliation and Democracy (LURD), 14, 23, 24, 96, 101, 102, 103, 106, 107, 223
Limba community (Sierra Leone), 193
Lofa Defense Force (LDF), 99
Loma community (Liberia), 22
Lomé Peace Agreement (1999), 180, 189
Lyons, Terrence, 22

Machar, Riek, 199, 200, 207–17 passim, 225–30 passim, 235, 238; and Bor Massacre, 213; and human rights abuses, 229, 236; as broker, 240; as vice-president, 205, 210, 223; use of securitized identities by, 211, 212, 233; use of spirituality by, 212; use of violence by, 218, 234, 237, 241
Machel, Samora, 125
Macuiane, Saimon, 143
Magalhaes, Viana, 137

Mai-Mai militias (Congo), 44, 45, 50, 51, 54, 55, 61
Major, Solomon, 238
Mali, 74
Mandela, Nelson, 18
Mandingo community (Liberia), 22, 97, 98, 99, 101, 107, 109, 111
Mané, Asumané, 163, 166–9 passim
Manning, Carrie, 133, 222
Mano community (Liberia), 98, 111, 112, 114
Margai, Charles, 186
Massaley, Abel, 104, 113, 114
Massoqui, Francois, 99
Matsangaissa, André, 123, 138
Mazimpaka, Patrick, 73
Mbusa Nyamwisi, Antipas, 42, 43, 47–63 passim, 224, 227, 229, 230, 232, 238, 239, 241, 243; as broker, 51, 52, 60, 240, 242; links to organized violence, 58, 59, 61, 228, 231, 235, 237; political marginalization of, 54, 56, 60, 61; political strategy of, 42, 51, 52, 60; presidential campaigns of, 53, 56
Mendés, Francisco, 162, 163
Mhlanga, Lucas, 123
Milaco, Armindo, 138
militarization, 43
Mobutu, Sese Seko, 43, 44, 48, 72
Momade, Ossufo, 137
Movement for Democracy in Liberia (MODEL), 101, 102, 103, 243
Movement for Democratic Change (MDC) (Zimbabwe), 133
Movement for the Liberation of the Congo (MLC), 44, 45, 51
Movement of 23 March (M23) (Congo), 58, 74, 228
Movement of Democratic Forces of Casamance (MDFC) (Senegal), 156, 167, 168
Mozambican Demobilized Soldiers Association (AMODEG), 128
Mozambican National Resistance (RENAMO), 121–51 passim, 224, 225, 232; and disarmament process, 128, 129, 130, 148, 152; electoral performance of (in 1994, 131, 133; in 1999, 133, 136; in 2003, 134; in 2008, 135; in 2009, 132; in 2014, 142, 149, 151, 152); human rights abuses by, 124, 125; reintegration of soldiers, 127, 128, 148, 150, 152

Mozambique, 6, 121, 123, 140, 227; 2015 conflict in, 145, 146, 147; civil war in, 124, 125; demobilization of soldiers in, 126, 127, 128, 151; disarmament in, 128, 129, 130, 151; elections (in 1994, 127, 130, 131, 133; in 1999, 133; in 2004, 133; in 2008, 133; in 2009, 132, 142; in 2013, 141; in 2014, 133, 141, 142); electoral system in, 141, 144; General Peace Accords, 126, 130; regional autonomy in, 144, 145, 148
Mozambique Liberation Front (FRELIMO), 122, 124, 125, 126, 128, 131, 132, 135, 136, 141–5 passim, 149, 151, 152
Mozambique National Resistance (MNR) see Mozambican National Resistance (RENAMO)
Muhire, Charles, 77
Muhola militia (Congo), 51
Munyarubaga, Gratien, 83
Murle community (South Sudan), 206, 212
Murrial, Agostinho, 134
Museveni, Yoweri, 47, 48, 49, 70, 71, 75
Musonera, Jonathan, 84
Muvingi, Enoch, 48, 49, 61, 62
Muzito, Adolphe, 56

Namburete, Eduardo, 143
Namibia, 6
Nande community (Congo), 47–50 passim, 53–60 passim
National Army for the Liberation of Uganda (NALU), 48, 51
National Congress for the Defense of the People (CNDP) (Congo), 46, 55, 58
National Democratic Party of Liberia (NDPL), 100
National Election Commission (Rwanda), 80
National Patriotic Front of Liberia (NPFL), 97–8, 99, 100, 110
National Patriotic Party (NPP) (Liberia), 95, 100, 102, 103
National Provisional Ruling Council (NPRC) (Sierra Leone), 178, 179, 185
National Resistance Army (NRA) (Uganda), 11, 70–1, 76, 79
National Transitional Government of Liberia (NTGL), 102, 103, 104, 107, 243

National Union for Democratic Progress (NUDP), 113, 114, 225
National Union for the Total Independence of Angola (UNITA), 121, 122
National Unity and Reconciliation Commission (Rwanda), 85
Netherlands, 74
Nigeria, 16, 98
Nimba County (Liberia), 98
Nimely, Thomas, 105, 243
Nkomati Accord (1984), 125
Nkubito, Alphonse Marie, 77
Nkurunziza, Pierre, 2
Norman, Samuel Hinga, 177, 180–4 passim, 192, 224, 226–32 passim, 238; arrest of for war crimes, 183, 184, 192, 224, 229, 234; as peacelord, 230; links to organized violence, 178, 192, 231, 235; use of securitized identities by, 178, 185, 192, 194
Ntaganda, Bernard, 86
Ntwali, Frank, 84
Nuer community (South Sudan), 199, 207–17 passim
Nyamwasa, Faustin Kayumba, 77, 78, 83, 84
Nyamwisi, Edouard, 58
Nyenabo, Isaac, 95, 104
Nyusi, Filipe, 144, 148, 149, 151

Oliveira, Paulo, 123
Operation Rachel (Mozambique), 128
outbidding, 22, 41, 46, 61, 202, 203, 211

Paluku Kahongya, Julien, 54, 57, 59, 62
Papel community (Guinea-Bissau), 163
parties, political, 3, 7, 8, 9, 10, 11, 15, 46
Party for Peace, Democracy and Development (PDD) (Mozambique), 137
patronage networks, 16, 24
peacebuilding, 3, 6, 15, 17, 240
peacelords, 17, 18, 222, 227, 229, 230
Pennue, Zoe, 104
People's Liberation Party (PLP) (Sierra Leone), 181
People's Movement for Democratic Change (PMDC) (Sierra Leone), 178, 185, 186, 224, 227
People's Movement for the Liberation of Angola (MPLA), 11

Perreira, Manuel, 134
Polisi, Denis, 73
politics: criminalization of, 22, 23, 26; party politics, 241; personalization of, 46
pompier-pyromane strategy, 43, 60, 62, 63, 232
Portugal, 159, 160, 161
Progressive Democratic Party (PRODEM) (Liberia), 14, 96, 104, 107, 109, 224, 225
Prunier, Gérard, 75, 81
Przeworski, Adam, 82

Quitine, Ossufo, 136
Quiwonkpa, Thomas, 109

Revolutionary Armed Forces of the People (FARP) (Guinea-Bissau), 160, 161
Revolutionary United Front (RUF) (Sierra Leone), 14, 101, 122, 178, 179, 188, 189, 191, 223
Revolutionary United Front Party (RUFP) (Sierra Leone), 14, 178, 181, 189, 190, 191, 224, 225
Rhodesia, 123
Rosberg, Carl, 15
Ross, Michael, 144
Rudasingwa, Theoneste, 73, 77, 84
Rwanda, 44, 47, 58, 69, 71, 72, 88; 1992 peace agreement in, 71; 1994 genocide in, 72; constitution of, 78, 80, 86; economic growth in, 87; elections (in 2003, 73, 79, 80, 82; in 2008, 79); electoral politics in, 82; ethnic identities in, 86; ethnic violence in, 70; Government of National Unity, 72, 75, 79, 80, 81; human rights abuses in, 83; reconciliation in, 85
Rwanda Inc., 73
Rwandan Defense Forces, 76
Rwandan National Congress, 84
Rwandan Patriotic Front (RPF), 11, 69, 71–9 passim, 81, 82, 83, 85, 87, 223
Rwigyema, Fred, 70, 71
Rwisereka, André Kagwa, 83

Saleh, Salim, 49, 58
Salomão, Tomás, 136
Sanha, Malam Bacai, 170
Sankoh, Foday, 122, 188, 189

Savimbi, Jonas, 122
Sawyer, Amos, 98, 103, 110, 112
Sebarenzi, Joseph, 79
Sendashonga, Seth, 77
Senegal, 156, 168
Sengulane, Dinis, 129
Sesay, Issa, 14, 190
Sezibera, Richard, 77
Shilluk community (South Sudan), 212
Sierra Leone, 14, 192, 193, 195, 241; 1992
    coup d'état in, 185; civil war in, 177, 179;
    elections (in 1996, 180, 186; in 2002,
    14, 178, 179, 181, 183, 190; in 2007, 178,
    181, 185, 203; in 2012, 177, 178, 181, 182,
    186, 187, 188, 191); warlord democrats
    in, 193, 194
Sierra Leone People's Party (SLPP), 14,
    178, 181–3 passim, 186, 187, 193, 194, 224
Simango, Daviz, 135
Simpser, Alberto, 83
Soares, Ivone, 143, 144
Social Democratic Party (Rwanda), 81
South Africa, 84, 123, 124, 125
South Sudan, 74, 199, 205, 210; 2011
    hostilities in, 206, 207; 2013 crisis in,
    207, 214; civil war in, 227; elections
    in, 205, 206, 209, 218; ethnic mix of,
    211; human rights abuses in, 200;
    militarization of, 200; patronage in, 215;
    relations with Sudan, 208; securitization
    of identities in, 200; social networks in,
    216, 217; use of amnesties in, 216, 218;
    violence in, 215, 216
South Sudan Democratic Movement/
    Army (SSDM/A), 206
South Sudan Liberation Movement/Army
    (SSLM/A), 206, 207
Special Court for Sierra Leone (SCSL),
    178, 181, 183
spoilers, 27, 116
statebuilding, 7, 10, 173
Stedman, Stephen, 27
Strasser, Valentine, 185
Sudan, 208
Sudan People's Liberation Movement/
    Army (SPLM/A), 199, 200, 205, 206,
    207, 209, 217, 218, 223
Sudan People's Liberation Movement/
    Army – In Opposition (SPLM/A-IO),
    199, 200, 206, 207, 208, 212, 213, 214,
    216, 217

Sudan People's Liberation Movement/
    Army – Nasir faction (SPLM/A-Nasir),
    209
Sudan People's Liberation Movement –
    Democratic Change (SPLM-DC), 205
Sweden, 74

Tagme Na Waie, Batista, 158, 170
Tamaboro militia (Sierra Leone), 182
Taylor, Charles, 2, 23, 24, 95, 97, 98, 100–3
    passim, 105, 109, 110, 116
Temne community (Sierra Leone), 193
Thaçi, Hashim, 22
Timor-Leste, 16
Tolbert, William, 97
trade, illicit, 22, 23, 25
Tri-Star Investments (Rwanda), 73
True Whig Party (Liberia), 100
Truth and Reconciliation Commission
    (TRC) (Liberia), 97, 102, 105, 113–16
    passim, 228
Truth and Reconciliation Commission
    (TRC) (Sierra Leone), 188
Truth and Reconciliation Commission
    (TRC) (South Africa), 123
Tshisekedi, Étienne, 56
Tubman, Winston, 114
Tutsi community, 48, 69, 70, 71, 72, 75,
    76, 81
Twagiramungu, Faustin, 86

Uganda, 44, 47, 48, 51, 58, 75, 208
United Bloc for the Renaissance and
    Emergence of the Congo (BUREC), 57
United Kingdom (UK), 74, 82
United Liberation Movement for
    Democracy (ULIMO), 98, 99
United Liberation Movement for
    Democracy – Johnson faction
    (ULIMO-J), 23, 99, 101
United Liberation Movement for
    Democracy – Kromah faction
    (ULIMO-K), 99, 100, 101
United Nations (UN) Group of Experts,
    74
UN Security Council, 101
UN Mission in Liberia (UNMIL), 102
UN Mission in Sierra Leone (UNAMSIL),
    180
UN Mission in the DRC (MONUSCO),
    59

UN Observer Mission in Sierra Leone
(UNOMSIL), 180
UN Operation in Mozambique
(ONUMOZ), 126, 128, 130
United States of America (USA), 74, 82, 97
Unity Party (UP) (Liberia), 100 UP, 104,
109

Vahamwiti Mukesyayira, Jean-
Chrysostome, 53
Vaz, Joaquim, 137
Vicente, Rogério Francisco João, 134
Vieira, João Bernardo, 4, 156–74 *passim*,
223, 226, 229, 230, 238, 239, 243,
244; as warlord democrat, 159, 170;
assassination of, 158, 172; electoral
performance of (in 1994, 165; in 2005,
169, 170); military career, 160, 161;
political career, 161–6 *passim*, 169,
170, 171; role in drugs trade, 158, 167,
171, 172, 236; role in human rights
violations, 166; use of securitized
identities by, 163
violence: electoral, 7; organized, 19, 20, 21,
26, 61, 200, 201, 202
Vurundo militia (Congo), 51

Wamba dia Wamba, Ernest, 47, 49
warlord democrats (WDs), 2, 3, 4, 5,
12, 13, 16, 20, 88, 200, 222, 225, 226,
230–43 *passim*; access to resources, 19;
agency of, 15; and benevolence, 237;
and criminalization of politics, 229;
and human rights abuses, 229; and
organized violence, 227, 228, 236; and
patronage networks, 239; as autocrats,
238, 239; as brokers, 239, 240, 242; as
two-faced, 231; directive functions
of, 201; electoral constraints on, 236,
237, 243; electoral strategies of, 14;
personality traits of, 26, 27, 238; social
networks of, 204; use of securitized
identities by, 228, 232, 233, 234; use of
state resources, 203, 204
Warren, Rick, 68
Weah, George, 104, 112, 115

Yauyau, David, 206

Zenawi, Meles, 88
Zimbabwe, 16
Zimbabwe African National Union
(ZANU), 11